Sport, Physical Recreation and the Law

It is important for anybody involved in sport and physical recreation to be aware of the legal context in which their activity takes place, to develop an understanding of their legal responsibilities and to know what might happen if something goes wrong. *Sport, Physical Recreation and the Law* is the first textbook on this difficult subject for students and practitioners in sport and physical recreation.

Covering a wide range of legal principles and cases, this textbook introduces the reader to legal systems, terminology, databases and the use of case law. Designed to encourage analysis, reflection and the application of examples and ideas from the reader's own experience, the book clearly and comprehensively explains key topics such as:

- Socio-legal aspects of sports violence and criminal liability

- Negligence and defences against negligence

- Manslaughter by individuals and organisations in sport

- Principles of natural justice, disciplinary tribunals and doping

- Discrimination, harassment and child protection

- Risk management, statutory duties and breaches of health and safety

- Criminal liability in recognised sports, hazing and cage fighting.

Including over 300 exercises, hypothetical scenarios, investigative tasks and seminar activities, this book is an essential course text for all students of sport, recreation and the law, and an invaluable reference for coaches, physical education teachers and those who play, lead or organise sport and physical recreation.

Hazel Hartley is a Principal Lecturer and research activist in Sport, Law and Ethics at Leeds Metropolitan University and a former Higher Education Academy Subject Specialist in Sport and the Law. She has more than 25 years' experience teaching this subject to students and practitioners.

£24.99.

Sport, Physical Recreation and the Law

Hazel Hartley

Routledge
Taylor & Francis Group

LONDON AND NEW YORK

First published 2009
by Routledge
2 Park Square, Milton Park, Abingdon, Oxon, OX14 4RN

Simultaneously published in the USA and Canada
by Routledge
270 Madison Avenue, New York, NY 10016

Routledge is an imprint of the Taylor & Francis Group, an informa business

Typeset in Univers, Eras and Rotis by
Keystroke, 28 High Street, Tettenhall, Wolverhampton
Printed and bound in Great Britain by
CPI Antony Rowe, Chippenham, Wiltshire

British Library Cataloguing in Publication Data
A catalogue record for this book is available from the British Library

Library of Congress Cataloging-in-Publication Data
Hartley, Hazel J.
   Sport, physical recreation and the law / Hazel Hartley.
       p. cm.
     Includes bibliographical references and index.
   1. Sports—Law and legislation—United States. 2. Physical education and training
Law and legislation—United States. 3. Recreation—Law and legislation—United States.
I. Title.
   KF3989.H37 2009
   344.73'099—dc22   2008054270

ISBN 978–0–415–32184–6 (hbk)
ISBN 978–0–415–32185–3 (pbk)
ISBN 978–0–203–29952–4 (ebk)

ISBN 0–415–32184–0 (hbk)
ISBN 0–415–32185–9 (pbk)
ISBN 0–203–29952–3 (ebk)

This book is dedicated to my wonderful twin sister Ann – born together, always together. Your creativity and kindness touch so many people.

Contents

List of cases

Foreword

There is virtually no part of our lives that is not affected by the law

All our human relationships and interactions from employment through to our love life have legal implications and, of course, the law regulates our relationship with the state in all its forms. The concept of the Rule of Law had its origins in Britain with a recognition that everyone had to be answerable to law, even the king.

Increasingly, professionals in every avenue are encouraged to have some grounding in the law, simply because it is good to know where we stand in relation to our rights and entitlements, as well as our legal responsibilities to each other. Law is the 'supreme regulator' and none of us escape its sinews, but it is not nuclear science. It is simply the rules by which we live. As a criminal trial lawyer, I have actually found the practice of law riveting because it is about the human condition and the cases are so infinitely variable and challenging.

Those who have careers in sports and physical recreation have particularly good reason for desiring some knowledge of the law as it affects their work. Increasingly, teachers, coaches and instructors are hamstrung by overbearing health and safety requirements, which seem to take so much of the fun out of sporting endeavour. However, those regulations are the consequence of the rise in the number of lawsuits alleging negligence against sports providers and organisations and anxiety by central and local government about the financial cost to the taxpayer. The school playing field, gymnasium and playground have become minefields with the threat of litigation haunting every fixture. The rush to law and the desire for compensation for injury has become one of the features of our changed society, where a price is put on everything and the desire to blame for all misfortune has become standard procedure. Risk aversion has become one of the themes of our times with risk management and risk assessment figuring large in the running of all institutions. Yet the willingness to take risks has always been at the heart of all achievement and creativity, and no thriving society should quell the desire to reach new heights. It is for this reason that an understanding of the law becomes so precious because knowing about something makes it less intimidating.

There are many other areas of sports where the law intervenes: the rough and tumble of sporting activity can also spill over into serious criminal behaviour, on and off the pitch, and an awareness of the legal parameters of the criminal law is vital. Competitiveness in sports is also leading to increasing attempts to enhance performance and disciplinary procedures for the use of drugs and other enhancers are now an integral part of the regulatory framework that controls sport. Just understanding the rules of natural justice and the way in which tribunals conduct their hearings is invaluable knowledge for those engaged in sport – in whatever capacity.

Another development in recent times is concern about sexual abuse or harassment where a person in a position of authority might abuse their power to take advantage of a pupil or trainee. Sexual abuse was certainly a buried problem for too long, with victims remaining silent because of the taboo that surrounded sexual allegations. However, the increase in complaints now means that those who teach or coach are fearful that normal behaviour will be perceived as transgression and caution is having a paralysing effect upon the willingness of people to volunteer to train young people.

However, for all these challenges there is no better guide to the law in the area of sport than Hazel Hartley. She takes you by the hand and leads you calmly through the different legal fields in a really accessible and enjoyable way. She explains how to do legal research, tells the story of our law's origins, explains how the different courts work and generally demystifies the whole business of law.

If law is taken out of its social context it becomes dry and arid, but when it is fleshed out with the accounts of cases and reflections upon what is currently happening in the news, it begins to live and breathe. The joy of Hazel Hartley's approach to the law is the way in which she draws upon the direct experiences of the students themselves. She convinces them they are their own academic resource, with knowledge and information gleaned from the sports pages of the press or sports autobiographies which can be just as valuable as academic texts. By gaining the confidence and interest of the student early on, she makes her subject utterly pleasurable. I just wish someone had written legal textbooks like this when I was a student.

At the heart of the book are the chapters on negligence. This falls under the ancient heading of the Law of Tort. Teachers, coaches and people involved in sports recreation invariably have 'duty of care' relationships with those they teach and train. If someone suffers an injury as a result of an accident, the central question is almost always whether there was a breach of the duty of care. Did the teacher or trainer fail to give proper advice as to technique, fail to provide safety equipment, fail to obtain help with sufficient alacrity? The variables are infinite. And not only might the teacher/trainer/individual be sued but the school or other establishment which employs that person will probably be joined in the action, because they will be more likely to be able to foot the bill or have the requisite insurance to do so. While few cases are exactly the same, our system of law – the common law system – is built upon precedents or legal cases which have been decided in the past by the higher courts. These precedents lay down the legal principles, which should help determine the law cases which follow on. In this way our law has developed like the skin on an onion, layer upon layer with parliament passing laws or statutes and the courts then interpreting the new law through the cases which come before them.

Hazel Hartley takes special care to explain the important concept of *volenti non fit injuria* which has special relevance in sports cases. Where a pupil or trainee or sports practitioner is a willing participant in an activity (*volenti*) and readily embraces the risks which attach to it, then an injury which befalls him or her will not be deemed the fault of others. The particular facts will be very important. It is important to distinguish between inherent risks and unacceptable risks. Similarly, the concept of contributory negligence is one which figures often in personal injury cases. If an injured party has contributed in some way to their own injury, the compensation ordered by the court will be reduced proportionately.

Law does not exist within a social vacuum and Hazel Hartley helps the student see the development of law through a sociological lens. The world is going through a period of dynamic change, presenting entirely new problems to nations and to the international community. Societies are now more complex and mixed than they were in the twentieth century; people are better educated, more demanding and more conscious of their rights. The position of women has changed radically. Attitudes to 'race', religion, homosexuality, age and disability have all altered. The rigid divisions between classes have broken down. The law has a central role to play in this new landscape, ensuring that opportunities are not blighted by discrimination, protecting human rights and upholding civil liberties. To be effective, laws have to resonate and reflect our changed communities, and this has to be done against a backdrop of principle.

Those who work in sport and physical education play a hugely important role in maintaining the general well-being of our nation. There is greater recognition today than ever before of the benefits of sport in creating well-rounded, confident and healthy citizens, who can work in teams, who understand the importance of rules in any social endeavour, who know the pleasure of achievement. It is vital that practitioners working in the field of sport have a comfortable knowledge of the law and do not see it as a block to those aims. So I congratulate Hazel Hartley on a great achievement – a law book that is carefully researched and scholarly but also accessible and relevant, placing the law squarely at the core of practical experience and, consequently, making it real.

Baroness Helena Kennedy QC
Doughty Street Chambers and the House of Lords, 2009

Acknowledgements

This is primarily a teaching text to encourage students to engage in this fascinating and challenging subject, which, as students often point out, is current and relevant to the real lives of those who work or engage in sport and physical recreation. I would like to thank the students in the Carnegie Faculty at Leeds Metropolitan University who took the plunge and opted for the sport and law modules. They have patiently acted as guinea pigs for several years as I tried out ideas and exercises for this book. Their observations, feedback and enthusiastic contributions have been invaluable and they are a pleasure to teach.

Also at Leeds Metropolitan University I appreciate the support of many people. Thank you to Sally Brown for encouraging me to write and publish, even if I am a late starter. Mark Snowden and John Slater kindly helped with technical advice and the formatting of the manuscript. Hayley Fitzgerald advised me on presentation and reminded me that it was time to let go of this book. Ashley Hardwell was always there to help me with work-related tasks so that I could get to the book. He also significantly reduced my stress levels by helping with the final stages of the preliminary pages.

Mark James and Yvonne Williams provided invaluable feedback and advice on the draft manuscript. Margaret Talbot always found time to send me interesting and timely little snippets from the press. Jan Doleschal was so generous in sharing her pioneering work on hazing and the law in the United States. Celia Brackenridge has always supported my work and encouraged me, through her pioneering work, to think of the socio-legal and risk assessment factors of child protection (safeguarding children) in sport. Delegates at various conferences have been so supportive in the early stages of my work and shared in my passion for the subject – including Ian Blackshaw, Karen Bill, Hilary Findlay, Simon Gardiner, Jim Gray, Mark James, Dave McArdle, Hadyn Opie, Hamish Telfer and Yvonne Williams. I am indebted to Sue Jack for her meticulous searching of internet and journal sources, particularly on hazing and child abuse in sport.

Thank you to those editors who gave permission to include my previous work from the *International Sports Law Journal* and *Sport and the Law Journal* in 1998. Permission was also granted from Nina Beckett at the Higher Education Academy HLST Subject Network to use parts of Hartley 2003, 2008 *Learning Resource Guide in Sport and Law*. A small section of Hartley 2001b *Exploring Sport and Leisure Disasters: A Socio-legal Perspective* (London: Cavendish) is included in Chapter 7. Parts of Hartley (2001a) Chapter 9 is used in Chapters 4 and 8 of this text.

I could not have completed this book without the support and practical advice of the editors at Routledge, Taylor and Francis Group. Samantha Grant and Simon Whitmore – thank you for trusting in me and waiting so long for this book. I acknowledge and appreciate the passion and commitment of all those who create positive experiences for participants in sport and physical recreation. Use the law to help you inform and support, rather then threaten, your endeavours. Finally – thank you to my family for their love and patience on this one – especially as I swore that I would never write another single-authored text!

Acknowledgments

Abbreviations

AALA	Adventure Activities Licensing Authority
AHD	[CAS] ad hoc division
ANZSLA	Australia and New Zealand Sports Law Association
BAF	British Athletics Federation
BALCO	Bay Area Laboratory Co-operative
BASL	British Association for Sport and Law
BBBC	British Board of Boxing Control
BBC	British Broadcasting Corporation
CA	Court of Appeal
CAS	Court of Arbitration for Sport
CCPR	Central Council of Physical Recreation
CLA	Copyright Licensing Authority
CPS	Crown Prosecution Service
CPSU	Child Protection in Sport Unit
DCMS	Department for Culture, Media and Sport
DID	Drug Information Database
DRC	Disability Rights Commission
EAT	Employment Appeals Tribunal
ECJ	European Court of Justice
EHRC	Equality and Human Rights Commission
EWCA	Court of Appeal of England and Wales
FEI	Federation De Equestrienne Internationale
FIFA	International Football Federation
FINA	Federation Internationale de Natation Amateur
FIS	Federation de Ski Internationale
HC	High Court
HL	House of Lords
HSE	Health and Safety Executive
IAAF	International Amateur Athletics Federation
IABA	International Amateur Boxing Association
IFC	International Football Commission
IOC	International Olympic Committee
ITU	International Shooting Union
LCCP	Law Commission Consultation Paper
NSLI	National Sport Law Institute
OMAC	Olympic Medical Advisory Council
SFT	Swiss Federation Tribunal
SRLA	Sport and Recreation Law Association
THG	Tetrahydrogestrinone
TQS	Tourism Quality Services
TUEs	Therapeutic Use Exceptions

UKA	United Kingdom Athletics
UKSDRP	United Kingdom Sports Dispute Resolution Panel
USADA	United States Anti-Doping Agency
USFSA	United States Figure Skating Association
USOC	United States Olympic Committee
WADA	World Anti-Doping Agency

Introduction

'Graduates of all programmes in Hospitality, Leisure, Sport and Tourism will be able to demonstrate an understanding and critical awareness of moral, ethical, environmental and *legal* aspects which underpin best practice' (Higher Education Academy, 2002: 6). This is one of the five areas of the 'generic knowledge base' included in the National Subject Benchmarks for all undergraduate degree programmes in Hospitality, Leisure, Sport and Tourism.

> Working with students on the legal aspects of sport and leisure is a challenging but immensely rewarding experience. It is not just about meeting the requirements of a Subject Benchmarking Statement. Once students start to build up their confidence, become acclimatised to the study skills required, and realise how much they have to contribute from their own experiences, they come to appreciate the central relevance of the subject to their employability, as well as being able to interrogate and justify their own conduct, as participants or managers in sport or leisure.
>
> (Hartley, 2005a: 4)

There are many aspects of law which could be applied to sport and physical recreation. Not all of them can or should be accommodated in one degree programme. Institutions will obviously be influenced by the course rationale, the needs of the external environment/industry, and the strengths of the staff in their teaching and research, as well as the key features which are part of the university identity. Law students also access electives or dissertation topics in sport and law, mainly at level three of undergraduate courses, and there are a range of post-graduate courses in sport and law in the UK. Students studying sport might study law in a discrete module and/or in a permeation model. The latter sees legal aspects of sport integrated where appropriate, in, for example, professional practice, personal development, event management, work experience or activity modules.

The study of legal aspects of sport and recreation provides excellent opportunities to meet another of the Subject Benchmarks, that is, 'an understanding of the need for multi-disciplinary and interdisciplinary approach to study, drawing, as appropriate, from service, research and professional contexts' (Higher Education Academy, 2002: 6). There are endless opportunities for collaboration between law and other disciplines such as sociology, philosophy, sports science, psychology and social work. Indeed, students and practitioners are the ones who make such connections themselves as they self-select materials to support their personal interests and what makes sense to them in their reflective practice.

This book has grown out of my passion for teaching legal aspects of sport to students and practitioners over the last two decades. It is a challenging and wonderful subject to study, research and teach. I would like to support others who go on this journey by sharing some of the materials and approaches which students have found useful and engaging. The invaluable contributions which students make to the learning process of this subject continue to amaze and motivate me. I believe that it is important in the learning process to acknowledge and use their experiences, observations, reflections and phenomenal resource base to help make sense of and apply quite intimidating legal concepts to their own varying roles in sport and physical recreation.

Although this is a student textbook, the materials and approaches have been tried and tested with a variety of practitioners, coaches, coach educators, sports leaders, players, managers and teachers in sport-related contexts. There is increasingly common ground between the student curriculum, and the legal education and training of, for example, sports coaches, leaders, volunteers, managers and physical education teachers. Legal principles, cases, incidents and issues in this text are predominantly located in sport and physical recreation, although this varies with the themes of each chapter. Some chapters, for example, two, three and seven, will have more cases arising from physical education, school sport or educational visits. The engagement of students and pupils in risk education and personal responsibility can hopefully impact on the decisions young people make about their conduct in informal physical recreation and leisure. Here they can and do, get into serious danger or can be charged with a criminal offence away from an institutionalised sport setting.

This textbook takes a particular approach which introduces the student to a set of legal generic or authority cases or relevant statutes as well as cases, incidents and issues in sport and recreation contexts. It provides exercises, hypothetical scenarios, seminar activities, investigative tasks and self-reflection at the end of each subtheme. Each chapter includes a range of illustrative summaries of sport and recreation cases, followed by a more detailed key case. The legal principles, cases and statutes draw materials predominantly from Anglo-Welsh law. There are, however, illustrative examples from other jurisdictions such as Canada, Australia and the United States. As required by the publisher house style, the sport and legal sources in the bibliography are presented in Harvard referencing style, so these may differ from the usual presentation of legal sources.

The book is divided into nine chapters. Some of the challenges of engaging students in this subject relate to their lack of familiarity with and fear of legal jargon, legal databases and case law. Chapter 1 is designed to orientate students to and build up their confidence in the resources they might use in the study of legal aspects of sport and physical recreation. This chapter can be used to prepare students to make the most of the chapters to follow in this text. It can be used as pre-module preparation or directed learning prior to, during and after the teaching and learning delivery of each subtheme. Students are encouraged to use their imagination and view as relevant a wide range of sources beyond traditional legal texts or databases.

A resource does not have to have the title 'sport, recreation and law' in order to be usefully applied to this subject. Chapter 1 is divided into three parts and in part one covers civil and criminal court systems, searching for legal cases, followed by some examples of legal journals and study texts. Part two dips into illustrative examples of sport, recreation, physical activity and the law-texts and journals from other academic disciplines. Part three highlights a range of websites of sport, recreation and law organisations and governing bodies or authorities within and beyond sport and recreation. Students are also encouraged to search media, film, autobiographies and people who research, teach or practice law applied to sport or recreation. They are reminded that one of the most important resources is their own experiences, observations and reflections which they can contribute to the study group. As we work together on the journey through a module, the confidence and enthusiasm of the students is enhanced as they find and contribute incidents, issues and cases from the real lives of athletes and sports organisations, on a weekly basis.

Chapters 2 and 3 introduce the tort of negligence. Chapter 2 focuses on the three elements of negligence drawing on generic principles and authority cases as well as examples from sport and recreation. It explores sport and recreation negligence cases under a number of practical themes such as deviation from standard and approved practice, supervision, provision of a safe environment providing lessons from case law. Chapter 3 examines two defences against negligence – *Volenti* and the partial defence of contributory negligence, rarely discussed by sport and recreation participants and leaders. The Occupier's Liability Act 1957 and 1984 are introduced with some key cases, particularly in relation to trespassers. The standard of care in sport – a very difficult topic, is covered in advance of two key rugby cases which clearly illustrate the themes of Chapter 2 and 3.

Moving on to the first topic from the criminal law, Chapter 4 takes a socio-legal lens to sports violence and criminal assault, a theme which has been particularly popular with students, games players and managers, or those engaging in sports business. It introduces sports violence as a contested concept before moving on to general principles of criminal liability and sports violence. Common assault and public order issues are briefly summarised before placing the Offences Against the Person Act 1861 at the heart of this chapter. Case law from the sports field illustrate the three offences under s.47, s.20 and s.18 of this Act, followed by two key cases from the soccer and ice hockey. A critical sociological lens is then pointed at hegemonic masculinity, power and male sport subculture to engage students in a theoretical critique of the danger of normalisation of violence from the sports field to the law courts.

A continuum of abuse or exploitation in Chapter 5 takes the student through a brief overview of discrimination, harassment and child protection issues. Again there are some links with the sociological lens through gender stereotyping and discrimination law. Challenges of defining and researching child abuse, child protection (safeguarding children) precedes a brief overview of those groups the research indicates might be at greater risk. The sociological lens of power, and subcultures (or subworlds), add a more contextual and critical approach which can assist an understanding of a lack of action or resistance to such issues within a sport or recreation community. Illustrative criminal cases under the Sexual Offences Act(s), legal and policy frameworks and standards for child protection and safeguarding children close this chapter.

Chapter 6 introduces an area of criminal law which is often perceived as only applying to school trips in outdoor activities – that of risk management, including the more formal end of risk assessment and a range of generic statutory duties in health and safety in the workplace. Hazards, risk and risk management in sport and recreation settings precede a more generic section on statutory duties in health and safety. The central part of this chapter includes prosecutions brought by the Health and Safety Executive (HSE) against managers, local authorities, universities or corporations in sport and physical recreation contexts. The final part of Chapter 6 illustrates some key issues in risk assessment, clearly highlighted by the HSE report into the tragedy at Glenridding, Cumbria during a school activity weekend in 2002.

Chapter 7 introduces a topic rarely covered in sport, recreation and law modules – that of manslaughter. Chapter 4 addressed non-fatal injuries. Chapter 7 deals with causing and investigating death through the topic of manslaughter by individuals and corporations. Most texts on sport and law mention one or two of the manslaughter cases against two soccer players in the 1880s. The central part of this chapter will summarise a range of manslaughter cases involving players, competitors, sport leaders, fans, parents, facility managers, local authorities and children as young as 10 or 11. It will focus in much more detail in the landmark case of individual and corporate manslaughter in 1993 arising from the Lyme Bay canoe tragedy of March 1993, which has lessons for all those involved in sport and recreation.

Chapter 8 introduces students to the principles of natural justice and takes them on a journey through sports disciplinary processes from an informal grievance to the Court of Arbitration for Sport (CAS). It will then focus attention on the issue of doping in sport, examining the strict liability rule followed by key illustrative cases, as well as raising questions around the harmonisation of doping rules with domestic, international law or human rights. Chapter 9 was almost an afterthought. I decided to include it very late in the process of writing this book for two reasons. First, alongside many other academics and practitioners from sport, physical recreation and the law, I submitted a lengthy response to the 1995 Law Commission Consultation Paper on Consent and Offences against the Person (Criminal Law). I paid particular attention to the conception of a recognised sport, and the sections on boxing, martial arts, horseplay, secondary liability and casual fighting.

Following the two consultations in 1994 and 1995 the Law Commission made some recommendations to parliament in 1999 of a generic nature. At the time of writing in 2008, however, there have been no recommendations by the Law Commission to parliament in the area of sports and games and related issues above. Therefore the only guidance on criminal assault, to those in sport, remains as before, that is, the Offences against the Person Acts 1861 and in particular the CA case of *R v (Mark) Barnes* [2004] EWCA Crim 3246; [2005] 1 WLR 910. Unrecognised martial arts and emerging spectacles such as 'cage fighting' remind us that the very thorough analysis and initial proposals of the Law Commission in 1995 need resurrecting. One of the most significant reviews of sport and law in the history of legal reform and policy making remains 'unfinished business'.

Second, during time taken writing this book, the law covered in Chapter 7, corporate manslaughter, manslaughter has been through a lengthy process of legal reform. In addition, only in August 2008, proposals which limit manslaughter and introduce first and second degree murder had just been published by the Law Commission (2008).

1 Resources at your finger tips: a guide to legal sources, databases and organisations

Introduction

Library staff in universities often advise academic staff that students under-use the range of print, media and electronic sources available to support their studies. Academics also try to encourage students to increase their engagement in the recommended reading for their modules. In the area of law applied to sport, physical education and recreation, there are a range of academic disciplines or fields of study which can make a contribution – such a sociology, psychology, management theory, policy, philosophy, social work, sport science, leadership and coaching theory. The print, media and electronic sources which can support this area of study are very wide-ranging and might not be pigeon-holed in one subject or location. Sources do not have to be titled law, sport and physical education or physical recreation to be relevant to those areas of study.

This chapter is designed as a basic introduction to a range of print, electronic and media sources and databases. It can be used to:

* prepare you for the rest of the text – with exercises relevant to subsequent chapters
* orientate yourself with legal system terminology
* support distance learning in advance of, or part of, a course or module
* support directed learning within a module
* orientate you to legal databases and other sources as part of a specific library induction at course or module level[1]
* build up your confidence and skills in the searching and use of print, media and electronic legal sources
* encourage you to find out about applied law by locating the people who work and teach in this very exciting and relevant subject
* encourage students, partners and practitioners to contribute ideas for resources which can be used for future modules
* identify sources and websites or locations which might be used in or as a link to Web CT or X-stream or other technology-enhanced learning.

This chapter is divided into three parts. Part one introduces criminal and civil law and the court systems and terminology. It introduces you to searching for legal cases and statutes, using such systems as *Lawtel* or *Westlaw UK*. It also covers the use of legal journals, and highlights some useful law study books and revision texts, which can help you to dip into clear summaries of topics where they need a concise summary of a more generic area of law. Part two lists some examples of sport, recreation, physical activity and the law, texts and journals in legal and other disciplines. Part three introduces you to some useful websites and other sources on organisations, people and the media. It will make the very pertinent point that one of the most important, valuable and relevant sources is *you*, your experiences, observations, reflections and the chain of thought and possible application to sport and physical education, which come into your mind as you read and discuss aspects of law with your peers and lecturers.

Part one: making sense of court systems, legal databases and law texts

Understanding court systems in criminal and civil law

'Definitions of crime and criminal law differ according to economic and ideological circumstances and may be influenced by prejudices and stereotypes' (Fitzgerald et al., 1981; Edwards, 1984[2]). An obvious and minimalist definition of a crime is that which is 'prohibited by the criminal code' or 'what the law says it is' (Fattah, 1997: 30). A crime can partly be understood by the nature of the threat and who should deal with it. Criminal liability is imposed on 'conduct felt to be against the general interests of society' as we cannot have people attacking or killing other citizens, stealing their car, trespassing on or breaking into someone's property and stealing their belongings (Elliot and Quinn, 2006: 1). Criminal conduct is 'such a serious danger to society that, in the public interest, the state must bear the full responsibility and costs of providing a deterrent and following through all stages of implementation' (Hartley, 2001b: 30). Crimes, usually categorised as offences against the person, property or the state, are not considered private matters which can be settled between parties (see Drewry 1975; Jefferson, 1992).

The Crown Prosecution Service, provided with relevant evidence by the police, can recommend whether or not to proceed with criminal charges and usually bases such decisions on three prosecutorial principles. It should be in the public interest to proceed with the prosecution. In addition, there should be sufficient corroborated evidence and a realistic chance of a conviction. Once a crown case proceeds, the alleged victims and defendants cannot change their minds and withdraw the charges or stop the proceedings. A crime has three elements. The *mens rea* is latin for 'guilty mind' and refers to the mental element, or state of mind of the person committing the crime, such as intention or recklessness (Elliott and Quinn, 2006). The *actus reus* requires proof that the defendant's conduct caused the harmful result, related to the circumstances and consequences. Finally, there is no lawful justification, defence or excuse (such as consent, provocation or diminished responsibility, depending on the offence).

In criminal cases the prosecution must prove their case, in both the *mens rea* and *actus reus* so that the magistrate or a jury are satisfied 'beyond reasonable doubt' of their existence (Elliott and Quinn, 2006: 9[3]). The punishment by the state can be a range of things from imprisonment, fines or community service, depending on the offence and sentencing policy and guidelines at the time. A selection of illustrative crimes in sport and recreation contexts will be covered in Chapters 4, 6 and 7 of this text. A range of crimes of assault arising from the Offences Against the Person Act 1861 will be covered in Chapter 4. Breaches of statutory duties in health and safety (criminal offences) are applied to sport, physical education and leisure contexts in Chapter 6. Manslaughter by individuals and corporations in sport, education and leisure contexts is the main focus of Chapter 7. The terminology in criminal cases is different from civil law cases. For example:

> *R v Kite, R v Stoddart, R v OLL Ltd* (unreported, 9 December 1994, Winchester Crown Court, Ognall J)

R stands for 'Regina' – the Queen [the embodiment of the State] v (versus) the named defendant. Sometimes the report of the case will just name one of the parties, for example *R v Kite* or *R v Kite and others*. This is then followed by the date the case was decided, the court where it was heard and the name of the judge; for example, Ognall J or Mr J (Justice) Ognall. The criminal cases covered in this text are usually heard in a court of the first instance – one of the crown courts divided into six 'circuit' courts, heard by circuit judges or recorders (part-timers). The Queen's Bench Division (QBD) of the High Court can hear appeals from a magistrates' court. The Court of Appeal (Criminal Division) has 37 Lord Justices of Appeal (LJJ) and cases are usually heard on matters of fact, law and sentence, by one Lord Justice (LJ) and two High Court judges, although five judges hear very important appeals (Darbyshire, 2007: 3[4]). The Civil Division of the Court of Appeal hears appeals from the Chancery, Queen's Bench and Family Division, county courts across England and Wales, as well as appeals from certain Tribunals (HM Courts Service see http://www.hmcourts-service.gov.uk/). The highest court in domestic criminal law is the House of Lords Appellate Court where there are 12 Lords of Appeal. These 'Law Lords' referred to as 'their Lordships', sit in panels of five and hear appeals for England, Scotland, and Northern Ireland (Darbyshire, 2007: 3[5]). The hierarchy of the courts is as listed below:

- House of Lords (Supreme Court from 2009)
- Court of Appeal (Criminal Division)
- Crown Court
- Magistrates' Court (lowest court).

In civil law, which deals with legal relations between citizens, proceedings are brought by an individual or group against another individual or group, rather than the state. Unless legal aid is accessed or a 'no-win no-fee' arrangement is agreed, the person or group bringing the case must fund the case themselves. Unlike a criminal case brought by the state, either party can decide to drop the case or negotiate an 'out-of-court' settlement at any time. The standard of proof is lower than that required in criminal cases. The case must be proven on the 'balance of probabilities'. A tort is 'a civil wrong that is committed against an individual, rather than the state. The gist of tort law is that a person has certain interests which are protected by law' (Cooke, 1995: 3). Civil law is part of common law and is often referred to as 'judge-made' law (Drewry, 1975; Rozenberg, 1994).

Tort law develops through the practical reasoning of judges, often using the same reasoning used by judges in previous cases. The doctrine of precedent depends on lower courts being bound by the precedent set by higher courts (see Farrar, 1990). The hierarchy of the courts is as listed below:

- House of Lords (or Supreme Court from 2009)
- Court of Appeal (Civil Division)
- High Court (Queen's Bench Division, Chancery Division, Family Division)
- County Court.

There are 218 county courts operating under the Courts and Legal Services Act 1990 and the Civil Procedure Rules 1998. The High Court sits in London with many district registries. The England and Wales Court of Appeal (EWCA) Civil Division hears appeals and consists of three judges, drawn mainly from Lord Justices, sometimes assisted by a High Court judge. The civil law cases included in this text are the tort of negligence in Chapters 2 and 3 and civil cases brought against governing bodies of sport in relation to natural justice principles and disciplinary processes, in Chapter 8. The case name is presented with both parties in italics, with the date of decision of the court in brackets, often with the name of the judge or judges. For example, a negligence case in a school sport context covered in Chapter 2:

Mountford v Newlands School and Another [2007] EWCA Civ 21, 24 July 2007, Waller LJ, Rix LJ, Hooper LJ.

Mountford is the claimant, a young rugby player at Newlands School. He sued Newlands School and the school physical education teacher for negligence after he sustained an elbow injury during a school rugby match. The school was found liable for negligence and appealed against the decision. The England and Wales Court of Appeal (EWCA) dismissed the appeal by the school on 24 July 2007. The case was heard in the EWCA by three Lord Justices, Waller LJ, Rix LJ, Hooper LJ.

> *Modahl v British Athletics Federation Ltd* [2001] EWCA Civ 1447; [2002] 2 WLR 1192

In this case, covered in Chapter 8, Diane Modahl, an athlete, was the plaintiff. She was seeking legal compensation for financial losses, alleging breach of contract and apparent bias in a sport doping disciplinary process. The defendant was the British Athletics Federation Ltd. The case was heard in the Court of Appeal on 12 October by three Lord Justices, Lance LJ, Latham LJ and Parker LJ. Diane Modahl lost her appeal and the case ended at that point.

The European Court of Justice sits in Luxembourg and is made up of 27 judges, sitting in chambers of three or five, with the more important cases being heard in the 'Grand Chamber' of 13. It can hear appeals from the European Court of the First Instance such as the sport doping case of *Meca-Medina and Majcen v Commission of European Communities* [2006] ECR I-6991 where it was argued that the IOC rules on doping control 'violated the European Community Rules on competition' (Dios Crespo, 2006: 116[6]). The European Court of Human Rights (ECHR) is located in Strasbourg and enforces states' obligations under the European Convention on Human Rights. It has 46 judges, who sit in chambers of seven, with a Grand Chamber of 17 for more important cases (see Darbyshire 2007: 5–6[7]).

Searching for legal cases

Less than ten per cent of cases are reported in law reports. You might expect to find a high profile negligence case in sport, in one of the law reports, yet often, you will only find the court hearings, online, in one of the legal databases such as *Lawtel* or *Westlaw UK* or in newspapers which include law reports. Criteria for including cases in the All England Law Reports include making new law by dealing with a novel situation of extending the application of existing principles, clarify conflicting decisions of the lower courts or an important point of procedure (see Clinch, 2001).

Printed law reports are usually located in university law libraries in alphabetical order by title, from *All England Law Reports* to *Weekly Law Reports*. A citation is a full case reference. For cases heard since 1947 you can start with the *Current Law Case Citator*. The *All England Reports Index* has cases from 1936 onwards and the *Law Reports Index* has ten-year indexes of cases from 1936–2003. The *All England Reports* can also be accessed online through the *All England Direct* on the web if your university library subscribes to this service. A digest or summary of a case can be found in the appropriate year book. For example, the *All England Annual Review* has a sport and law section. Newspapers such as *The Times*[8] or *The Guardian* contain a law section with law reports. These cases are collected in the *Daily Reports Index*.

The *Current Law Monthly Digest* is usually in hard copy in university law libraries and includes a Cumulative Table of Cases. See if your case name appears in the latest issue. If it does:

the reference given is to the monthly issue of the CLMD and to the individual item number within that issue, where you will find a summary of the case and a note of where it has been reported. For example, suppose the Table of Cases gives your case a reference such as: Jan 129. This means that if you look in the January issue of the *Monthly Digest*, item 129 (not page 129) is the summary of the case, with a list of places where the case is reported in full.

(Thomas and Knowles, 2001: 50)

If a case is reported in one of the law reports it is usually cited in the following way. Here is a civil law nogligence case from the game of rugby league, covered in Chapter 3 of this text.

Simms v Leigh RFC Ltd [1969] 2 All ER 932
1   2   3   4 5   6

1   This is the plaintiff's name Simms, a rugby league player.
2   This is the name of the defendant Leigh Rugby Football Club Ltd.
3   This is the date the report appeared in the All England Law Reports. Where the date is in square brackets it represents the year the case was published in a law report. If the date is located within normal curved brackets it represents the year the judgement was delivered by the court. This depends on how the individual law report numbers its volumes.
4   This is the volume of the law report.
5   This is the law report, that is, the All England Law Reports.
6   This is the page number of the law report where the case starts.

Here is a criminal assault case from a football context, covered in Chapter 4.

R v (Mark) Barnes [2005] 1 WLR 910
1   2   3   4 5   6

1   This is 'Regina' the Queen.
2   This is defendant's name Mark Barnes, a football player who was appealing against his conviction for s.20 offence, unlawful and malicious wounding.
3   This the date the case appeared in the law report.
4   This is the volume in which the case appeared.
5   This is the title of the law report series, the *Weekly Law Reports*.
6   This is the page number in the WLR where the case starts.

The full reference or citation of the case, in a law report, is usually followed by:

- catchwords – these are keywords added by the law reporter which summarise the key legal issues involved. These can also be useful additions to your search vocabulary.
- headnote – summarises the facts of the case leading to the action, and following the word 'held' you will see the decision of this court.

Cases referred to in the judgment list the previous decisions on which this court relied. (If the case is online these are usually in blue-type and you should be able to click on them and access them directly):

- Other cases to which the arguments of counsel referred
- Details of the legal proceedings
- The judgment
- Names of the solicitors

- Name of the law reporter[9]
- Accessing online legal databases.

Two of the easiest online sources to use to find cases which might not be reported in the law reports are the legal databases *Lawtel* and *Westlaw UK*. Most universities with law courses subscribe to one if not both of these services. If not, you may have to subscribe as an individual. *Lawtel* has access to daily updates, summaries and full texts of judged cases as well as press and journal articles on various aspects of law. In addition, the British and Irish Legal Information Institute provides a free online database of most reported cases including a range of world law resources of cases from different countries (see www.bailii.org).

Lawtel legal database

If you are accessing from your university you will probably need an Athens password to connect to this service. Make sure you read the terms and conditions and that you check you can access from your home computer as well as on campus.

EXERCISE 1.1

Work in pairs and take turns to watch and use the computer.

On the home page, go to the left-hand column and click 'Lawtel UK'.

On the main search page, click on each of the following topics and click both 'case law' and 'articles' (each person could take two of the topics):

- negligence and sport
- doping and sport
- natural justice and sport
- violence and sport.

Download and print off the list of resulting articles and cases. From the case law search only, each person should take two of the following cases. Locate and save an electronic version of your cases (the full text):

- *Smoldon v Whitworth and Nolan* [1996] EWCA Civ 1225; [1997] PIQR 133 (rugby union negligence case covered in Chapter 3).
- *Vowles v Evans* [2003] EWCA Civ 318; [2003] 1 WLR 1607 (rugby union negligence case, covered in Chapter 3).
- *Watson v British Boxing Board of Control* [2000] EWCA Civ 2116 (negligence case in boxing, covered in Chapter 2).
- *Modahl v British Athletics Federation Ltd* [2001] EWCA Civ 1447; [2002] 1 WLR 1192 (legal case for compensation following doping ban, covered in Chapter 8).

You can also search cases using the case citator search on *Lawtel*.

Westlaw UK

If your university subscribes to *Westlaw UK*, you should be able to access it online using your Athens or equivalent password. Please read the terms and conditions carefully.

The cases on *Westlaw UK* provide a text of the full case judgment, as well as 'case comment'. Under 'case comment' you will find a list of articles about the case and a direct link to those cases. The Current Law Case Citator can be accessed on *Westlaw UK*. On *Westlaw UK* use the current law case citatory to locate the following key sport assault case covered in Chapter 4 of this text:

R v (Mark) Barnes [2004] EWCA Crim 3246 (court hearing)
R v (Mark) Barnes [2005] 1 WLR 910 (law report)

If you just have the name 'Barnes', you can still search the law case citator but you will have to find the 'Mark' Barnes case on the full list of case references which appears on the left-hand side of the screen under 'results'. Once you have the full case, download it, save it and print off a hard copy to read for Chapter 4. Then, on the screen of the main case text, scroll down the left-hand side of the screen to the list of headings in blue typing and click 'case comment', where the articles related to the Mark Barnes case are listed.

EXERCISE 1.2

Work in pairs. Take one of the following articles each. Locate, download, save and print off your article. Provide a copy of your article to your study partner. Read the article and summarise the case in relation to proving the elements of a crime. The articles comment on the appeal case of *R v (Mark) Barnes* [2004] EWCA Crim 3246; [2005] 1 WLR 910, a soccer case, covered in Chapter 4 of this text:

'Case Comment: *R v (Mark) Barnes* [2004] EWCA Crim 3246; [2005] 1 WLR 910' in *International Sports Law Review* (ISLR) 2 (May), 2005, 53–67.

Leake and Omerod (2005) 'Contact Sports: Application of the defence of consent'.

(*R v (Mark) Barnes* [2004] EWCA Crim 3246; [2005] 1 WLR 910; *Criminal Law Review* May, 381–384.)

EXERCISE 1.3

Take one case each from the assault cases listed below. Using *Westlaw UK* law case citatory or the main search facility locate, download, save and print off your case. Share your case with your study partner and discuss the application of the elements of *mens rea* and *actus reus* to these cases.

R v Lincoln (1990) 12 Cr App R (S) 250.

R v Ahmed [2002] EWCA Crim 779.

You can also search for case reports on the LexisNexis Professional (Butterworths) if your university subscribes to this service. This service includes easy online tutorials on how to use the service to access case law and statutes. The British and Irish Legal Information database (baili) is also useful for finding cases and has good links to cases in other jurisdictions.

Statutes

When a Bill has been approved by both the House of Commons and the House of Lords and 'has received the Royal Assent, it becomes an Act of Parliament. The Act is made available on the HMSO website[10] and the first printed version is published by The Stationery Office, within a few days of receiving the Royal Assent' (Thomas and Knowles, 2001: 57). If you are searching for a statute on the HMSO website, you will need the full name and year of the statute. The *Statute Law Database* (SLD) is the official revised edition of United Kingdom Statutes. It is developed by the Statutory Publications Office, part of the Lord Chancellor's Department, and lists legislation in force from 1 February 1991. *Westlaw UK* includes a current law statute citatory in the form of the *UK Legislator Locator* database.

You can also search for legislation on the LexisNexis Professional service by clicking 'UK Legislation' under 'Assisted searches' if your university library subscribes to this service. There is a link to this service from the Butterworths website.[11] This service includes *Halsbury's Laws Direct*. A separate database *UK Statutory Instruments* has printed Statutory Instruments from 1997, with all new statutory instruments online. *Halsbury's Statutes of England* is a printed annotated series of statutes. This source is particularly important as it includes 'correct and amended text of all legislation in force', as well as 'notes which provide, for example, judicial interpretation of words and phrases, details of statutory instruments made under the Act, case law and cross-references to other sections' (Thomas and Knowles, 2001: 65). In addition, the UK Parliament has information about the work of the House of Commons and the House of Lords and the progress of Bills.

EXERCISE 1.4

In groups of four, using any of the above sources, search for, download and save one statute each from the statutes listed below and send them electronically to other members of the group to save. These statutes will be used in Chapters 4, 6 and 8 of this text. Each person provides a concise, referenced summary of one charge, duty, regulation or Article and gives an example of its application to your sporting interest:

- Offences Against the Person Act 1861
- Health and Safety at Work Act 1974
- Management of Health and Safety at Work Regulations 1999
- Human Rights Act 1998.

Legal journals

When you look at legal references, you will see that the journal titles are presented in an abbreviated form with initials only. The Cardiff Index to Legal Abbreviations should include the full titles of legal journals and can be accessed online via your university law subject pages. In addition, shorter lists of abbreviations can be found in *Osborn's Concise Law Dictionary* as well as *Legal Journals Index*. You may be familiar with the usual academic journal searches through various abstracts and indexes and through EBSCO to 'Sport Discus' and may well access legal or socio-legal articles through these routes, when searching by author or subject. If you are looking for generic journals which often include articles related to sport and law, then you may find the following journals particularly useful:

- *New Law Journal* (NLJ)
- *Criminal Law Review* (CLR)
- *Journal of Criminal Law* (JCL)
- *Law Quarterly Review* (LQR)
- *Personal Injury Quarterly Review* (PIQR)
- *Journal of Personal Injury Litigation* (JPIL)
- *Solicitors Journal* (SJ)
- *Entertainment and Sport Law Journal* (ESLJ)
- *Socio-legal Studies* (SLS)
- *Journal of Law and Society* (JLS)
- *Professional Negligence* (PN)

Lists of legal journal articles can be accessed through various sites but:

> the easiest and most comprehensive way to find articles on an English case is to use the *Legal Journals Index* (LGI), which indexes all the major British legal journals. The online source of the LGI on *Westlaw UK* runs from 1998 and the print version of *Legal Journals Index* was first published in 1986. If your library does not hold the LGI you could use the *Index to Legal Periodicals*. In addition the *Index to Legal Periodicals and Books*, which commenced in 1908, is published in the United States but includes journals from the United Kingdom, Canada, Ireland, Australia and New Zealand.
>
> (see Thomas and Knowles, 2001: 89)

Lawtel includes an articles index box to tick on the main search page of *Lawtel UK* which contains references to the contents of 57 UK publications. It also includes references to the legal sections and law reports from *The Guardian*, *The Independent* and *The Times*. *Westlaw UK* has the most comprehensive legal journals index and many libraries locate their online legal journals index source as *Westlaw UK*.

You have already used *Lawtel* earlier in this chapter to search for subjects and cases in sport contexts.

EXERCISE 1.5

In pairs, one person takes Lee and Felix (1999) and Charlish (2003) and the other person takes Gardiner (2005 and 2007). These articles will be central to Chapters 3 and 4 in this text. Search, save and share your articles which you will search using the 'Legal Journals Index' on *Westlaw UK* or EBSCO 'Sports Discus' or equivalent in your institution.

Lee, T. and Felix, A. (1999) 'Case comment: Smoldon v Whitworth and Nolan' *Journal of Personal Injury Litigation* 3: 218–221 (in preparation for Chapter 3).

Charlish, P. (2003) 'Case comment–Richard Vowles–Rugby Case' *Journal of Personal Injury Litigation* 2 (85–89): 1–6 (in preparation for Chapter 3).

Gardiner, S. (2005) 'Should more matches end up in court?' *New Law Journal* July, 155, no. 7183: 998–1000 (in preparation for Chapter 4).

Gardiner, S. (2007) 'Sports participation and criminal liability' Analysis *Sport and the Law Journal* 15 (1): 19–30.

Legal revision texts, law study books and law dictionaries

It is often difficult when studying sport and law on a sports studies or similar course to find an accessible and reasonably priced general law guide to the legal topics you are applying to sport or recreation on your modules or dissertation. It is unlikely that you will find everything you need in one text. However, there are some relatively short and accessible generic legal guides that are suitable for quick reference to principles or summaries covering the areas of law commonly applied to sport contexts. For example, the following three texts from the 'Nutshells' series by Sweet and Maxwell are very good, accessible, general guides and, in particular, can support you in working on the areas supporting Chapters 2, 3, 4 and 5 of this text:

Bermingham, V. (2008) *Torts* 9th edn, London: Sweet and Maxwell.
Darbyshire, P. (2007) *English Legal System* 7th edn, London: Sweet and Maxwell.
Dobson, P. (2008) *Criminal Law* 9th edn, London: Sweet and Maxwell.

In addition, Routledge-Cavendish also publish a 'law cards' series of small ring-bound booklets in areas such as employment law, criminal law, torts, etc. There are a range of general law texts aimed at supporting the delivery of A-level law which undergraduate sports studies students engaging in law may find useful as a concise introduction to the areas of law applied in their sport law modules. For example:

Barker, D. and Padfield C. (2002) *Law Made Simple* 11th edn, Oxford: Elsevier.
Cavendish Law Cards *AS Level Law* London: Cavendish.
Routledge-Cavendish Law Card Series (2006) Law Cards *Employment Law* 5th edn, Oxon: Routledge-Cavendish.
Turner, C. (2003) *Tort Law* London: Hodder and Stoughton.

It is useful to explore the range of law study guides for courses and using law libraries, as well as law dictionaries. For example:

Clinch, P. (2001) *Using a Law Library: a student's guide to legal research skills* London: Blackstone Press.
Mozley and Whitley's (1993) *Law Dictionary* 11th edn, London: Butterworths.
Thomas, P. and Knowles, J. (2001) *Dane and Thomas: How to use a Law Library* London: Sweet and Maxwell.

Part two: sport, recreation and law books and journals

The literature supporting the study of legal aspects of sport, recreation and leisure has been steadily growing over the last 20 years. Since almost any aspect of law can be applied to sport and recreation contexts, the literature can be generated from, among other things:

- controversial incidents and debates or issues arising from such incidents (e.g. violence on the field, fraud or betting issues, doping)
- judged case law
- commentaries by practitioners and professional or sport governing bodies
- sport law interests of academics from disciplines related to sport law
- research interests of individual academics and partnerships with practitioners
- media interest and television documentaries.

The books you access on your modules or dissertation will vary according to the module reading lists selected by academic staff and the sources you find and feed into your work. Sport and recreation law texts which cover a range of topics in one text are listed below and include those from other jurisdictions.

Examples of general sport law texts suitable for use by students on sport, physical education and recreation-related courses

Anderson, P. (1999) *Sports Law and Regulation* Milwaukee: Marquette University Press.*

Anderson, P. (1999) *Sports Law: A Desktop Handbook* Milwaukee: National Sport Law Institute.*

Barnes, J. (1996) *Sports and the Law in Canada* 3rd edn, Toronto: Butterworths.*

Beloff, M., Kerr, T. and Demetriou M. (1999) *Sports Law* Oxford: Hart Publishing.

Collins, V. (1993) *Recreation and the Law* London: Routledge.

Corbett, R., Findlay, H. and Lech, D. (2007) *Legal Issues in Sport* Toronto: Montgomery see Centre for Sport and Law www.sportlaw.ca.

Cox, N. and Schuster, A. (2004) *Sport and the Law* Dublin: First Law.

Dougherty, N. (2002) *Sport, Physical Activity and the Law* Champaign, Illinois: Sagamore Publishing.

Gardiner, S., O'Leary, J., Welch, R., Blackshaw, I. and Boyes, S. (2006) *Sports Law* 3rd edn, London: Cavendish.

Gibson, A. and Gee-Clough, D. (1999) *Australian Sports Law* CCH.*

Grayson, E. (2000) *Sport and the Law* 2nd edn, London: Butterworths.

Greenfield, S. and Osborne, G. (eds) (2000) *Sport and Law in Contemporary Society* London: Frank Cass.

Healey, D. (2005) *Sport and the Law* 3rd edn, Sydney: University of New South Wales Press.

Kevan, T., Adamson, D. and Cottrell (2002) *Sports Personal Injury: Law and Practice* London: Sweet and Maxwell.

Lewis, A. and Taylor, J. (eds) (2003) *Sport: Law and Practice* London: Butterworths, LexisNexis.

Moore, C. (2000) *Sports Law and Litigation* 2nd edn, Welwyn Garden City: CLT Professional Publishers.

Nygaard, G. and Boone, T.H. (1995) *A Coach's Guide to Sport Law* Champaign, Illinois: Human Kinetics Publishers.*

* Sports law books in other jurisdictions.

Books covering a particular theme on legal aspects of sport or recreation

Lead texts

Kitchen, J. and Corbett, R. (1995) *Negligence and Liability – A Guide for Recreation and Sport Organisations* St Mary's, Ontario: Centre for Sport and Law, Canada.[12]

McArdle, D. (2000) *Football, Society and the Law* London: Cavendish.

O'Leary, J. (ed.) (2001) *Drugs and Doping in Sport: A socio-legal perspective* London: Cavendish.

Whitlam, P. (2005) *Case Law in Physical Education and School Sport* Leeds: Coachwise 1st4 sport.

Additional texts

Benedict, J.R. (1998) *Athletes and Acquaintance Rape* London: Sage.

Blackshaw, I. (2002) *Mediating National and International Sports Disputes* Dodrecht: TMC Asser Press, Netherlands.

Blackshaw, I., Seikman, R. and Soek, J.W. (2006) *The Court of Arbitration for Sport 1984–2004* The Hague: TMC Asser Press.

Caiger, A. and Gardiner, S. (eds) (2000) *Professional Sport in the European Union: Regulation and Re-regulation* The Hague: TMC Asser Press.

Fraser, D. (2005) *Cricket and the Law: The Man in White is always Right* Oxon: Routledge.

Gray, J.T. (1996) *The Stadium Game* Milwaukee: National Sports Law Institute.

Gray, J.T. (1999) *Sports Law Practice* 2nd edn, Charlottesville, Virginia: Lexis Law Publishing.

Grayson, E. (1999) *School Sport and the Law* Kingston: Croner Publishing.

Hartley, H.J. (2001) *Exploring Sport and Leisure Disasters: A socio-legal perspective* London: Cavendish.

Karin, Volkheim-Caplan (2002) *Sexual Harassment in Sport: Impacts, issues and challenges* Oxford: Meyer & Meyer Sport.

Pittman, A.T., Spengler, J.O. and Young, S.J. (2002) *A Casebook Approach to Legal Concepts in Sport: The most important cases of the 20th Century* Gainsville, Florida: Florida Books (textbook and CD Rom).

Soek, J.W. (2006) *The Strict Liability Principle and the Human Rights of Athletes in Doping Cases* The Hague: T.M.C. Asser Press.

Examples of chapters in books relevant to legal aspects of sport

Hartley, H.J. (2001) 'Legal principles and issues: Managing disciplinaries in sport and recreation', in K. Hylton, P. Bramham, D. Jackson and M. Nesti (eds) *Sport Development: Principles, Policy and Process* London: Routledge, pp.170–194.

Messner, M.A. (1992) 'The embodiment of masculinity', in M.A. Messner (ed.) *Power at Play: Sports and the Problem of Masculinity* Boston: Beacon Press.

Messner, M.A. (2002) 'Playing center: The triad of violence in men's sports', in Messner *Taking the Field*, Women, Men and Sports, Sport and Culture Series, vol. 4, Minneapolis: University of Minnesota Press.

Moore, C. (2000) 'Sport and the Law of Tort', in C. Moore (ed.) *Sports Law and Litigation* Welwyn Garden City: CLT Professional Publishers.

Parry, S.J. (1998) 'Violence and aggression in contemporary sport', in M.J. McNamee and S.J. Parry (eds) *Ethics and Sport* London: Routledge, pp. 205–224.

Young, K. (2004) 'Sport and Violence', in J. Coakley and E. Dunning (eds) *Handbook of Sports Studies*, pp. 282–407.

Do you regularly check publishers' websites for new books? Do you check if publishers have 'e-books' where you may be able to access, view, or print, at a cost, chapters of books, if you do not need to purchase the whole text?

Examples of non-legal titles which are relevant to legal aspects of sport and recreation

Appenzeller, H. (ed) (2005) *Risk Management in Sport: Issues and Strategies* 2nd edn, Durham: NC Academic Press.

B.A.A.L.P.E. (2004) *Safe Practice in Physical Education and School Sport* Leeds: Coachwise Solutions Ltd.

Boxhill, J. (ed.) (2003) *Sports Ethics: An Anthology* Oxford: Blackwell.

Brackenridge, C. (2001) *Spoilsports: Understanding and Preventing Sexual Exploitation in Sport* London: Routledge.

Brackenridge, C., Pitchford, A., Russell, K. and Nutt, G. (2007) *Child Welfare in Football* Oxon: Routledge.

Darby, P., Johnes, M. and Mellor, G. (eds) (2005) *Soccer and Disaster: International Perspectives* Oxon: Routledge.

Frosdick, S. and Whalley, J. (eds) *Sport and Safety Management* London: Butterworths-Heinemann.

Houlihan, B. (2002) *Dying to Win: Doping in Sport and the Development of Anti-doping Policy in Europe* Strasbourg: Council of Europe.

Kerr, J.J. (2005) *Rethinking Aggression and Violence in Sport* Oxon: Routledge.

Scraton, P. (2000) *Hillsborough: The Truth* Edinburgh: Mainstream.

Scraton, P., Jemphrey, A. and Coleman, S. (1995) *No Last Rights: The Denial of Justice and Promulgation of Myth in the Aftermath of the Hillsborough Disaster* Liverpool City Council, Hillsborough Project, Centre for Studies in Crime and Social Justice, Ormskirk, Lancs.

Severs, J. (2003) *Safety and Risk in Primary School Physical Education – A Guide for Teachers* London: Routledge.

Severs, J., Whitlam P. and Woodhouse J. (2003) *Safety and Risk in Primary School Physical Education: A guide for teachers* London: Routledge.

Spengler, J.O., Connaughton, D.P. and Pittman, A.T. (2006) *Risk Management in Sport and Recreation* Champaign, Illinois: Human Kinetics.

Examples of sport, recreation and law journals

*Entertainment and Sport Law Journal**
International Sport Law Journal
International Sports Law Review
*Journal of Legal Aspects of Sport**
Marquette Sports Law Review
*Sport and the Law Journal**
Sport Law, Administration and Practice
Sports Law Bulletin

* These are the leading academic sport and law journals which are peer-refereed.

EXERCISE 1.6

Search for the following journal articles. Download and save them. Read them in relation to relevant chapters and exercises later in this text:

Beloff, M. (1996) 'The CAS at the Olympics' *Sport and the Law Journal* 4 (3): 5–9 (used in Chapter 8).

Ruff, A. (2002) 'Facial injuries and football before school' *Entertainment Law* 2 (1): 89–97 (used in Chapter 2 or 3).

Examples of non-legal journals which include articles on legal aspects of sport and recreation, often linked to other relevant disciplines

European Journal of Sport Management
Journal of Sport and Social Issues
Journal of Sport Management
Leisure Studies
Managing Leisure
Sociology of Sport Journal
Sport and Society

You should be exploring all the services of the university library. For example, are there collaborative lending arrangements with other university libraries? Can you check their catalogues? Are you using the Inter-Library loans (ILL) service for books and journals which are not included in your own university stock? If you only have a limit of six ILLs per student, are you working collaboratively with other students on your module/year group to access and share resources effectively?

EXERCISE 1.7

In groups of four, take one article each from the following list. Search for your article, download it, save it, and share it with other students in your group. Read them in relation to Chapter 4 exercises:

Coakley, J. and Hughes, R. (1991) 'Positive deviance among athletes: the implications of over-conformity to the sport ethic' *Sociology of Sport Journal* 8: 307–325.

Messner, M.A. (1990) 'When bodies are weapons: masculinity, violence and sport' *International Review for the Sociology of Sport* 25: 203–221.

Rosenberg, D. (2003) 'The banality of violence and the McSorley Affair' *Avante* 9 (2): 30–42.

Welch, M. (1997) 'Violence against women by professional football players: a gender analysis of hypermasculinity, positional status, narcissism and entitlement' *Journal of Sport and Social Issues* 21 (4): 392–411.

Part three: organisations, people and the media

Sport and law websites

British Association for Sport and Law

Despite its domestic label the BASL www.britishsportslaw.org has had a very international membership and journal since its inception in 1993 at Old Trafford, the home of Manchester United FC. It aims to 'assist the development of sports law as a legal discipline and provide a network for practitioners, academics and sports administrators' (BASL website, accessed 21 August 2007). The BASL has an annual conference each October as well as regional seminars and networking events, hosted by corporate members. The journal *Sport and the Law Journal* has various sections including opinion and practice, analysis section (for longer refereed articles), case reports and book reviews. If you are accessing the journal (electronically available from 2002 onwards), you will need either your individual username and password, or the username and password of your institution or university, if they have paid an annual subscription for the hard copy and electronic journal. There are reduced rates of membership for academics and students.[13]

EXERCISE 1.8

In groups of four, select one article each from the list below. Locate, download and save your article and share it with the rest of the group:

Barker, S. (2005) 'Is there a case for more criminal justice system involvement in sporting incidents?' Opinion and Practice, *Sport and the Law Journal* 13 (2): 13–15.

Brackenridge, C.H. and Kirkby, S. (1997) 'Playing safe: assessing the risk of sexual exploitation to elite athletes' *International Review for the Sociology of Sport* 32: 407–418.

Bradford, M. (2005) 'Sport, gender and the law' *The International Sports Law Journal* 1–2: 78–83.

Williams, Y. (2006) 'The potential of the safeguarding vulnerable groups Bill for children's sport' *Entertainment and Sports Law Journal* 4 (1): 1–4.

EXERCISE 1.9

In the 'Sport and the Law Journal Law Reports' in vol. 15, issue 1, 2007, p.103, find the case of *Stretford v Football Association Ltd* [2007] EWCA Civ 238; [2007] 2 Lloyd's Rep 31. Were the human rights of Paul Stretford breached, under Article 6, when disciplinary proceedings against him, relating to circumstances surrounding his acquisition of the right to represent Wayne Rooney, were halted and submitted to arbitration under Rule K of the FA Rules?

Higher Education Academy, Hospitality, Leisure, Sport and Tourism Subject Network

The Higher Education Academy Subject Network for Hospitality, Leisure, Sport and Tourism[14] (www.hlst.heacademy.ac.uk) is based at Oxford Brookes University, Wheatley Campus, Wheatley, Oxford, England. It supports Lecturers in Further and Higher Education in the UK working in these subject areas and has an excellent and well-designed website of resources as well as highly subsidised seminars and workshops. Students also use their website resources. The Learning Guides, reusable learning objects, *LINK* issues, and the international online refereed journal are all very popular. In addition, there are links to relevant publishers, book reviews, consultations and opportunities to bid for funded projects and collaborate with other institutions.

EXERCISE 1.10

Browse the HLST HEA website and make sure you know where to find:

- The *LINK* issues
- The Resource Guides
- The international e-journal.

EXERCISE 1.11

Locate the 'Event Archives'. Locate the Events 2000–2005. Find out who presented papers at 'Teaching Legal Aspects of Sport' 18 May 2005, Leeds Metropolitan University, Headingley Carnegie Stadium.

EXERCISE 1.12

Locate, download and save:

Hartley, H.J. (2008) *Sport and Law: Learning Resource Guide.*

Hartley, H.J. (2005) 'Collaborations in the curriculum–sport and law: an emerging area?' *LINK* issue 12.

EXERCISE 1.13

Locate, download and save the learning resource guides on:

• Governance and sport
• Ethics and sport
• Event management

These resource guides cover areas related to legal aspects of sport such as ethics or risk management, as well as access to relevant professional organisations or policy makers in sport.

The Centre for Sport and Law, Canada

The CSL (www.sportlaw.ca) is headed by Dr Hilary Findlay Phd LLB, and is run by a team of lawyers, agents, professors who all have relevant sport experience, is based in St Catharine's, Ontario, Canada, and in 2007, celebrated 15 years of providing consulting services and practical resources on legal and risk management issues to all levels of the Canadian sport system. The website is very clear, well designed and easy to navigate. The articles, which are free to download, are grouped usefully under themes and there is a free e-mail newsletter. The bookstore includes ten CSL '40-minute' handbooks. Each handbook follows a particular theme and is written in clear accessible language, suitable for coaching/sport practitioners and sports students who may be engaging in legal aspects of sport and recreation for the first time.[15]

EXERCISE 1.14

Familiarise yourself with all areas of the CSL website, especially the articles and handbooks sections. Check out all the 'writings' under the headings of bullying, harassment and violence (Chapters 4 and 5 in this text), doping (Chapter 8), liability for negligence (Chapters 2 and 3), procedural fairness (Chapter 8) and risk management (Chapter 6 in this text).

1 Locate, download and save the following articles:
   - 'Violence in sport – it's your responsibility too'
   - 'Violence in sport – Part II: Dealing with violence as a legal issue'
   - 'Playing Russian roulette with supplements: coaches need to know'
   - 'The coach–athlete relationship – a legal view'
   - 'Legal liability and risk management: a handbook for directors'
   - 'What is the standard of care?'
   - 'The standard of care for coaches'
   - 'Maintaining fairness in investigations and hearings'
   - 'Suspending a coach before a hearing'
   - 'Risk management for sport organisations and sport facilities'

OR

2 Access or share a copy of Corbett, R., Findlay, H. and Lech, D. (2007) *Legal Issues in Sport: A Toolkit for Sport Managers* Edmond Montgomery Publications (www.emp.ca).

National Sport Law Institute

The NSLI (http://law.marquette.edu/), at Marquette University Law School, founded in 1989, is the only institute of its kind associated with an American law school and has extensive, high-profile national and international networks, well beyond the sports law alumni association. The NSLI is affiliated to the Marquette University Law School Sport Law programme, which provides sports law courses and internships with local sports organisations. The NSLI sponsors many local, national sport and law events, including conferences and symposia for the sports industry, drawing on its research and study of legal, ethical and business issues, affecting amateur and professional sports. It has a well-respected, edited journal *The Marquette Sports Law Review*, which regularly has international or comparative law contributions, as well as a *For the Record Facility Report* and a newsletter, *You Make the Call*. Conference proceedings from the annual NSLI fall conference can be purchased overseas. There are two categories of student membership: those students enrolled on the sports law programme, as well as international student members.

EXERCISE 1.15

Familiarise yourself with the National Sport Law Institute website and save it to your favourites list.

Examine the annual fall conference proceedings since 2003 and note presenters' names, papers, publications and institutions which relate to your areas of interest. Check out the websites of presenters' institutions or firms for more details of up-to-date publications.

EXERCISE 1.16

Brief yourself on the background of Professor Paul Anderson and Professor Matthew Mitten of the National Sports Law Institute, recording at least four of their publications, which match your module or course of study.

EXERCISE 1.17

Find out how to order a copy of the one of the following articles from the *Marquette Sports Law Review* (perhaps through inter-library loan system, if the item is not stocked in your library):

McLaren, R. (2004) 'The CAS AD HOC Division at the Athens Olympic Games' *Marquette Sports Law Review* 15, Fall (1): 175–203.
Opie, H. (2002) 'Australian medico-legal issues in sport: the view from the grandstand' *Marquette Sports Law Review* 13: 113–148.

Sport and Recreation Law Association

The SRLA[16] (http://srlaweb.org/) aims to further the study and dissemination of information regarding legal aspects of sport and recreation within both the public and the private sectors. The membership includes, for example, practising attorneys, university lecturers, administrators, athletic directors and recreation professionals. The SRLA has a refereed journal the *Journal of Legal Aspects of Sport* edited by Professor Paul Anderson, Assistant Director of the NSLI at Marquette University Law School. The Annual SRLA conference abstracts, like the journal, display a wide range of interests, clearly relevant to academics and practitioners in schools, universities, and public or private sport and recreation.

EXERCISE 1.18

Familiarise yourself with the SRLA website. Look in particular at the conference information (and abstracts), the *Journal of Legal Aspects of Sport*, the 'Teaching Tips' by SRLA members and related links.

Locate the SRLA Annual Conference on Sport, Physical Activity, Recreation and the Law, 28 February 2007, University of North Carolina at Chapel Hill. Browse the abstracts and select one topic which interests you which links to an area of study or personal sport interest or experience. Stay on this conference site and locate the following abstracts and complete the tasks below:

Lovett, M.D. (2007) 'Terrain Park lawsuit at Jackson Hole Mountain Resort: Negligence of Inherent Risk?' 9.05 Friday 3 March.

1   Outline the circumstances and decisions to date in this skiing negligence case of *Dunbar v Jackson Hole Mountain Resort* 392 F3d 1145 (10th cir 2004). What is your opinion on the decisions so far? Should this injury on a half-pipe be regarded as an inherent risk of skiing?

Carroll, M.S., Connaughton, D.P. and Spengler, J.O. (2007) 'Hazing in sport: implications for sport organisations and practitioners' 12.10 Saturday 3 March.

2   In a study conducted by Alfred University in 1999, what percentage of college athletes reported being subjected to some form of hazing (initiation rites)?

The Asser International Sports Law Centre

The AISLC (www.sportslaw.nl) in the Netherlands has a range of high-profile seminars and conferences and produces the *International Sports Law Journal* (ISLJ) as well as the Asser series of international sports law books, published by TMC Asser Press. The website is well designed and easy to navigate. There is an extensive international bibliography of sports law topics provided by the Peace Palace Library, as well as access on the website to documents, case law and news updates. It is useful to browse the detailed database of national and international sport law associations, centres, journals and courses.

EXERCISE 1.19

Familiarise yourself with the AISLC website. Make sure you can locate and navigate the sports law bibliography, the journals, national and international sports law associations and centres.

Using the sports law bibliography locate and check access to the following references:

Anderson, J. (2006) 'Recent developments in tort liability for foul play' *International Sports Law Journal* 1–2: 41–48 (under the search theme of 'negligence').
Hartley, H.J. (2004) 'An innocent abroad? The Diane Modahl doping case 1994–2001: sports science and the law' *International Sports Law Journal* 3–4: 61–65

(under the search theme of 'strict liability').

EXERCISE 1.20

Divide into groups of three. Each person should provide a summary of one of the following:

1   a sports law organisation (excluding the United States)
2   a sports law journal
3   a sports law centre.

Search for and locate the following journal articles from the AISLC *International Sports Law Journal*:

Vrijman, E. (2007) 'The "Official Statement from WADA on the Vrijman Report": Unintentional proof to the contrary?' *International Sports Law Journal* 1–2: 3–10.
Zagklis, A.K. (2006) 'The CAS ad hoc division at the XX Olympic Winter Games in Turin' *International Sports Law Journal* 3 (4): 47–52.

The International Association of Sports Law

The IASL (www.iasl.org) was founded at an International Congress of Sports Law in December 1992 in Greece and is based in Athens. It has a particular interest in the links between the Olympics and the law. Members are people who actively participate in research, teaching and practical application of sports law. The IASL organises seminars and conferences, as well as collaborating with other sports law organisations.[17]

The Australian and New Zealand Sports Law Association

ANZSLA (www.anzsla.com.au) was formed in 1990 and is based in Randwick, New South Wales, Australia. Members include lawyers, administrators, academics and government representatives. The contributions to the annual conferences reinforce the links between sport law, government and those working in policy, practice and administration of sport. Members have access to 'sport law shorts' updates on cases and issues, the newsletter and the *ANZSLA Commentator*, the refereed ANZSLA sports law journal. The 2007 ANZSLA Conference is on the Gold Coast Australia in November and has 'Sport-Risky Business' as the theme. Most sections of the website are accessible by members only with the exception of information on the annual conference and an excellent list of relevant links to sports law.

Sports governing body or legal organisation websites

World Anti-Doping Agency

WADA (www.wada-ama.org) is an essential part of your web browsing if you are studying any topic related to the legal aspects of doping in sport. Make sure you familiarise yourself with all the sections of this website. It contains the WADA Code, the Prohibited List and the Therapeutic Use Exemptions (TUEs). Under 'resources' there are information resources for athletes and anti-doping organisations, including questions and answers on TUEs and medication, as well as the *Play True* WADA magazine. WADA also has a range of funded research projects, located under the 'education' section and reports on WADA international conferences. The press releases and news updates are very interesting and highlight the currency, relevance, controversy and dynamic nature of anti-doping in the international sport arena.

EXERCISE 1.21

Locate, download and save the Prohibited List and the Therapeutic Use Exemptions (TUEs) which runs from 1 January 2009, from the WADA website.

EXERCISE 1.22

Locate, download and save the WADA Code, known as 'The Code'.

EXERCISE 1.23

Complete and submit the doping quiz on the WADA website.

EXERCISE 1.24

Locate, download and save one of the *Play True* issues in an area of your interest or one which supports a theme from Chapter 8 of this text.

EXERCISE 1.25

Click 'education' then 'social science research', 'completed research projects', click 'overview' then click 'funded research projects'. Find the executive summary of the first research project led by Dr Sue Backhouse at Leeds Metropolitan University. Outline the research project and its main findings.

The Court of Arbitration for Sport

The Court of Arbitration for Sport (www.tas-cas.org) (covered in Chapter 8) is based in Lausanne, Switzerland. The website section on 'presentation' outlines the workings of CAS using a very helpful question-and-answer approach, whilst the 'statistics' section provides data on numbers of cases since 1986. The case law section includes more recent cases which have not been included in the *Digest of CAS Awards* edited by the Secretary General, Matthieu Reeb.[18] All CAS arbitrators are listed under 'members' and the 'media' section provides short pieces on incidents and issues which have or will be referred to the CAS.

EXERCISE 1.26

Find the answers to the following questions under the 'presentation' section of the CAS website.

1 Who can refer a case to CAS?
2 How are the arbitrators chosen?
3 Are all arbitration processes confidential?

EXERCISE 1.27

There are around ten CAS arbitrators from Great Britain. Access the list of 'members' on the CAS website and locate a judge, a barrister and a solicitor, from Great Britain, who are on the list of CAS arbitrators.

EXERCISE 1.28

Locate and access the 'media' section. Why have a group of Austrian skiers filed an appeal to CAS arising out of a police investigation at the 2006 Winter Olympics in Turin, Italy?

EXERCISE 1.29

Locate and access the statistics section. How many cases were filed with CAS in 1996 and 2006?

UK Sport

UK Sport (www.uksport.gov.uk), established in 1996, is responsible for managing and distributing public investment and is a statutory distributor of funds raised by the National Lottery. It is accountable to parliament through the Department for Culture, Media and Sport (UK Sport website home page, accessed 28 August 2007).The UK Sport website is well designed and easy to navigate. The drug-free sport section houses the UK Sport anti-doping policy with links to the main 'athlete zone' and '100 per cent ME', containing the drug-information-database (DID). This includes important and useful information on natural supplements, Therapeutic Use Exemptions, Athletes' Whereabouts Rules for out-of-competition testing and informative 'question and answer' sections. The UK Sport website also includes the National Equality Standards in Sport, and information on investment in sport and sport events.

Sports Coach UK

Sports Coach UK (www.sportscoachuk.org) (formerly the National Coaching Foundation) is 'a charitable organisation and is the lead agency for development of the UK Coaching System' (SCUK website, accessed 28 August 2007). It is responsible for all UK Sports Coach Education, including the UK Coaching Certificate, coach education workshops and also provides a wide range of resources and support, including information on research projects related to coaching. Books, videotapes, leaflets, on a very wide range of coaching topics, can be purchased via the website and particularly through *Coachwise*.[19] The online newsletter is free but access to *Coaching Edge*, the quarterly coaching magazine, is by subscription only.

Child Protection in Sport Unit

The CPSU (www.thecpsu.org.uk) was set up in 2001, as a partnership between the National Society for the Prevention of Cruelty to Children (NSPCC) and Sport England.[20] They aim to be the first point of contact for sports organisations (and individuals) on child protection issues, co-ordinate information and training for sports organisations, commission research into child protection (CP) in sport issues, and develop and promote standards for child protection procedures and training in all sports (CPSU website, accessed 28 August 2007). This website has a range of essential materials, including the ten standards for safeguarding and protecting children in sport, a practical guide to taking children on trips, a guide to developing child protection policy, recruiting volunteers, and a very useful section on frequently asked questions. There are briefing papers on Criminal Records Bureau checks and guidelines on photographs and images of children in sport. The CPSU has well-established links with academic research on child protection issues in sport and provides a very good section on NSPCC and ongoing research, guidance for students and researchers, including a research checklist, suggested research areas, a good practice research checklist and links with useful related books, articles and websites.

EXERCISE 1.30

Go onto the UK Sport website and locate the Drug Information Database (DID). Find out what is meant by an 'unclassified substance' and a 'topical preparation', providing an example of each.

Explain the two kinds of Therapeutic Use Exemptions.

Identify one problem with a competitive athlete taking supplements.

EXERCISE 1.31

Under 'publications' find the Latest Anti-Doping Quarterly Report (February 2007). Table 2. Is it true that 29 per cent of potential doping violations were in the category of anabolic agents and 24 per cent in the category of stimulants?

EXERCISE 1.32

Go onto the Sports Coach UK website link to their 'Coachwise' resources and find the revised 2007 version of *Safeguarding and Protecting Children: A Guide for Sports People*. Why is the word 'safeguarding' now used in current documents and education?

EXERCISE 1.33

Click onto the Sports UK workshops in your region or your equivalent coaching body. Are there any workshops or resources on 'coaching and the law'? Find out details on content, dates, access and costs.

EXERCISE 1.34

Go onto the Child Protection in Sport Unit website at www.thecpsu.org.uk

Locate the 'Frequently asked questions' section. Find the responses to the questions:

1 Are the risks of abuse greater in some sports than others?
2 What can an organisation do to safeguard the interest of children?
3 How are the allegations of child abuse in sport investigated?

EXERCISE 1.35

Locate, download and save the following from the CPSU publications:

CPSU (2002) 'Standards for Safeguarding and Protecting Children in Sport'

EXERCISE 1.36

Locate the section of the CPSU website on 'Advice for Students and Researchers'.

Download and save:

- Good practice checklist
- Suggested topics for study
- Existing research and research in progress
- Useful books and articles.

Royal Society for the Prevention of Accidents

RoSPA (www.rospa.com) is a registered charity established over 80 years ago. 'By providing information, advice, resources, and training, RoSPA is actively involved in the promotion of safety and the prevention of accidents in all areas of life – at work, in the home, on the roads, in schools, at leisure and on (or near) water' (RoSPA website, accessed 28 August 2007). The website has an extensive database on accidents and injuries, an online resource for young (adolescent) workers, and 18 key safety points which act as a guide to outside organisations, drawing on established ideas about risk analysis, perception and management. The RoSPA website has a dedicated theme of 'water and leisure' with a range of fact sheets, news items, case studies, statistics, and safety information.

Health and Safety Executive

The Health and Safety Executive HSE (www.hse.gov.uk) website has extensive information on health and safety, risk assessment, industry specific items (see education), including a site on 'school trips' and learning from serious incidents, such as the death of ten-year-old Lancashire schoolboy Max Palmer, at a plunge pool in Glenridding, Cumbria, in May 2002.[21] It provides access to short, clearly presented leaflets on a range of health and safety topics, as well as other items, which can be ordered from the HSE bookshop.

EXERCISE 1.37

Familiarise yourself with the main themes on the RoSPA website home page.

Locate the 'Water and Leisure' section. See if you can find the fact sheet on 'Child Holiday Swimming Pool Safety' and answer the following questions:

1   How many children under ten have died in holiday swimming pools abroad in the last ten years?
2   Which kind of facility has the highest number of those drownings?
3   Why are two–three year olds most at risk?

EXERCISE 1.38

On the 'Water and Leisure' section, find the Leisure Safety Information sheet on Trampoline Safety and find out the four key safety issues.

EXERCISE 1.39

Explore the accident statistics database experimenting with the categories (e.g. gender, activity, part of body injured) and find an accident statistic, which relates to an area of interest to you or a chapter in this text.

EXERCISE 1.40

Find the 'aboutrospa' section on the home page of the RoSPA website. Locate, download and save the two pages on RoSPA safety point, that is, 'RoSPAs approach to safety – the 18 key safety points'.

EXERCISE 1.41

Go on the Health and Safety Executive website at www.hse.gov.uk.

Locate and download the leaflet 'Five steps to risk assessment' INDG 163 (rev2) June 2006, in preparation for Chapter 6 on risk assessment. See www.hse.gov.uk/pubns. Check out the related website of *Workplace Health Connect* to explore other resources on risk assessment or health and safety advice for small businesses. See www.workplacehealthconnect.co.uk.

EXERCISE 1.42

On the main HSE website locate 'your industry'. Click on this and click on 'Education'. Click on 'School Trips' and find the 'Glenridding Site'. What is this site for? Locate 'Glenridding Beck – the facts' and download and save 'Glenridding Beck–Investigation' pdf file, to use in Chapter 6 on risk assessment and Chapter 7 on manslaughter (see www.hse.gov.uk/schooltrips/investigation/index.htm).

Professional and voluntary bodies and government departments

Professional and voluntary bodies and relevant government department websites provide a more up-to-date picture of policy, management and legal issues than books or journals. You should be checking them regularly, drawing on, for example, press releases, research reports, conferences and conference proceedings, public consultations, publications, leaflets, guides, training opportunities and press coverage of key individuals in those organisations and departments. If key academics are researching and publishing in areas of law, policy, management etc used to inform policy or campaigns for change, then follow up the names of those academics in their own institutional website, where you will find more current and related research references. Voluntary and campaign groups websites also often provide a more critical view of the context or adequacy of relevant legislation, as well as recording key cases.

EXERCISE 1.43

Divide into pairs and each pair take one governing body or professional organisation in or related to a sport and recreation context. You can check up the organisations listed in the learning resource guides on 'Sport Governance' and 'Sport Development' on the HEA subject website at www.hlst.heacademy.ac.uk.

Or, focus on one of the following, depending on your areas of study:

• Central Council for Physical Recreation (CCPR)
• Leisure Studies Association (LSA)
• Institute for Leisure and Amenities Management (ILAM)
• Institute for Sport and Physical Activity Leadership (ISPAL)
• Volunteering England (VE)
• Disability Rights Commission (or Equality Commission) (DRC or EC)
• UK Sport (UKS)
• Sports Coach UK (SCUK)
• Department for Culture, Media and Sport (DCMS).

Check your chosen website for any research, publications, press releases, courses, conferences, newsletter items, which highlight or are relevant to a legal aspect of sport and recreation or themes covered in the other chapters of this text (negligence, criminal assault, sport subcultures, breaches of health and safety, safeguarding children, discrimination, harassment, risk assessment, manslaughter etc). Download and save the item and explain the item to your study partner, including the relevance to your module or dissertation topic.

EXERCISE 1.44

In pairs, work on the Centre for Corporate Accountability (CCA) website and locate and save one press release each from the following items. Share it with your study partner:

- Corporate Manslaughter charges relating to the outbreak of Legionnaires Disease at the Forum Centre in Cumbria, England
- The manslaughter charges against a first officer on a P&O European Ferry, arising from the sinking of the *Ouzo* yacht in 2006.

Explain the case to your study partner.

EXERCISE 1.45

Check the Law Commission and Home Office websites for reports or press releases on the proposals for first and second degree murder and manslaughter. Why have these proposals been made? What implications are there for violence on the sports field?

EXERCISE 1.46

Go on the Volunteering England *or* the Child Protection in Sport Unit website and find a model child protection policy or good practice on a child protection policy.

EXERCISE 1.47

Go on the CCPR or DCMS website and find out about the requirements of The Safeguarding Vulnerable Groups Act 2006 and the Independent Safeguarding Authority (ISA) in the UK. What is the ISA? What will it do?

Who is working in sport, law and recreation?

It is important to be informed about who is working in sport, recreation and the law. This may involve searches for lawyers, solicitors, academics, law firms, in various jurisdictions and keeping up to date with, among other things, conferences, journals, books, websites, press releases and press coverage of quotes and commentaries following incidents or cases.

EXERCISE 1.48

Each student in the group takes one person each from the academics listed below, who work in the areas of legal aspects of sport. Search for your academic. Locate and save information on:

1 their main areas of interest
2 one conference presentation
3 one journal article
4 one book or chapter in a book.

United Kingdom
Jack Anderson, Karen Bill, Ian Blackshaw, Simon Boyes, Celia Brackenridge, Andrew Caiger, Walter Cairns, Peter Charlish, Simon Gardiner, Hazel Hartley, Mark James, Patricia Leighton, Dave McArdle, John O'Leary, Richard Parrish, Geoff Pearson, Stephen Wetherill, Roger Welch, Yvonne Williams.

Canada
John Barnes, Rachel Corbett, Hilary Findlay, David Lech, Richard McLaren, Kevin Young.

Australia and New Zealand
Hayden Opie, Andy Gibson, Debra Healey, Paul Jonson, Ian Warren.

Netherlands
Robert Seikmann, Jan Willem Soek, Emile Vrijman.

Malaysia
Wardah Salman.

South Africa
Steve Cornelius, Stephen Nkosi, Paul Singh.

United States of America
Robert Ammon Jnr, Paul Anderson, Daniel Connaughton, Neil Dougherty, Gil Fried, James Gray, Lisa Pike Masteralexis, Lori Miller, James Nafziger, Andrew Pittman, Betty Van Der Smissen, John Wolohan.

EXERCISE 1.49

Choose one practitioner each from the list below and find out:

1 Where do they work?
2 Solicitor, barrister, judge . . . ?
3 What are their areas of speciality?
4 Find examples of their published work and/or references made to their comments in relation to legal case, issue, press release or report etc.

Darren Bailey, Nick Bitel, Sir Michael Beloff QC, Edward Broome, Nicholas de Marco, Charles Flint QC, Kate Gallafent, Edward Grayson, David Griffith–Jones, Mel Goldberg, Serena Hedley–Dent, Paul Harris, Andrew Hunter, Paul Kitson, Peter Leaver, Adam Lewis, Karen Moorhouse, Jane Mulcahy, Urvasi

Naidoo, David Pannick QC, Simon Pentol, Richard Pound QC, Murray Rosen QC, Kuldip Singh QC, Jonathan Taylor, Karena Vleck.

These are just to get you started. There are many more. Find a legal practitioner who works in the area of law applied to sport or education and provide a referenced 'pen portrait' of no more than one side of A4, which includes name, firm, location, a case or incident connected to him/her, one publication or press source,

Generic professional legal websites

In addition to using resources outlined so far in this chapter, you may also find the more generic professional legal websites useful:

- The Association of Women Solicitors at www.womensolicitors.org.uk
- Bar Council at www.barcouncil.org.uk
- Crown Prosecution Service at www.cps.gov.uk
- Home Office at www.homeoffice.gov.uk
- Law Commission at www.lawcom.gov.uk
- Law Society www.lawsociety.org.uk/home.law
- Legal Services Research Centre at www.lsrc.org.uk.

Law, sport and recreation in the news: using media and films

Print media

The print media cover a vast range of sporting events, incidents and issues and are a useful resource to help you illustrate the application of the law to past and current incidents and cases. This resource is also very useful for collecting examples of responses to sport incidents, as well as opinions on disciplinaries, cases and issues. It is advisable to keep a file of cuttings relevant to the themes studied on your sport, recreation and law modules; for example, violence, assault, doping and sport disciplinaries. It is advisable to focus on the broadsheets rather than the tabloids, for example, in England *The Times*, *The Guardian*, *The Daily Telegraph*, *The Independent*, or *The Observer* newspapers.[22]

Most university libraries subscribe to LexisNexis and list it under 'L' in their library online. It is usually listed as LexisNexis Executive or LexisNexis Newspapers. Libraries also have microfiche records of older newspaper articles. In addition, most newspapers have websites with some current articles online, often linked to past relevant articles, as well as providing a separate search facility, although there may be a subscription charge for some newspaper archives. Newspaper articles are also included in the articles search on *Lawtel*.

Television news media

You are advised to keep an eye on national and regional news programmes for coverage of legal matters relating to sport and recreation. In particular, look out for reports, articles on the day, or the day following, a significant, high-profile sporting matter, such as a violent incident, criminal charges or court judgment, announcement of disciplinary proceedings against an athlete, a doping incident, or during coverage of a legal issue at major sporting events such as the Olympic and Paralympic Games. Websites of a range of television companies are extremely useful for printable formats of reports, for educational use only, on current incidents and cases, for example in the UK, the *BBC*,[23] in the USA, *CNN* or *Fox*.[24]

Television and radio documentaries and current affairs programmes

Television and radio documentaries and current affairs programmes are a rich resource which you can use in the application of generic legal themes to or illustrate legal issues within sport and recreation contexts. Some examples of television or radio documentaries in the UK, relevant to sport, recreation and the law include:

- whistle blowing about safety in a sport context
- doping cases and issues in sport
- regulation of management development courses in the outdoors
- the legality of boxing
- assault cases in male sports
- the subculture, class, gender and lack of democracy in an English golf club
- corruption, bribes and scandals related to Olympic bids by host cities
- legal processes and issues relating to sport and leisure disasters
- child abuse in sport
- male university sports teams involved in sexual assault cases
- initiation rites, punishments and bullying in institutional settings
- radio programme on the inquiry into the death of a university student in Snowdonia during a university walking club activity.

Television dramas and films

Legal aspects of sport and recreation relate to other disciplines, such as sociology, psychology, sports science, sport and recreation management and policy making (see also Winfield and Osborne, 2001). Drama and films can assist you in:

- your understanding and illustration of a legal principle
- the application of a legal principle to a sport or recreation context
- appreciating a more personal or critical treatment of a case or the power relations facing those involved in seeking compensation or justice
- developing empathy for those parties involved in a legal case, issue or sports disciplinary
- providing a starting point for discussion from popular culture which might be more meaningful, relevant or current
- providing a springboard to encourage you and your peers to make connections with other disciplines, or, for example, organisational culture, structures, rules, management, bullying, resources issues in sport and recreation, which can impact on legal responsibilities.

EXERCISE 1.50

Go onto LexisNexis or Nexis if provided by your library online (using your Athens password). Click LexisNexis Executive. Use the search facility. Find one person or incident in sport or recreation which is linked to a legal theme in this text or on your sport and law module(s):

- Select English speaking
- Select major stories only
- Limit the dates of the search.

Once you have a list of articles, select one or two articles only from the quality broadsheets. Save them electronically and, if possible, contribute them to the group on the module, in consultation with your tutor, and with advice regarding the Copyright Licensing Authority (CLA) rules for educational purposes.

EXERCISE 1.51

Repeat the same search techniques on LexisNexis Executive on the following topics/names:

- 'Ben Thatcher' (the elbow collision with Perdo Mendes in soccer in April 2006)
- 'Willie Mason' (two incidents on the field in a world cup rugby match 2006)
- 'Lee Bower' or 'Kieran Dyer' (April 2005, two Newcastle United players fighting each other during a soccer match)
- 'Christine Oroghuru' (IAAF World Athletics Championships 400m Women–gold medal winner and the 12–month ban for failure to attend doping control out-of competition testing, Thursday 30 August, 2007)

OR

Use the same search facilities or ones which you know to locate coverage of a current incident or legal issue in your area of sport or recreation interest or useful for the physical education curriculum.

EXERCISE 1.52

Note one example of a documentary or current affairs programme which covered a topic related to legal aspects of sport and recreation. Explain the legal issue to your study partner or group and discuss ways in which it made you reflect on your own practices or those you have observed in sport and recreation.

EXERCISE 1.53

Go onto the news website of one of the leading television networks relevant to your location. Search for news coverage of one item, incident, or issue from the following themes in a sport or recreation context or that might be applied to one and report back to your study partner with a fully referenced one-page summary:

- Child protection (now safeguarding children and vulnerable adults)
- Discrimination
- Harassment
- Doping
- Violence or criminal assault in a sport or recreation context
- Breach of a statutory duty regarding health and safety
- Individual or corporate manslaughter
- Negligence
- Natural justice and disciplinaries
- Court of Arbitration for Sport.

EXERCISE 1.54

Get into groups of three. One person talk for two minutes. One person time the two minutes and make notes. One person listen and ask the speaker questions. Focus on the following topics. Swap roles once for the second topic:

1 In the film *Erin Brockovich* (starring Julia Roberts and Albert Finney) a group of local residents bring a mass/group negligence case against a large corporation (T&N), for allegedly causing illness and death in the community through the treatment of water from the T&N local plant. Outline the elements of negligence, which had to be proven. Focus particularly on, first, the issue of proving the cause of the illness and, second, proving that the T&N Corporate Board of Executives were aware of the risks of harm or injury, for which compensation is sought.
   Follow-up activity: follow this initial reflection with reading Chapter 2 on the three elements of negligence, particularly proving causation, and Chapter 7 on principles of corporate manslaughter.
2 *A Few Good Men* (starring Tom Cruise, Demi Moore and Kevin Bacon) is a drama in which two US marines are charged with the murder of a Corporal Santiago. What happened on the night in question? What was the relevance of the tradition of 'Code Red'? What does 'Code Red' tell you about organisational subculture and power? Was there more than one cause of Corporal Santiago's death?
   Follow-up activity: following this initial reporting and reflection, read Chapter 4 and focus on hegemonic masculinity, supported by subculture and different kinds of power. Revisit 'Code Red' using these and other relevant sociological concepts from your reading of Chapter 4. Consider the application of these ideas to initiation rites in sport or recreation contexts.

EXERCISE 1.55

If you are familiar with YouTube or Facebook or Myface[25] or similar sites or websites where people post blogs, then use these or other sites which might be useful. Try to find out about the information and commentary on the following:

1 'Tombstoning'. What is it? Who does it? Why? What is the view and actions of the authorities or rescue services? Is it or ought it to be a recognised sport?

2 'Parkour' or 'City Running'. What is this? Who takes part in it? Is it a recognised sport or a physical recreation activity?

3 Ball tampering in cricket. What is it? Give some examples? Specify the actual rule it breaks? Do players get caught and disciplined for this activity? Give examples.

4 Dwain Chambers – should he have gone to the Beijing Olympics as part of Team GB in 2008?

5 'Oscar Pistorius wins appeal and right to compete against able-bodied athletes in the international arena'. What is this story about from May 2008? Why is it so significant? Here is a very good example of the links between sports science and the law (see also *Modahl v British Athletics Federation Ltd* [2001] EWCA Civ 1447; [2002] 1 WLR 1192, in Chapter 8 of this text). Is sports science the only lens to bring to the case of Oscar Pistorius? Identify and explain the contribution of other academic disciplines to his story.

It is good to build up your skills and confidence in identifying and accessing many of the resources included in this chapter. It is, however, very important to remember, one of the most invaluable resources of interest to your peers, lecturers and researchers is *you*, your experiences, observations, reflections and the chain of thought and possible application to sport and physical education, which come to mind as you read and discuss aspects of law and various incidents and issues with your peers and lecturers. Each academic year, you and your peers who might study law applied to sport and physical education are invaluable contributors to this field of knowledge and to the resources of your group and those who follow in your footsteps.

Summary

- You, your experiences, observations and reflections and those of your peers are one of *the most invaluable resources* you can bring to the study of law applied to sport, physical education and recreation!
- A resource does not have to include the words 'sport' and 'law' to be relevant to this subject.
- It is crucial to build up your skills and confidence, investigating, searching, using and applying a wide range of print, electronic and media resources. You need to invest time in this and to practise your skills.
- Criminal and civil law have different principles, definitions, terminology, processes and outcomes. Do not mix them up.
- Less then 10 per cent of cases end up in the Law Reports. You can still find many unreported cases, case commentaries, incidents and issues in legal databases, relevant literature, media coverage, *The Times* or *The Guardian Law Reports*.
- You need to know the difference between a court report and a law report.
- LexisNexis Professional or Nexis newspaper database, television and print news online provide very current sources and commentaries on incidents and issues which may not come to court.
- It is important to become familiar with using key generic legal texts which you will self-select at your level of knowledge and experience. Revision texts, law cards, a law dictionary or law study books are useful to assist you in quick summaries of generic principles or cases.
- Use your library and library staff/learning advisers or skills sessions. They are usually free and you can organise yourselves into small study groups for more efficient access to such resources.

- Make use of search facilities and abstracts from a range of disciplines which can throw light on law applied to sport, physical education and recreation, such as sociology, psychology, sports science, policy studies, management theory, social work, socio-legal studies.
- In addition to reading books and journals, make use of electronic resources from the websites of sports governing bodies, government departments, professional organisations, charities, including press releases, especially around the time of a high-profile legal incident, case or issue.
- Some of the best resources (apart from you) are a range of sport and law organisations – their websites, their conferences and seminars – you can present and write too! Look for student membership and student conferences and make your own network.
- Do not forget the organisations and networks such as the Higher Education Academy HLST Subject Network, The Royal Society for the Prevention of Accidents (generic and water and leisure section) and the Health and Safety Executive websites for free and very useful information.
- Television documentaries and mainstream films can provide current, relevant and meaningful illustrations of legal principles, cases and issues applied to sport, physical education and recreation.
- Your experience and skills in using such resources as YouTube, Facebook, Myface, discussion sites and blogs can help you access a range of examples of incidents, issues and commentaries which might not be available in more traditional locations. Used with care, acknowledging limitations, these resources can enhance and illustrate, rather than substitute, key academic readings.

2 Taking reasonable care?
Principles of negligence in sport, physical education and recreation

Introduction

> The most common cause of action to recover compensation for injuries suffered in the course of play is negligence.
>
> (James, 2001: 695)

Those who engage in sport and recreation as participants, spectators, organisers, coaches, officials etc may well suffer physical or psychological harm or injury. An accident or incident resulting in some kind of harm does not necessarily mean that it was caused by another sport participant's negligence.

> Everyone who participates in any form of sport and recreation, be it as an amateur or a professional, runs the risk of injury, and the task which faces lawyers is to distinguish between those injuries which the participant must accept as 'occupational hazards' and those which may seek compensation.
>
> (Collins, 1984: 18)

What does it mean to be negligent? What must an injured person prove in a claim against a defendant? The elements or conditions of negligence form the basis of this chapter. There are three elements of negligence. Sometimes these are expressed as logically necessary and sufficient conditions for a successful claim, as they must all be present. They are:

1 A duty of care must be owed by the defendant to the plaintiff/claimant.
2 There was a breach of duty by the defendant.
3 *Thereby* causing the injury/harm/loss to the plaintiff.

Sometimes this is presented as four requirements.

1 There exists a duty of care towards the athlete.
2 This duty imposes a standard of care and this standard has been breached.
3 A harm or loss is suffered by the athlete.
4 The breach of the duty of care causes, or substantially contributes to, the athlete's harm or loss.

(Centre for Sport and Law, Canada, 1995: 1)

A claim for negligence might be defended if it can be shown that there was no duty of care owed in a relationship, there was no breach of duty or, that, even if there was a breach of duty owed, that did not cause the harm or injury. The term *thereby* in condition three above is very important.

EXERCISE 2.1

Outline the three elements or conditions of negligence.

Illustrate them by using any judged negligence case in sport, recreation, or physical education, from a printed or an electronic sources (e.g. Westlaw UK, Lawtel, All England Law Reports, British and Irish Legal Information etc).

EXERCISE 2.2

Keep a resource file throughout your module on current incidents, cases or issues and note their relevance to negligence. Draw on print, electronic and media news sources as well as the sport law websites and the LexisNexis Executive or Nexis newspaper search facility, if your university subscribes to this service.

A defence to negligence is to establish, to the satisfaction of the court, that the injuries resulted from the normal, inherent risks of the sport or recreation activity, to which the claimant reasonably consented. These led to the injury or harm. There was no negligence by the defendant. This complete defence is known as *volenti* and will be covered in Chapter 3. In addition, damages awarded to an injured person can be reduced if it is established that the injured person contributed negligently to his/her injury, under s.1(1) of the Law Reform (Contributory Negligence) Act 1945. Contributory Negligence will also be covered in Chapter 3.

Duty of care: the first condition of negligence

The first element or condition of negligence is that a duty of care must be owed by the defendant to the claimant who has suffered the injury or harm identified in the claim. A duty of care arises by virtue of a relationship between parties, and the coach–athlete relationship is clearly one which establishes a duty of care. Here are some examples of other duty of care relationships in sport and recreation:

- Player to player
- Teacher to pupil
- Sport or recreation event organiser to spectator
- Private gym/health club to club member
- Governing body to participant
- Team doctor to athletics team
- Referee to player
- Adventure tourism tour operator to tourist
- Manufacturer of a sport product to a consumer
- Employer to police on duty at a soccer match
- Adult to adult on a skiing holiday together
- Occupiers of sports centre to lawful visitors, even trespassers
- Sport/recreation governing body to member

- Hypnotist/theatre/club to audience volunteers
- Teenagers to other teenagers in informal leisure/recreation.

The modern duty of care was established in the case of *Donoghue v Stevenson* [1932] AC 562. In this case Mrs Donoghue drank half a bottle of ginger beer from an opaque bottle, at a cafe, and found the remains of a partly decomposed snail as she poured out the rest of the drink. She claimed that this caused her illness (gastro-enteritis and nervous shock). The drink had been bottled at source, by the manufacturer, then sold on to the cafe. Mrs Donoghue sued the manufacturer of the ginger beer and won her appeal. The Law Lords held that the manufacturer 'should be held liable for the injury to the ultimate consumer of the product, as a result of its defective condition' (Jones, 2002: 32).

> The judgment is important not just for the decision itself but for identifying negligence as a separate tort in its own right, but also for devising the appropriate tests for determining whether negligence has actually occurred.
>
> (Turner, 2003: 10)

In this landmark case, Lord Atkin formulated the 'neighbour principle' to be used as a test for determining whether a duty of care was owed.

> You must take reasonable care to avoid acts or omissions, which you can reasonably foresee would be likely to injure your neighbour. Who then in law is my neighbour? The answer seems to be – persons so closely and directly affected by my act that I have them in contemplation as being so affected when directing my mind to the acts and omissions which are called into question.
>
> (Lord Atkin, *Donoghue v Stevenson*)

The decision in *Donoghue* and the formulation of the 'neighbour principle' framed negligence in terms of a failure to take reasonable care to avoid reasonably foreseeable harm to people closely and directly affected by our acts or omissions. Prior to this case there was 'no generalised duty of care' (Jones, 2002: 32). *Donoghue* allowed argument for liability for negligence in new situations and relationships not covered by previous case law (see Jones 2002: 34; Cooke, 2003: 31; Harpwood, 2003: 21; or Bermingham, 2005: 14). Since *Donoghue* was decided it should come as no surprise to those engaged in sport and recreation to see negligence cases brought by, for example, players against coaches, referees, sport governing bodies or sports goods manufacturers. The test applied today to establish the existence of a duty of care is a 'three-stage test' which asks the following questions in deciding the existence of a duty of care. Is there reasonable foresight of harm? Is there proximity between the parties? Is it fair, just and reasonable to impose a duty of care?

EXERCISE 2.3

Outline the evidence in the case of *Donoghue v Stevenson* [1932] AC 562. Explain the significance of this landmark case, including the 'neighbour principle'.

EXERCISE 2.4

List examples of five 'duty of care' relationships in sport, recreation and physical education contexts. Is it likely that the courts would find no duty of care exists in any of these relationships? Explain your answer.

EXERCISE 2.5

Find the negligence case of either *Smoldon* or *Vowles* from Chapter 3 and locate the paragraphs which refer to the question 'is it fair, just and reasonable to impose a duty?' What did the court consider and conclude on this matter? Do you agree? Give reasons for your answer.

In deciding whether or not a duty of care *should* be owed by one party to another, judges are really making 'policy' decisions. In doing so they need to consider the effect of their judgments on the way law operates in our society, moral and practical considerations, insurance loss allocation, fear of floodgates [of claims], avoiding creating an indeterminate [endless] liability. In addition, for reasons of public policy, immunity in some situations is provided by the courts to certain groups of public service providers (see Bermingham, 2005: 31–35).

Peter Kite, the managing director of OLL Ltd, the outdoor activities centre in Lyme Bay, Dorset, where four teenagers died whilst canoeing there in 1993, was convicted of involuntary manslaughter in Winchester Crown Court in 1994, as outlined in Chapter 7. Peter Kite brought a claim for negligence against HM Coastguard on the grounds of their alleged bungled rescue attempt (*OLL Ltd v Secretary of State for Transport* [1997] 3 All ER 897). The Court of the first instance held that HM Coastguard owed no duty of care, as it could lead to a defensive approach (as in *Harris v Evans* [1998] EWCA Civ 709, a case involving Health and Safety Executive inspectors) (see Bermingham, 2005: 33). However, in *Kent v Griffiths* [2001] QB 36, the court held that 'in certain circumstances, the ambulance service could be held liable for negligence' (Bermingham, 2005: 34).[1]

Negligence cases may be brought against defendants in sport and recreation, where other parties such as the police and emergency services may be involved in the chain of causation which leads the defendant to raise issues regarding their conduct, so an awareness of such 'duty of care' professional immunity cases is important.

EXERCISE 2.6

Work in pairs. If an emergency service is involved in an incident which leads to serious injury or death in, for example, a sport, physical education or recreation activity, could this lead to liability for negligence for that emergency service. Do all emergency services have professional immunity from liability for negligence? Each person should take one of the following cases: *OLL Ltd v Secretary of State for Transport* [1997] 3 All ER 897 and *Kent v Griffiths* [2001] QB 36. You may find it useful to read the section on the 1993 Lyme Bay Canoe tragedy in Chapter 7 of this text, as you reflect on the *OLL Ltd* case above. After reading that section of Chapter 7, report what you have found and share your opinion on the decision in *OLL Ltd v Secretary of State for Tranport.*

EXERCISE 2.7

Hypothetical

'Jennifer' was an experienced professional tennis player, ranked in the top 50 in the world. She met her ex-husband 'Jeff' on the tennis circuit but they had been separated for a few months. They were no longer living together but she had been stalked by him for months, suffering harassment via phone, e-mail, text messages and in person on several occasions. The matter had been reported to the police and she had made it clear to them that she thought that her life was in danger. The police took no action and a few weeks later 'Jeff' waited outside Jennifer's house and shot her as she left the house to go tennis training. She died an hour later in hospital. Discuss potential liability for negligence and the chances of the courts granting the police professional immunity if a negligence case was brought by Jennifer's mother. Make reference to previous relevant case law in relation to possible professional immunity of emergency/public services, including the police. You might usefully revisit this hypothetical in Chapter 5, in relation to the application of the Protection from Harassment Act 1997.

EXERCISE 2.8

Hypothetical

'Imran' was attending hockey training at his local club. Towards the end of the practice he suffered a very severe asthma attack. The hockey club coach phoned 999 and requested an ambulance. The call was received in ambulance control at 7.30 pm.

However, the ambulance did not arrive until 8.15 pm, by which time 'Imran' had died. The ambulance service had just introduced a new computer system which failed on that evening, leaving many people in emergencies stranded, for up to an hour and a half, when the national target was to reach emergencies within eight minutes. Ambulance control centre staff had to resort to manual procedures. The company which installed the system assured the ambulance service that it was reliable and would improve their quality of service.

Discuss potential liability with particular reference to duty of care, drawing on judged cases relating to the ambulance and emergency services. Do you think the emergency services should have professional immunity from liability for negligence? Give reasons for and against such immunity.

It is clear that the decisions of the courts are unpredictable and 'duty of care' policy decisions, as those above, may vary in different contexts, decades and in relation to human rights. However, it is highly unlikely that those who participate in sport and recreation will be included in the groups to which the courts grant immunity on policy grounds. This is particularly so in activities with an element of risk, where rules are designed to protect players and the relationship is very formal or structured, as that between a referee and players in a physical contact sport.

> The role of a referee is to enforce the rules. Where a referee undertakes to perform that role, it seems to us manifestly fair, just and reasonable that the players be entitled to rely upon that referee to exercise reasonable care in so doing. Rarely if ever does the law absolve from any obligations of care a person whose acts or omissions are capable of causing physical harm to others in a structured relationship into which they have entered.[2]
>
> (*Per* Lord Philips in *Vowles v Evans* [2003] EWCA Civ 318; [2003] 1 WLR 1607)

The courts have also had to decide whether schools, in law, have a duty of care to insure pupils against possible injury. In *Van Oppen v Clerk to the Bedford Charities Trust* [1990] 1 WLR 235 (CA), the 'claimant argued that his serious spinal injury and partial paralysis resulted from a coach allegedly failing to teach him tackling correctly. The attempt failed on the facts of the case' (Gardiner, 1993: 11). The Court of Appeal found that this point failed on the evidence and that the school could not be blamed for a mis-timed tackle, a 'tragic accident'.

The second point of the claimant's case, that the school failed to insure him against possible injury, or advise his father of the risks, also failed because there was no duty in law on parents to insure their children. 'It would be neither just nor reasonable to impose a duty upon the school, a greater duty than that which rested on a parent' (*Van Oppen* as *per* Lord Balcombe, CA, June 23, 1989). In using what a parent would do as a guide, the courts are applying the doctrine of the careful parent.[3]

Breach of duty: the second condition of negligence

'The trickiest element of negligence is perhaps the second point: the breach of [duty] standard of care' (University of Alberta, Legal Resource Centre, 1993: 3). Negligence is based on the notion of reasonableness. What would a reasonable coach/sports leader or PE teacher do or not do in similar relevant circumstances faced by the defendant. 'As adults we are all credited with the same general intelligence and sensibility, and thus the law expects each of us to behave in a reasonable fashion when confronted with similar circumstances' (Centre for Sport Law, 1995: 1). 'Negligence is an omission to do something which a reasonable man, guided upon those considerations which ordinarily regulate human affairs, would do, or doing something which a prudent and reasonable man would not do' (*Per* Alderson B in *Blythe v Birmimgham Waterworks* (1856) 11 Ex 781). The law does not expect perfection. However, BAALPE (2004: 10) suggest that 'it does impose on those involved in physical education a duty of care to: a. identify foreseeable risks that may result in injury. b. take reasonably practicable steps to reduce the risk to an acceptable level'.

Negligence is an act or omission which leads to foreseeable harm which a careful person would have avoided. It is regarded as 'culpable carelessness'. The defendant did not *mean* to harm anyone, but did not advert to unreasonable risks, which would have been obvious to the prudent (careful) coach or sports leader, in similar circumstances. The plaintiff or claimant does not have to prove, on the balance of probabilities, that the defendant did not care, only that the standard of care (conduct, not thought), was not high enough. It is often described as a blank state of mind but a culpable, blamable one at that. The second condition of negligence, the 'breach of duty' embraces that culpability or fault element.

The standard of care is an objective one as it does not depend upon 'the idiosyncrasies of the particular person whose conduct comes under question' (*Glasgow Corporation v Muir* [1943] AC 448, 457 *per* Lord McMillan).

James (2001: 698) observes that:

> the court (in *Condon v Basi* [1985] 1 WLR 866; [1985] 2 All ER 543 (CA)) comes out in favour of determining a breach of duty of care objectively. This seems to be a common sense position. All participants in a game must be deemed to consent to playing the game according to the same standard of care. It is illogical that each participant should have their own version of what is acceptable and what is unlawful as that could completely change the nature of the sport being played.

James (2001: 699) observes that:

> One of the most serious areas of confusion that arose from the decision in *Condon v Basi* was that a higher degree of care was said to be required of a player in the First Division match than that of a player in a local league football match.[4] This would introduce a variable standard of care for an activity, depending on the skill of the particular individuals involved in the incident. This would appear to be in direct conflict with the generally acceptable test laid down in *Nettleship v Weston* [1976] 2 QB 691, where it was held that the driving of a learner driver is to be judged by the standard of the ordinary, reasonable, competent (qualified) driver. Thus all participants [in sport] ought to be judged by the same basic standard, that of the ordinary reasonable competent participant in that activity. This point has been reinforced in later judgments.[5]

BAALPE (2004) agrees with this identification of the *Nettleship* standard for those with less experience. 'Newly qualified teachers are normally expected to demonstrate the same level of competence as teachers with significant experience. Inexperience is not a defence against a charge of not meeting the expected professional standard of care' (BAALPE 2004: 11). In addition, 'when a volunteer or paid coach is in charge of a group, that person owes the same duty of care to the pupils as if they were a teacher' (BAALPE, 2004: 11). In the case of *Williams v Eady* (1893) 10 TLR 41, Mr J Cave stated that 'a person must take such care of the pupil as the careful parent would take care of the same' (cited BAALPE 2004: 10). *Lyes v Middlesex County Council* (1962) 61 LGR 443 'modified this to mean that the teacher must take care as would a reasonable, prudent parent in the same situation as the teacher' (ibid: 10).

James (2006b: 635) notes that 'it quickly became accepted that all participants ought to be judged by the same basic standard of the ordinary, reasonable competent participant in the particular activity' (see Felix and Gardiner, 1994 on *Elliot v Saunders and Liverpool FC* HC January 1994, Drake, J). Since the case of *Caldwell v Maguire and Fitzgerald* [2001] EWCA Civ 1054; [2001] PIQR 45, the courts have accepted a variable standard of care.

EXERCISE 2.9

Explain the meaning of negligence and the objective test of the reasonable, prudent person/sports leader. A first year physical education student is on teaching practice and a second year undergraduate student is on work placement. A volunteer helps out at a local leisure centre on a Friday evening. Explain the standard of care which the law expects from each of these three people, with reference to relevant case law and literature.

EXERCISE 2.10

The popular TV programmes in the UK, such as *You've Been Framed* (ITV) and *Auntie's Sporting Bloomers* (BBC 1), display incidents where people have got themselves into difficulties and usually end up having a mishap. Viewers offer videotape evidence of their 'mishaps' having assured the programme that no one has been hurt in the process. Some incidents shown are genuine accidents (for example several players going up for the ball in a rugby union line-out in the mud, and clashing heads and all falling in the mud). Others are situations where you could pause the film before a situation unfolds and think 'I know exactly what is going to happen next, anyone could see that!' potentially fitting into the second condition of negligence – a breach of duty by failing to take reasonable care in the relevant circumstances to prevent reasonably *foreseeable* harm.

Make up a hypothetical example of a sport or recreation activity just like those on the above television programmes which, hypothetically, leads to a serious injury and can potentially lead to a negligence case. Provide as much detail as you can about the activity/incident, the age and characteristics of the participant, and the nature of the resulting harm/injury.

Apply the three elements of negligence – duty of care, breach of duty, thereby causing injury/harm. Discuss the seriousness and likelihood of risk, the social utility of the activity and the costs and practicability test outlined above and in using the next section of this chapter, referring to relevant principles and cases. In your opinion, is there a duty of care owed which has been breached, which caused the injury? Is there a potential negligence case?

EXERCISE 2.11

Discuss the following. Do programmes such as *You've Been Framed* and *Auntie's Sporting Bloomers*, or films such as *Dumb and Dumber* and the film *Jackass* help us to appreciate the potentially harmful consequences of our conduct and take carelessness seriously. Can they glorify, celebrate and encourage negligent and even reckless conduct? Try to view your critical reflection through the lens of subcultures (masculine or otherwise), including norms and values, covered in Chapter 4 of this text.

Although the test for negligence is said to be 'objective' there is still a subjective element since 'it is left to the individual judge to decide what is reasonable or what could have been foreseen' (Jones, 2002: 192). The courts in reality need to assess if the defendant exposed the claimant to an unreasonable risk of harm. This engages them in a difficult task of weighing up the balance between the following three factors to help them make a value judgment on what a 'reasonable man' would have done in the circumstances:

1 The magnitude (seriousness) of the risk and the likelihood of it happening.
2 The social utility or value (if any) of the activity.
3 The costs and practicability of minimising or removing the risk.

A reasonable person is not expected to take expensive and unreasonable steps in anticipation of a risk, which is foreseeable but remote. The life of a reasonable person 'would be impossible if he were to attempt to take precautions against every risk he can foresee. He takes precautions against risks which are reasonably likely to happen' (*per*

Lord Oaksey in *Bolton v Stone* [1951] AC 850; [1951] 1 All ER 1078). In *Bolton* the plaintiff was injured when a cricket ball was hit right out of the ground onto the road outside, where she was standing. Evidence was heard that the ball had only travelled out of this cricket ground approximately six times in the previous 30 years. Therefore the chances of this happening were so remote that the defendants had not acted unreasonably in failing to guard against it. However, in *Miller v Jackson* [1977] QB 966 (CA), a nuisance case, the ball had regularly been hit out of the ground eight or nine times each season, and the defendants were held liable (Griffiths-Jones, 2003: 1037).

Liability for negligence can arise out of informal recreation or leisure activities as well as organised or regulated sport. In *Hilder v Associated Portland Cement Manufacturers Ltd* [1961] 1 WLR 1434, children were permitted to play football on the defendant's land. The ball was kicked over a low boundary wall and fatally injured the plaintiff's husband who was riding past on his motorcycle. 'As there was a strong possibility of injury to road users the defendants were negligent as they had taken no additional precautions to ensure the safety of road users' (Cooke, 2003: 116). Rachel Gillan, a police officer controlling the perimeter of a soccer ground, was facing the crowd when, without warning, a soccer player chasing the ball, which bounced off the field of play, collided with her, knocking her unconscious. She brought the negligence case against the Chief Constable of Strathclyde Police and Airdre Football Club, arguing that a segregation barrier should have been erected by the club between the field of play and the track, for the safety of police officers (Duff, 1995b: 31).

In this Scottish case it was agreed that, as a matter of law, following *Bolton v Stone*, liability depended on 'whether or not the risk of injury was such as to warrant precautions being taken' (Duff, 1997a: 25).The case failed as it was held that the risk was 'so minimal that it could be ignored by the police and the football club' (*Gillan v Chief Constable Strathclyde Police and Airdrie Football Club* 1996 RepLR 165). When a one-eyed garage worker became totally blind after being struck in the eye by a metal chip which flew from a bolt he was trying to hammer loose, the defendants were held liable for failing to provide him with safety goggles (*Paris v Stepney Borough Council* [1951] AC 367). 'Although the risk was small the injury to this particular plaintiff was very serious' due to the characteristics of the plaintiff (Bermingham, 2005: 39). Those who organise and participate in high-risk sports such as boxing, mountaineering and formula one racing are expected to take more care in response to significant risks.[6]

'The social utility of the defendant's activity may justify taking greater risks than would otherwise be the case' (Jones, 2002: 198). Risky measures may be necessary in an emergency to save lives. 'One must balance the risk against the end to be achieved. The saving of life or limb justified the taking of considerable risks, and in cases of emergency, the standard of care demanded is adjusted accordingly' (*per* Lord Denning in *Watt v Hertfordshire County Council* [1954] 1 WLR 835 (CA)). However, this leniency of the courts is not without limits. In *Griffin v Mersey Regional Ambulance Service* [1997] EWCA Civ 2441; [1998] PIQR 34, an ambulance service was held liable for 40 per cent of the damages when a plaintiff in a car was crossing a road junction and was injured in a collision with an ambulance. The third factor in evaluating the standard of care is the cost of taking precautions to prevent reasonably foreseeable harm. When an employee slipped on an oily film on the floor of a factory, he sued the company arguing that the factory should have been closed down. The oily film was the result of water from an exceptionally heavy storm and such an extreme measure was found to be unnecessary. The Court of Appeal held that the company 'had done all that a reasonable person would have done in the circumstances' in covering wet areas with sawdust' (*Latimer v AEC Ltd* [1953] AC 643).

The three guidelines above, the seriousness and likelihood of the risk, the social utility or value of the activity and the costs and practicability of minimising the risk, assist the courts in deciding if there was a breach of duty, as the objective 'reasonable man' from *Blythe* is expected to have realised the risks and acted to avoid or reduce them.

Sport is not regarded as a special case. It is judged by general legal principles, in negligence, those of 'reasonableness'. 'The cases tell us very clearly that, in considering issues of liability, sport is not a special case with its own discrete area of jurisprudence, divorced from established general principles' (Griffith-Jones, 2003: 1031). Swift J emphasises this point in the case of *Cleghorn v Oldham* (1927) 43 TLR 465 at 466 when he stated 'ordinary principles apply . . . whilst recognising that the circumstances of the sporting context go into the melting pot when judging the issues of reasonableness' and 'reasonableness . . . requires that all relevant circumstances are taken into account' (ibid: 1031). Griffith-Jones (ibid: 1031–1032) also points out that reasonableness 'may also be influenced by individual judgments and changing values' as well as public perceptions. Conduct which was perceived to be acceptable in, for example, the 1970s or 1980s may not be acceptable now.

EXERCISE 2.12

Give an example of changing perceptions and attitudes towards on–the–field conduct, which can lead to or has already resulted in personal injury in a sport, which was acceptable at one time in the past but was later regarded as unacceptable.

Give reasons for your answer and explain how you/we come to know that such perceptions have changed. Are or should such perceptions rest solely on the 'subculture' or 'working culture' (James, 2006) of that sport, club or level? Can or should this be brought into the notion of what is a normal game with normal risks? What does this all have to do with the notion of 'reasonableness' when a judge is viewing a negligence case in court?

Although the legal standard of care of 'taking reasonable care in all the relevant circumstances', those circumstances in sport, which the courts consider, include the competitor's conduct taking place in the 'heat of the moment' or the 'flurry of excitement'. Here attention is naturally focusing on the defined challenge of the competition.

Decisions taken in a fraction of a second where skill is exercised 'at the extremes of physical endeavour', may involve errors of judgment and skill which the spectator and competitor in sport contexts will have to accept. In the Canadian case of *Agar v Canning* (1965) 54 WWR 302 at 304, the court held that 'the conduct of the player in the heat of the game is instinctive and unpremeditated and should not be judged by the standards suited to polite social intercourse' (cited Griffith-Jones, 2003: 1039).

An error of judgment or lapse of skill, taking place in the heat of the moment, by a competitor, in a competition which results in injury are not regarded as negligent. In the case of *Wooldridge v Sumner* [1963] 2 QB 43, a rider in an equestrian show jumping event lost control of his horse, hitting and injuring a press photographer. Negligence was claimed against the defendant. The Court of Appeal held that a spectator accepts the risk of a lapse of judgment or skill in a competitor who is going all out to win, but does not have to accept the risk of a participant having a reckless disregard for his safety' (James, 2003: 702[7]).

In the case of *Caldwell v Maguire and Fitzgerald*, both defendants were jockeys in a race where they:

> pulled across in front of Byrne before they were fully clear of him, causing his horse to veer suddenly away from the rails and unseat him. The claimant, who had been in fourth place, was unable to avoid the unseated rider and was also brought down sustaining very serious injuries that caused him to retire from being a jockey.
>
> (*Caldwell v Maguire and Fitzgerald*, cited James, 2006b: 632)

The test applied in the Court of Appeal was:

> negligence taking into account the prevailing circumstances. The judge did not say that the claimant had to establish recklessness. There will be no liability for errors of judgement, oversights or lapses of which any participant might be guilty in a fast-moving context. Something more serious is required.
>
> (*Caldwell v Maguire and Fitzgerald*, cited James, 2006b: 633)

In evaluating the existence of a breach of duty, as a matter of fact, the courts may use different standards depending on the location of the incident or injury. For example, in *Johnson v First Choice Holidays and Flights Ltd* (unreported, 22 August 2003, Northampton County Court), a claimant brought a case against the tour operator, after he slipped near the edge of a swimming pool and injured himself, whilst on holiday in Fuertaventura, in the Canary Islands (Spain). He argued that this was a result of the absence of non-slip materials around the pool, handrails and warning notices. The county court found the claimant had not proved that the defendant had failed to comply with relevant local standards relating to the particular issues of his complaint. 'The standard of care and therefore, breach of duty, were to be assessed by reference to local, Spanish, rather than British Safety Standards.'[8]

In evaluating whether or not the defendant in sport has breached a duty of care to another person in that sporting activity, the courts may draw on several things to help them decide what is reasonable. The Centre for Sport Law (1995: 2) suggest that although there is no 'black and white answer', 'there are places to look for guidance' including 'written standards, and unwritten standards, case law and common sense, which, taken together, indicate the standard of care the coach must meet'. Written indicators may include equipment standards, technical rules, an organisation or local authority's internal policies, emergency procedures, codes of practice, coaching manuals, event guidelines on first aid, Coaching Code of Ethics, or a job description. 'Written standards promote prudent behaviour by telling coaches how to behave before an accident happens. Disregarding written standards is strong evidence of negligent behaviour' (Centre for Sport and Law, 1995: 2). Unwritten standards or guides include, for example, common practices of other coaches, teachers, sports leaders, institutionalised practices, conventions, role models etc.

Cases illustrating the significance of both formal rules and standard and approved practice in assessing a breach of duty, by the courts, are included in the second half of this chapter.

The courts can use expert witnesses to help them with questions such as 'Is X conduct of the defendant standard and approved practice in this sport?' This is especially important where new practices at the cutting edge of coaching sport are involved and are not yet recorded within written sources of standard and approved practice. Witnesses and expert witnesses for the claimant and the defendant can, and often do, disagree in their opinion on the same matter and the judge has to decide which version or opinion to accept. In the county court and High Court, one judge resides over the case and must decide which version to accept. In *Allport v Wilbraham* [2004] EWCA Civ 1668, the Court of Appeal held that the trial judge was 'entitled to prefer oral evidence of the defendant to that of a witness for the claimant and had given adequate reasons for that preference'. Judges can also make decisions about what evidence is admissible and also what format of evidence upon which, they prefer to rely. In *Elliott v Saunders* 1994 (unreported, 10 June 1994, High Court, Drake J), the judge preferred to rely on oral evidence, rather than the video evidence at the civil trial. He regarded the latter as 'two-dimensional' and 'therefore open to unlimited subjective interpretation. The judge believed it right to base the evaluation of what happened on the perception of officials [and other witnesses] present at the match' (Gardiner and Felix, 1994: 1).

Causation: the third condition of negligence

'*Thereby* causing harm for which the plaintiff seeks compensation' is the third condition or element of negligence. Proving causation is not necessarily a straightforward scientific or medical matter to be ticked off if a breach of duty has been established. The process of understanding and proving causation can be a lengthy, costly, complex process, with contrasting expert opinions on medical or scientific matters. The first principle to understand in causation is 'factual causation', sometimes referred to as 'but for' causation. 'If damage would not have happened *but for* the particular fault [breach of duty] then that fault is the cause of the damage; if it would have happened all the same, fault or no fault, the fault is not the cause of the damage' (*per* Lord Denning in *Cork v Kirby MacLean Limited* [1952] 2 All ER 402 (CA)).

In other words, if the outcome would be the same, negligent act or no negligent act, then the defendant would not be liable. A night watchman went to the accident and emergency department of a hospital with stomach pains and vomiting. The casualty doctor refused to examine him and advised him to see his own doctor the next morning if he felt unwell. He died of arsenic poisoning five hours later. The court held that the hospital was not liable since he probably would have died anyway, even if prompt treatment had been given. The breach of duty was not the cause of his death (*Barnett v Chelsea and Kensington Hospital Management Committee* [1969] 1 QB 428).

The 'but-for' or 'factual causation' test has presented the courts with some interesting challenges in situations of multiple defendants or where the cause was not known medically at the time. In *Fairchild v Glenhaven Funeral Services Ltd* [2002] UKHL 22; [2003] 1 AC 32, the court heard evidence that more than one employer contributed to the inhalation of asbestos, which resulted in mesothelioma (a form of cancer). Because of the limits of human science at the time, it could not be shown which employer's breach caused the disease. It was held by the House of Lords that it was 'sufficient to prove that the defendant materially increased the risk of harm' (Bermingham, 2005: 46).

EXERCISE 2.13

Explain the 'but for' principle of causation, supported by reading and relevant case law.

EXERCISE 2.14

Hypothetical

Imagine an employee who had worked in several canoe companies over the years, making and maintaining canoes. She developed permanent respiratory problems, caused by working with fibre glass, without the appropriate masks or ventilation. Would a potential negligence case fail as the claimant could not establish which one of her previous employees caused the illness? Support your answer with reference to relevant case law.

Hypothetical

A group of 15-year-old surfers taking part in a surfing programme provided over the summer, by the local leisure services authority, often gave their surfboards 'a bit of a bashing' on the water, leading to damage to the boards. The local leisure services authority are a bit strapped for cash so are quite relieved when they see the boys and girls repairing their own surf boards in one of the local garages belonging to the local authority. Over the long hot summer, the surfers repeatedly sanded down and refilled holes with resin. The sanding down of the surfboard surface, released fibre glass particles in the closed confined space of the garage. They later presented with symptoms of serious respiratory disorders and claimed for negligence.

Discuss the chances of a successful claim.

EXERCISE 2.15

Hypothetical

'Susie' was a very experienced health-related exercise leader in her local health club. Her aerobic step class was very popular, especially the advanced class on a Friday evening. 'Andy' aged 48, moved to the area and joined the club on a 'two-week trial' offer. He did not go through a screening procedure or complete a medical/injuries questionnaire. 'Andy' had managed to avoid any form of physical exercise since leaving school. However, 'Pete' his friend, aged 30, persuaded him to join him at his advanced step-class. 'Andy' reckoned it would be a poor show if he could not keep up with 'Pete'. They both arrived late and rushed into the advanced step class. 'Pete' said to 'Susie', 'he's with me!' During the class, 'Andy' experienced severe chest pain. First aid was administered and an ambulance was called immediately. Despite the efforts of the paramedics and hospital staff, 'Andy' was pronounced dead (of a heart attack) at the local hospital that evening. His wife sued the health club for negligence.

Did the health club owe 'Andy' a duty of care?

If yes, did they, in your opinion, breach that duty? Give reasons using relevant reading on negligence principles.

If yes, did that breach of duty cause the harm to the claimant? Consider codes of practice on screening participants in physical activity. What other medical information might the court need in relation to causation?

Would a negligence claim against the health club be likely to succeed? Give reasons in support of your answer.

The second element of causation is called 'legal' or 'proximate' causation. Even if a breach of duty is shown to cause the damage or harm to the claimant (as a matter of fact), the courts can still decide that the defendant *ought* not to be liable for such injury or harm. For policy reasons a line must be drawn in the chain of causation in order to 'contain the defendant's liability within reasonable bounds' and, as a matter of law, this cut-off point will exclude damage caused beyond this point as it is said to be 'too remote'.[9] (Bermingham, 2002: 45; Cooke, 2003: 137). The courts have to consider questions around the type of damage, the way in which it is caused, the extent of the damage and multiple or new intervening causes. The precise nature of the damage need not be foreseeable, provided it is 'of the type' which could have been foreseen (Bermingham, 2005: 49). A van driver sent on a long journey in an unheated vehicle in severe weather successfully recovered damages for frostbite. Even though it was not in itself foreseeable, it was within the broad class of foreseeable risk arising from exposure to extreme cold (*Bradford v Robinson Rentals Ltd* [1967] 1 All ER 267).

However, in *Tremain v Pike* [1969] 1 WLR 1556, the plaintiff contracted a rare disease (Weil's disease) from rats' urine during his work as a farm labourer on a farm which the defendant allegedly neglected, allowing it to become infested by rats. The employee lost his case since J Payne decided that, although the 'rat bite was foreseeable, the method by which this disease was contracted was not' (Harpwood, 2003: 153). An unusual case involving the same disease in a recreation context was *Darby v National Trust* [2001] EWCA Civ 189; [2001] PIQR 372. The claim for damages was brought by a widow whose husband had drowned whilst swimming in a pond in the grounds of a stately home, under the control of the defendant. The claimant argued that her husband would not have swum in the defendant's pond (and drowned) if the defendant had put up a sign warning about the risk of contracting Weil's disease.

However, the Court of Appeal held that 'the risk of contracting Weil's disease and the risk of drowning were fundamentally different – an alleged duty to take reasonable care to warn against the risk of contracting the disease could not form the basis of a claim for damages, attributable to a different cause, that is, drowning' (Jones, 2002: 229).[10] The risks were 'intrinsically different, so were any dependent duties' (*Current Year Law Book* 2001: 1519, para 4504). Although the decision in *Tremain* has come in for some criticism,[11] it is important to note for sport and recreation participants and organisers, that the knowledge and awareness of the nature and risks of Weil's disease,[12] is now more widespread than in the 1960s. This is particularly so among canoeists, surfers and triathletes. Coaches, participants and those organising water-based events are expected to take reasonable care to reduce the known risks and consider such risks in their risk assessment.

John Illman reported in 1992 that GPs often associate leptospirosos (Weil's disease) with workplaces such as agriculture, but not with workers from any context who may go, for example, wind-surfing in their leisure time (Illman, 1992). In the same year the British Canoe Union reported that around eight or nine water sports enthusiasts contract Weil's disease each year 'with a risk of developing the disease at one in 200,000' (ibid: 25). To reduce the risk it is advisable, if taking part in water sports to 'keep broken skin covered with waterproof plasters, avoid rat-infested waters, avoid capsize drill or rolling in slow or stagnant water, wear footwear and shower after canoeing, falling in, swimming, windsurfing or water-skiing' (ibid: 25).

In 1991, a survey published in the *British Medical Journal* showed that people entering the water for a paddle were 25 per cent more at risk from infection than those staying on the beach – with 31 per cent for swimmers and surfers at 80 per cent more risk, because of the more active sports increasing the risk of the ingestion of contaminated waters (Surfers Against Sewage, 2005). The SAS are calling for the revised Bathing Water Directive to 'incorporate the concept of "recreational waters" as opposed to "designated bathing beaches" so that all recreational water users will be safe when in the water, wherever they choose to practice their sport' (ibid).

EXERCISE 2.16

Hypothetical

A triathlon event was hosted in an inland quay alongside a run-down industrial area, next to a former brewery. In this stagnant water the competitors swam face down doing front-crawl for up to half an hour. Revellers had been out the night before and there were broken glass bottles between the changing rooms and the start line. The water had not been tested for the presence of relevant organisms. Two competitors, 'Michelle' and 'Rachel', cut their feet before entering the water. A few days later they became ill with 'flu-like' symptoms and had a yellow skin colour by the end of the week. 'Michelle's GP was an experienced canoeist and recognised the symptoms of Weil's disease. He sent her blood off to a laboratory for urgent tests. They proved positive for Weil's disease and she was successfully treated. 'Rachel's doctor did not realise the significance of her symptoms. She died a week later. Discuss potential liability for negligently causing 'Rachel's death making reference to three elements of negligence, particularly matters of causation. Look on the British Canoe Union (BCU) and British Triathlon Association (BTA) website for relevant background information on Weil's disease and other water-based organisms or viruses.

Imagine you are advising 'Rachel's family on bringing a potential negligence case. Identify appropriate defendants and evaluate the potential for a negligence case.

EXERCISE 2.17

'Tracy', a competitive board sailor, returned from a two-week holiday for 18–30 year olds in Benidorm to take part in the British Championships in Windsurfing in a resort on the south coast. It was a major achievement to reach this level of fitness and even participate as in recent years – 'Tracy' fought and won a long battle with heroin addiction. She won the silver medal but that is not why the event is memorable for her. She claims she contracted hepatitis from untreated sewage in the water. 'It was awful. I was very, very ill for many weeks. I had to stick to a very strict diet and drink several pints of water each day.' The Water Company, 'Regional Water', responsible for sewage outfalls in the locality of the sports competition stated in an interview with the local television news 'We are very sorry that "Tracy" became ill, but we believe there is no link between swimming in the sea and this illness. Our operations use long sea outfalls, in line with EC regulations.' Some critics, including environmental campaigners and surfing groups, argue that long sea outfalls which are designed to meet the bare minimum standards to avoid prosecution under EC law should be replaced by the use of ultraviolet light to kill bacteria in sewage and tackle the viruses that make people ill.

EXERCISE 2.18

Imagine you are advising 'Tracy' on the potential suing for negligence. Address each of the conditions for negligence outlined in this chapter, with a particular focus on condition no 3, *thereby* causing harm.

Is there a duty of care owed? If yes, explain this.

Was there a breach of duty – a failure to take reasonable care, to prevent reasonably foreseeable harm, in the relevant circumstances?

If there is a breach, did this breach cause the harm (hepatitis) for which the claimant may be seeking compensation?

What are the difficulties facing 'Tracy' in relation to 'but for' causation and multiple causes? What other information might you need to make this assessment? Where and from whom will you get such information or opinion? What could 'Regional Water' say in their defence, which illustrates the difficulties of proving 'but for' causation and expected standards?

In some cases there may be more than one cause of the injury or harm and the courts have to work out whose conduct (acts or omissions) caused the injury and which defendants should actually be liable in law and pay compensation. In a very interesting case from a recreation context, Bristol Crown Court heard that 20-year-old Mr Day attended a ball organised by the Territorial Army, who had hired a bouncy castle, as part of the evening entertainment for adults (*Day v 266 Operations Battery Royal Artillery and Brandon Hire* (unreported, 11 March 1996, Queen's Bench Division, Rougier J)[13]).

Mr Day admitted he had had 'a few beers' and went on the bouncy castle, where some of his friends 'made a pyramid. But I was not on that. We were just bouncing around having a bit of fun when one of my friends fell on top of me'; 'we didn't realize it was dangerous' (Mr Day the claimant, cited in Weaver, 1996: 1). The bouncy castle was hired out by the other defendant in the case, Brandon Hire. The decision of Rougier J held both defendants liable for negligence in 1995, and in 1996 allocated two-thirds of the compensation to be paid by Brandon Hire and one-third to 226 Operations Battery, Royal Artillery, the ball organisers.

'The company should have made sure that the bouncy castle was not to be used by adults, as they knew there was a risk. The Territorial Army, although unaware of the dangers, should have checked with Brandon Hire, particularly when the instructions said there should be supervision and that the use should be limited to children. I have much doubt if the instructions were read at all' (Rougier J in *Day v 266 Operations Battery Royal Artillery and Brandon Hire*, cited in Weaver, 1996: 1). In response to the finding Mr Nathan, Chair of Brandon Hire, commented: 'A bouncy castle is a children's toy and is hired out as such. The TA hired it for an adult ball. It was sent with instructions that it was only to be used by people with an average weight of a seven year old' (Weaver, 1996: 1).

EXERCISE 2.19

Day v 266 Operations Battery Royal Artillery and Brandon Hire (unreported, 11 March 1996, Queen's Bench Division, Rougier J).

Get into groups of three. One person should report the evidence and the decision in *Day*. One person should critically comment on the case from the perspective of Brandon Hire. One person critically comment on the case from the perspective of the claimant and the Territorial Army. As a group of three, vote on whether or not you think this was a fair judgment in relation to division of liability and payment of compensation. Give reasons.

Reflect on the issues this case might have raised in your minds around after dinner entertainment activities such as bouncy boxing, 'barflying', bouncy castles, sumo wrestling suits.

EXERCISE 2.20

Summarise the case of *Kinnear v Falconfilms NV* [1996] 1 WLR 920 below.

Compare and contrast *Kinnear v Falconfilms NV* with *Day v 266 Operations Battery Royal Artillery and Brandon Hire* above.

In September 1988 the actor Roy Kinnear was thrown from his horse and sustained serious pelvic injuries whilst filming a riding sequence for the film *The Return of the Musketeers*. He was taken to hospital and subsequently died from his pelvic injuries and a massive haemorrhage. It was argued in court, for the plaintiff, that her husband was never advised that a stand-in should be used for the high-speed ride across a bridge.

The court heard that 'it was foreseeable that he would lose his footing. He was an inexperienced, incompetent and nervous rider. They should never have allowed him to thunder across the bridge' (see *The Guardian*, 4 October 1994: 3). The defendant argued that 'Mr Kinnear consented to the risk and his death was due to medical negligence on the part of the Madrid hospital which transferred him to a clinic which was ill-equipped to deal with his injuries (ibid: 3). Hidden J in the High Court 21 December 1994 held that 'the failure of the hospital to diagnose massive internal bleeding helped cause Mr Kinnear's death; had he been given an immediate transfusion he would not have died' and ordered the hospital to pay 60 per cent of the £650,000 compensation. The *Kinnear* case illustrates 'multiple causes', involving medical treatment, where the first defendant, at the beginning of the chain of causation, remains liable for negligence.

Negligence cases in sport, recreation and physical education

The illustrative case law from Anglo-Welsh courts, Scotland, Canada and Australia, in the second half of this chapter, identifies emerging areas or guides to alert sports leaders, physical education teachers, participants and organisers of sport to potential areas of negligence claims. Sport and recreation governing or professional bodies and many local authorities also keep an eye on emerging case law and provide summaries of relevant cases, providing comments on the implications for the members of that particular sport, recreation or authority.

However illustrative these cases are, it must be recognised that each case is decided on the relevant facts and circumstances, within the policy lens of that time. Still, they are useful in highlighting areas of potential liability. Equally, and more importantly, identifying common situations which meet the criteria of negligence (or not) can assist coaches, sports leaders and physical education teachers in the development of their own proactive risk assessment lens (see Chapter 6). Most cases tend to illustrate more than one thing either legally or in relation to practical implications in sport and recreation. In addition, as emphasised in Chapter 1, it is essential that the case is followed through to the final court decision as decisions can be reversed on appeal. In addition, what is reported by the press and media, leading up to a case and following a judicial decision, may not be an accurate reflection of the issues and evidence, which were admissible in the court, or considered by the judge.

There are many ways of categorising cases into subthemes according to which legal or practical themes they tend to highlight. Nygaard and Boone (1985) identified seven 'legal duties' of coaches, listing areas and cases where coaches have been found negligent in the United States. These were supervision, sound planning, warning of the inherent risks of the activity, provision of a safe and appropriate environment, evaluation of capacity or incapacity to participate, matching or equating opponents for competition and training, and, finally, provision of first aid and implementation of emergency medical procedures. The cases which follow are examined using some of these themes in an attempt to unpack, in an applied manner, the 'reasonableness' test and to illustrate it in a more practical way in sport, recreation and physical education contexts:

- Deviation from or changes to standard and approved practice
- Breaching the rules of the game or sport
- Supervision
- Incapacity to participate and inadequate matching of participants
- Facility management in sport and recreation: provision of a safe environment or equipment
- High-risk sports: a key negligence case in boxing.

Deviation from or changes to standard and approved practice

Regular and approved practice is 'typical of that seen nationally rather than locally' and is 'deemed to be widely used because it is sound. Such practice is typical of that evident in local education authority schemes of work and national governing body or national association guidelines' (Whitlam, 2005: 26). Standard and approved practice is 'where a practice has been commonly adopted by teachers throughout the country and has proved by time and experience to be safe and efficient' (BAALPE 1985: 26). Such practices are officially approved and are not just common. They can afford some protection against claims of negligence. However, in industrial settings practices adopted within an industry have been questioned by the courts in negligence or involuntary manslaughter cases.[14] Standard and approved practice is disseminated in many ways through sport, recreation and physical education contexts – through coaching or leadership courses, information from technical committees of governing bodies via general and local secretaries, and working with other coaches or physical education.

There may be disagreements regarding standard and approved practice and in court the expert witnesses for the plaintiff and defendant often give different opinions on whether or not X conduct followed standard and approved practice. In *Wright v Cheshire Council* [1952] 2 All ER 789, the plaintiff was injured when another pupil who should have been waiting at the vault to support him suddenly left the gym at the sound of the school bell. Of central importance was the acceptance by the Court of Appeal of the defence of standard and approved practice, since it had been seen as safe for years for 11-year-old boys to support each other at the buck, as long as they had been trained to do so (see Brierley, 1993: 20).

Is it standard and approved practice to use an upturned bench as a goal in indoor hockey? When a 13-year-old pupil fractured her left elbow when she tripped over the protruding leg of such a bench in a game of indoor hockey the Court of Appeal accepted the judge's findings that although some schools used it, there was no evidence that this was standard and approved practice throughout the country (*Cassidy v Manchester City Council* (unreported, 1995, Court of Appeal)). In high-risk sport and recreation activities, where codes of practice are related to safety, participants and organisers could be in a very weak position in a court case if they failed to follow such codes. A scuba diving instructor deviated from the code of practice by allowing a novice out of his sight during her first open dive lesson and was held liable for her death (*Bacon v White and Chartfield Associates* (unreported, 21 May 1998, Queen's Bench Division).

A skydiver who collided with and injured another skydiver was found negligent for those injuries by a Canadian court, since he made a turn contrary to well-established safety procedures (*Dyck v Laidlaw* [2000] 9 WWR 517). Standard and approved practice does not only apply to participant conduct. It also embraces, among other things, equipment and a safe environment. When a 9-year-old boy was injured in a motorcycle race, the sports governing body was held liable for the injury, as they deviated from the code of practice by using an inflexible rope as a boundary, where a flexible rope was recommended (*Hinchcliffe v British Schoolboys Motorcycle Association* (unreported, 12 April 2000, Queen's Bench Division, Smith J); Griffith-Jones 2003: 1052).

Breaching the rules of the game or sport

Griffith-Jones (2003: 1040) suggests that the implication of the decision in *Condon v Basi*[15] is that 'it will be almost impossible to establish liability unless the actions of the defendant are outside the rules of the game' and indeed the Court of Appeal 'appeared to be saying that a breach of rules is virtually a necessary, albeit not necessarily a sufficient requirement for liability to attach'. A late tackle, regarded as a foul, which ended a footballer's career was not judged as liable by the courts in the case of *Pitcher v Huddersfield Town Football Club* (unreported, 17 July 2001, Queen's Bench Division, Hallet J). The judge held that this was 'the kind of tackle which, although against the rules of the game, occurs up and down the country every Saturday of the football season in Division One matches' (JPIL 2002: 226). The tackle came 0.2 seconds after the ball was played. It was 'an error of judgment in the context of a fast moving game where Paul Reid (defendant) had to react to events in a matter of a split second' and had not crossed the 'high threshold' to be actionable in negligence (ibid: 226).

In contrast, following a soccer tournament in 2001, in which a player sustained a serious leg injury, another example of rule-breaking tackle was seen by the courts to cross that very high threshold. The judge ruled that the offending player:

> went to tackle Mr Leabody from behind, using both legs and that the tackle was deliberately aimed at the man rather than the ball, which was two or three yards ahead

of the claimant – the tackle was unlawful, outside the rules of the Association Football and dangerous in all the circumstances.

(Leabody v Ministry of Defence (unreported, 9 July 2001, Bristol Crown Court, Burcell J), Cairns 2002: 57)

In 1999 a judgment in the High Court held that a uni-hockey player in a police inter-club match was negligent in causing an eye injury to the plaintiff by raising his stick above waist level, breaking a safety rule 'at the heart of and itself central to the spirit and purpose of the game' (*Leatherlands v Edwards* Unreported, 28 November, High Court, QBD, Newman J, *Sports Law Bulletin*, February 1999b: 5). James (2001) suggests that conduct which goes beyond the written rules but is regarded as within the 'playing cultures' of the activity may act as a guide to the courts as to what is to be expected by participants.

A breach of rules may not only involve the technical rules of a game or sport. It could apply to more general rules of a disciplinary nature or a very specific safety rule, which is, for example, related to maintenance, hygiene or cleanliness of a facility. Such rules may also be found in relevant statutes. In 1999 a swimming pool operator was found liable for neck and head injuries to a visitor, caused by slipping on the floor tiles at the side of a swimming pool. They had been regularly cleaned but this had not been done in accordance with the prescribed regime of the tile manufacturer and a build up of body fats made the surface slippery (*Taylor v Bath and North East Somerset District Council* (unreported, 27 January 1999, Judge Chambers)[16]).

Deviation from, or knowledge of, the rules or conventions of an activity do not only apply to organised or regulated sports competitions. They are also relevant to informal recreation and leisure activities, including physical horseplay and messing about, by either adults or children. In *Blake v Galloway* [2004] EWCA Civ 814; [2004] 1 WLR 2844, the Court of Appeal addressed issues of negligence, implied consent, and the standard of care for participants in an informal game. Could a child bring an action for negligence against another child, having been injured by a piece of bark being thrown during informal horseplay? The Court of Appeal held that such horseplay was conducted with certain tacitly agreed understandings or conventions, with no expectation of skill or judgment being exercised and a very small risk of injury, which could have easily been objectively assessed by the child claimant. Principles from sport and games case law were used and applied and it was decided that there was no negligence in this case (see also Hill and Revere, 2004).

In February 2005, Jarrod McCracken, a member of the West Tigers rugby league team in Australia, successfully sued two opposing players of the Melbourne Storm rugby league team for negligence arising out of a spear tackle which resulted in spine and neck injuries and ended McCracken's playing career.[17] The New South Wales Supreme Court heard that the defendant players swivelled the unbalanced player around the midriff, and dumped him on his head. The defendants argued that the tackle was truly accidental – an error of judgment. However, Hulme J rejected this argument for three reasons. First, the tackle was inherently dangerous. Second, the defendants had 'pleaded guilty to an internal NRL disciplinary hearing charge of effecting a dangerous throw, contrary to s.15 of the Laws of the Game of Australian Rugby League' (Anderson, 2006: 44). Third, Hulme J rejected the argument that the conduct was 'normal, and to an appreciable degree unavoidable, incident of an event involving three heavy players' (ibid: 44).

The videotape shown to the court, in the opinion of Hulme J, clearly demonstrated that the spear tackle was 'not necessary in preventing McCracken's momentum' and had the clear intent that the plaintiff should 'fall heavily onto the ground' (*McCracken v Melbourne Storm Rugby League Football Club and Others* [2005] NSWSC 107 at para 37, cited ibid: 45).The employer, Melbourne Storm RL club, was found vicariously liable for the actions of its employees. Anderson (2006: 47) advises that 'sports organizations in England should be aware that the English Court of Appeal has held that sports bodies owe a strict duty of care to adopt rules and policies that protect the health and safety of participants' (see *Watson v British Boxing Board of Control* [2000] EWCA Civ 2116; [2001] QB 1134).

EXERCISE 2.21

Give an example of each of the following:

1 A sport competition rule which is designed to standardise the test, that is, make all competitors face the same test of physical skill.
2 A sport competition rule which is designed to maintain flow, aesthetic appeal or maintain the physical skill or challenge the right level.
3 A sport competition rule which is designed for health and safety reasons.

Focus on 3, your example of a health and safety rule. Justify this health and safety rule. Give an example of a situation where this rule could be breached and lead to significant injury. In your opinion would such an injury caused by such a breach of a sports rule be beyond an inherent risk accepted and consented to as part of the normal game or sport? Give reasons supported by reading a relevant case law. Why does the Law Commission see control of risks by rules and officials as the most relevant UK Sports Council for a recognised sport in their 1995 review of consent and the criminal law, applied to assault in sport or recreation contexts?

EXERCISE 2.22

Think of an example where either a. a new safety rule was introduced in a sport OR b. a safety rule was changed or adapted. Give reasons for the new rule or the adaptation of the rule. Did it work? How was information about this change disseminated to the sporting community? How long did it take from recognising the need to implementing the rule change or new rule? Read the cases of *Hamstra* and *Agar* and discuss the difficulties facing national and international governing bodies in changing safety rules. Do you think the courts were fair to the governing bodies in *Hamstra* and *Agar*? Should rule-makers be liable for injuries related to the need for or speed of implementation of rule changes in sport?

EXERCISE 2.23

Find an example from a sport where a safety rule was regularly flouted or broken, but this was not spotted by or addressed by the officials or authorities or appeared to be tolerated by the authorities. If this led to a serious injury, critically discuss 'Is this an acceptable, inherent risk of the sport?' Explain the relevance of this to negligence.

EXERCISE 2.24

Record all the possible reasons for rule breaking in sport competition. Is and should all rule–breaking be regarded as 'negligent'? Refer to relevant case law such as *Condon, Pitcher, Leabody*, and *Caldwell v Maguire and Fitzgerald* [2001] EWCA Civ 1054; [2001] PIQR 45.

Supervision

Supervision is a common theme illustrated in the judged cases on negligence in sport, recreation and physical education contexts. It can be of a more general kind such as supervising school playgrounds, changing rooms or buses, coaching or refereeing sports team or match or of a very specific kind such as physically supporting a gymnast on a 1:1 basis in a difficult move. A young adult left unsupervised in a sports centre sustained a serious spinal injury when he attempted an unsupervised forward somersault on mats and over-rotated too close to the wall. Although an employee of the sports centre, who was qualified to teach trampolining, but not gymnastics, had previously instructed the claimant, he had not warned him about the risks or safe placement of mats.

The Court of Appeal focused on three issues – the danger of the activity, the failure to expressly forbid practising this manoeuvre in the absence of a supervisor, and the fact that previous instruction had been given to the plaintiff (but without adequate warnings). Although the plaintiff was seen to have contributed negligently to his own injury and had his damages reduced by one-third,[18] the County Council was still held liable for two-thirds of the damages (*Fowles v Bedfordshire County Council* [1996] ELR 51).

In *Lam v University of Windsor* (unreported, March 9 2001, Ontario Superior Court) the defendants were found liable for failing to monitor or supervise a judo club on its premises. A much earlier case highlighting the need for direct 1:1 supervision was *Gibbs v Barking Corporation* [1936] All ER 115, where a pupil was injured landing from a vault in gymnastics because of a 'lack of promptitude by the teacher in preventing the stumble' (Grayson, 2001: 13).

A PE teacher replaced worn-out elastic on a trampette in the school gymnasium. The old elastic was thrown in the bin just outside the gym, on the edge of the school playground. At break time the normal supervision in the playground failed to materialise for ten minutes, by which time some 11-year-old boys had spotted the elastic and were playing with it, resulting in the plaintiff losing the sight in one eye. The presence of this thick elastic in the open bin, together with a failure to provide adequate supervision, amounted to negligence (*Beaumont v Surrey County Council* (1968) 66 LGR 580). There have also been some interesting and sometimes worrying cases where liability for supervision outside strictly formal settings has been examined by the courts. Schools and local authorities anxiously awaited the outcome of an appeal by Kent County Council in October 2002. A 14-year-old pupil at a boys' grammar school suffered a serious eye injury when struck by a full-size leather football. It happened at 8.40 am whilst the pupils were on the school premises before school formally commenced at 8.55 am. The claimant was successful in his claim and the defendants appealed, arguing that it was unreasonable to expect staff to supervise pupils in a pre-school period.

Although there had been previous case law, which established such a duty, it depended on what was 'reasonable'. The court heard that there was a school ban on leather footballs in the school playground. The boys were warned about the ban twice a year, yet regularly flouted it. No action was taken by the school after previous facial incidents and the judge in the first instance on the facts thought plainly that the ban was not being effectively enforced by the school and that the boys did not take it seriously. The appeal was dismissed (*Kearn-Price v Kent County Council* [2002] EWCA Civ 1539).

EXERCISE 2.25

Read Ruff, A. 2002 'Facial Injuries and Football Before School' *Entertainment Law* 2 (1): 89–97. Critically comment on the decision in *Kearn-Price* and discuss the implications for school/club supervision outside formal scheduled time.

On a school skiing trip Simon Chittock, aged 17, sustained a serious spinal injury when he collided with another skier as he was overtaking on a bend. Schools and local authorities were very concerned about the future of school skiing trips when, on 25 July 2001, QBD, Leveson J held the defendants, Woodbridge School, liable for negligence, subject to a 50 per cent reduction in damages for the claimant's own contributory negligence. Prior to the accident the claimant was involved in some incidents. In one incident he was caught smoking in the bedrooms. On two occasions he was caught skiing 'off-piste'. The teacher told the court he had 'threatened to confiscate their ski passes, but had decided not to do so as he was trying to treat them as adults and they assured him that they would not ski off-piste again' (ibid: para 9).

Leveson J held that the teacher's 'disciplinary response to Simon's unauthorised skiing off-piste had been negligent' and that he 'should have confiscated his ski pass or have arranged for him to ski under supervision on the following day and that his failure to take one of those steps was negligent' (ibid: para 15). If he had done this the accident would not have occurred and that 'his negligence was the cause of it' (ibid: para 15). The Court of Appeal allowed the appeal by the school and noted that 'the accident the next day had nothing to do with skiing off-piste or with deliberately irresponsible behaviour of that sort. It had to do with carelessness where the claimant lost control and made a misjudgement' (*Woodbridge School v Chittock* [2002] EWCA Civ 915, para 11).

> Although ultimately and not suprisingly, the decision was overturned on appeal, examples such as this fuel the anxiety of schools and other organizations, who appear increasingly to be deterred from organizing ski-ing and similar trips for their pupils and from permitting them to engage in other high risk sports, partly because of the risk of possible litigation in the event of injury.
>
> (Griffith-Jones, 2003: 1055)

EXERCISE 2.26

Outline the evidence in *Woodbridge School v Chittock* [2002] EWCA Civ 915. Explain the reversal of the High Court decision in the EWCA, with reference to the incident in question, causation principles and the normal acceptable risks of skiing.

Incapacity to participate and inadequate matching of participants

It is important to have effective systems for screening participants or assessing that there is no reason which would incapacitate them or make their participation inappropriate on safety grounds.

> A pupil with a congenital hip defect injured her ankle attempting a handstand in a PE lesson. The mother of the pupil had made it clear to the school, in writing, that the girl should not on any account do any form of physical education or games.
>
> (Barrell and Partington 1970: 401)

This restriction had been noted in the school records. However, the pupil told the teacher she could participate, took part and suffered the injury. The teacher 'should have made arrangements for the child's account to be checked with the mother before allowing her into the class' (*per* Lord Denning in *Moore v Hampshire County Council* (1981) 80 LGR 481 (CA)). In some sports, such as boxing, medical screening for fitness to compete is a well established practice. The claimant in a negligence case against the Ministry of Defence was injured in an inter-unit boxing competition and claimed that his temperature of 37.4 degrees centigrade, before the fight, was a sign of dehydration or infection, which would have affected his alertness in the ring. It 'could not be proved by the claimant that his increase in temperature contributed to his injury' (James, 2002: 8). The Court of Appeal held that the MOD was not liable for his injuries and the doctor 'had been entitled to conclude that the claimant's body temperature was in the band of normality and, in the absence of signs of infection or dehydration, he was fit to box (*Fox v Ministry of Defence* [2002] EWCA Civ 435).

A PE teacher, who was 'a local club player, was taking a group of 15-year-old pupils for a practice game. He picked himself on one of the sides for the game. During the game he got the ball, put up a high kick, followed it up and high tackled the boy' who was much weaker than himself, causing a serious spinal injury (Brierley, 1993: 20). Such conduct was held to be negligent in the high Court (*Affutu-Nartoy v Clarke and Anor*, The Times, 8 February 1984 (QBD) Hodgson J[19]).

In 1986 Mark Hamstra, a young Canadian, suffered a serious spinal injury resulting in quadraplegia.

> He sued, among others the coach, alleging that the scrum collapsed as a result of a coaching error in mismatching the athletes playing the prop positions alongside him . . . claiming they were neither skilled nor fit enough to play the prop position competently, and that the coach ought to have known risk of a collapsed scrum leading to the very type of injury Hamstra suffered. Furthermore, such knowledge carried with it a very high degree of care. In making this argument, Hamstra referred to a written memorandum from the English RFU and experimental variations of the junior game, designed for safety, which were taking place overseas.
>
> (Centre for Sport and Law, Brock University Canada, 2001: 2)

The court decided that the coach was not or should not necessarily have been aware of information from abroad on the risk of spinal injuries and he had followed written standards of the Canadian sports governing body at the time of the accident (ibid. 2001: 1). In response to the mismatching claim, the defendants argued that 'skill in the scrum depended upon technique, strength and weight in that order and even with differences in weight neither side clearly dominated the scrum throughout the match' (ibid, 2001: 2).

Explain in detail how the rugby sport governing body defended itself in the *Hamstra* case.

Identify potential risks relating to mismatching participants in any sporting situation, which are not really addressed by the formal rules or standard and approved practice. Suggest any ways of addressing such risks, if possible. Discuss the implications of the *Affutu-Nartoy* case for 'staff–pupil/old-boy or girls' matches or charity events which match boys against girls or staff against pupils.

Facility management in sport and recreation: provision of a safe environment and equipment

In a case involving multi-activities sharing a facility, the standard of care owed to disabled athletes was examined by the courts in December 1993. The claimant, Miss Morrell, who was a disabled paraplegic, took part in an archery session organised by the defendant sport governing body. An archery activity held at the same time as a discus activity, separated by a fish-net curtain (rather than using a proper, heavier dividing curtain). The claimant, an archer, had received no safety instruction and was not informed of the dangers of the discus activity. She suffered, among other things, permanent brain damage, when a discus caused the net to billow into the archers' section of the hall, striking her on the temple, an event which the judge regarded as 'entirely foreseeable' (see Farrell, 1994: 9). The judge emphasised that 'such coaches owed a greater duty of care to disabled participants than would be owed to able bodied athletes' and found all three defendants liable – the archery and discus coach, as well as the treasurer of the BSLA (see *Morrell v Owen*, The Times, 14 December 1993, Farrell, 1994: 9).

In a very significant Australian case which went to appeal in the High Court,[20] a sports company which organised an indoor cricket session was not held liable for the eye injury caused by a mis-hit 'pull shot' to an adult participant. The plaintiff argued that there was a failure to warn him of such risks and that helmets should have been provided by the defendants. The judge decided it was 'not reasonable to expect *Multi-Sport* to provide helmets as no suitable helmet had been designed for the game; none were worn by any players elsewhere; the rules of the game did not provide for such headwear, and the way in which the game is played means that there are reasons of safety and convenience why such headwear is not worn' (*Woods v Multi-Sports Holdings Pty Ltd* [2002] HCA 9; 208 CLR 460, in Cairns 2002).

In the case of *Futcher v Hertfordshire LEA* (unreported, 1997, Luton Crown Court) the defendants were found liable in Luton County Court for a knee injury to a participant in an athletics competition, caused by the use of builders sand in a long jump pit which had not been dug over (Whitlam, 2005: 119–120). A successful negligence claim was made against a local council who had failed to maintain a rugby post which had become rusty. The claimant was in a group of younger boys playing under the posts while older boys sat on the cross-bar (Whitlam, (2005: 147–148). The rusty cross-bar collapsed injuring the claimant (*Steed v Cheltenham Borough Council* (unreported, July 2000, Gloucester County Court)[21]).

EXERCISE 2.28

Is and should a higher duty of care be owed to disabled participants in sport and recreation? Explain your answer with reference to quotes from *Morrell v Owen*, The Times, 14 December 1993 and the principle of reasonable foreseeability.

EXERCISE 2.29

Is it reasonable for a sports organiser or coach to provide indoor cricket helmets if such equipment has not yet been designed and is not required by the rules or standard an approved practice? Explain your answer with reference to *Woods v Multi-Sports Holdings Pty Ltd* [2002] HCA 9; 208 CLR 460.

EXERCISE 2.30

An adult basketball club held a practice session in a local school, as their normal venue was being refurbished. During the practice, two players collided with a folded up trampoline, which the school physical education teacher had stored just over the sideline of the basketball court, and one of the players sustained a serious head injury. Evaluate potential liability for negligence, making reference to the three elements of negligence and the cases above, relating to a safe environment.

EXERCISE 2.31

A junior motor bike scrambling event held on a very hot June day ran into difficulties when, a few seconds after the start, the competitors raised so much dust that no one could see anything. The 11-year-old racers could not see. There was no system for stopping the race in such circumstances and before the competitors eventually came to a halt, several boys collided and three were seriously injured. Evaluate the potential for a negligence claim, with reference to the three elements of negligence and the duty to provide a safe environment.

Example of a key sport negligence case – Medical provision in a high-risk sport: liability of a sport governing body in *Watson v British Boxing Board of Control* [2000] EWCA Civ 2116; [2001] QB 1134

The high-profile case of *Watson v British Boxing Board of Control* [2000] EWCA Civ 2116; [2001] QB 1134 brought into sharp focus the liability for injury of a sports governing body which is seen to control, through its rules and regulations, medical provision in a high-risk sport. On 21 September 1991 the World Boxing Organisation (WBO) boxing match between Chris Eubank and Michael Watson was stopped in the twelfth and final round.

Disorder ensued between rival supporters and there was chaos in the ring for some time. The claimant's trainer became aware that Watson was slipping into unconsciousness. It took a considerable time (agreed as being around seven minutes) for a doctor to be summoned. As a result of a blow to the head sustained during the bout, the claimant suffered a subdural haemorrhage and is now an invalid.

(Sport Law Bulletin, 1999a: 3)

Because of lack of suitable medical equipment and assistance, the appropriate medical treatment 'was not applied until Michael Watson arrived at hospital some 25–30 minutes after his collapse in the ring' (*Watson v BBBC*). He also underwent emergency surgery twice to remove blood clots from his brain. Michael Watson has never worked again and suffered permanent brain damage with paralysis down the left side, after losing half of his brain function. He sued the British Boxing Board of Control (BBBC) for significant damages, which could potentially bankrupt the uninsured sport governing body. The decision by Kennedy J in December 1999 to hold the BBBC liable for the injury was upheld on appeal by the defendants, in December 2000.

In relation to the first element of negligence – a duty of care – the court decided that the BBBC did owe a duty of care to Michael Watson. Although they were not contracted to organise or promote the actual boxing matches, as the only body governing the professional sport, everyone had to accept their rules, including those relating to medical support at events. This power and control was enough for the court to impose a duty of care. The fact that the Board was not insured and had charitable status failed to stop a duty of care being owed on a matter of policy.

On the second element of negligence, a breach of duty, it was held that the duty to take reasonable care in all the circumstances had been breached by the Board in failing to provide *standard medical protocol* (emphasis added) which would be recommended by any medical expert.

> Serious brain damage represented the most serious risk posed by the sport, and the judge was entitled to find that it should have been addressed by the adoption of a resuscitation facility at the ringside, something that anyone with the appropriate expertise would have advised.
> (*Watson v British Boxing Board of Control* [2000] EWCA Civ 2116; [2001] QB 1134)

At the time of the injury the BBBC required promoters, among other things, to have three approved doctors, who have knowledge of sports medicine, and an ambulance to be in attendance at all bouts.[22] In taking this approach, the BBBC was seen by Kennedy J to be rather complacent in not going outside their own practices and getting expert medical advice on standard protocol recommended for sports with a recognised risk of such serious injury. Expert medical witnesses established that 'the importance of timely resuscitation to the outcome of serious injuries of all sorts has been well accepted since the 1970s' (*Watson v British Boxing Board of Control* (unreported, 12 October 1999, Queen's Bench Division, Kennedy J), p. 19, para G).

If such protocol had been 'made available ringside, the claimant would have been treated within, at the latest, three minutes [rather than 25–30 minutes] of his collapse' (*Sports Law Bulletin* 1999a: 3). It was not considered impractical to provide such expertise and support. In relation to the third element of negligence, causation, the Court of Appeal accepted the judge's findings that 'but for the absence of appropriate and immediate treatment, Mr Watson would have made a good recovery' (Griffith-Jones, 2003: 1662). The outcome of his injuries would have been 'significantly better' (*Watson v BBBC* (CA) p. 2). It was held that the Board 'was liable for the totality of disabilities suffered, and not just those flowing from the initial injury'.[23]

Although the claimant:

> clearly consented to the risk of injury at the hands of his opponent, he did not consent to the risk of injury flowing from the Board's failure to ensure that its safety arrangements were as carefully worked out as they might have been.
>
> (Kennedy J 24 September 1999)

EXERCISE 2.32

Explain the grounds used by the courts to decide that a duty of care was owed by the BBBC to Michael Watson.

'Following a sport governing body's own standard and approved practice is clearly not enough to avoid a successful negligence claim.' Explain this statement with reference to the breach of duty in the *Watson* case.

Would the claimant, Michael Watson, have suffered *no injuries* if standard medical protocol had been used? Explain the principles of causation in relation to the final injury outcome in the *Watson* case.

Summary

- Negligence is a tort – a civil wrong.
- There are three conditions for negligence to apply – duty of care owed by defendant to a claimant; a breach of duty by the defendant; *thereby* causing injury.
- The landmark case of *Donoghue v Stevenson* established negligence as a separate tort as well as the modern duty of care using the neighbour principle.
- Some groups in some circumstances may have immunity from liability for negligence, but this is gradually changing.
- Negligence is regarded as culpable carelessness and is an act or omission to do something which a reasonable person would do or not do in similar or relevant circumstances. The standard of care is an objective test.
- Three factors help the courts to decide what a reasonable person might have done in the circumstances – magnitude of risk and the likelihood of it happening; the social utility (value) of the activity; and the costs and practicability of minimising or removing the risk.
- An error of judgment by a sports competitor, in the heat of the moment, is not negligence.
- There are various sources to assist us in sport and the courts in evaluating what is reasonable including written and unwritten standards, case law, and common sense, coaching courses, standard and approved practice, codes of practice, and more experienced leaders, teachers and coaches.
- Proving causation and the link to a breach of duty can be a challenging and complicated matter in a negligence case.
- Multiple causes can lead to shared liability and proportional payment of compensation in a successful negligence case.
- Negligence cases in sport, physical education and recreation tend to illustrate a failure or breach in a set of common categories such as: deviation from standard or approved practice, breaching the rules of the game or sport, particularly safety rules, supervision,

incapacity to participate and inadequate matching of participants, or facility management and provision of a safe environment.

- Following standard and approved practice is not a fail safe way of avoiding liability for negligence. The standard and approved practice of sport governing body or school may be itself questionable.

3 Taking care of ourselves in sport: *volenti non fit injuria*, contributory negligence and occupier's liability

Introduction

The absence of a duty of care owed by the defendant to the claimant, no breach of duty and no link between the breach of duty and harm or injury caused to the claimant can obviously lead to a finding of no liability for negligence. In addition, *volenti non fit injuria* is a complete defence against a claim for negligence. It is rarely discussed in the sport community or on academic courses in sport and physical education and yet it is an important part of understanding the difference between making a decision to consent to the normal risks of a sport or game and those risks which are extraneous or unacceptable, and the implications for insurance and the outcome of negligence claims.

A partial defence – contributory negligence – will be discussed in this chapter. Although the defendant is still liable for negligence, a claimant can have their compensation reduced proportionally to the degree to which they negligently contributed to their injury. It is important to appreciate that the courts have found children as young as 11 to have contributed to their own injuries. The Occupier's Liability Acts of 1957 and 1984 are introduced, including some interesting cases which highlight the challenges facing the courts in dealing with the liabilities of occupiers when visitors, including trespassers, come onto their property and are injured. The difficult topic of the standard of care in sport is then reviewed before moving on two key cases in negligence in sport, the rugby union cases of *Smoldon* and *Vowles*.

Two defences against a negligence claim

Voluntary assumption of risk (*volenti non fit injuria*)

Volenti is a complete defence against negligence. It means that 'no harm is done to a person who has assumed the risk' and operates to 'exonerate the defendant from liability for what would otherwise have been an actionable breach of duty' (James, 2000: 163[1]). *Volenti* can only be pleaded once negligence is established. 'Contributory negligence (below) means that the courts can apportion damage, holding the plaintiff responsible for some loss and the defendant for the rest. *Volenti non fit injuria*, however, is a complete defence, meaning the defendant is not liable at all' (Tayfoor, 1995: 26). If participants agreed implicitly or explicitly to assume, or accept or agree to the ordinary risks inherent in a sport activity, if they are injured or harmed as a result of those risks, they cannot then sue for such injury or harm. *Volenti* has three elements or logical conditions.

First, as indicated in the name, the consent must be voluntary and made by sane, rational people, who are able to make such a choice. Whitlam (2005: 25) suggests that 'it would be difficult to apply this defence to pupils in physical education lessons that require participation as part of the National Curriculum. It would also be difficult to show that young people, particularly, were fully cognisant of the risks involved and were legally competent to accept them'. Second, the players or participants must be fully informed of the risks of the sport or recreation activity. Third, players or participants are only expected to consent to the *inherent* risks normally associated with that activity (see Nygaard and Boone, 1985; Hartley, 2001a). Inherent risks are difficult to define but are central to the meaning of *volenti*. Hartley (2001a: 180) suggests that they are:

> those risks which are left, when everyone involved in the sport contest has taken reasonable care to avoid reasonably foreseeable harm; to remove those risks would take away the agreed physical challenges which are valued and justified as good things for individuals and society.

These risks are irreducible if we are to retain the defined physical challenge of that sport or recreation activity valued by society. They are 'such an integral part of the game that players cannot possibly avoid it' (Gardiner 1994: 513). A cricket player, batting in a competitive game, is suddenly struck by the ball on his chest, during a normal, lawful delivery within the rules, directly hitting him on the heart, causing his death through heart failure.[2] A competitive diver performing a reverse three and a quarter tucked dive off the high board hits his head on the concrete board during the fast rotating dive. The subsequent brain damage caused leads to his death. Are these risks the inherent, irreducible risks normally associated with the sports of cricket and competitive diving?

It is important for those participating in and organising sport, or teaching physical education, to engage in discussions around the nature and examples of inherent risks, as compared to unacceptable risks, in various sporting activities. This is not only to meet the three criteria for a *volenti* defence. It is also important to educate participants to collectively and actively embrace risk management as part of their legal and moral responsibilities as players, so that they play a role in recognising risk and helping to reduce risks to a minimum. It should also encourage participants to reflect on the core aims and values of the sport or physical activity and so be more able to recognise when something is threatening those things (such as unacceptable but tolerated violence). This applies to civil matters (such as negligence), as well as criminal matters (such as statutory duties in risk assessment,[3] Offences Against the Person 1861,[4] and manslaughter[5]).

In addition, if we continually interrogate such boundaries of *volenti* in the sport community, expert witnesses who attend civil and criminal courts may, hopefully, be expressing an opinion which arises out of well-argued boundaries regularly discussed in that sport community. The boundaries of a 'normal' game embracing those inherent risks may be highlighted by norms or 'playing cultures' of the game, as well as formal rules (see James, 2000, 2001; Hartley, 1998, 2001a). Whatever is useful in identifying the boundaries of voluntary assumption of risk, it appears that such a process might usefully draw on conceptual questions, empirical questions and evaluative questions. For example:

- What are the core aims, the original defined, physical challenges of this sport or game, captured partly in the formal rules? (conceptual)
- What ought to be included as an inherent irreducible risk in this sport or game? What are the things which we value and wish to protect in this sport activity? (evaluative)
- What are the statistical risks of injury in this activity? (empirical). Do we know and understand these for our individual sports, let alone make informed comparisons between different sports?

Many negligence cases discussed so far in Chapter 2, where the defendant has been found liable, indicate that there was a breach of duty and those risks that led to that particular injury or harm to those successful claimants were not considered by the courts to be inherent, irreducible risks, to which the claimant ought to have consented. Case law can illustrate how the courts, in particular circumstances, have viewed the risks which led to the claimant's injury or harm as the 'ordinary' risks, inherent to the sport activity, or regarded them as 'extraneous' or unacceptable risks.

In *Simms v Leigh RFC* a rugby league player brought a claim for negligence arguing that his leg was broken when he was tackled and made contact with a brick wall 7'3" from the pitch boundary. The byelaws allowed walls to be no less than 7' from the boundary. However, the case was not proven on the facts and the court concluded that the injury was caused by a normal tackle, which did not result in contact being made with the wall. This was regarded as part of the normal risks of playing rugby and there was no breach of duty. In *Murray and Another v Harringay Arena* [1951] 2 KB 529, being hit by a puck which had broken through the boundary netting (considered to be standard equipment at that time[6]) was considered an acceptable risk of watching an ice hockey match. There was no breach of duty. A cricket ball or football or tennis ball hitting a spectator in the course of play would probably be viewed in the same way, but not if the tennis player for example hit the ball in anger outside the course of play. In the case of *Watson v BBBC* discussed in Chapter 2, *volenti* might be accepted in relation to injury caused by an opponent in a normal regulated boxing match, but not for an injury resulting from inadequate safety arrangements by the sport's governing body (Bermingham, 2005: 61).

Participants and spectators are expected to consent to the ordinary risks inherent in a sporting activity which cannot be avoided. In *Hall v Brooklands Auto-Racing Club* [1933] 1 KB 205 it was decided that those running or competing in sports events were not obliged to 'protect against the inherent danger to the entertainment which any reasonable spectator foresees and of which he takes the risk'. In the Australian case of *Rootes v Shelton* [1968] ALR 33, a waterskier:

> sued the boat driver for damages arising out of an incident where the skier collided with an object, of which he had given no warning. The claim failed, the risk in question being held to be inherent in or part and parcel of the sport.
>
> (Griffith-Jones 2003: 1040)

In contrast, a spectator at a hockey match was successful in a claim for negligence when it was accepted by a Canadian court that his injuries resulted 'not from an ordinary incident of the game of ice hockey but of a result of a fight between two players' (*Payne v Maple Leaf Gardens Ltd* [1949] DLR 369). How would and should the courts view the same circumstances as *Payne* today?

When using an indoor climbing wall, an experienced female adult climber had climbed 30 feet before she suddenly realised that she was not tied on to her belayer on the ground below. Despite an attempted rescue by the duty manager of the centre, she fell 30 feet and suffered a serious brain injury. It was claimed that 'when the duty manager attempted the rescue the claimant froze to the wall and that the method of rescue was inappropriate and caused her to fall' (*Day v High Performance Sports Ltd* [2003] EWHC 197 (QB)). She was a reasonably experienced climber and had accepted the conditions and rules, which 'clearly put an onus on her to make sure she was tied on' (ibid, 2003: 1). However, the decisions and actions of the duty manager when attempting a rescue 'had to be assessed in the context of the emergency facing him and not in the light of hindsight' and any error would be 'one of judgment rather than one that amounted to negligence' (ibid, 2003: 1). There was no breach of duty and the claim was dismissed.

EXERCISE 3.1

Explain the defence of *volenti non fit injuria* with reference to the three essential elements. Illustrate your answer with reference to relevant judged cases and literature.

For each of the following examples reflect on the question – are these inherent risks to which you would reasonably expect a participant to consent? Give reasons for your answer with reference to the readings (literature and cases) on *volenti*.

1 During an adult basketball practice in a local school, two players collided with a folded up trampoline, which the school physical education teacher had stored just over the sideline of the basketball court. One of the players sustained a serious head injury from hitting the metal legs of the trampoline.
2 A boxer sustained a serious head injury during an exhibition match, hosted at an outdoor stadium, when a parachutist taking part in a display at the event made an error of judgment and landed on the boxer in the ring instead of on the edge of the arena.
3 An employee who was required to go on an outdoor pursuits management development residential course took part in a 'fire-walking' challenge on the first night designed to test team motivation and badly burnt her feet on the hot coals.
4 A competitive backstroke swimmer suffered deep lacerations from an underwater camera whilst competing at a major international event. The camera ran on a rail at the centre of lane five, according to FINA guidelines. At other (domestic) swimming events the camera is located under the lane divider, to avoid such accidents.

EXERCISE 3.2

Using the sport, recreation or physical education activity with which you are most familiar or experienced, as a participant or an observer, attempt the following task. Identify a) an example of inherent risks and typical injuries which follow from those risks and b) an example of extraneous or unacceptable risks and associated injuries, to which you would *not* reasonably expect a participant to consent. Give reasons for your examples with reference to *volenti* principles and cases.

Contributory negligence

Under s. 1 (1) of the Law Reform (Contributory Negligence) Act 1945 damages paid in compensation by the defendant can be reduced 'according to the extent to which the claimant contributed to his or her own harm' (Turner, 2003: 47). People who do not conduct themselves in a reasonable manner and who should have foreseen that this might injure them are seen to be liable for 'contributory negligence'. It is for the defendant to prove that the claimant had also been negligent and therefore was partly to blame. The courts have a good deal of discretion in apportioning blame and percentage of damages between defendant(s) and claimant. In making such decisions the courts may use the degree to which the claimant's conduct caused the injury and the degree of deviation below the expected standard of care by the claimant (Bermingham, 2005: 59).

A failure to wear a seat belt, which contributed to the injuries, resulted in a reduction in damages for a claimant who was a passenger in a car.[7] This reduction in damages also applied to a passenger on a motor cycle whose failure to wear a helmet resulted in much greater injuries.[8] Furthermore, a passenger who gets a lift from a driver who the passenger knows has been drinking is contributorily negligent, 'even if the passenger is so intoxicated as to not appreciate the driver is unfit to drive' (Bermingham, 2005: 58[9]) In *Fowles v Bedfordshire County Council* the adult claimant's damages were reduced because of his contribution to his own spinal injuries when using a trampette, unsupervised in a local sports centre.[10] A 36-year-old experienced swimmer who injured his face when slamming into the side of a deck level pool had his damages reduced by 50 per cent where it was established by the court that the tiles defining the edge of the pool should have been wider and the water was murky. However, the claimant was experienced and was aware of the murkiness of the water and the nature of this 'leisure pool' and should have taken more care (*Greening v Stockton-on-Tees Borough Council* [1998] EWCA Civ 1704[11]).

The reduction in damages can be significant as in *Craven v Riches* [2001] EWCA Civ 375, where the Court of Appeal reduced the damages of an amateur motor cycling participant by two-thirds, as a result of his careless riding. The defendants remained one-third to blame in allowing drivers of different standards, experience and therefore speeds on the track at the same time (see Griffiths-Jones, 2003). In a leading Canadian case on sports instruction a claimant parachutist failed to steer her parachute properly, as she had been instructed. The courts reduced her damages by 30 per cent and allocated 70 per cent to the defendant parachuting school and instructor, who, among other things, misjudged her readiness to jump, although she was highly motivated and shared in the decision to jump (see *Smith v Horizon Aero Sports Ltd* (1981) DLR (3d) 91). A skiing holiday organised by a group of friends ended with one of the group suffering very serious fractures and a change in personality. The defendant argued that the claimant was 50 per cent responsible for his injuries as he had, when celebrating the achievement of a particular skiing skill, stopped and 'jumped for joy' on the slope. In the end the case was settled out of court (see *Freud v White* (unreported, 1988)[12]).

The objective test applied in all negligence cases is also used for assessing contributory negligence by children. In *McHale v Watson* (1966) 115 CLR 199, it was held that the standard of care was 'such care as can reasonably be expected of any ordinary child of the same age as the claimant' (Jones, 2002: 21). However, the courts have not been consistent in their findings of contributory negligence in children of different ages. A 13-year-old girl who stepped out into the road into the path of a negligent driver, after being beckoned by the driver of a stationary van, was found not to have contributed negligently to her own injury (see *Gough v Thorne* [1966] 1 WLR 1387). In contrast to this an 11-year-old boy in *Morales v Ecclestone* [1991] RTR 151, who was struck by a negligent driver while kicking a ball along the dotted line in the middle of the road, had his damages reduced by 75 per cent.

A more recent case, *Mullin v Richards* [1997] EWCA Civ 2662; [1998] 1 WLR 1304, found no negligence or contributory negligence in the conduct of two 15-year-old girls, who were playing at fencing with plastic rulers, when one of the rulers broke and a piece of plastic entered the plaintiff's eye. This was because of the risk of injury not being regarded by the CA as reasonably foreseeable.[13] In *Gannon v Rotherham Metropolitan Borough Council* Halsbury's Monthly Review, 91/1717 a 14-year-old pupil who suffered spinal injuries when diving into the shallow end of a swimming pool had his damages reduced by 25 per cent due to his contributory negligence.

There have been some interesting and worrying judgments on contributory negligence in relation to duties owed to drunken adults, where adults are located in the residential care of an institution. For example, in *Barrett v Ministry of Defence* [1995] 1 WLR 1217; [1995] 3 All ER 87 (CA), an off-duty naval airman in Norway got drunk to the point of collapse and passed out. He was placed in his room unsupervised, where he eventually asphyxiated on his own vomit (Muir, 2001). The MOD was held to be one-third liable for negligence, as once the deceased had passed out, they voluntarily assumed a duty of care towards him, when purporting to look after him. However, the deceased was regarded by the courts to be two-thirds to blame for contributing to his own negligence, in drinking to the point of collapse (ibid, 2001: 7[14]).

EXERCISES 3.3

Explain the principle of contributory negligence supported by relevant literature. What guides the courts in the allocation of blame and percentage allocation of damages?

EXERCISE 3.4

Review the cases of *Fowles v Bedfordshire County Council* [1996] ELR 51 and *Greening v Stockton-on-Tees Borough Council* [1998] EWCA Civ 1704 providing detailed notes from *Lawtel* or *Westlaw UK* (or equivalent) case summaries to illustrate the application of contributory negligence in these sports cases.

EXERCISE 3.5

Can children be found to contribute to a defendant's negligence? At what age? Support your answer with reference to case law involving children. Can and should education and physical education, Personal and Social Education (PSE) curriculum include contributory negligence and the responsibility of children as young as 11 in reducing risks in physical education and sport?

EXERCISE 3.6

Review the cases of *Barrett v Ministry of Defence* 1 WLR 1217; 3 All ER 87 (CA) and *Jepson v Ministry of Defence* [2000] 1 WLR 2055 then consider the following hypothetical.

EXERCISE 3.7

Hypothetical

A student union rugby club organises a residential weekend to coincide with the last match of the season. A series of drinking games on the last night results in most of the second team getting very drunk. Outside the pub some of the players decide to engage in some 'roof-running' along the tops of cars in the street. 'Andy' and 'Phil' are so drunk they are seriously injured after falling from one of the vehicles. Members of the club committee use their minibus to take the injured players to the local hospital, leaving the rest of the, very drunk, second team to go back to the hotel. After working out how long it would take to walk to the hotel, three of them persuade the second team captain to drive them back to the hotel, even though he has been drinking as much as everyone else. During the journey they are involved in a road traffic accident and the club secretary 'Pete' suffers serious facial injuries as he was not wearing a seat belt. During the night one of the second team players, 'Thomas' who had gone to sleep on his back, died due to choking on his own vomit. Discuss potential liabilities for negligence of the rugby club committee members and the student union. What are the likely outcomes in terms of allocation of blame and damages due to contributory negligence for each of the injuries to 'Andy', 'Phil', 'Pete' and 'Thomas'?

EXERCISE 3.8

Hypothetical

'Tricia' a 19-year-old part-time model and hockey goalkeeper had been advised to wear the normal protective gear when practising in goal. One night after they had finished training and she had removed her protective gear her coach's young son arrived and asked if he could try to get the ball past 'Tricia' before she went into the changing rooms. She and the coach 'Pat', agreed to let him have a go, only for a couple of minutes. At the second attempt the boy hit the hockey ball hard and it struck 'Tricia' in the face, causing a fractured cheek bone and eye socket, with some scarring. Discuss potential liability for negligence and the possibility of reduced damages for the contributory negligence of 'Tricia'.

Occupier's liability acts, 1957 and 1984

Civil law negligence cases can be brought in relation to statutory duties of occupiers under the 1957 or 1984 Acts. An occupier can be held liable under the 1957 Act for loss or injury suffered by lawful visitors to the premises. The statutory duty is to take reasonable care, and although in statutory form, this tort (civil wrong) has arisen out of common law negligence and so many of the principles are the same (Turner, 2003: 81).[15] An occupier has 'a duty to take reasonable care as in all circumstances of the case it is reasonable to see that the visitor will be reasonably safe in using the premises for the purposes for which he is invited or permitted to be there' (Bermingham, 2005: 85). This duty may extend to taking steps to see that a visitor does not deliberately harm other visitors by their foreseeably harmful conduct as in *Cunningham v Reading Football Club Ltd*, The Times, 22 March 1991 (HC) (Bermingham, 2005: 85). In this case a police officer was injured whilst on duty at a football match on the occupier's premises, when visiting fans threw a large piece of concrete at him. The defendants had failed in their duty to maintain the premises in a reasonable state, allowing fans access to sections of concrete from the poorly maintained wall.[16]

There is no statutory definition of an occupier but it applies to anyone who has sufficient control of the premises at the time of the damage or loss, and does not require an occupier to be physically present (Jones, 2002; Turner, 2003[17]). A warning will not be enough to absolve the occupier of any duty unless that warning is enough to enable the visitor to be reasonably safe as in *Jones v Northampton Borough Council*, The Times, 21 May 1990. Here the defendant was held not liable for injuries caused by slipping on a wet floor during a game of five-a-side football, as a warning had been given regarding the leak and the danger.

The case of *Wattleworth v (1) Goodwood Racing Co Ltd (2) RAC Motor Sports Association Ltd and (3) Federation Internationale De L'automobile* [2004] EWHC 140 (QB), arose out of the death of an experienced amateur racing driver, as a result of crashing into a long-tyred earth bank for the third time, where it 'pocketed' rather than allowing the car to slide along it.

> The actions against the first defendant under the Occupier's Liability Act 1957, s.2, for breaching a duty to provide a safe place to ride motor vehicles, and against the second and third defendant, for failing to carry out sufficient or adequate inspections of the Goodwood circuit, thereby breaching their duty of care towards the owners of the track.
> (James, 2006b: 651)

All claims were dismissed as appropriate technical recommendations were carried out and in meeting international standards, were considered by the court to be appropriate for an event at this level. The duty of care was not breached.

There have been various cases involving adult claimants suffering serious spinal injuries when diving into swimming pools, some in domestic pools and others on tour holidays abroad.[18] In a slightly different setting a local authority failed to maintain a tidal (boating) pond next to the sea and allowed silt to build up. The claimant dived into the shallow end of the pond (in which the defendants had allowed silt to build up, making the depth variable and uneven) resulting in serious spinal injuries. He argued that the defendants should have continued the former practice of dredging the pool and erected warning and depth signs or alternatively prohibited swimming and diving in the pool and enforced the ban ('Law Report', 1997). The defendants were found to be in breach of their common law duty under the Occupier's Liability Act 1957 and held liable for 80 per cent of the damages. The claimant was found to have contributed negligently to his injury for the other 20 per cent (see *Farrant v Thanet District Council* (unreported, 1996, Queen's Bench Division)).

Trespassers are not covered by the 1957 Act but they are afforded 'limited rights' under the Occupier's Liability Act 1984 (Griffith-Jones, 2003: 1047), although an occupier is still 'entitled to act reasonably in his own protection' (Turner, 2003: 88). The duty applies to people other than visitors for 'injury on the premises by reason of any danger due to the state of the premises or things done or omitted to be done on them'. In contrast to the 1957 Act, compensation is *for injury only* and not for damage to property. In *Tomlinson v Congleton Borough Council* [2003] UKHL 47; [2004] 1 AC 46, a local authority won an appeal in the House of Lords against the previous decision by the Court of Appeal which held them liable for a severe spinal injury to an 18-year-old claimant. He had ignored 'no-swimming and diving' signs at their lake and park and dived in, striking his head on the bottom of the lake.

The Court of Appeal held the defendants liable under the 1984 Act as they were aware of risk, knew that the warnings were generally ignored and delayed starting work on a scheme to make the lake inaccessible, because of lack of funds (Turner, 2003: 89). The House of Lords held that the injuries had arisen out of the claimant's decision 'to dive into a shallow lake when the risk was obvious' and not from the state of the premises or things done or not done by the defendants. A claimant, who willingly accepted that he was a trespasser, was injured when he dived into shallow water to retrieve a football, later argued in court that the injury was caused by a danger under the 1984 Act, that is, a fibre-glass container on the bed of the lake. However, it was held that the defendant was unaware of the existence of the container and had no reason to suspect a danger. A duty of care under section 1(3) had not been established (see *Rhind v Astbury Water Park Ltd* [2004] EWCA Civ 756 in Bermingham, 2005: 90–91).

A student who had been out drinking with other students, late one night in the middle of winter, knew that the college outdoor pool was locked and entry prohibited at the time he trespassed. He climbed over the locked gate and although conscious of the word 'warning', did not read the notice and dived in at the shallow end, suffering tetraplegic injuries. Section 1(16) of the 1984 Act allows for a defence of *volenti*. It was successful in this case as the claimant was aware of the nature of the risk and had voluntarily accepted it.[19]

Scott and Swainger v Associated British Ports (unreported, 18 March 1999, Queen's Bench Division, Deputy Judge Rafferty) was a trespasser case relating to the 1984 Act involving two teenagers. These claimants, aged 15 and 14 respectively at the time of the accidents, had truanted from school and were held to understand and consent to the dangers of train 'surfing' (attempting to jump aboard and ride moving trains). They argued that the defendants owed and breached their duty of care under s.1(1) (6) and s.1(3)a of the 1984 Act as they were aware that trespassers were regularly on their land and should have erected fences and that the trial judge defined the nature of the danger too narrowly. The Court of Appeal agreed with the trial judge that even if it were accepted that ABP should have discharged their duty in that way, the boys would not have been deterred from venturing onto the railway track, notwithstanding the provision of suitable barriers.[20]

EXERCISE 3.9

Explain the common law duties under the 1957 Occupier's Liability Act. Does the occupier have to be on the premises at the time of the injury/loss? Can an occupier be liable for the acts of a visitor? See *Cunningham v Reading Football Club Ltd*, The Times, 22 March 1991.

EXERCISE 3.10

Describe the common law duties under the 1984 Occupier's Liability Act. What is the difference, in duty owed and boundaries of compensation, between the 1957 and 1984 Act?

EXERCISE 3.11

How did the defendants breach their duty in relation to a boating pond in the case of *Farrant v Thanet District Council* (unreported, 1996, Queen's Bench Division)? What was the allocation of blame and damages?

EXERCISE 3.12

Compare and contrast the case of *Tomlinson v Congleton Borough Council* [2003] UKHL 47; [2004] 1 AC 46 with *Rhind v Astbury Water Park Ltd* [2004] EWCA Civ 756.

EXERCISE 3.13

Locate the case of *Ratcliff v McConnell* [1997] EWCA Civ 2679; [1999] 1 WLR 670. Print off a copy of the full text from one of the legal databases – for example, *Westlaw* or *Lawtel* or equivalent – for educational purposes only, and provide detailed notes, illustrating the application of the relevant duties and principles in relation to the 1984 Occupier's Liability Act to this case.

Critically review the decision of the first instance court (HC) using direct quotes from that judgment. What were the reasons for the HC judgment? Do you think it was fair to the defendants? What is your opinion of the CA reversing the decision of the HC in *McConnell*? Critically reflect on the issues this case raises in your mind around drunken student pranks on and off-campus.

EXERCISE 3.14

Hypothetical
Having watched the 'Jump Britain' television documentary and seen the French 'City Runners' ('Parkour') in action, a small group of teenage 'jumpers' and skateboarders planned a route across the roof, walkway and bridge linking the local leisure centre, sports hall and cinema. They did not have permission to stage an official exhibition/promotion event and trespassed on the premises when the facilities were closed to the public. The premises were well maintained and had clear signs saying 'no trespassing'. The teenagers used climbing ropes to get up the bridge onto the main walkway. 'Nicole' and 'Simon' were seriously injured when they fell from the roof of the walkway. Discuss a possible negligence case brought by the injured teenagers against the local council under the 1984 Occupier's Liability Act.

EXERCISE 3.15

Hypothetical
'Darren', a 17-year-old sports studies college student, had worked hard at a soccer summer camp for six weeks. He decided to celebrate his birthday at the local bar but wasn't used to the local beer and got very drunk. He was separated from his friends and was going to be late at their meeting outside a club. To save time, he decided to take a short cut over a disused railway bridge, which, like the fence alongside it, was in a state of disrepair. There were signs up saying 'No Trespassing' but he knew where the holes in the fence were and climbed through onto the bridge. He fell through the bridge onto the road below sustaining serious spinal injuries. How might this case be viewed in relation to a negligence claim brought by 'Darren' against the occupiers of the railway premises in relation to the 1984 Occupier's Liability Act? Identify two things which could invalidate his holiday insurance for personal injury and medical costs.[21]

Standard of care in sport: ordinary negligence or a special category of reckless disregard?

Failure to take reasonable care to prevent reasonably foreseeable harm in all the relevant circumstances is accepted as the ordinary negligence test for a breach of duty, that is, the legal standard of care in negligence, as outlined in Chapter 2. Clearly located in tort law, a 'civil wrong', it is associated with a blank state of mind, sometimes described as inadvertence. In contrast, criminal liability is associated with states of mind such as intention or recklessness. Since a test of 'reckless disregard' for the health and safety of others was apparently introduced as the appropriate test in the sports case of *Wooldridge v Sumner* the courts, in a limited number of sports negligence cases, have grappled with this issue. Was a special category or test of reckless disregard more appropriate to criminal law really introduced in *Wooldridge*? How have the courts and legal commentators approached this issue since *Wooldridge*? What is the test now?

In contrast to *Wooldridge* the Australian courts in *Rootes v Shelton* expressly rejected a test of 'reckless disregard' and used reasonableness in the special circumstances, adopting the general standard of care of Lord Atkin in *Donoghue*, later adopted by Lord Donaldson in *Condon v Basi* that:

> you are under a duty to take care, taking account of the circumstances, in which you are placed; which, in a game of football, are quite different from those which affect you when you are going for a walk in the countryside.
>
> (*per* Kitto J in *Rootes v Shelton*, preferred by
> Lord Donaldson in *Condon v Basi*)

It has been argued that *Wooldridge* did not really introduce a special category of reckless disregard for sport. It still used the ordinary test for negligence, but in unpacking the 'special circumstances' or 'practical content' of the duty of care in sport, emphasised the use of a very high threshold of liability, that of 'reckless disregard' (see James and Deeley, 2002; Griffith-Jones, 2003; McArdle, 2005; James, 2006b). Either way, it seems that a test or guide more appropriate to criminal law was introduced to sport cases, with no basis in tort law. In *Elliott v Saunders* Drake J rejected the variable standard of care adopted in *Condon* but held that the plaintiff would have to show that 'the defendant had been guilty of dangerous and reckless play' (Gardiner and Felix, 1994: 2). Gardiner and Felix (1994: 2) appear to support the use of such test when they made the following observations:

> The construction of negligence in terms of dangerous or reckless play reflects the developments of the law of negligence for sports injury in American Tort Law. In order that a balance be maintained between the safety of the players and the competitive edge of the sport, the defendant should only be liable where he has shown reckless disregard for the safety of the plaintiff. It should not be enough to merely show negligence. Reckless disregard is held to exist when the player knows an act is harmful and intends to commit that act but does not intend to harm his opponent with that act.[22]

Although Drake J in *Elliott* used the test of reckless disregard, and questioned the variable standard of care, *Condon* remained the higher (CA) authority as observed by Moore (2000: 79). Drake J seems to be agreeing with the use of the need to show reckless disregard 'whereas, of course, standing his opinion, he only needs to find a lack of reasonable care, he did not have to adopt these remarks' (Duff, 1999: 46). James (2006b: 639) observes that Drake J 'did accept the ordinary standard of negligence standard used in *Condon v*

Basi but went on to find that the defendant was not guilty of dangerous and reckless play and was therefore not on breach of the duty of care owed'.

Gardiner and Felix (1994), and Felix (1996, 1998) regard the lower standard of care, one of reckless disregard, as the appropriate one for the standard of care between competitors in a fast-moving sports contest where players, particularly professional players, are assumed to consent to more harm that is reasonably foreseeable than non-sporting activities.

> Ordinary negligence standards cannot be applicable to establishing the standard of care in the sporting context. The standard of care is determined by reference to reasonable foreseeability of harm. In the context of sports and participants in sport, a greater degree of harm is foreseeable by reason of participation in the game. Therefore, the standard of care should be lower . . . this can be justified by reference to the fact that society as a whole regards participation in sport as a valid activity although the risk can be foreseen. On this basis then the lower reckless disregard standard set out in *Wooldridge v Sumner* must be regarded as applicable law.
>
> (Felix, 1996: 35)

Felix (1996: 32) argued that Drake J's sole reliance on *Condon* goes no further in assisting us with the appropriate standard of care in a sporting context in English law and, furthermore, *Condon v Basi* 'is not good authority for the standard of care in sporting contexts in English law'.[23] Lord Donaldson in *Condon*:

> in relying on the Australian High Court Decision of *Rootes v Shelton* failed to establish the standard of care. Indeed, the failure to consider the English authorities of *Wooldridge v Sumner, Wilks v Cheltenham Home Guard*[24] and *Harrison v Vincent*[25] renders the decision *per incuriam*. As such it would be legitimate to argue that the standard of care in English law is the reckless disregard in *Wooldridge v Sumner* and *Harrison v Vincent* [1982] RTR 8.
>
> (Felix, 1996: 35–36)

The cases of *Wooldridge* and *Wilks* above related to injuries to spectators and not participants in a sport competition and the comments by the judges were not binding. James (2006b) summarises the arguments for and against a lower standard of reckless disregard in sporting contexts. Proponents for reckless disregard:

- Defendants have a greater degree of carelessness before liability is imposed than does ordinary negligence.
- Less pressure will be put on players to alter their style of play through fear of civil litigation. Most injuries are caused in the heat of the moment and are not intentional. Players can concentrate on playing the game or playing to win and not hold back due to considerations of the possibility of legal action.
- Reckless disregard would allow greater leeway and the ordinary test is too easy to meet in the context of a fast-moving sport contest.
- Reckless disregard is a more subjective text with the need to show awareness of the risk on the part of the defendant, risks which were unacceptable according to the playing culture of the game.

(James, 2006b: 640)

Criticisms of the reckless disregard test include:

- The consideration of the nature and value of fast-moving sport contests where conduct can be located in the heat of the moment is already catered for in the ordinary test of negligence of failing to take reasonable care in all the relevant circumstances.

- This test blurs the distinction between criminal liability and tort as subjective recklessness is a state of mind associated with criminal liability.
- Moving from an objective to a subjective test creates the possibility of sports participants defining their own subjective version of acceptable conduct yet negligence is based on an external objective test of an expected standard of care.

(James, 2005: 640)

Furthermore, the recognition by society of the value of sporting activity and sport contests, highlighted by Felix (1996), was already included in the principles guiding the courts in ordinary negligence around magnitude and probability of the risks, social utility and value of the activity, and practicability-costs of removing the risks.[26] With judgments continuing to use the ordinary standard of care, but adding comments which emphasise the need to establish that a defendant showed 'reckless disregard', would obviously lead to counsel for plaintiff's selecting the ordinary test of negligence and lawyers for defendants going for the 'reckless disregard' test in their arguments to the courts (see James, 2006b).

The landmark rugby case of *Smoldon v Whitworth and Nolan* [1996] EWCA Civ 1225; [1997] PIQR 133, discussed in detail in the next section of this chapter, relied on *Condon* with the plaintiff lawyer arguing for the ordinary test of negligence and the defendant arguing for a test of reckless disregard. The test framed by Lord Bingham in *Smoldon* rejected recklessness and held that the duty owed by a referee towards players was 'appropriate care in all the circumstances, taking full account of the factual context in which he was exercising his functions as a referee' (Moore, 2000: 95). Lord Bingham saw no inconsistencies between this conclusion and those reached in *Wooldridge* and *Wilks* as they were about the participants and spectators and the position of the referee in was different, with responsibilities to safeguard the players, through application of safety rules. The legal duty was the same but the practical content differed.

The plaintiff's case failed in *Elliott* but was successful in *McCord v Swansea City AFC Ltd and Cornforth*, The Times, 11 February 1997 where the error made by the defendant soccer player missed the ball and collided with the plaintiff in what was described as a dreadful tackle. The test used by Kennedy J was 'a duty to take such care towards one's neighbour as in reasonable in all the circumstances could fit the relationship of player and spectator and player and player in every sport'. The conduct of the defendant was 'unmistakably inconsistent with his taking reasonable care towards the plaintiff' who sustained a career-ending injury (Kitson and Allen, 1997: 5).

In the case of *Watson & Bradford City Association v Gray and Huddersfield Town AFC Ltd* (unreported, October 1998, High Court), Hooper J preferred the formulation of the test presented by the counsel for the plaintiff that 'it must be proved on the balance of probabilities that a reasonable professional player would have known that there was a significant risk that what Kevin Gray did would result in a serious injury to Gordon Watson' (cited Felix, 1999a: 223). The judge's findings appeared to be based on the ordinary test of negligence and returned to a variable standard of care adopted by Lord Donaldson in *Condon* (See Felix 1999; Moore 2000).

Finally, a negligence case involving two professional jockeys as defendants (*Caldwell v Maguire and Fitzgerald*) has come 'the closest to defining the true scope of negligence in this area' and found five applicable propositions from earlier sports cases (James, 2006b: 632–633). The duty of care is objectively reasonable in the prevailing circumstances and include the nature, object of the sport, the demands made on contestants, inherent dangers, rules, conventions, customs, the obligation of the jockey to race for the best possible place in the race, and the standards expected of a professional jockey. The threshold for liability is very high and does not include errors of judgment or momentary lapses of skill, which are inherent and expected in racing. The fifth and final proposition agreed with previous observations of, among others, Griffith-Jones (2003) and James (2006b). 'In practice, it will be difficult to prove a breach of duty without proof of conduct that in point of fact amounts to reckless disregard for the other contestant's safety. However, it must be emphasized that there is a distinction between the expression of legal principle and the practicalities of the evidential burden' (*per* Tuckey LJ, para 23; James, 2006b: 633).

'Reckless disregard is only a reflection of the amount of evidence potentially required to prove negligence in sport, not a new standard of care. In reality there is little practical difference between reckless disregard and negligence in all the circumstances' (James, 2006b: 640). Regardless of whether the phrase reckless disregard is seen as a new or alternative test or presented as one of the guidelines to the courts on the circumstances for consideration of the duty and standard or care, an element appears to have been introduced which has no basis in tort law and is more logically located in the criminal law. If the operation of the emergency services such as fire and ambulance are subject to the ordinary standard of care from the general tort of negligence, should sport be treated more leniently. Surely the former is at least of equal value to society, yet does not receive special treatment by the courts?

EXERCISE 3.16

Consider the following two statements

A. 'The test of "reckless disregard" introduced in *Wooldridge v Sumner* [1963] 2 QB 43, sits uneasily in civil law negligence.' This test is more at home in the criminal law, for example, in assault charges under the OAPA 1861. Is there and ought there to be a special (and arguably) more lenient test for sport?

B. '*Wooldridge* did not really introduce a special category of reckless disregard for sport. It still used the ordinary test for negligence, but unpacking the special circumstances or practical content of duty in sport, emphasised the use of a very high threshold of liability, that of reckless disregard' (see James and Deeley, 2002; Griffith-Jones, 2003; cited Hartley 2001a earlier in this chapter).

Get into two groups. Each group takes one of the arguments above and defends it. Make use of James (2006b) on the range of arguments for and against each of the approaches above, as well as Felix (1996). What do you think?

EXERCISE 3.17

Does case law distinguish in any way between the test used for competitive participants and those who organise or officiate at sport competitions? If so, can you give reasons for such a distinction?

EXERCISE 3.18

Outline the five applicable propositions articulated in the case of *Caldwell v Maguire and Fitzgerald* [2001] EWCA Civ 1054; [2001] PIQR 45. Was Tuckey LJ proposing a new standard of care?

Key cases: liability of rugby union referees in U19 (colts) and the adult amateur game

Smoldon v Whitworth and Nolan [1996] EWCA Civ 1225; [1997] PIQR 133

'Some 490,000 people take part in rugby every weekend. This is for eight months of the year. 3036 schools are affiliated to the ERFSU. 1958 clubs are affiliated to the RFU. Approximately 45 very serious injuries from clubs and schools are reported each season' (Tracey and Baker, 2002: 1). In 1996, almost out of nowhere, *Smoldon v Whitworth and Nolan* was 'the first case of its kind brought against a rugby referee' (Felix and Lee, 1999: 1; James, 2001). The plaintiff, Ben Smoldon sued Thomas Whitworth, the opposing forward and Michael Nolan, the referee of the colts match, for causing his catastrophic spinal injuries, during a scrum collapse.

> Scrums can be dangerous – the referees know it and the players know it. Scrums can collapse for a variety of reasons, either through foul play, or when there has been no foul play, due to pitch conditions, one pack being stronger than the other, players losing their grip or binding.

> (Tracey and Baker, 2002: 2)

In the High Court, in April 1996, Curtis J found the referee liable, but decided that the first defendant, Thomas Whitworth, did not cause the injury and that the plaintiff was not contributorily negligent. The referee lost his appeal in December 1996. Ben Smoldon was awarded £1.8 million in damages for negligence, but received only £1 million, the maximum available under the English Rugby Football Union's insurance scheme.

There were disputes over the evidence, particularly in relation to the number of collapsed scrums, warnings from the touch judge to the referee and any complaints during the match. However, the court accepted the following facts. On 19 October 1991, the match between Sutton Coldfield and Burton was described to the court as starting off 'at 100 mph' and set the pattern for the match, sometimes violent and at other times played with a very competitive spirit. A player was sent off for punching early on in the game. After ten minutes the plaintiff replaced another player as hooker, this being his usual playing position. There were problems of the scrums coming together 'in a rushed way and with excessive force' as well as head butting and punching in the scrum (which could make binding difficult). In response to these difficulties, the touch judge warned the referee that 'someone in the front row would get hurt if he did not do something about it', that is, the number of collapsing scrums (CA judgment, 17 December 1996: 10). The referee told the court that he has awarded penalties for this conduct (three against Sutton and two against Burton) but responded to the touch judge's warning by saying 'I know but I can't see who is doing it' (CA judgment, 17 December 1996: 11).

Seven months before this match a directive on the new crouch-touch-pause-engage (CTPE) sequence for U19 colts rugby was introduced, under Law 20 of the game of rugby.

This was disseminated to the referee, via the minutes of a meeting in the West Midlands Rugby Football Union on 2 September 1991. At the time of the injury it was his first colts match under these new rules. Law 20 was designed to respond to the known risk of serious spinal injury due to collapsing of scrums (where this age group was particularly vulnerable) by controlling the engagement of the scrum. Witnesses gave 'clear, unshakeable evidence' that the referee 'did not, during the course of this match, insist on the CTPE sequence being followed and it was not' (CA judgment, 17 December 1996: 10). Expert witnesses informed the court that five or six collapsed scrums would be considered normal and the 25 collapsed scrums in this match an abnormal number, which would have made the packs physically weary and vulnerable and would indicate that there was a problem with the refereeing.

Prior to the final three attempts to engage the scrum, the plaintiff had told his pack to calm things down. On the third attempt, with no CTPE engagement and a strong impact, the scrum went down immediately injuring Ben Smoldon, who reported that he could not feel his legs. On matters of law the courts had to engage with the articulating a test for a breach of duty, with past cases dealing only with player to player or player to spectator duties and not the duty of a referee/official to players. Not surprisingly, counsel for the (second defendant) referee used the cases of *Wooldridge v Sumner* and *Wilks v Cheltenham Homeguard Motor Cycle and Light Car Club* [1971] 1 WLR 668 and argued that 'nothing short of reckless disregard of the plaintiff's safety would suffice' (CA 17 December 1996: 8). Lee (1997) reported that at this point LCJ Bingham asked the defendants if they were postulating that there was a new tort of 'recklessness'? They did not fall into that trap.

The counsel for the plaintiff argued that the referee owed 'a duty to exercise such a degree of care as was appropriate in the circumstances', drawing on *Condon v Basi* and *Rootes v Shelton*. The CA agreed with the decision of J Curtis to adopt the test proposed by the plaintiff and clarified that, in their opinion, there was 'no inconsistency between this conclusion and that reached by the CA in *Wooldridge* and *Wilks*'. The position of a referee towards players was not the same as that of a sport participant to spectators, with the former having 'responsibilities to safeguard the players'. The CA decided that the legal duty was the same, but the practical content of the duty differs due to the quite different circumstances (CA judgment, 17 December 1996: 8). The level of care was 'that which was appropriate in all the circumstances, the circumstances being of crucial importance' with a full account being taken of the 'factual context in which a referee fulfils his function' (Bingham, LCJ, CA 17 December 1996, cited Felix and Lee, 1999: 220). This was a clear message that the Court of Appeal was using the ordinary test of negligence and not 'reckless disregard' supposedly used in *Wooldridge* and *Wilks*.

The referee argued that the law should not interfere with a hard contact game supervised by a responsible body and involving volunteer referees. Was it fair to impose a duty on the referee when he may be 'at the whim of players who actually wish to play in an illegal or dirty way, particularly since he would not actually inflict the injury on the plaintiff himself' (Felix and Lee, 1999: 219)? Curtis J balanced this against the need for laws to protect players, rejected public policy arguments regarding imposing a duty. The referee argued that the judge was wrong to reject his defence of *volenti non fit injuria*. Since the plaintiff had 'consented to the risk of injury . . . by voluntarily playing as a member of the front row . . . and by voluntarily participating in the collapsing thereby also increasing the risk that the opposing front row might do the same' (CA 17 December 1996: 16). The Court of Appeal accepted that plaintiff consented to the ordinary incidents in a game of rugby football. However, since the rules were framed to protect him, he 'cannot possibly have consented to a breach of duty on the part of the official whose duty it was to apply the rules and ensure as far as possible that these are observed' (CA 17 December 1996: 16).

The judge concluded that:

> the plaintiff succeeds against the second defendant, who in important respects relating to the scrums failed to exercise reasonable care and skill in the prevention of collapses by sufficient instruction to the front rows, and in the use of CTPE thereby reducing the impact of engagement of the pack to an acceptable level for a Colts' game.
>
> (CA 17 December 1996: 11)

With reference to the unfolding risk during the match, the judge found that the referee 'failed to appreciate the true nature of the situation arising from the number of collapses, and in particular, to enforce the CTPE sequence' (Felix and Lee, 1998: 8). In the judge's view there was not a risk of a floodgate of claims provided 'all concerned appreciated how difficult it was for a plaintiff to establish that a referee had failed to exercise the care and skill reasonably expected of him in a hotly contested game of rugby football' (CA 17 December 1996: 16, cited in Moore, 2000: 91).

Curtis J could not stress too strongly that his decision was based upon 'special considerations of the case, mainly the facts of the case, that it was a Colts game, the law of rugby modified for the Colts and the laws and customs of rugby in the 1991/2 season' (Felix and Lee, 1999: 218). The Court of Appeal rejected the arguments of the referee that the judge should not have attached significance to the physical immaturity of the colts, the absence of complaint (there had been at least five), or the advice from the touchline. The Court of Appeal also considered the strength of evidence, including expert witnesses in support of the judge's conclusions on the failure to enforce the CTPE rules, as well as the causal link between such failures and the resulting abnormal number of collapsed scrums (CA 17 December 1996: 15). In contrast, the referee's criticism of the judge for *not* relying on reports from other matches was rejected on appeal, since that was 'unhelpful' and it was right to concentrate on evidence from this particular match.

However, the Court of Appeal did have some sympathy with the sixth criticism raised by counsel for the second defendant. Although the power to call 'no-side' was provided in the rules, that course of action, argued the referee, was 'unrealistic in the circumstances' and was 'so rarely followed it was not fair to criticize [him]' for 'failing to adopt it'. It was plainly 'a power to be exercised as a last resort, when and only when all other measures have failed' but the Court of Appeal held that the judge 'placed little reliance on this, in his conclusion to the judgment, because the referee had not adopted all the measures which he could have adopted' (Kitson and Allen 1997: 7). Although the judge had emphasised the special circumstances and facts of the case, this decision in *Smoldon* in 1996 caused an outcry in the press at the time and attracted comment from the sport and legal community.

In one letter to *The Times* newspaper, 20 April 1996, Simon Jenkins stated that 'individuals should be left with some responsibility for their actions' and referred to 'the phalanx of wheelchairs at the Twickenham touchline, none of whose occupants have ever sued the game'. Kevin Mitchell, in *The Observer Sport* newspaper believed that the *Smoldon* judgment was 'only good news for the burgeoning army of smart-talking lawyers now invading the playing fields' and 'confirms the growing suspicion, that, for all their smart talk, lawyers are unwelcome guests in sport' (1996: 2). Mitchell suggested that the way the courts used the terms 'reasonable', 'acceptable' and 'responsible' was to 'make them relatively redundant in the real world'. These people from the field of 'legal niceties' were seen as 'intruding on the turf of another' in the 'grey areas of interpreting and enforcing the rules and regulations of a pursuit as relatively innocent as a game of rugby' (ibid: 2). He expressed a common concern about the 'danger of litigants in other sports', encouraged by lawyers, 'bounding into court at the drop of a writ' but it was his summary of 'the evidence' which was most illuminating:

> His [Smoldon's] counsel estimated that there had been 25 such scrum collapses. The referee, Michael Nolan . . . recall only eight such incidents, and he said, he could not remember the linesman warning him that players could be hurt if he did not intervene. That, basically, was the evidence.

(ibid: 2)

Concerns around the possible implications of the *Smoldon* judgment for rugby and other sports drew significant comments from sport organisations, coaches, teachers, lawyers and the media (see Uttley, 1996). One of the major concerns was around the potential effects on the recruitment and retention of volunteer referees in both rugby and football. However, Felix and Lee (1998: 8) did not feel that would be a problem and pointed out that litigation against surgeons had not affected application to medical schools. In 2001 James recognised shortage of referees was a fear after *Smoldon* but, 'sport had not ended, officials still officiate' (2001: 711).

In addition, the case emphasised the importance of referees having to 'observe the laws of the game meticulously and keep strict control' of the game. In addition 'schools may have to prove, for insurance purposes, that all teachers taking games fully understand the intricacies of sports rules' (Edward Grayson, quoted in Colley 2002). Usher (1996) emphasised the importance of awareness, understanding and applying the rules.

Since the *Smoldon* case the English Rugby Football Union has encouraged all players to have their own policies of insurance and have increased the maximum payout under their own policy to £5 million (James, 2001: 711). The need to review both player and referee insurance, double premiums and to insure for catastrophic personal injury, whether or not caused by negligence, were common themes in the legal and press commentary. David Hincliffe, Labour MP for Wakefield and secretary of the all-party Parliamentary Rugby Group, 'called for an urgent review of scrummaging rules, suggesting rugby union moved closer to rugby league type scrums' (Press Association News, 19 April 1996).

Most commentary on the implications for other sports focused mainly on cricket, boxing, rugby league and hockey. For example, if a referee in boxing failed to stop a fight early enough, or a cricket umpire failed to control the number of bouncers to an acceptable level, they may be held liable for injuries caused as a result of such player/competitor conduct. Equally, if a referee in soccer failed to address repeated violent conduct, or in rugby league failed to respond appropriately or early enough to spear tackles or a hockey referee to address hitting shots above the waist, they may be held liable for resulting injuries or at least partly liable.

Steve Double, Football Association Spokesman, commented 'We find it difficult to see a similar situation arising in football. Physical contact is part and parcel of rugby' and he also quoted Law Five, Clause 13 of the Rules of Association Football 'The referee shall not be held liable for any injury of any kind suffered by a player, official or spectator..which may be due to any decision which he takes in terms of the laws of the game' (quoted in Llewellyn, 1996).

It would indeed be interesting to see that tested in court in a negligence case involving a failure of a referee to control or respond appropriately to, or making the wrong decision in relation to repeated dangerous or violent conduct of a player, leading to an injury of another player in a soccer match.

EXERCISE 3.19

What was significant about the *Smoldon* case?

EXERCISE 3.20

Summarise the evidence, accepted by the courts, on the following points:

The Evidence:

1   The sendings off early in the match.
2   The atmosphere of the match.
3   The introduction and dissemination of the new safety rule – Law 20, by the sport governing body.
4   The nature and reason for the CTPE rule, Law 20.
5   The collapsed scrums. What is regarded as 'normal'? According to the expert witnesses in this case, what would 25 collapsed scrums indicate?
6   The warnings from the touch judge regarding the collapsed scrums and risk of injury.
7   Complaints from the sidelines and the match report.
8   The circumstances of Ben Smoldon's serious spinal injury.

EXERCISE 3.21

The Law:

1   Counsel for the plaintiff (Ben Smoldon) and counsel for the defendant (referee), selected and presented to the court *different* tests for the standard of care. Explain this with reference back to the previous section on 'reckless disregard'. Which test did the courts use in *Smoldon*?
2   Was it fair, just and reasonable to impose a duty of care on a referee in these circumstances?
3   Was the first defendant, Thomas Whitworth, the opposing prop, found to have caused the injury or been liable in any way?
4   Did Ben Smoldon contribute to his own injuries?
5   Explain the defence of *volenti non fit injuria* put forward by counsel for the second defendant, the referee. Summarise the decision of the CA on the matter of *volenti*. What do you think?
6   Critically comment on the referee's reasons for his failure to call 'no-side' (abandon the match) in the face of collapsing scrums. In dealing with this issue does the court use 'norms' or 'playing subcultures' as a guide or stick with the formal written rules of the game?
7   Summarise concisely, using quotes from the CA judgment, how the referee breached his duty.
8   Discuss the implications of the *Smoldon* case for insurance matters, floodgates, dissemination of new safety rules by a sport governing body, recruitment of volunteer referees in rugby in the future and application of this case to referees in other sports and games.
9   Comment critically on the points made by Simon Jenkins in his letter to *The Times* following the HC judgment in *Smoldon*.
10 Summarise and give your opinion on the approach taken by Kevin Mitchell in his article in *The Observer Sport* following the HC judgment in *Smoldon*. Having read the case, critically analyse Mitchell (1996). What view do you think he is trying to communicate to readers?

11 Discuss the options open to a referee in dealing with collapsing scrums in these circumstances. Are there pressures on a referee not to abandon the game? Is the need to find out which individual is collapsing the scrum, in order to take action, helpful or a hindrance to a referee trying to engage in good risk management?

12 What are the main things which you have learnt from reading about the *Smoldon* case? What has it made you reflect upon as a player, coach or observer of rugby?

Vowles v Evans [2003] EWCA Civ 318; [2003] 1 WLR 1607

Following the *Smoldon* case there was no floodgate of cases against rugby football referees. There was an incremental extension, in 2002, with the first negligence case against a rugby referee in an amateur *adult* match. Richard Vowles, from Lanharan, Wales, sustained serious and permanent spinal injuries when playing rugby union in January 1998. The first defendant, referee David Evans, was held liable for negligence by the High Court in December 2002, a decision which was upheld in the Court of Appeal in March 2003. The second defendants, the Welsh Rugby Union, accepted vicarious liability (*Vowles v Evans*). The claimant had reportedly been awarded £91,000 in September 1998 'according to the disability cover provided by the Welsh Rugby Union to all its member clubs' (*Insurance Day* 13 March 2003, cited Elvin 2003: 560).

Approximately 30 minutes into an amateur match between Llanharan and Tondhu, the Llanharan loose-head prop was injured and had to leave the field. There was no experienced or trained front row forward to replace the prop, so the flanker, Christopher Jones, who had never trained but occasionally played as a front row forward, took his place. The referee 'discussed with the Llanharan team the possibility of agreeing to finish the match with non-contested scrummages, but this was declined because any league points would have been forfeited' (*Vowles v Evans* summarised at www.lawtel2002.com). The claimant, Richard Vowles, aged 25 at the time, played hooker for the Llanharan team. The game continued and was described as a 'forwards game' which was 'hard fought but not dirty' played in 'very muddy or boggy conditions' (Williams, 2003: 50).

In evidence to the High Court, the plaintiff reported that Mr Jones's timing and binding was wrong going down, making scrummaging difficult. This meant that the plaintiff was effectively taking the weight of the opposing hooker and props. One witness, the Llanharan second team coach, thought that there were slightly more scrum collapses than normal, but conditions were slippery and players had difficulty keeping their feet. There were approximately 55 collapsed scrums during the match.[27] Set scrummages started to go wrong as soon as Christopher Jones took up the position in the front row, with problems of engagement and mistiming, which was to prove crucial in the judgment (see Watson 2003: 1). 'In the final scrummages of the game the front rows failed to engage properly and C (Richard Vowles) sustained a dislocation of the neck. As a result C sustained permanent, incomplete tetraplegia' (www.lawtel2002.com).

On the issue of duty 'the Court applied the *Caparo v Dickman* [1990] 2 A.C. 605 test of whether it was fair, just and reasonable to impose, on an amateur referee, a duty of care towards the players in the game refereed. The Court decided that it was' (Elvin 2003: 560). No distinction was made between Colts and adults in deciding this (see Charlish 2003: 87; Williams, 2003: 50). Morland J, in the first instance judgment, did not consider it logical to draw a distinction between amateur and professional rugby. However, he commented that he considered the risk of very serious spinal and cervical injuries to the front row forwards was more likely to occur in the amateur game than in the professional game – albeit extremely infrequently.[28]

The first defendant, the referee, submitted that the supply of voluntary referees would diminish if referees were potentially liable for negligence. It was not fair, just and reasonable that unpaid, amateur referees risked being ruined by legal liability. Following the decision in the High Court, Glanmoor Griffiths, Chair of WRU, feared it would lead to 'an increase in insurance premiums and make it difficult to recruit referees and umpires' (BBC News, 24 February 2004, cited Elvin, 2003. 561). Evidence indicated that the Welsh Rugby Union was facing financial difficulties and public liability insurers were considering excluding cover for sporting injuries. However, Lord Philips indicated that judges could not take notice of such financial problems or the intentions of public liability insurers (see Chaudray, 2003).

The Court used *Agar v Hyde* [2000] HCA 41; (2000) 201 CLR 552 and considered *Smoldon* in deciding that such a duty was owed. The standard of care expected of the referee depended on 'all the circumstances of the case'. The threshold of liability was a high one. 'The evidential test was that applied from *Smoldon* but is in line with recent statements from *Caldwell v Maguire and Fitzgerald* [2001] PIQR 45' (James, 2003: 167). In *Smoldon* it was held that:

> A full account must be taken of the factual context in which a referee exercises his functions, and he could not properly be held liable for errors of judgement, oversights or lapses of which any referee might be guilty in the context of a fast moving and vigorous contest. The threshold of liability is a high one. It will not be easily crossed.
> (*Per* Bingham LCJ [1997] PIQR 137 at 139, cited James 2003: 167)

The referee was 'in breach of duty in failing to properly apply the provision of law 3 (12). He did not ask the Llanharan captain whether he had anyone suitably trained or experienced to be tried in the front row' and he 'should not have offered Llanharan the option to continue with non-contested scrums or to try Jones as a prop' (*Vowles v Evans*).[29] The referee had not checked the suitability of the replacement and failed to make uncontested scrums mandatory for the remainder of the match. 'It is clear from the decision that a referee's duty extends even as far as overruling what, in effect, were consenting players' and quotes RFU guidance acknowledging that 'at times, referees may have to protect players from themselves' (Charlish, 2003: 3). The following comments, by Lord Philips, lie at the heart of this important judgment by the Court of Appeal:

> A rugby referee owed a duty of care towards his players. Rugby was a dangerous sport and the rules of the game were designed to minimize the dangers. Players were dependent for their safety on the rules being enforced, and enforcement of the rules fell to the referee. Rugby was no exception to the fact that the law rarely, if ever, absolves from a duty of care a person whose actions or omissions were capable of causing physical harm to others in a structured relationship into which they had entered.
> (*Per* Lord Philips MR, *Vowles v Evans* [2003] EWCA Civ 318;
> [2003] 1 WLR 1607 at para 25)

The decision to continue with contested scrums in those circumstances was not made in the heat of the moment, and in the opinion of the Court of Appeal there was 'time to give considered thought to it' (Williams, 2003: 50). Charlish (2003: 2) observes that 'the standard of ordinary negligence will apply as the referee's conduct did not take place in the heat of the moment. There was opportunity for reflection and thought.' An interesting, and rather puzzling point was made by Lord Philips in relation to situations where spectators, who are volunteers, might be called in to referee a rugby match should the referee fail to turn up. 'In such circumstances the volunteer cannot reasonably be expected to show the skill of one who holds himself out as a referee, or perhaps be fully conversant with the Laws of the Game' (*per* Lord Philips in *Vowles* CA, cited Elvin, 2003: 563). Elvin observes that this is:

> difficult to understand. If a spectator volunteers to be a referee, then surely he is holding himself out to be a referee. He should not volunteer to be a referee if he is not fully conversant with those laws of the game pertaining to safety, since the health and safety of the players depends on their due enforcement.
>
> (2003: 563)

Aside from the safety issues raised by Elvin (2003), it is not clear in making these observations in *Vowles* whether or not Lord Philips is rejecting or doubting *Nettleship*, which, as outlined in Chapter 2, held that a beginner/learner driver owed the same standard of care as an experienced and competent driver. BAALPE (2004) applied this principle confirming that learners, beginners, students or volunteers in school sport and physical education, owed the same standard of care as experienced and competent sports leaders or teachers.

On the issue of causation, the court considered Morland J's findings *critical* that the scrummages had started to go wrong as soon as Christopher Jones had taken up position in the front row (Watson, 2003: 1). The increasing tiredness of the forwards and the worsening condition of the pitch were factors also considered by the court. On the balance of probabilities the court accepted that 'Jones's lack of prop techniques was the material cause of the failure to engage it properly' (Williams, 2003: 50). This was a 'significant contributory cause of the unsatisfactory nature of the set scrummages' and of the 'mistimed engagement which was the cause of the claimant's accident' (ibid: 50).

> Any case of a serious rugby injury involves a detailed analysis of the rules in the calm of the courtroom, against the precise circumstances of the game and the exact sequence of events leading to injury. Thus those who run and regulate the game cannot avoid having some cause for anxiety.
>
> (ibid: 50)

The decision in *Vowles* was regarded as 'an extraordinarily paternalistic approach' (Charlish, 2003: 4). It was not expected to open any floodgates, but it 'will cause all our members to look again very closely at their regulations and insurance policies' (Nigel Hook, General Secretary of the Central Council for Physical Recreation (CCPR) quoted in *The Times* December 14, 2002, cited Charlish, 2003: 87). In relation to knowledge and application of rules or laws of the game Charlish (2003: 87) pointed out that:

> it may worry referees of rugby union however, that it is now clear that they must have a very detailed knowledge of all laws of the game, particularly laws relating to safety. It may well be that this will be a deterrent to referees in a sport where official laws of the game currently run to 176 pages.

James (2003: 167) acknowledges the possibility that referees may control the game in a more defensive manner, but 'if this is to prevent such injuries from occurring, then that could be said to be a positive step'. Following the Court of Appeal decision in *Vowles*, the Welsh Rugby Union Chair Glanmoor Griffiths stated: 'This has been a landmark case for sport in the UK, which may force the governing bodies of many sports to re-examine their rules and regulations and take a long hard look at training practices for players, coaches and officials' (Associated Press Worldstream, 12 March 2003: 2).

'*Vowles* significantly develops the law. A referee of a game of rugby football now owes a duty of care to players' (Elvin, 2003: 560). This is not the case. *Smoldon* in 1996 established that a referee owed a duty of care to Colts players. *Vowles* incrementally, on the facts, merely extends the context to adult amateur rugby football and does not significantly develop the law as, for example, *Donoghue* did in 1932. As Charlish (2003: 87) observes, '*Smoldon* has already established that a referee owed a duty of care to youth level players. It is hardly a great leap of legal principle to extend this duty to apply to amateur adult players'. Watson (2003: 1) more accurately suggests that 'this case is a good example of an incremental extension to the circumstances in which a duty of care is owed' and anticipates that 'in future cases claimants will seek to extend this precedent to other sports'.

Elvin (2003: 561) also sees referees of other contact sports owing a duty of care to participants as they also 'have chosen to enter a relationship with the players that is structured by the rules of the sport concerned'.

> Once again there has been much consternation that the end of the sport as we know it will be brought about by the decisions such as this. In reality, nothing could be further from the truth. Just as *Smoldon* did not signal the end of junior level sport, so *Vowles* will not bring amateur sport to an end.
>
> (James, 2003: 167)

EXERCISE 3.22

Does the *Vowles* case make new law in the same way as *Donoghue v Stevenson* [1932] AC 562, or does it just apply *Donoghue* and extend the facts to an amateur referee of adult rugby? Support your answer with properly referenced quotes.

EXERCISE 3.23

Summarise the relevant evidence with referenced materials, quoted directly or paraphrased, from the full text judgment (or relevant literature), on each of the following issues:

1   The substitution following the injury to the forward.
2   The effect of this substitution. Was this and its effects the material cause of the claimant's spinal injury?
3   Was it 'fair, just and reasonable' to impose a duty on a referee in these circumstances? Report the arguments for and against imposing such a duty.
4   Explain and precisely quote Law 3 (12) from the rule book itself, if possible. What did the referee do in relation to this Law? Why was this considered a breach of duty by the courts?
5   In your opinion, is there a potential conflict between Law 3 (12) and the rule which withdraws league points in the case of uncontested scrums being implemented?
6   Consider the responsibilities of the team captains, coaches and clubs. Were they defendants in this case?

7   Read Charlish, P. 2003 'Case Comment Richard Vowles-Rugby Case' JPIL 2, 85–92. What points does Charlish make in relation to contributory negligence and the *Vowles* case? What do you think of such points, reflecting back to the principles of contributory negligence and cases earlier in this chapter?

8   Go on LexisNexis Executive or Nexis and other press/media databases online. Locate at least two examples of responses or commentaries on the *Vowles* case. Clearly summarise, referencing appropriately. Critically comment on the implications of the *Vowles* case for refereeing, training and updating officials, insurance and rule-making.

9   Ask another student involved in rugby union as a player or coach about a. what they know about the *Vowles* case. b. if they are aware of it, what effect this case has had or might have on refereeing or substitution practices. (Responses should be anonymous.)

10 Find examples of commentaries or responses to *Vowles* on or in governing body websites or publications.

11 Identify and explain on what areas has *Vowles* encouraged you to reflect as a sports student or practitioner.

Summary

- *Volenti non fit injuria* is a complete defence against a claim of negligence. It means that no harm is done to a person who has assumed the risk.
- There are three requirements for *volenti*. It must be voluntary, fully informed and relate to the inherent risks of the game or sport.
- Learning about inherent risks is not just about defending a negligence case. It is important for all participants to appreciate their own responsibilities and actively play a part in reducing the risks to those inherent in the sport or game.
- Contributory negligence is a partial defence against negligence, where damages paid to a plaintiff or claimant may be reduced according to the degree to which the claimant negligently contributed to his or her own injury.
- Children as young as 11 have been found to be contributorily negligent.
- Under the Occupier's Liability Act 1957 an occupier can be held liable for loss or injury suffered by lawful visitors to the premises. This duty can be exercised to include failing to take steps to make sure that another visitor does not deliberately harm other visitors.
- Trespassers are afforded limited rights under the Occupier's Liability Act 1984 related to dangers arising from the state of the premises or things done or omitted to be done to them.
- There are contrasting views as to the existence of a special category of 'reckless disregard' for the safety of others in negligence applied to sport, or indeed if there should be such a category.
- The Smoldon case in 1996 was the first time a rugby referee had been found liable for negligence.
- The Vowles case in 2003 was the first time a rugby referee of an amateur adult game had been found liable for negligence.

4 Sports violence and criminal assault: a socio-legal perspective

Introduction

> If a person intentionally or recklessly caused harm to another person in order to prevent them from reaching the ball or for reason of sheer thuggery, then these actions are in breach of the criminal law. Clearly, the administrators of sport have failed to control this evil within their own sports. The concept that sporting supervisory bodies should usurp the power of the courts and the system of British justice cannot be supported by any cogent argument. Why should offenders who commit a crime within their game not be punished for their villainy? The law of the land never stops at the touchline.
>
> (Grayson and Bond, 1993: 693)

In June 2005 the Crown Prosecution Service (CPS) of England and Wales held a conference on 'Crime in Sport' focusing on a range of issues around criminal liability, but it was 'the regulation of on-field violence that raised the most media interest' (Gardiner, 2005: 998). The CPS reported that it was reviewing policy concerning when and where criminal prosecutions should be brought for on-field violence. 'The growing feeling among the public is that players are getting away with crime – that footballers in particular escape punishment by criminal justice – and that is wrong' (Nazir Afzal, Sector Director for the CPS in London, speaking at the conference, cited in Gardiner, 2005: 998). Concerned about an ad hoc approach of existing policy, which lacked clarity and provided little guidance for police, the CPS were reported as focusing on both off-the-ball punch-ups and violent on-the-ball incidents (ibid: 998).

Some lawyers argued at the conference that the criminal justice system 'does not have the resources to deal with sporting incidents' and it was 'time for the law to leave the field of play' leaving 'discipline on the field of play' to be dealt with by 'the sport's professional governing bodies, not the criminal justice system' (Steve Barker, defence lawyer, speaking at the conference[1]). Barker argues that there is no case for more involvement of the criminal law in sporting incidents: 'An FA disciplinary tribunal composed of persons who have engaged in the sport themselves for many years and who understand the pressures of the game is in a far better position to decide such issues than a magistrate or jury' (2006: 15).

The CPS view of 'a need for firmer action concerning violent and abusive behaviour on the sports field' was countered by the views of some criminal justice delegates that 'any increased involvement of the criminal law' in sports field activity would be 'highly problematic' in 'adversely affecting the dynamics of the sport and an inappropriate use of resources' (Gardiner, 2005: 1000). Gardiner (2005: 998, 1000) raised doubts about any assumed increase in sports-related violence and argued that there were two major concerns – the confusion around the law of assault and consent, in particular, and drawing the line on when should conduct be prosecuted.

Sports violence: a contested concept?

'What is sports "violence"? What is called violence and what is not is no trivial matter. The extent to which behaviour is perceived as violence has a great deal to do with what people are willing to do about it' (Smith, 1979, 2003: 215). 'Misnaming the disease can lead to the wrong medication or none at all' (ibid, 2003: 215). Critcher (1995: 30–31) suggests that many [violent] acts in sport can be deviant but only some are labelled as such. It is important that we have some conceptual understanding of violence in sport. Philosophers, lawyers, psychologists and players may approach this word game differently. The concept of 'sports violence' is 'elusive . . . everyone thinks they know what it is until challenged to define it, or faced with having to do something about it' (Young, 2004: 382). Parry (1998: 209) suggests that violence is 'centrally to do with intentional hurt of injury to others, as well as attempts to harm, recklessness to harm, and negligence'.

Parry (1998) makes an important distinction between 'violent acts' and 'acts of violence'. Violent acts describe 'actions performed with lots of vigour, energy, and fierceness', while acts of violence are 'distinguished by intentional behaviour that cause or result in harm, injury and suffering' and are 'not considered to be part of the game' (Rosenberg, 2003: 34). It seems that a violent act then could include aggression in a bodily contact sport which cannot be avoided, as long as the force is reasonable.

Violence is seen as morally wrong in most social circumstances, in contrast to violence from assertion or aggression, that are, for the most part, morally acceptable practices in sport (Parry 1998; Rosenberg 2003: 31).

> Violence in sport is a physical assault or other physically harmful actions by a player that takes place in a sports context and that is intended to cause physical pain or injury to another player (or fan, coach, game official etc.) where such harmful actions bear no direct relationship to the rules and associated competitive goals of the sport.
>
> (Canadian Centre for Ethics in Sport 1999: 1)

Smith's socio-legal work in 1983 included a typology of violence, ranging from legitimised to illegitimate violence. Brutal bodily contact within the rules of sport is a legitimate form of violence which includes body checks and collisions in [ice] hockey, tackling in rugby, punching in boxing – all of which are viewed as consensual in an implied way and an inherent part of the sport (Young, 2004: 390–391). Borderline violence involves acts prohibited by the official rules of a given sport but which occur routinely and are more or less accepted by most people concerned. For example, a bouncer in cricket, a wandering elbow in basketball, a fist-fight in ice hockey (Young, 2004: 390). Borderline violence is essentially seen as the province of referees, umpires, game officials and sports governing body officials and the law rarely becoming involved (Smith, 2003, in Boxhill, 2003: 207).

Quasi-criminal violence is that which 'violates not only the formal rules of a given sport (and the law of the land), but, to a significant degree, the informal norms of player conduct' which draws attention of high-level sports governing body officials, generates public outrage and puts pressure on legal authorities to become involved (ibid: 208). In contrast criminal violence is not seen as legitimate and is regarded as 'so seriously and obviously outside the rules of the game that it is handled as criminal from the outset by the law' (Smith, 1979, 2003: 213).

Sports psychologists tend to use the terms assertion, aggression and violence and interchange aggression with violence. Aggression can be seen as 'unprovoked hostility or attacks on another person which is not sanctioned by society' (Kerr, 1997: 115–116). However, in a sports context aggression in team contact sports is intrinsic and sanctioned, provided the play remains permissible within the boundaries of certain rules, which act as a kind of contract in the pursuit of aggression and violence between consenting adults (Kerr, 1997: 115–116). Kerr (2005) then distinguishes between 'sanctioned' and 'unsanctioned' aggression and violence. Bakker et al. argues that 'sanctioned' aggression and violence includes both the written rules or laws of sport and any unwritten rules or player norms, whereas 'unsanctioned' aggression and violence is 'any act outside the written and unwritten rules or laws and player norms' (1990, cited Kerr, 2005:115–116). Smith (1983: 3) locates physical violence at the 'end point on a continuum of aggressive behaviour, it is the most extreme form of aggression'.

EXERCISE 4.1

Summarise and critically comment on the conceptions of violence put forward by Parry (1998), Young (2004), Canadian Centre for Ethics in Sport (1999), Kerr (1997, 2005) and Smith (1978, 2003). Propose your own conception of violence which could be applied to contact sports, giving reasons for your choice.

EXERCISE 4.2

Categorise the following examples of sport conduct as a 'violent act' or 'act of violence' (Parry, 1998). Give reasons for your answers:

In rugby union:

1 a hard tackle within the rules
2 punching off-the-ball
3 ear-biting

In ice hockey:

1 body checking
2 fist-fighting
3 stick-fighting.

EXERCISE 4.3

Supported by relevant reading and/or case law discuss the following statements:

A. 'Violent acts on the sports field = sanctioned aggression = brutal bodily contact = reasonable force = regarded as inherent risks and a normal part of the sport/game = within the rules = legitimate/lawful.'
B. 'Acts of violence on the sports field = unsanctioned aggression = unreasonable force = unacceptable or extraneous risks outside the normal game = outside the rules = illegitimate/unlawful.'

EXERCISE 4.4

Select one sport. Explain the meaning of the following terms and identify one example of each of the following from your chosen sport:

1 sportsmanship
2 gamesmanship
3 assertion
4 intimidation
5 aggression
6 violence.

What is a crime?

Can legal cases and judicial and legal academic commentaries help us to address the question, 'when should violence in sport be regarded as "criminal" conduct, and lead to criminal assault charges?' Who should deal with violence on the sports field – sports governing bodies, civil claims for compensation for negligence, the criminal law, or all of these processes? There are three stages to proving criminal liability:

1 The mental element or *mens rea*. This is the state of mind of the accused, such as intention or recklessness, as required by the relevant offence. Recklessness is the conscious taking of an unreasonable or an unjustifiable risk (see Gardiner, 1994: 1; Leake and Omerod, 2005: 3).
2 The *actus reus* or the causing of the resulting harm. Criminal liability for Offences Against the Person is a very individual matter. For example, it must be proved, beyond reasonable doubt, that the accused or defendant did, for example, punch or kick the victim and that this is what caused the resulting harm specified in the offence.
3 The absence of a lawful justification, excuse, mitigation or defence. For example, consent, self-defence, reasonable chastisement, or consensual horseplay, can all be used in response to Offences Against the Person, such as s.47, s.20 or GBH with intent, (s.18) in relation to conduct on the sports field.

When should sports violence lead to criminal charges for assault?

Basically a player may be charged with a criminal offence for sports violence if he/she shows intentional or reckless conduct, causing serious bodily harm (or harm defined by the offence), beyond the inherent risks of injury. As a matter of law, a person could not consent to having bodily harm inflicted upon him/her and any exceptions to this would be based on public policy (*R v Brown* [1994] AC 212). One of the exceptions to that general rule was physical injury in the course of contact sports. However, if what occurred 'went beyond what a player could reasonably be regarded as having accepted by taking part in the sport, that indicated that the conduct would not be covered by the defence' (*Times Law Report, R v (Mark) Barnes*, Monday 10 January 2005[2]).

Players are deemed to consent to force of a kind which could reasonably be expected to happen during a game. Some cases will cross the line and a decisive distinction may be that between force in and outside the course of play. Punching a player and breaking his jaw during a rugby match was regarded by the judge in *R v Billingshurst* [1978] Crim LR 553 in Newport Crown Court as crossing the line, and beyond the boundaries of consent. Kicking an innocent victim in the head with great force, when he was lying on the ground, in an off-the-ball incident, was regarded by the criminal courts as 'vicious and barbaric' and 'had nothing to do with the rugby football or play in progress' (*R v Lloyd* (1989) 11 Cr App R (S) 36).

> Consent to bodily contact and to violence is inferred from participation in play subject to the rules and working cultures within the game. Penalties exist within the rules of the game to penalise infringement. Players expect that in the heat of the action some contact will take place in on-the-ball incidents, which is dangerous and will therefore occasionally cause injury, even severe injury. There is invariably no intent or reckless-ness towards the resultant injury. This conduct may well call for a penalty, but not criminal charges, for it is such an integral part of the game that a player cannot expect to avoid it and therefore must be deemed to have given his consent
>
> (Gardiner, 1994: 2)

Gardiner (1994: 2) contrasts these on-the-ball incidents with those involving retaliation, intended to do bodily harm and are off-the-ball. The majority of criminal convictions secured in relation to charges brought under the Offences Against the Person Act 1861, in England and Wales from 1978 to 2004, were in amateur rugby union and soccer. Nearly all of those cases involved clear off-the-ball incidents of punching or kicking away from the course of play (see Gardiner, 2005; James, 2006a).

> The consent by players in sports to the use of moderate force is clearly valid, and the players are even deemed to consent to an application of force, that is in breach of the rules of the game, if it is the sort of thing that may be expected to happen during a game.
>
> (Williams, 1962: 80)

It has been argued that rule-breaking conduct which leads to bodily injury can still be lawful as what is commonly expected in the normal course of the game is located in and indicated by the 'playing cultures' or 'norms' of players (Gardiner, 1993, 1994, 2005, 2007; James, 2003, 2006a). They suggested that perhaps it should be the 'working cultures' of the sports governing body which provides a guide to the boundary of consent and not only what the players are prepared to accept.[3] Two key Canadian ice hockey cases, *R v Cey* (1989) 48 CCC (3d) 480 and *R v Cicarrelli* (1989[4]) developed objective tests for the boundary of consent in sports and influenced later cases in Anglo-Welsh law such as *R v Brown*, and the Law Commission's Consultation Paper no. 134 in 1994–1995.

In *R v Cey*[5] the defendant, Cey, cross-checked the victim from behind to the boards, causing facial injuries, whiplash and concussion. The victim was facing the boards and trying to retrieve the puck. The defendant skated towards him at speed and used his stick to push the victim's head into the boards. Contact with the victim's head was said to be intentional. A defence of consent was argued. It was determined by the court that the consent of the victim should be implied and that the boundaries or scope of that consent could be determined using a set of objective criteria. These were:

- The conditions under which the game was played.
- The nature of the act which forms the subject matter of the charge.
- The extent of force employed.
- The degree of risk and probability of serious harm occurring.

(James, 2006a: 609–610, Centre for Sport and Law, 2002)

The reasoning in *Cey* was applied in *R v Leclerc* (1991) 67 CCC (3d) 563 (CA).[6] The court concluded that a hockey player consents 'to some bodily contact necessarily incidental to the game, but not overtly violent acts' and a deliberate purpose to inflict injury will be generally held to be outside the scope of implied consent in the sports arena. In using *Cey*, the cross-checking of pushing of a victim across the neck in close proximity to the boards was so inherently dangerous as to be excluded from implied consent. In the case of *R v Cicarrelli* [1989][7] the standards established in both *Cey* were applied and framed the issue of consent. Striking a player on the head three times with a stick, in an act of retaliation, after the whistle had halted play according to the rules of the game, was considered to be so potentially dangerous as to be outside the normal playing culture and professional culture of professional ice hockey and beyond the boundaries of consent (see Centre for Sport Law, 2002; James, 2006a: 610).

The set of objective criteria developed in *Cey* was extended to include the nature of the game played, the nature of the particular acts and their surrounding circumstances, the degree of force employed, the degree of risk of injury and the state of mind of the accused. 'Participants do not have a free licence to commit assault in the name of sport, only to commit those acts which are within the rules, or the objectively determined implied consent' (James, 2006a: 610–611). In all three cases, *Cey*, *Leclerc* and *Cicarrelli*, the courts recognised that 'even where a particular level of violence is expected and indeed may have been consented to, it may be so inherently dangerous as to preclude consent' (Centre for Sport Law, 2002: 2).

The rules of sport (particularly the safety rules) are a crucial guide to criminal liability but not the sole criterion (Williams, 1962; Gardiner, 1994, 2005; James, 2003, 2006a).

> In the absence of proof of intent or recklessness to injure, participants who cause injury to others within a reasonable application of the rules of a sport can rely on the victim's consent to potential harm. An injury caused due to an illegal tackle that amounts to a foul within the rules of a sport is also likely to be seen as consensual. It may be contrary to the rules of the game, but may well be inside the 'code of conduct' or 'working culture' of the sport. Consent is not limited solely by the formal rules in contact sports.
> (Gardiner, 1994: 2)

If it is an 'illegal tackle', how can it be a foul 'within the rules' of the game? Is it really appropriate that an 'open' or 'professional' foul, although, outside the technical, formal rules of the game, would normally be dealt with by the regulative or prohibitive rules which are designed to deal with foul play (Fraleigh, 1984)? Surely any foul play per se should not be assumed to be consensual in a criminal sense, simply because there is a remedy available to officials or sports governing bodies, such as sending off, suspension, banning, fines etc? Considerable reliance and trust is placed on internal regulatory mechanisms of sports governing bodies.

> In determining the approach of the courts the starting point [in *R v Barnes* [2004] EWCA Crim 3246; [2005] 1 WLR 910] was that most organised sports had their own disciplinary procedures for enforcing their particular rules and standards of conduct. As a result, in the majority of situations there was not only no need for criminal proceedings, it was undesirable that there should be any criminal proceedings.
> (*R v Barnes*, The Times, January 10 2005)

'Criminal law is a last resort and one that should consistently defer to robust internal disciplinary sporting punishments' (Gardiner, 2005: 1000). The Crown Prosecution Service supports the view that referees, administrators and players have the initial and major responsibilities to avoid and deal with excessive violence or serious disorderly conduct on the part of players, coaches and managers. During a consultation process on prosecution policy for sports violence, among other things, the CPS concluded that governing bodies 'take these responsibilities seriously and any prosecutorial guidance does not wish to interfere with or diminish the authority of sports governing bodies' (Crown Prosecution Service and ACPO, Draft Guide to Prosecutors and Police Officers-Crime in Sport, 2005: 1). However, 'even if those involved seek to discharge their responsibilities seriously those participating in sporting activities cannot be regarded as exempt from compliance with the criminal law' (ibid, 2005: 1).

In deciding whether or not a criminal offence has been committed on the sports field, the CPS must apply the criminal law, as laid down by statute and decided case law. In addition, in deciding to prosecute the CPS must use the usual tests set out in the Code for Crown Prosecutors, namely, when there is sufficient evidence to provide a realistic prospect of a conviction and when it is in the public interest to prosecute. The relevant statutes which will be included in the next section of this chapter are the Public Order Act 1986, the Criminal Justice Act 1988, and illustrative case law involving s.47, s.20 and s.18 of the Offences Against the Person Act 1861.

EXERCISE 4.5

Explain the three stages in proving criminal liability.

EXERCISE 4.6

As a matter of law a person cannot consent to the infliction of bodily harm. What is the lawful exception to this rule in relation to contact sports?

EXERCISE 4.7

Using relevant academic commentary and case law, put together a guide to the boundaries of consent for sports players using the following themes:

1 Within and beyond the course of play or a normal game.
2 'On the ball' or 'off the ball'.
3 Technical rules of the game or sport.
4 Moderate or reasonable force.
5 Commonly accepted by the playing culture or subcultural norms of that sport.
6 The objective test developed in *Cey* and *Cicarrelli*.

EXERCISE 4.8

Should an open, professional foul, even if it leads to serious injury, be dealt with by the internal disciplinary mechanisms of a sports governing body, rather than the criminal law in relation to assault, or both? Support your argument with relevant literature and case law, including Gardiner 1994, 2005, James 2003, 2006a, and *R v (Mark) Barnes* [2004] EWCA Crim 3246; [2005] 1 WLR 910.

Public order offences and common assault

In 1996 the Manchester United Player Eric Cantona was initially jailed for 14 days for assault, a sentence which was later amended, on appeal, to 120 hours of community service, following his conviction for common assault, a common law offence brought under s.39 of the Criminal Justice Act 1988.

> Assault is an act that causes the victim to apprehend the immediate infliction of unlawful personal force, that is [the fear] or threat of violence. Battery is the actual infliction of unlawful force to the body of another, that is, the use of violence. Common assault is charged where there is little or no harm to the victim.
>
> (James, 2006a: 598)

During a soccer match Eric Cantona 'jumped over the advertising hoardings and attacked a spectator in the crowd who had verbally and racially abused him' (Gardiner, 2005: 999). Cantona performed a 'kung-fu'-style kick into the chest of a Crystal Palace supporter at Selhurst Park on 25 January 1995. The spectator was standing 11 rows back from the advertising hoardings. Jeffrey McCann, for the prosecution, told the court that it is alleged that the fan, Matthew Simmons ran to the front of the hoarding and was using foul language directed towards Cantona, as well as gesticulating and shouting highly offensive phrases, heard by other spectators in the crowd (Duce, 1996: 1). Television pictures of the incident, witnessed by millions, were played several times to the court. Cantona was banned by France and Manchester United for the rest of the season. A Football Association Disciplinary Tribunal also suspended him from playing football until 30 September 1995 and fined him £10,000 (Duce, 1996: 1).

On 8 June 2005 Lee Bowyer was summoned to appear in court for a s.4 offence of the Public Order Act 1986. He had been involved in a highly publicised incident, where he was fighting with his own team mate at Newcastle United, Kieron Dyer, during Newcastle United's match against Aston Villa on 2 April 2005. Bowyer had received a four-match ban, as it was his second red card, whilst Dyer had a three-match ban. Bowyer's legal representative pointed out at the times of the summons that his client had already been fined by Newcastle United and the Football Association and suspended for several matches and noted that if it had happened in the street 'I don't think any policeman would prosecute'.[8]

Bowyer received a six-week fine by his club, 'believed to be around £20,000 and a final warning. No court in the country would impose a fine of this level for an incident that lasted seven seconds and in which there were no injuries, no weapon, no pre-meditation, no criminal intention, and no vulnerable victim' (Defence lawyer, speaking at the Crown Prosecution Service, *Crime in Sport* Conference, 6 March 2005).[9] Gardiner (2005: 999) regards the Bowyer–Dyer incident, although 'legally a common assault, as little more than a scuffle, or using the vernacular, "handbags" with none or only minor resulting harm'. Although it is true that the degree of physical harm caused in such incidents is minimal, the public order concerns remain central in any public policy lens taken by prosecutors. Just because a public order incident did not actually follow, does not mean that there was a real risk or a genuine concern. In addition, it is interesting to note the common practice here of 'normalising' fighting as just 'a minor scuffle' and labelling it as 'handbagging', implying they were fighting like a woman, an example of a misogynistic lens, located centrally in the locker room culture of masculine athletic identity as outlined by Messner (1990, 2002) and Welch (1997).

'A breach of the peace occurs when there is a threat to a person or his property' where a defendant can be bound over to keep the peace, with a promise of good future behaviour, which, if broken, can result in the loss of the surety paid or imprisonment or both (James, 2006a: 597).[10] When three professional footballers were involved in a goalmouth fight, in front of a crowd at a Glasgow Rangers FC v Glasgow Celtic FC Scottish Premier Division match, one of the players was convicted and 'bound over' one was found not guilty and the third case was 'not proven'. It was held that 'because of the history of sectarian violence between rival fans . . . the players' behaviour was likely to cause a serious breach of the peace in the form of crowd disturbance' (James, 2006a: 598).[11]

EXERCISE 4.9

Explain what is meant by the offence of 'common assault'.

EXERCISE 4.10

Illustrate your understanding of the term common assault and the Crown Prosecutor's Code in the decision to bring charges in *R v Cantona* (unreported, 1995, Court of Appeal), following the infamous 'kung–fu' kick of a football spectator at Selhurst Park in 1995.

EXERCISE 4.11

Conduct a search of the relevant archives including LexisNexis Executive or Nexis for reporting and commentary of the fighting incident between Lee Bowyer and Kieron Dyer, in April 2005, including the CPS Crime in Sport Conference 2005 and Gardiner 2005. Gardiner (2005: 999) regarded the Bowyer–Dyer incident 'although legally common assault, as little more than a scuffle, or to use the vernacular "handbags"'. It resulted in little or no physical injury. Using these and other relevant sources, such as Barker (2006), critically address the question 'should this incident have led to the application of the criminal law, in addition to the disciplinary action taken by the football club and the Football Association against Lee Bowyer and Kieron Dyer?'

Offences against the person act 1861

Section 47 Assault occasioning actual bodily harm

Section 47 of the OAPA 1861 makes it an offence to 'commit an assault occasioning actual bodily harm' and is punishable by a maximum of five years imprisonment (Dobson, 2005: 78).The *mens rea* for s.47 is intention or recklessness as to whether force will be applied to or contact made with another person. The *actus reus* only requires that actual bodily harm be done to the victim and it 'need not be permanent but must be more than merely transient and trifling' (*R v Donovan* [1934] KB 498). Section 47 offences can 'cover a wide range of injuries from serious bruising to minor fractures' (James, 2006a: 599) and can also include psychiatric injury, though not mere emotions such as fear, distress or panic.[12] There is 'no need to prove that the defendant foresaw any bodily harm'[13] (Dobson 2005: 78). This requirement for the harm to be 'occasioned but not intended or foreseen can make it relatively easy for [sports] participants to commit this offence', although players are reluctant to report incidents under s.47 as the injuries are relatively minor and are often little more than players expect as an integral part of playing contact sports (James, 2006a: 599).

On 14 June 2006, Justice Beatrice Bolton threw out an assault case against a rugby player, ordering the jury to clear the defendant, Andrew Evans, of the charges of assault causing actual bodily harm and common assault, at Newcastle Crown Court. 'I am flabbergasted that the CPS wished to continue with this. That bruise was the sort that happens within the rough-and-tumble of rugby and is neither here nor there.' Justice Bolton told the court (Jenkins, 2006: 8). The prosecution case was that Evans deliberately stamped on the victim's head during a ruck, just as Ryton scored a try. Evans was originally charged with causing grievous bodily harm following a deep wound to the victim's eye. However, a videotape of the incident, from a rugby union match in December 2004, between Billingham and Ryton, showed that the injury was caused by one of Mr McKie's own teammates (*The Daily Mail* 15 June 2006: 24). It appeared that the stamping by the defendant had only led to a bruise on the forehead.

In *R v Lincoln* (1990) 12 Cr App R (S) 250 the Crown Court in Lewes heard that Mr Lincoln was sentenced to four months imprisonment for a s.47 offence 'assault occasioning actual bodily harm'. Five minutes into a football game between two amateur sides in the district league, the defendant took a throw-in and the victim took up a position immediately in front of him. This restricted his freedom to throw-in. After taking the throw-in, both players then made their way up the field, probably towards the ball. When Mr Lincoln drew alongside the victim he said to him 'Nobody does that to me', or words to that effect, and punched the victim, breaking his jaw in two places. The incident was witnessed by the manager and the linesman, although it was never brought to the attention of the referee or the football authorities, who supervised the league.

Five days after the match, when the victim realised the gravity of the injury, he reported the injury to the police. Following his conviction for assault occasioning actual bodily harm, Mr Lincoln argued in the Court of Appeal that the sentence was excessive having citing 'the cumulative effect of various mitigating factors'.[14] It was argued that only one blow was struck in the heat of the moment, the extent of damage may have given a false impression of the force of the blow and the witnesses did not regard it as serious enough to report.[15] In *R v Davies* [1991] Crim LR 70[16] towards the end of a soccer game in the Nottingham Sunday Combination League, tempers apparently became heated and there was a collision between Mr Walker and another player, resulting in the award of a free kick, which Mr Walker did not take. He ran across to take up his position while another player took the free kick. When he had taken up his position, Mr Davies 'quite deliberately aimed a blow with his fist at Mr Walker's face. Mr Walker fell to the ground. No action was taken by the referee and the game continued to its conclusion'.[17]

Even though the victim suffered blurred vision and pain he completed the match. However, he was diagnosed with a fractured cheekbone, which required an operation and two weeks off work. The Court of Appeal noted that the trial judge, Tudor Evans J, concluded that the blow 'had nothing to do with the game of football. It was when they were both away from the ball. It was a deliberate punch aimed at Mr Walker's face'.[18] Mr Davies had pleaded not guilty to a s.18 offence, grievous bodily harm with intent, but later pleaded guilty to the s.47 offence of assault occasioning actual bodily harm. The Court of Appeal did not wish to intervene in the sentence of six months imprisonment, and regarded this as 'an offence of the utmost seriousness', where the two players were 'not in any sense involved in playing football'.[19]

Section 20 Unlawful and malicious wounding of inflicting grievous bodily harm

A player who unlawfully inflicts and maliciously wounds or inflicts any grievous bodily harm on another person, with or without any weapon or instrument, shall be guilty of an offence contrary to s.20. The *actus reus* for s.20 is therefore wounding or inflicting grievous bodily harm, the 'degree of harm being much more serious than for s.47' (James, 2006a: 600). A wound involves 'a complete break in the skin. A graze would be insufficient unless the skin is broken. Similarly a broken collar-bone is not a wound unless the skin is broken. It could, however, amount to grievous bodily harm' (Dobson, 2005: 79). The *mens rea* for s.20 requires 'intention or recklessness as to whether contact is made with another person' and at the time of the act, the player must 'foresee some bodily harm but not necessarily grievous or serious bodily harm' (James, 2006a: 600). Nearly all the charges brought under s.20 (and s.47) are related to off-the-ball incidents such as punching and kicking and almost all are in soccer or rugby union matches at an amateur level (James, 2006a: 600; Gardiner 2005). Recklessness by a player, during a challenge on-the-ball, beyond the rules, without the establishment of consent or self-defence, could lead to a criminal charge under s.20 against that player (see James, 2006a: 600).

Mark Moss was convicted of assault inflicting grievous bodily harm, contrary to s.20 of the OAPA 1861, and was sentenced to eight months in prison. It was the prosecution's case that following a 'ruck' the victim was the last person to stand up and as he did so Mark Moss punched him in the face, resulting in a fractured eye socket, which required a titanium mesh to build it up again. The jury at trial concluded that Mark Moss had punched the victim in the face and he failed to get the prison sentence reduced on appeal. Comments made by the Court of Appeal included the acknowledgement that 'although rugby was a contact sport, it was not a licence for 'thuggery'. Moss was guilty of committing an 'off-the-ball offence so serious that a custodial sentence could be justified'.[20]

Jason Tasker was convicted of unlawful wounding under s.20 and won his appeal to have his sentence of 12 months imprisonment reduced to six months. Mr Tasker was playing soccer in the local Sunday League in County Durham on 1 April 2001. In the second half his team thought that the goal scored by the opposing team should have been disallowed.

Following this, things deteriorated, and Mr Tasker was cautioned once and spoken to later by the referee before a foul led to a flare-up between players during which the victim was pulled to the ground. Before he could get up again Mr Tasker 'came across the field and kicked him in the face, resulting in serious injuries' and surgery on a fractured eye socket and possible fracture of the cheekbone. There were several grounds of appeal, including his previous good character, his plea of guilty and the circumstances 'a single kick to the face of an opponent in a football match'.

> In our view each case has to be looked at on its own facts. Here the appellant had earlier been cautioned. He was not involved in the incident which caused the victim to fall over. He deliberately went across and kicked him on the face. He did so when the victim was lying on the ground. There was no provocation at the time when he did so. As a result very serious injuries were caused.
>
> (*R v Tasker* [2001] EWCA Crim 2213; [2002] 1 Cr App R (S) 120, Westlaw UK, 2004: 2)

In the unusual case of *R v Ahmed* [2002] EWCA Crim 779,[21] an amateur soccer player was found not guilty of the more serious charge of causing grievous bodily harm with intent but convicted of unlawfully inflicting grievous bodily harm for attacking the opposing goalkeeper twice. He was also found guilty of common assault of the referee at the same match. Mr Ahmed was initially involved in a scuffle with the opposing goalkeeper where he punched him, breaking his nose and causing it to bleed. The referee sent Mr Ahmed off the pitch by holding up a red card. At the moment the referee held up the red card, Mr Ahmed punched the referee in the face. Then as he was leaving the pitch, he passed by the area behind the goal where the goalkeeper was receiving treatment, moved quickly towards him and kicked him with force in the face. This resulted in serious injuries to the goalkeeper, who spent three nights in hospital, received treatment and surgery under a general anaesthetic, for a broken jaw, broken eye socket and broken nose. His jaws were wired together and three metal plates and 13 screws were inserted to hold his face together.

In relation to consent and previous case authorities making some allowances for misconduct on a football or rugby pitch, the EWCA noted the following:

> We must note on the present facts, so far as the referee is concerned, he of course does not consent to any physical contact, and in this particular case he was particularly defenceless, having one arm raised in the air with a red card in it. So far as the goalkeeper is concerned, the more violent of the two blows was inflicted when he was off the field of play, lying on the ground completely defenceless behind the goal. Accordingly, if some lesser tariff applicable to those who are actually engaged in sport, it would not on the present facts avail this appellant.[22]

The EWCA did not consider the 30-month sentence for the s.20 offence or the four-month sentence for the common assault on the referee, to be 'a day too long' and in dismissing the appeal for a reduction in sentence concluded that he was 'a manifest danger on the football pitch and the Football Association's approach to the matter is to be commended'.[23]

EXERCISE 4.12

Explain the offence of occasioning actual bodily harm, contrary to s.47 of the Offences Against the Person Act 1861.

EXERCISE 4.13

With referenced support from the full case report of either *R v Lincoln* (1990) 12 Cr App R (S) 250 or *R v Davies* [1991] Crim LR 70, argue the case for the prosecution, making reference to the *mens rea*, *actus reus*, and guidance on the boundary of consent covered so far in this chapter.

EXERCISE 4.14

Why are there so few charges brought under s.47 in relation to conduct on the sports field, particularly in contact sports?

EXERCISE 4.15

What are the elements of a s.20 offence?

EXERCISE 4.16

In which circumstances and sports are most of the s.20 offences located?

EXERCISE 4.17

In the case of *R v Tasker* [2001] EWCA Crim 2213; [2002] 1 Cr App R (S) 120, explain the conviction for a s.20 offence and the dismissal of the appeal, with reference to *mens rea*, *actus reus* and the boundaries of consent being related to 'playing the game'.

EXERCISE 4.18

Explain why the defendant in *R v Ahmed* [2002] EWCA Crim 779 was convicted of a s.20 offence *and* common assault, with detailed reference to the elements of the offence.

EXERCISE 4.19

Divide into groups of five. Each person should take one of the following s.20 cases, using the full text report from Westlaw UK or Lawtel. Summarise and critically comment on the case for the prosecution and the defence in relation to the elements of the offence and any discussion around what is 'part of the game' and what is 'off-the-ball' conduct:

1   *R v Chapman* (1989) 11 Cr App R (S) 93
2   *R v Shervill* (1989) 11 Cr App R (S) 284
3   *R v Goodwin* (1995) 16 Cr App R (S) 885 (CA)
4   *R v McHugh* (unreported, 1998)
5   *R v Moss* [2000] 1 Cr App R (S) 64

EXERCISE 4.20

What does recklessness mean? Make up a hypothetical incident from rugby, soccer or ice hockey, where an 'on-the-ball' incident, leading to bodily harm under s.20, which is arguably reckless, and could lead to a criminal assault charge contrary to s.20. Present an argument for the prosecution and the defence, relating to this hypothetical sports incident. What would Gardiner, 1994, 2005 and James, 2003, 2006a have to say about such 'on-the-ball' incidents and any resulting criminal charges?

EXERCISE 4.21

In groups of three, one person takes notes, one person tells their story and one person checks the details against the elements of a s.20 offence. As a player or observer, can you recall any incidents, particularly in soccer, rugby union or league, leading to injury which, in your opinion, might or should have led to charges under section 20 of the OAPA 1861? How often have you witnessed such incidents? Most charges are brought for off-the-ball incidents in rugby or soccer. There are relatively few criminal charges brought in sport contexts. Discuss reasons for this.

Section 18 Unlawful and Malicious Wounding or Causing of Grievous Bodily Harm with Intent

In contrast to s.47 and s.20 offences, only intention can satisfy the *mens rea* requirement of an s.18 offence. 'One of the following forms of intention must be proved: an intent to cause GBH or an intent to resist or prevent a (lawful) arrest or detention' (Dobson, 2005: 82).The maximum sentence for this offence is life imprisonment.

> Cases involving s.18 will be unusual in sport. Even where players intend to criminally assault each other, such as during a fight, it will be a rare case indeed where they intend to cause each other the very high degree of injury necessary for this offence. It is even less likely that the requisite intent for s.18 would be present for an on-the-ball challenge, and even where it is the police will usually consider that it is not in the public interest to proceed.
>
> (James, 2006a: 600–601)

The *actus reus* of a s.18 offence is the same as s.20, that is, a 'wound' or causing of 'grievous bodily harm'. In November 1985 in a rugby match between South Wales Police team and Newport Police team, Keith Jones tackled Richard Johnson, trying to free the ball from his grasp. As they were on their feet, side by side, the court heard that:

> the defendant, Richard Johnson, turned his head towards Keith Jones and bit the lower lobe of Jones's right ear. He then moved his head to the right and then sharply to the left, tearing away a portion of Jones's right ear lobe. Jones admitted at that stage having punched out at Richard Johnson, hitting him in the face . . .

> The two men fell to the ground. A struggle took place, which was broken up by other players and the referee. Jones at this stage cried out 'that bastard's bit my ear'. Johnson remained on the ground with his face covered, saying in his turn that Jones had gouged him in the eye, a matter which he reported later to the police. When the referee spoke to Johnson about the incident immediately afterwards, he said he could not have done it, because he was wearing a gum shield.[24]

The six month prison sentence was upheld by the Court of Appeal. In their judgment they made the following comments.

> The circumstances of the present case were that it was done in the course of the game, and it is perfectly true . . . the adrenaline was pumping and that people do things on the spur of the moment which they might not otherwise do. But unlawful violence of this sort on the football field needs discouraging as much as unlawful violence on the terraces or indeed anywhere else.[25]

In 1992 Gary Blisset was acquitted of an s.18 offence, following an incident in a soccer match where, during an aerial challenge, his elbow made contact with the victim, who sustained career-ending injuries of a fractured cheekbone and eye socket. 'The most controversial comment in the trial was by a witness for the defence, the FA chief executive, Graham Kelly. He described the defendant's conduct as an "ordinary aerial challenge" which he would see 200 times a week if he attended four matches' (Gardiner, 2005: 999). Edward Grayson believed that the evidence of Graham Kelly should have been excluded, as he was not providing an opinion in his own area of expertise, which is football administration (Conn, 1993). Such expert evidence as that put forward by Graham Kelly 'seems to suggest that if a certain type of act is committed regularly enough, it will become legitimized and as such immune from both internal disciplinary and criminal matters' (James, 2006a: 601).

Rugby Union player Simon Devereux was convicted of Grievous Bodily Harm with Intent contrary to s.18 of the OAPA 1861. The prosecution's case was that after the referee had blown the whistle, at the end of a ruck, Simon Devereux 'came up to the Rosslyn Park Captain, James Cowie, from behind and punched him. There was no excuse for this off-the-ball incident' (Mr J Baker, 2001: 100). He told the court that 'when he fell to the ground he saw the Gloucester No. 6 [Devereux] follow through' and later it was 'put to him that after the rucking incident, he was punching out at the Gloucester players. This was denied and became the central issue in the case' (ibid: 100).

> At the ruck there was a bit of a fracas with pushing and shoving on both sides. It happened in rugby quite often. Then he saw the Gloucester No 6 come in from the side and hit Cowie on the jaw. His impression was that Cowie, as captain, was stepping in to calm things down. He saw the punch and heard a crack.
>
> (Evidence given by a linesman who was a witness for the prosecution, Baker, J 2001: 100)

The perception of this witness was that 'everything had died down before No 6 stepped forward and Cowie had no chance to defend himself' (ibid: 100). 'There was no question that violence was offered by the defendant which caused the injuries but it was not unlawful. So-called self-defence extends to the defence of others' (opening speech to the jury by the defence counsel, reported by Baker, J 2001: 101). Witnesses for the defence reported to the court that there was 'a general fracas with 5–6 players involved throwing punches. The referee blew for a penalty to Gloucester. Then he saw an injured player emerge from a group of people'. The jury returned a guilty verdict on the more serious s.18 offence, which was unanimous.

Mr J Baker (2001: 102) was 'rather unprepared for the strident, and if I may say so, some-times uninformed outburst of criticism' which followed his decision to sentence Simon Devereux to nine months in prison. He pointed out that offences under s.18 are 'often met with lengthy terms of imprisonment because of the element of intent' with community sentences seldom being passed (Baker J 2001: 102). 'Devereux's place was in the scrum and not in gaol', 'Outrage as Devereux goes to jail' and 'A travesty of justice' were some media responses to the prison sentence, cited by Baker J (2001: 102) but letters were also written in support of the judgment and sentence such as 'a punch in the game of rugby is no different to one thrown outside the Rose & Crown on a Saturday night' (George Crawford, referee, cited in Baker J 2001: 102).

EXERCISE 4.22

Explain the *mens rea* and *actus reus* of an s.18 offence.

EXERCISE 4.23

Drawing on full text reports and relevant literature or academic commentaries, justify the outcome of and critically compare the following s.18 sport cases in relation to the three elements of the crime:

1   *R v Johnson* (1986) 8 Cr App R (S) 343
2   *R v Blisset* (1992) The Independent, 4 December
3   *R v Devereux* (unreported, February 1996, Kingston Crown Court, Judge Baker)

Why was the *Blisset* case so controversial? What issues does it raise about expert witnesses verifying a defendant's conduct merely by common practice?

Was the sentence passed in *Devereux* justified? Give reasons for your answer.

EXERCISE 4.24

The following quote is from the serialisation of Roy Keane's autobiography in *The Times* 12 August 2002, cited James (2002: 73). Keane was commenting on an incident involving Alfie Haaland, where the latter received a significant knee injury.

I'd waited almost 180 minutes for Alfie, three years if you looked at it another way. Now he had the ball on the far touchline. Alfie was taking the piss. I'd waited long enough. I fucking hit him hard. The ball was there (I think). Take that you cunt. And don't you ever stand over me again sneering about fake injuries. And tell your pal Wetherall, there's some for him as well. I didn't wait for Mr Elleray to show the card. I turned and walked to the dressing room.

Completely unexpectedly, Keane had admitted what many had suspected all along. The challenge on Haaland had been deliberate, it was intended to hurt and had been almost two years in the planning. Keane had apparently confessed to assaulting a fellow player during the course of a game, that he had not cared whether or not the ball was playable and that he knew that his challenge was an automatic sending off offence.

(James, 2002: 73)

Hypothetically, imagine you are a Crown Prosecution Service lawyer. Advise the CPS on whether or not to proceed with a criminal prosecution under any relevant section of the Offences Against the Person Act 1861 – s.47, s.20 or s.18. Critically apply the elements of the crime:

1 The mental element or *mens rea* of the crime.
2 The *actus reus* or harmful result/injury required by the specific offence.
3 Does this fall within the boundaries of consent to the risks of the normal game of football? Is there any mitigation, excuse, justification for this conduct by Keane?
4 The prosecutorial guidelines for proceeding with a prosecution.
5 Search for accounts of this incident and use such references appropriately.
6 Are you missing any key evidence or information needed to assess the grounds for a prosecution? If so, explain your answer. Give a detailed answer drawing on principles of criminal assault applied to sport, using key cases and commentaries.

EXERCISE 4.25

On 3 February 1998, Kevin Yates, a Bath rugby union player, was found guilty of biting Simon Fenn on the ear, during a match against London Scottish, on 10 January 1998 and was suspended for six months. The victim, who received the bite during a collapsed scrum, required 25 stitches to his ear. Hypothetically, imagine you are a Crown Prosecution Service lawyer. Advise the CPS on whether or not there is a case for prosecuting Yates for any offence in relation to the Offences Against the Person Act 1861. Apply the elements of the relevant offence and the CPS guidance for prosecutions. In addition, which previous case in rugby union may provide assistance in this decision and why? (Sports Law Bulletin, 1, no 2 March/April 1998: 1)

Examples of key cases: criminal assault

R v (Mark) Barnes [2004] EWCA Crim 3246

A criminal case involving an 'on-the-ball' incident does not come to court very often and is likely to create a challenge for the criminal courts. In *R v (Mark) Barnes*[26] Mark Barnes was convicted on one count of unlawfully and maliciously inflicting grievous bodily harm upon Christopher Bygraves, contrary to s.20 of the Offences Against the Person Act 1861.[27] The defendant successfully appealed against the conviction in the EWCA which related to specific aspects of the trial judge's summing up. The *Barnes* case arose out of an amateur soccer match which took place on 7 December 2002. Following a time-wasting incident by the victim and a foul on the victim by Mark Barnes (the appellant), heated words were exchanged between the two and the referee told Barnes to 'grow up'.

Ten minutes later the victim received the ball and ran with it, approximately six yards from the opposition penalty area and at about seven yards from the goalmouth, and kicked the ball into the net with his left foot. After he kicked the ball, the appellant tackled him from behind, making contact with his right ankle. The victim said he heard a snapping noise and fell to the ground. The appellant was also on the ground, but stood up and said words to the victim to the effect 'have that'. The victim suffered a serious injury to his right ankle and right fibula. The prosecution contended that the injury was a result of a 'crushing tackle, which was late, unnecessary, reckless and high up the legs'.[28] The appellant admitted the tackle but claimed that it was 'a fair, if hard, challenge, in the form of a sliding tackle in the course of play, and that any injury caused was accidental'.[29]

Although witnesses were called from both sides, the EWCA judgment notes that perhaps the most important witness was the referee who had 34 years of experience in refereeing soccer matches. He reported to the court that:

> he had a clear, unobstructed view of the incident and, in view of what he saw, he sent the appellant off for violent conduct. He would not agree that the appellant had made a sliding tackle. It was his view that the appellant had gone in with two feet.[30] The judge in his summing up, reminded the jury in relation to s.20, there was no dispute on the facts, that the appellant had caused the victim's injury. He made it clear that the appellant could only be guilty if his actions were 'not done by way of legitimate sport' and the prosecution had alleged that the conduct was so reckless that it could not have been in legitimate sport and it was tantamount to assault.[31]

James (2006a: 611) observes that the Court of Appeal 'criticised the trial judge for failing to explain or to give examples of what is meant by legitimate sport and acceptable conduct in sport, yet failed to elaborate on those terms itself'. There were several different complaints made in the grounds of the appeal, collectively arguing that the judge's summing up was inadequate, by failing to deal with:

> the real issue, the importance and relevance of the defence of consent, where an injury had occurred in the course of a lawful sport. It had not been made clear to the jury that there could lawfully be breaches, even serious breaches, of the rules of the sport, without there necessarily being the commission of a criminal offence.[32]

The EWCA considered that, among other things, the summing up 'should also have made it clear that even if a tackle results in a player being sent off, it may still not reach the necessary threshold to constitute criminal conduct'.[33] In addition, the jury needed to be told 'why it was important to determine where the ball was at the material time and the importance of the distinction between the appellant going for the ball, albeit late, and his going for the victim' (Leake and Omerod, 2005: 2). It was:

> difficult to determine what they thought they had to decide in order to find the appellant guilty. This being the position, we are forced to come to the conclusion that the summing up was inadequate, and that as a result the conviction is unsafe. Accordingly the appeal will be allowed and the orders made set aside.[34]

The courts recognise that there is so little authoritative guidance in law, in the appellate courts, regarding when it is appropriate to institute criminal proceedings after an injury was caused to one player by another player in the course of a sporting event. This may be partly due to the very low number of prosecutions in those circumstances to date, although there is a modest flow of cases to the courts and there was a need for some guidance. However, although there may have been several cases coming to court to date under the Offences Against the Person Act 1861, nearly all of them involved clear off-the-ball incidents (James, 2006a; Gardiner 2005, 2007).

The Court of Appeal in *Barnes* gave guidance in determining whether conduct during the course of a contact sport was criminal. It should be regarded as an objective test, which did not depend on the views of individual players, but which did depend on all the circumstances. What kind of circumstances? The Court of Appeal concluded that it was necessary to take into account the type of sport being played, the level at which it was played, the nature of the act, the degree of force used, the extent of the risk of injury and the state of mind of the defendant. 'Although passing reference is made to *R v Cey* and in paragraph 15 of the judgment a composite test is propounded that draws on *R v Ciccarelli* (1989) 54 CCC (3d) 121 and discussions of playing culture outlined in earlier editions of this book, it is then not applied in the instant case' (James, 2006a: 611).

The Court of Appeal recognised that there would be cases that 'fell in a grey area' and in relation to matters of fact the jury would have to ask themselves, among other things, 'whether the contact was so obviously late and/or violent that it could not be regarded as an instinctive reaction, error or misjudgement in the heat of the game' (*R v (Mark) Barnes*, The Times, 10 January 2005: 54). Criminal proceedings should only be brought against a player who injured another player in sport if his conduct 'was sufficiently grave to be properly categorised as criminal' (ibid: 54, CA). The starting point for the approach of the courts was that:

> most sports governing bodies had their own disciplinary procedures for enforcing their particular standards of conduct. As a result, in the majority of situations, there was not only no need for criminal proceedings, it was undesirable that there should be any criminal proceedings.
>
> (ibid: 54)

In addition, it was 'on the basis of public policy that physical injury sustained in the course of participation in a contact sport was an exception to the general principle that a person could not consent to having bodily injury inflicted upon him'.[35] However, if what occurred went 'beyond what a player could reasonably be regarded as having accepted by taking part in the sport' it was indicated that the conduct 'would not be covered by the defence' (Leake and Omerod, 2005: 2). The current position after *Barnes* is summarised as:

> i. All injuries inflicted by contacts unconnected with the playing of the game are criminal. ii. All injuries caused by unreasonable contacts or contacts that carry an unreasonable degree of risk are criminal. iii. All injuries caused by contacts that are part of the normal, reasonable playing of the game are not criminal.
>
> (James, 2006a: 612)

James (2006a: 611) argues that an opportunity was missed in the Court of Appeal to 'explain and develop the concept of playing culture in English criminal law'. The technical rules of the game are seen as too narrow or strict a boundary for delineating consent to the 'normal game' or 'playing the game'. Is it helpful to use the playing culture, that is, be guided by the norms of players and coaches, which are part of the sport-specific sub-culture or organisational culture? In the next section of this chapter a critical, sociological lens will be applied to hegemonic masculinity, subcultures in some male contact sports, in order to explore the notion of normalising violent conduct, in sporting arenas where self-regulation and internal disciplinary processes are part of the policy lens which keeps the criminal law at a distance. Is it safe to leave the boundaries of a 'normal game' or 'playing the game' to the 'playing culture'?

The Marty McSorley Case

Before moving on to the sociological lens on hegemonic masculinity, sport specific sub-cultures and normalising violence in sport, the Canadian ice hockey case of *R v McSorley* (unreported, 6 October 2000, British Columbia Provincial Court Criminal Division, Judge William Kitchen) provides an interesting and rare example of a successful criminal conviction following sports violence on an ice rink. Marty McSorley, playing for the Boston Bruins, clubbed Donald Brashear, of the Vancouver Canucks, on the right temple, during an ice hockey game on 21 February 2000. Brashear hit his head on the ice and suffered a seizure and serious concussion (Rosenberg, 2003: 35). The act occurred well away from the puck and McSorley stated later, in an interview 'Yes – I meant to slash him.' 'Did I mean to hurt him with my stick? No' (Kennedy, 2000: 60 cited Kerr, 2005: 10). He went up to him to try to get him to fight, as he had earlier in the game (Kerr, 2000: S1, cited Rosenberg, 2003: 36). Kennedy (2000: 60) claimed that McSorley aimed to slash at Brashear's shoulder before making contact with his face. 'If what McSorley says is true, his act of unsanctioned aggression was not undertaken with intent to injure' (Kerr 2005: 10).

The NHL Commissioner acknowledged that McSorley's intent was 'difficult to determine, he must be held responsible for the consequences of delivering a deliberate slash' (Rosenberg, 2003: 36). It is unclear whether the charge is equivalent to an s.20 offence or GBH with intent, s.18 offence. The latter requires intent as the *mens rea*. In the former, recklessness will do. The National Hockey League (NHL) suspended McSorley for 23 games, the rest of the season and he forfeited $72,000 of his salary. This was 'the longest suspension in NHL history and [he] had to apply for a hearing in order to be reinstated' (Deacon, 2000, cited Rosenberg, 2003: 23). McSorley tried to argue that he could produce evidence of past attacks which were more brutal than his but resulted in less severe sanctions than he had received, but this was rejected as the game had changed and that the NHL was 'merely fulfilling its commitment to penalize more stringently irresponsible blows to the head' (Bettman, 2000: 5, cited Rosenberg, 2003: 37).

The NHL Commissioner, Gary Bettman, observed that his decision had been informed by several factors, including McSorley being disciplined eight times previously (four for stick-related incidents), that McSorley should be held responsible for the consequences of delivering a deliberate slash, and that the attack was not a common occurrence in the NHL, it was not part of the game, or the ethos of the game (Bettman, 2000: 4–5, cited Rosenberg, 2003: 36–37). In the criminal trial in October 2000, the Crown submitted that McSorley's act 'is precisely why the law, the criminal law has a place in the hockey rink'.[36] The fact that this was hockey at the highest level, witnessed by millions of people, who valued the game and played it themselves, all featured in the public policy lens which justified a criminal prosecution.

The Crown considered that McSorley's conduct was 'way beyond the scope of this game' and 'completely irrelevant to the game that was taking place on the ice'.[37] Mr J Kitchen considered many sources of evidence including the testimony of both Donald Brashear and Marty McSorley. He also considered the rules of hockey, both written and unwritten, and their application, as well as videotapes and witnesses who could determine the atmosphere of the game (ibid: 3). McSorley was critical of the judge, who he claimed, 'did not acknowledge the true nature of professional hockey' (ibid: 35). On 6 October 2000, McSorley was convicted of 'assault with a weapon, but was granted conditional discharge that carried no criminal record or jail time if he remained "clean" for 18 months'. Interestingly, the judge ordered McSorley not only to keep the peace, but also not to participate in any sporting events where Donald Brashear was playing.[38]

EXERCISE 4.26

An English soccer case: *R v (Mark) Barnes* [2004] EWCA Crim 3246; [2005] 1 WLR 910
In the case of *R v (Mark) Barnes* there is no doubt that the defendant's contact with the victim's leg caused the bodily harm required for an s.20 offence. However, there were two versions of the defendant's conduct presented to the court. What were they and how do they relate to the elements of the offence?

EXERCISE 4.27

Explain with referenced support from the full text law reports case commentaries on *Barnes* (e.g. Leake and Omerod, 2005; James, 2005), the arguments presented on behalf of *Barnes* in the EWCA, in relation to:

1 What counts as legitimate sport.
2 Breaching the rules of a sport – and the commission of a criminal offence.
3 The sending off of a player and the commission of a criminal offence.
4 Where the ball was at the relevant time and the difference between going for the ball and going for the victim.
5 Explain the six areas making up the objective test of all the circumstances, informing criminality, outlined in *Barnes*. Are they useful? Which precedent case is used?
6 What is the current position on sports field injuries and criminal prosecutions following *Barnes*?

EXERCISE 4.28

A Canadian ice hockey case: *R v McSorley* (unreported, 6 October 2000, British Columbia Provincial Court Criminal Division, Judge William Kitchen)
Summarise the 'off-the-puck' incident involving Marty McSorley and Donald Brashear on 21 February 2000.

EXERCISE 4.29

Report the outcome of the National Hockey League (NHL) hearing. Support your response with reasons.

EXERCISE 4.30

Critically evaluate McSorley's comments to the NHL in defence of his conduct.

EXERCISE 4.31

Does the criminal law have a place in the ice hockey rink? Identify and explain the public policy lens in the decision to prosecute McSorley.

EXERCISE 4.32

Did the Crown view McSorley's on ice violence as part of the normal game of ice hockey? Critically evaluate the approach of the Crown on this matter.

EXERCISE 4.33

Explain the issues in this case around intent. What, in particular, did the judge order McSorley to do as part of his conditional discharge? Critically discuss this as an effective deterrent. What is your opinion of the outcome of the criminal case against McSorley?

Masculinity, violence and consent: a sociological lens on sport

Hegemony is 'the achievement by a class . . . of leadership over the rest of society, in accordance with its perceived interests' (Hargreaves, 1986: 7). Hegemonic masculinity or masculinist hegemony sustains itself as the dominant form through two main routes. First, players are located in a masculine sports specific subculture, where they learn very quickly 'how things are done here' through unwritten rules/norms, expectations, shared values, role models, traditions, attitudes, reactions to incidents of violence, which they internalise from the moment they join that group. It is this '*complicity* of other men, some (or many) of whom might be uncomfortable with some of the beliefs and practices that sustain hegemonic masculinity' (Messner, 2002: 30). Second, if the sports specific subculture does not persuade the player to engage in violence, there is always a range of different kinds of power, over the player/athlete, including positional power, resources power, legitimate power, expert power, charismatic or personal power, reward power, or referent power (see Brackenridge, 2001: 83). 'On his or her own, the coach has the greatest potential to influence behaviour and attitudes on the field' (Centre for Sport and Law, 2002: 1). Messner (1992: 72–73) suggests that most athletes tend to:

adopt the visions and values that coaches are offering: to take orders, to take pain, to take out opponents, to take the game seriously, to take women, and to take their place on the team. And if they can't take it, then the rewards of athletic camaraderie, prestidge, scholarships, pro contracts and community recognition are not forthcoming.

Critcher (1995) suggests that an overemphasis on success (Functionalism) is a factor which can affect deviance in sport. 'The Game is played to win, but is not played to win at all costs' suggests the Centre for Sport and Law (2002: 1) but often a commitment to playing the game, becomes an overcommitment to winning at all costs. If only some violent acts are labelled as deviant, does this mean that others are normalised or legitimised where it is possible for 'a whole area of human activity for an organised group to become institutionally corrupt, committed to a system of breaking the rules' (Critcher, 1995: 30–31)? The question is rarely asked 'Why is it that some male sports, steeped in masculine subculture, have very different norms, values and behaviour regarding rule-breaking and violence?' In particular, 'how do some sports retain a strong sense of order such as golf and martial arts?' (Critcher, 1995: 34). Violence which may occur in other sports such as soccer, ice hockey, rugby union and American football, may be one of 'misplaced masculinity' in which 'being a man has come to mean deviating from the rules when your sense of self is at stake' (ibid: 34).

Deviant behaviour is 'a situation where there is a violation of normative expectations surrounding the organisation and this behaviour has peer and elite support, conditions that facilitate rule-breaking and the adoption of goals inconsistent with societal values' (Ermann and Lundman, 1978, cited Frey, 1994). Drawing on their research into elite make players in North American sports, Coakley and Hughes (1991) developed a working definition of 'positive deviance, which involves excessive conformity to the norms and values embodied in sport itself' which they called the 'sport ethic'. This 'sport ethic' involved players in:

a. Making sacrifices for the game
b. Striving for distinction
c. Accepting risks and playing through pain
d. Refusing to accept (human) limits in the pursuit of possibilities.

(Coakley and Hughes, 1991: 309–310)

They argued that conforming to the 'sport ethic' is likely to 'set one apart as a real athlete' but also 'creates a clear-cut vulnerability to several kinds of deviant behaviour' (ibid: 308). In this context, violence on and off the sportsfield and the use of performance-enhancing drugs are seen as 'positive deviance', that is, a kind of overconformity to the sport ethic, that is, the norms and values of the sport subculture, even though they deviate from both societal norms and sport competition rules and values. Messner (2002: 28) supports this notion of positive deviance when he argues that 'far from being an aberration perpetrated by some marginal deviants, male athletes off-the field violence is generated from the normal everyday dynamics at the centre of male athletic culture'.

Messner (1990: 303) argues that players tolerate extreme conditions and injuries. Socialisation into masculinity involves routinely giving and accepting injury, where self-esteem and power are derived from doing violence to the bodies of co-workers'. For Young (1993: 374) sport is a site for the 'expression and reproduction of hegemonic masculinity where violence and its results, including injury, are legitimized and make sense'. He argues that the 'health and safety of professional sports workers is repeatedly compromised, as they are expected to face intolerable working conditions, severe and unreasonable punishment, and dish out and accept violence on a regular basis' (ibid: 376). Professional players who fail to conform could end up being unemployed as 'player to player violence continues to be rationalized by many athletes and coaches' (ibid: 376).

Messner (1992: 72) talks of players 'giving up their bodies' and 'playing hurt', where their athletic body was at the centre of their athletic identity.

It could go either way. Playing at their peak and gaining respect as an aggressive winner gives them a sense of male athletic identity, which can easily be unravelled if the body breaks down through violence and injury, negatively impacting on self-esteem (Messner 1992: 72–75). Players who occupied certain positions (such as offensive linesmen) or were coached in roles of 'hatchetmen', 'warriors' or 'goons' had higher status, exhibited hypermasculinity, and displayed a more extreme 'normalisation' of risk and violence (Welch, 1997; Messner 1990, 2002). Messner (2002) argues that boys and men are socialised into a 'triad of violence' which consists of 'men's violence against themselves, other men and against women' and is held together by group-based process of misogyny, homophobia and suppression of empathy' (Messner, 2002: 76).

> When you learn to ignore other people and other people's pain you lose your capacity of empathy. When you learn to ignore your own pain as well, you lose your understanding of what it is to cause pain and it becomes of value to cause pain.
> (Michael Messner, *On the Line* 'Bad Sports' BBC 2 26 January, 1994)

The objectification of women, located in misogynist attitudes, can arise out of locker room culture which perpetuates negative descriptions of 'others' outside their own elite group as 'playing like a girl' or not fighting properly (merely a bit of 'handbagging'). Benedict (1998) outlines a subcultural process which gradually removes nearly all responsibilities from male players as they progress through school, college scholarships to professional contracts, where they become entitled to many privileges on and off the field, as long as they 'do the business' and deliver the goods on match-day.

Normalising violence from the sports field to the law courts

What does the critical sociological lens on hegemonic masculinity, sport subcultures, complicity and positional and role power have to do with substantive law and legal policy on criminal liability for assault related to violence on and off the sports field? From the moment a player joins a sports team they pick up messages, through the organisational or sport subculture, about how things are done here (Beech and Chadwick, 2004). The unwritten norms, the expectations, role models, feedback to behaviour and attitudes, can all contribute to a failure to challenge violent conduct. If those do not work, the operations of hegemonic masculinity through the normalisation of violence can also depend on various kinds of power (positional, resources, expert, charismatic power) exerted over players by coaches, club and sports governing body officials, employees etc as outlined by Brackenridge (2001).

Those in formal positions of power are able to use that formal or positional power in two ways. First, they can make players conform to violent conduct through the threat of withdrawing opportunities, resources, including future employment. Second, they often represent the sport community in civil or criminal court cases and give the courts their expert opinion on whether X conduct by a defendant was part of the normal game or approved practice. Was the defendant playing the reasonable, normal game, leading to accidental injuries to which players are reasonably expected to consent?

Clarity around what is regarded as 'beyond the normal game' or not 'playing the game' is a crucial part of defining and recognising when sports violence should be 'criminal'. However, often accounts of a normal game, by players or expert witnesses, simply make an empirical observation of incidents or conduct which happen quite a lot, and assume that this will suffice as a legal and moral justification. 'It is part of the normal game because it happens a lot – so what else do you want to know?'[39] If the technical rules are considered too narrow a boundary for a 'normal game', or 'playing the game', then will the player norms or 'playing culture' do the job and guide the internal disciplinary processes or the criminal courts?

If, as indicated earlier, the reliance of the law on the internal regulatory and disciplinary processes of a sports governing body provides a public policy reason to generally keep the criminal law on the other side of the touchline in relation to sports violence, then those disciplinary processes, as well as the use of rules and officials to reduce risks to an inherent minimum, need to be constantly scrutinised. 'Some people appeal to the attitude "everyone is doing it" which implies that certain behaviour cannot be wrong' (Rosenberg, 2003: 33). Sports coaches and sports governing bodies, or witnesses in court cases, should be challenging rather than legitimising acts of violence. If the sports governing bodies and the law courts frame the boundaries of consent to injury in sport by merely using what players commonly accept in their playing culture (as suggested by Gardiner, 1994, 2006; James 2006), there is a danger of an empirical observation of what commonly happens becoming the guide for the courts of what *ought* to be accepted in precedent setting cases as part of the normal game. Although this is not unique to sport contexts, it could be regarded as a slide from an 'is' to an 'ought' guide on consent, without critical reflection or justification.

As far back as 1969, in Canada, players or officials who normalised fist-fighting in the ice hockey sport subculture also took that message to the criminal courts in their role as expert witnesses and even persuaded the courts to chopping an opponent on the head with a hockey stick as being part of the normal game to which players are expected to consent. In an ice hockey case, being hit and receiving fight-related injuries, even chopping a player on the head with a stick, was viewed by the courts in the following way:

> No hockey player enters onto the ice without the knowledge of the possibility that he is going to be hit in one of the many ways he is on the ice . . . we can come to the conclusion that this is an ordinary happening in a hockey game and the players really think nothing of it.

> (Horrow, 1980, cited Young, 1993: 396)

In another case reported by Horrow, the court argued that 'fist-fighting was so frequent in the NHL as to be viewed as "normal" as long as the force used in the fight did not exceed that level authorised by other players' (1980: 186, cited in Young, 2004: 396). The apparent normalisation of fighting as part of the normal game has regularly drawn critical commentary from academics and sometimes, more rarely, journalists. For example, 'hockey actually seems to celebrate fighting as part of the normal part of the game . . . there isn't even the pretense that fighting is morally or ethically inappropriate' (Gruneau and Witson, 1993: 189, cited Rosenberg 2003: 39). Rosenberg (2003: 39) argues that one of the unique aspects of [ice] hockey is that it:

> regulates and has institutionalised on-ice bare knuckle fighting. Whereas most sports call for the ejection and suspension of athletes who brawl on the playing field, fighting in ice hockey often results in in-game penalties that, once served, permit athletes to return to competition. This regulation of fighting is part of the rationale some offer to claim that fighting is part of the game.

However, not only is the claim that fist-fighting in ice hockey is not really an injury issue as players wear helmets, a myth (see Young, 2004) but, like punching in any sport outside boxing, it is not actually regulated. Nor is it one of the defined physical skills of the sport, originally framed within the constitutive rules of the sport, which should be informing the voluntary and moral contract to compete and informing the basis of consent (see Fraleigh, 1984; Hartley, 1998, 2001a). In response to the Marty McSorley case, Deacon (2000, cited in Rosenberg, 2003: 37) observed 'when the game rewards men for beating each others' heads with bare fists, should we be surprised when fighters occasionally resort to sticks'. Although the McSorley case indicates a harsher attitude to stick fighting, compared to the late 1960s or early 1970s in the Canadian Criminal Courts, in that it led to the longest suspension in history by the NHL and a successful criminal prosecution for assault with a weapon, that conviction only resulted in an 18-month suspended sentence, without the player even having a criminal record.

The defined and agreed physical challenges or skills, which created and codified the exciting and popular sport of rugby union in the United Kingdom, include passing, running, tackling, rucking, mawling, goal-kicking, scrums and line-outs etc. They do not, and never will, include the 'skills' of punching, ear-biting, eye-gouging or stamping on players' faces. Yet this sort of conduct regularly features in matches and, punching in particular, provides examples of processes of legitimising, normalising outlined earlier by Messner (1990, 2002) and Young (1993, 2004). From the sports field all the way to the law courts, players, coaches, sports administrators, and expert witnesses, attempt to legitimise punching (a clear 'act of violence' Parry, 1998) as part of the normal game of rugby, with no more than a mere empirical observation that it is common.

> I know that, if I ended up on the floor, even if it was well away from the ball, someone was going to come along and boot me. Being a fly-half, you get used to it, especially if you kick goals as well. People always seem to be out to get you, but that's all part of the normal game.
> (Rob Andrew, England rugby union fly-half, in Stewart and Silver, 1993)

However, when Jonathan Collard received a serious facial injury, as a result of being raked in a rugby union match in 1993, he commented that he would not 'stand by and let so-called officials put this down to rugby being a hard game . . . or just a normal game of rugby' (cited Hartley, 2001a: 178). In the case of *R v Billingshurst* in Newport Crown Court, a rugby union player was charged with assault, following an incident on the field where the defendant punched another player and broke his jaw in three places. An expert witness for the defence informed the judge that punching was the rule rather than the exception, implying that it was part of the normal game, but this was not accepted by the court and the player was found guilty. When complaining about the conduct of the All-Blacks rugby team (whom he described as 'boot boys') after they caused facial injuries to Philip De Glanville, an English rugby union player, Butler (a former player) observed that 'the ruck in question did not appear to be heinous at the time; there was no flurry of retaliatory punches, which normally provide a sequel to excess and a warning of scandal' (Butler, 1993: 2).

Butler (1993) appears to be indicating, without critical comment, that punching was not only a normal part of the game, but was an acceptable means for players to communicate to their peers that the preceding incident was 'off the scale'. In 1985, during a televised rugby union match in Wales, George Crawford, the referee, walked off the pitch, abandoning the match, after warning the players he would do just this if they did not stop punching and actually 'play the game' of rugby.

> I took my action as a protest against violence in the game. I said that someone would be killed if severe action was not taken against all players who commit acts of foul play

... and expressed concerns that many of my referring colleagues see fit to merely caution people for a punch on the rugby field. There seems to be a reluctance to send people off for punching (unlike soccer).

(George Crawford, in an interview for
'Sport in the Dock' *On the Line*, BBC 2, 1992)

However, when interviewed for the same television programme, Dudley Woods, the then secretary of the Rugby Football Union (RFU), commented:

In the heat of the moment, things of this instance would *inevitably* occur. I don't think you would achieve anything, quite honestly, by, instantly a punch was thrown, a player was sent off the field, except perhaps a *lack of commitment* (emphasis added).

(Dudley Woods, in an interview for
'Sport in the Dock' *On the Line* BBC 2, 1992)

Punching in rugby union is often rationalised by such comments as 'it's just a bit of fisticuffs . . . the lads will settle down soon' (sports commentator) or an unconvincing biological deterministic argument such as 'where hormones flow aggression will follow' (Butler, 1993: 2), with no attempt to distinguish between aggression and acts of violence, when commenting on punching on the rugby field. George Crawford, the referee who made his protest (above) in 1985, warned that 'someone would be killed if severe action was not taken' in relation to foul play, tragically, was proved right in 1993 when Seamus Lavelle was felled by a punch when playing rugby union, suffered severe swelling of the brain and died two days later (see Cleary, 1995). During the early days of the police investigation, the police took some time to establish that it was, indeed, Hardy the defendant, who threw the punch which killed the victim, because so many players were punching at that time.

The defendant, who was initially arrested for murder, eventually faced a charge of (involuntary) manslaughter, told the court in July 1994 that during this ill-tempered match he saw 'one of his side, punched and kicked by three Hendon forwards' and he told the court 'I told them to leave it out and play rugby. But one of their players came towards me looking menacing. I thought he was going to hit me' and as he squared up he was 'hit from behind by two punches from Lavelle, and this caused the hooker (Hardy) to 'lash out blindly' (*R v Hardy* (unreported, 24 July 1994, Central Criminal Court)). He argued that he acted in self-defence when he told the court 'I hit out because I thought I was going to be hit some more . . . whether or not you call that self-defence, I don't know' (Cleary, 1995). Hardy was acquitted of manslaughter on the grounds of self-defence.[40]

Sports governing bodies are expected to be self-regulating, partly through their use of rules, officials and disciplinary procedures. Such processes are seen by the law to be the first port of call in dealing with violence, making it undesirable for the criminal courts to intervene initially (Gardiner, 2005; Leake and Omerod 2005; James 2005 on *Barnes*). If sports governing bodies experience any difficulty stepping outside the influence of their sport-specific subcultures and positional powers to truly self-regulate and, instead, normalise unacceptable, violent conduct, is it safe to leave control of risk and violence in their hands through internal, disciplinary procedures, as preferable to the intervention of the criminal law?

EXERCISE 4.34

Explain the role of sport-specific subculture and positional power in sustaining hegemonic masculinity and normalising unacceptable acts of violence on the sports field.

EXERCISE 4.35

Explain the concept of 'positive deviance' involving excessive overconformity to the 'sport ethic' or subcultural norms. How does this link to legitimising violence as part of the reproduction of hegemonic masculinity in male contact sports?

EXERCISE 4.36

Read Messner, 1990, 1992, 2002 and Young, 1993. Give examples of 'hatchetmen' or 'warriors' displaying hypermasculunity and suppression of empathy – and 'giving up their bodies', as part of socialisation into athletic male identity.

EXERCISE 4.37

What is the 'tricky triad'? How does it relate to Kretchmar's work on the development of 'moral callouses' in explaining complicity of male athletes in acts of sports violence?

EXERCISE 4.38

Explain how the critical sociological lens covered in 4.35, 4.36 and 4.37 above can throw light on the very small number of criminal assault cases arising out of violence on the sports field with reference to the accounts by expert witnesses in disciplinary and court cases of whether or not a defendant's conduct is regarded as part of the normal game being played at the time of the alleged offence.

EXERCISE 4.39

If the technical rules of a sport/game are too narrow to operate as a boundary of consent, should 'playing cultures' or sport-specific subcultural norms be the sole guide to the boundary of consent to what should be regarded as the normal in X game/sport?

EXERCISE 4.40

Identify examples from relevant literature and case law of attempts to normalise:

1 fist-fighting in ice hockey.
2 fist-fighting in rugby union.

EXERCISE 4.41

Critically analyse the following excuses provided in defence of sports violence in disciplinary or criminal cases:

1 It happens a lot. It is common practice.
2 It is normal part of the game/sport. The players accept it.
3 The referee did not see it or respond to it. No one was sent off.
4 It was a rash moment of madness.
5 It was done in the heat of the moment when emotions were high in a very competitive situation.
6 Players or clubs rarely report such conduct to the police.

EXERCISE 4.42

Critically comment on context leading to the concerns of George Crawford, rugby union referee, after he walked off the pitch in protest in 1986 and the issues around the case of *R v Hardy* (unreported, 24 July 1994, Central Criminal Court).

EXERCISE 4.43

Critically review the arguments and comments used by Gardiner 2005 in the light of relevant critical sociological lens applied to normalisation of sports violence, particularly in relation to the Lee Bowyer–Kieron Dyer fighting incident in April 2005.

EXERCISE 4.44

Critically discuss the role of sport subculture and positional power in the normalisation of violence from the sports field to criminal assault cases drawing on the work of Messner, 1990, 1992, 2002; Young, 1993, 2004; Coakley and Hughes, 1991; Welch, 1997; Benedict, 1998; and Hartley, 1998, 2001a.

Summary

- Sports violence is a contested concept. It will be defined variably across different academic disciplines such as philosophy, law, psychology and sociology.
- It is useful to engage in an analysis of a concept of violence in relation to other concepts such as assertion, aggression, intimidation, or 'gamesmanship'.
- There are three stages to establishing a crime: i. a mental element or *mens rea*; ii. an *actus reus* or causing of the resulting harm defined in the offence; iii. the absence of any lawful justification, mitigation, defence, such as consent.
- The set of objective principles used in the Canadian cases of *R v Cey* and *R v Cicarelli* (1989) for consent informed the lead EWCA case of *R v (Mark) Barnes*.
- Considerable trust is placed in the internal regulatory mechanisms of sports governing bodies, with little intervention expected from the criminal law for violence on the sports field (*R v (Mark) Barnes*).
- Criminal assault on the sports field is covered under a range of offences and statutes. Common assault (Criminal Justice Act 1988) and public order or affray offences (Public Order Act 1986) and also Offences Against the Person Act 1861 which has s.47, s.20 and s.18 offences.
- The majority of criminal charges for assault in sport, under the OAPA 1861 arise out of off-the-ball incidents and more commonly in the sports of rugby union and soccer at amateur level in the UK.
- Sports sociology can provide a critical lens for viewing violence on and off the sports field.
- In particular hegemonic masculinity, masculine sports subculture and power provide a theoretical lens which helps to explain the normalisation and celebration of risk and violence on and off the sports field.
- Socio-legal perspectives help to see the ways in hegemonic masculinity, the use of power and subcultural practices can attempt to normalise unacceptable risks and violence. This is not confined to the sports field but extends to the courts as those from the sport community either do not report or challenge potentially criminal behaviour, or continue to normalise it in their roles as expert witnesses or defendants, in criminal trials.

5 Discrimination, harassment and child protection in sport and physical recreation

Introduction

This chapter is divided into two parts. Part one begins with relevant statutes and cases on sexual discrimination, racial discrimination and disability discrimination. It moves on to discrimination on the grounds of sexuality and the legal rights of transsexual people in their acquired gender. Harassment is viewed as a form of discrimination and as part of a separate statute – the Protection from Harassment Act 1997, which, from June 2006, now applies not only to stalking but also to harassment in the workplace. Part two focuses on safeguarding children (child protection) in sport and starts with the challenge of definition, research and evaluating risk. Illustrative criminal cases are followed by the legal and policy frameworks and the standards now used in sport in the UK.

Part one: discrimination and harassment

Sex Discrimination Act 1975

The Sex Discrimination Act 1975[1] makes it unlawful to discriminate against a person on the grounds of their sex or marital status. A person discriminates against a woman if, on the grounds of her sex, she is treated less favourably than a man would be treated (direct discrimination). It also specifically protects women from 'being treated unfavourably because they are pregnant or on maternity leave' and, more recently, it 'prohibits discrimination based on the fact that someone is intending to undergo or has undergone gender reassignment' (TUC, 2008: 141). Sexual harassment on the grounds of a victim's sex is a form of sex discrimination in employment. The Sex Discrimination Act 'specifically defines sexual harassment as unlawful conduct' (Russell et al., 2008c: 1). In the case of *James v Eastleigh Borough Council* [1990] 2 AC 751, the House of Lords ruled that Mr James was 'directly discriminated against when he was charged a higher price than his wife for admission to a swimming pool' the reason being a concessionary price for pensioners, with no discriminatory intent on the part of the council. If he had not been a man, Mr James would have been treated the same as his wife. This was at a time when retirement ages were different for men and women.

Indirect discrimination occurs when a 'provision, criterion or practice, puts someone of a certain sex . . . at a particular disadvantage, when compared to others' (TUC, 2008: 137–8). Such requirements or conditions 'seem to be applied equally to both sexes but actually result in members of one sex being less likely to be able to comply with them' (McArdle, 2000: 132[2]). Indirect discrimination in employment 'occurs typically with respect to issues such as job-sharing, part-time working and forms of dress and appearance' (Welch, 2006: 563[3]). Statutory exceptions to the Sex Discrimination Act 1975 include Genuine Occupational Qualifications for a job (for reasons of physiology, decency or privacy) and s.44 which is a general exception for:

acts relating to participation as a competitor in certain sporting events which are confined to one sex. The sports to which the exception applies are those in which physical strength, stamina or physique are important so that the average woman would be at a disadvantage in competition with the average man.

(SDA 1975, s.44)

Initial interpretations of the Act and s.44 were highly influenced by myths and stereotypes, rather than by known capacity.[4] Individual's enactment and interpretation of sex, gender and identity in sport is framed by the eternal triangle of myths about performance, sex at birth (chromosomes and hormones) and the social construction of sport and the law (Talbot, 2006). It was assumed that s.44 applies after puberty. Mixed sex participation is still an issue for many organisations in the UK yet is common in other countries (Talbot, 2006). The application of s.44 is 'restricted to very specific circumstances' and indeed *Bennet v Football Association* (unreported, 1978, Court of Appeal) is the only case where it has been successful (McArdle, 2000: 136). In this case Theresa Bennet, aged 11, played football with the boys and wanted to join the boys' side that played in the local league (see Talbot, 1998). Mixed teams were not permitted under regional and national rules so the FA banned her from playing in the boys' team. The Court of Appeal heard medical evidence that:

> The strength, stamina and physique of pre-pubescent girls is not markedly different from that of pre-pubescent boys and that there are at least as many physiological differences within the sexes as there are between them. However, while accepting that the main purpose of the 1975 Act was to prevent the application of sex-based stereotypical assumptions, the Court of Appeal ruled that s.44 had been drafted in a way that obliged it to take these very stereotypes into account. Football was a sport in which the strength of the *average* woman put her at a disadvantage to the *average* man and Bennet's individual attributes could not be taken into account.

(McArdle, 2000: 137)

Bradford (2005) uses feminist and Foucauldian theoretical approaches as a basis for analysing sport as a cultured institution and 'inherently gendered notions' resulting in the Australian legislative equivalent of a s.44 SDA 1975[5] (see for example, Foucault, 1980; McKinnon, 1987, 1989; Bourdieu, 1987; Costa and Guthrie, 1994). In addition, the leading legal practitioner and author, Dame Helena Kennedy QC (1992), provides a practitioner's insight into the gendered lens of the Anglo-Welsh judiciary.

> Although anti-discrimination legislation focuses on differences in sex, amongst other attributes, it is the construction of gender that perpetuates division in sport. Gender encompasses the stereotypes and attitudes about the characteristics, attributes and behaviours that are appropriate for members of each sex.

(Bradford, 2005: 79).

In a landmark case of *Taylor v Moorabbin Saints Junior Football League and Football Victoria Ltd* [2004] VCAT 158, in the Victorian Civil and Administrative Tribunal (Australia), Morris J ruled that 'a 13 year-old girl could not be excluded from competing in a junior Australian Rules football league, but that 14 year-old and 15 year-old girls could be excluded' (Bradford, 2005: 79). The Equal Opportunities Act (Victoria) included a s.44 SDA 1975 Act exception equivalent, which allows exclusion of people of one sex from 'competing in a sporting activity in which the strength, stamina or physique of competitors is relevant'.[6]

> Whilst Morris, J held that this discriminatory law was valid, he did not consider there to be a relative difference between the strength, stamina and physique of boys and

girls playing Australian Rules football until the age of 14, thus this section should not be used to exclude girls aged 13 years old.

(Bradford, 2005: 79)

Bradford (2005: 79) suggests that *Taylor* and several other recent [Australian] legal decisions may indicate that the view of the judiciary towards issues of gender in sport is slowly changing from earlier notions, such as that of Lord Denning in *Bennet v Football Association*.[7] The inherently gendered notions which contribute to beliefs which frame the discriminatory Acts exceptions were all rejected by Morris J in *Taylor*. Those included beliefs that girls will get hurt, boys will modify their behaviour, it is unnatural for women to compete and women are weaker and inferior (Bradford, 2005: 79).

A series of earlier cases illustrating sports organisations engaging in sexual discrimination in relation to qualifications and authorisations or licences to compete or officiate in women only sport competitions, further exposed myths and prejudices and illustrated the limited application of s.44. In the case of *British Judo Association v Petty* [1981] ICR 660 (EAT), the British Judo Association were prepared to award a national refereeing certificate to a woman on condition that she did not actually referee men's matches. The BJA argued for a s.44 exception to the SDA 1975, on the basis that a woman would not have the strength to separate two male competitors. Lord Browne Wilkinson stated that s.44 'related to the participation of a person as a competitor in that activity'[judo] and 'we cannot see how provisions as to referees relate to the participation of the competitors in the contest'. The EAT held that the refusal to allow Petty to referee men's matches amounted to unlawful (sex) discrimination.

Jane Couch became Women's World Welterweight Boxing Champion in May 1996 and successfully defended her title twice, but all fights took place in the United States and to fight in recognised boxing contest in the UK she needed a licence from the British Boxing Board of Control (Felix, 1998: 1). Her application for a licence was refused. At the Tribunal, the BBBC reported that the refusal of a licence was based primarily on medical concerns of dangers to women's health posed by boxing. These included hormonal changes, fluid retention (affecting weight categories), premenstrual tension and emotions leading to a greater risk of accidents or injury, painful periods (where medication was banned by the sports doping rules) and the taking of contraceptive pills (also they claimed contraindicated by the rules). In addition Jane Couch was not given a medical examination.

The BBBC also argued that 'the licensing of female boxers would require a drastic change to the rules to allow the wearing of something above the waistband! In the same evidence it was said that the "man" with the most points would be the winner!' (Felix,1998: 6). The Tribunal did not view such rule changes as drastic and thought that there was 'no medical evidence to support the view that it is more dangerous for women to box than men' (Felix 1998: 6). McArdle (2000: 138) points out that:

> the House of Lords in *James v Eastleigh BC* . . . had already established that neither chivalry nor paternalism justifies sex discrimination. Even if there were any truth to the medical arguments, a desire to protect women from the consequences of an informed choice about consent and the voluntary assumption of risk provided no defence to a discrimination claim.

Appropriate rule changes had already been made in countries such as the US, Denmark, Belgium, Holland and Hungary, where women's boxing was more widely accepted

(McArdle, 2000: 138). 'The real reason for her refusal was on the grounds of sex . . . the "medical grounds" are all gender-based stereotypical assumptions [and are] not capable of amounting to valid defences to a claim of discrimination' (*Couch v British Boxing Board of Control* (unreported, 1998, Industrial Tribunal, IT No 2304231/97), cited McArdle, 2000: 138). The Board was a 'qualifying body' under the SDA 1975 Act as boxing was a profession or trade. The Tribunal concluded that there was 'incontrovertible evidence that led to only one conclusion – that Couch was treated less favourably . . . than a comparable man . . . and that such unfavourable treatment was on the grounds of her sex' (Felix 1998: 6). The refusal to grant a licence was discriminatory contrary to s.13 of the SDA 1975 (Rose and Weir, 2003: 901[8]). The s.44 exception was rejected as Jane Couch was applying for a licence to box against other women. In the Australian case of *Ferneley v Boxing Authority of New South Wales* [2001] FCA 1740,

> the law that stated only males were eligible for boxing licenses, was challenged. Although the application was eventually dismissed on the ground that it was brought in the incorrect jurisdiction, the Court examined the policy behind such a discriminatory provision.
>
> (Bradford, 2005: 80)

The rationale for the exclusion of females from obtaining a licence clearly illustrates gendered assumptions and was articulated in the court's discussion of policy in *Ferneley*. 'The spectacle of women attacking each other is simply not acceptable to the majority of people in our community . . . [there is a] risk of [women] becoming freaks in some sort of Roman circus disguised as a sporting contest' (Bradford, 2005: 80).

In the same year, an Employment Appeal Tribunal decided that Vanessa Hardwick, a school teacher and intermediate FA coach, had been a victim of direct discrimination under s.1 of the SDA Act 1975, in the treatment and circumstances which led to the FA failing her on an FA advanced coaching licence course in 1996, by a body that awarded qualifications or vocational training (see *Hardwick v Football Association* (unreported, 25 June 1999, Employment Appeal Tribunal, IT No 2200651/96), McArdle, 2000: 139–141[9]). In June 1999, Hardwick was awarded £16,000 compensation. The Tribunal also ruled that the FA should present her with her advanced coaching licence within 28 days (*The Guardian*, 29 June: 5, cited McArdle, 2000: 142). The SDA 1975 Act and the Race Relations Act 1976 did not initially contain definitions of sexual or racial harassment, so it is 'through case law that acts of harassment are deemed to constitute a detriment on the grounds of sex and race and thus unlawful direct discrimination' (Welch, 2006: 567). 'Discrimination laws protect you from harassment linked to your sex, race, disability, age, religion/belief or sexual orientation' (TUC, 2008: 139).

Race Relations Act 1976

The Race Relations Act 1976 prohibits discrimination on the grounds of colour, race, nationality or ethnic or national origins.[10] The discrimination can be direct, indirect or through harassment (s.3A). Mr Singh was withdrawn from the Football League's 'National List' of referees towards the end of the 1999 season, which meant he was not eligible to referee professional football teams.

> At this time he was the only person of Asian ethnic origin on the List. The reason given for the decision not to re-appoint him was that there had been a marked deterioration

in his position on the merit list over the previous three years. Singh denied that there had been any such deterioration in his performance and successfully claimed direct race discrimination under s.1 of the RRA against the Football League.

(*Singh v The Football League, The Football Association and others* (unreported, December 2001, ET Case No 5203953/99), cited Welch, 2006: 560)

Sports clubs who discriminate against contract workers, employees and those applying for employment are treated like any other employer, and in *Sterling v Leeds Rugby League Club* [2001] ILSR 201, Mr Sterling was successful in his claim for 'race discrimination against the club and its coach following the club's decision that he would not be selected for the first team, apparently irrespective of his performance during the season' and was 'awarded £10,000 for injury to feelings' (Rose and Weir, 2003: 901[11]). Discrimination by way of victimisation occurs when a person is treated less favourably, not on the grounds of his or her race or sex, but because he or she has raised an issue of concern – made or is about to make a complaint about the racial or sexual discrimination.

James Hussaney was an apprentice player at Chester City FC. In January 1997 when he was due to play for the reserves along with the first team manager, Kevin Ratcliffe. 'As part of his duties Hussaney was required to change the studs on Ratcliffe's boots, but, despite being told what to do, he fitted then wrongly. Ratcliffe angrily shouted, "Where's James, the black cunt?"' (McArdle, 2000: 114). Hussaney made an informal complaint to the club and a few months later the club informed him he would not be offered a professional contract, 'following discussions between Ratcliffe, the youth team coach and the assistant manager, about his merits as a player' (McArdle, 2000: 114). Hussaney brought an action before an industrial tribunal that 'both the words used and the failure to offer him a contract were acts of direct racial discrimination' (McArdle, 2000: 114). The tribunal held that the abusive language 'amounted to discrimination by both Ratcliffe and the club on the grounds of race and made a compensatory award of £2,500 for injury to feelings' (Welch, 2006: 568). The initial tribunal rejected the claim that the decision not to offer Hussaney a professional contract was victimisation as a result of his informal complaint, concluding that the decision was based on 'purely footballing grounds' (Welch, 2006: 568).

In January 2001, the Employment Appeal Tribunal upheld Hussaney's appeal. In the view of the EAT the original tribunal had erred by providing sufficient reasons as to why it had reached the conclusion that there was no unlawful unconscious motivation and remitted the case to the Tribunal for rehearing (see Rose and Weir, 2003: 895; Welch, 2006: 568). In the case of *Burton v De Vere Hotels* [1997] ICR 1 (EAT), an employer, a hotel chain, was held liable for the racial abuse of third parties, when the hotel management failed to protect black staff from racist 'jokes' told by a comedian by, for example, withdrawing them from the function, during Bernard Manning's after-dinner speech. The employer was seen to have a degree of control over a situation such that it could have taken steps to protect employees from third party abuse but failed to do so (Welch, 2006: 570). The decision in *Burton v De Vere Hotels Ltd* was later disapproved in the House of Lords in *Macdonald v Atourney-General for Scotland; Pearce v Governing Body of Mayfield School* [2003] UKHL 34; [2004] 1 All ER 339, where they held that an employer 'can only be held liable for third party harassment where the failure to protect the employee is itself racially motivated' (Welch, 2006: 570).

EXERCISE 5.1

What are the three categories of discrimination arising out of the Sex Discrimination Act 1975 and related or updated statutes or regulations? Which groups of people, in particular, does the SDA 1975 Act aim to protect?

EXERCISE 5.2

Explain the grounds on which James Eastleigh won his case for direct discrimination, contrary to the SDA 1975 Act, in relation to the price he was charged by a local council, to use their swimming pool.

EXERCISE 5.3

What is indirect discrimination? Give an example of indirect discrimination in a sport or physical education context.

EXERCISE 5.4

In pairs, each identify one Genuine Occupational Qualification in a sport or physical education context which would be an acceptable exception to the SDA 1975 and explain it to your partner.

EXERCISE 5.5

What is the s.44 exemption rule in the SDA 1975 Act? Critically discuss the application of s.44 in the football case of *Bennet v Football Association* (unreported, 1978, Court of Appeal).

EXERCISE 5.6

Is s.44 applicable to a female refereeing a male judo contest? Explain your answer with support from a referenced case.

EXERCISE 5.7

Jane Couch won her case against the British Boxing Board of Control (BBBC) for sex discrimination, contrary to s.13 of the SDA 1975. Summarise and critically analyse the arguments put forward by the BBBC relating to medical issues, risks and rule changes. Why were they rejected by the Tribunal? Is s.44 applicable to women boxing women?

EXERCISE 5.8

Read McArdle (2000: 139–142) or access the case on Lawtel/Westlaw UK and explain why Vanessa Hardwick won her case of direct discrimination against the Football Association, after they failed her on an advanced coaching licence course in 1996.

EXERCISE 5.9

Explain one of the following cases with reference to the Race Relations Act 1976:

1 *Singh v The Football League, The Football Association and others* (unreported, December 2001, ET Case No 5203953/99).
2 *Hussaney v Chester City FC and Ratcliffe* (unreported, 15 January 2001, Employment Appeal Tribunal, EAT/203/908, Charles J).

EXERCISE 5.10

What does the case of *Burton v De Vere Hotels* [1997] ICR 1 (EAT) establish in relation to the liability of employers for the discrimination by third parties under the Race Relations Act 1976? How was the test revised in *McDonald v AG for Scotland*; *Pearce v Governing Body of Mayfield School* [2003] UKHL 34; [2004] 1 All ER 339?

Disability Discrimination Act 1995, 2004

Under the Disability Discrimination Act 1995 it is unlawful to discriminate against a disabled person by way of less favourable treatment, by way of a failure to make reasonable adjustments, and by victimisation. A disabled person is someone with a disability. A disability is a physical or mental impairment, which has a substantial and long-term adverse effect on his/her ability to carry out normal day-to-day activities and now includes progressive illnesses such as cancer or those controlled by medication (Russell et al., 2008d).[12] In the Australian case of *Hall v Victorian Amateur Football Association* [1999] VCAT 627 an Australian Rules Football club refused to allow a player to register because he had an HIV-positive status. The Victorian Civil and Administrative Tribunal found the club had unlawfully discriminated against Hall, the player, by treating him less favourably due to his disability.

The key requirements of the Disability Discrimination Act 1995 (Part III) were implemented in England and Wales over three key dates. In December 1996 it was unlawful for service providers to treat disabled people less favourably for a reason related to their disability. In October 1999 service providers have had to make:

'reasonable adjustments' for disabled people, such as providing extra help or making changes to the way they provide services. In October 2004, service providers may have to make other 'reasonable adjustments' to overcome physical barriers to access.

(CCPR, 2008: 1, Disability Discrimination Act at
http://ccpr.org.uk/ accessed 11 July 2008)

Part III does not apply to private clubs, but most voluntary sports clubs are likely to be viewed as providing a service under the Act (CCPR, 2008: 1). There is now no exclusion for small employers (Russell et al., 2008d). Driver (2005) highlights the need for London's facilities for the Paralympics in 2012 to be fully accessible to disabled athletes in relation to the obligation under the DDA 1995, for service providers to make 'reasonable adjustments' to premises, and transport and accommodation considerations. The Disability Discrimination Act was significantly extended in 2005, covering rights for disabled people in the areas of employment, education, access to goods, facilities and services, including larger private clubs and transport services, buying or renting land or property and the functions of public bodies, such as the issuing of licences (see www.direct.gov.uk, accessed 17 July 2008).

In Australia, in 2000, a disabled spectator with eyesight difficulties, who was passionate about following the Olympics, was unable to read reports or order tickets online due to the inaccessibility of the Sydney Olympics website. He was successful in bringing a case of discrimination against the Sydney Olympics Organising Committee in 2000 (see *Maguire v Sydney Organising Committee for the Olympic Games* (unreported, 18 October 1999, Human Right and Equal Opportunities Commission, No H 99/115)).

In the United States a very important case was brought against the Professional Golf Association (PGA) Tour Inc by a disabled golfer Casey Martin. The Americans with Disabilities Act 1990 requires covered businesses to make reasonable modifications to policies, practices or procedures as are necessary to afford goods, services and privileges to individuals with disabilities; but explicitly does not require modifications that would fundamentally alter the nature of the goods, services and privileges. Would allowing a disabled golfer, with a vascular disease, to use a cart to get round a golf course, alter the nature of golf? In May 2001, the US Supreme Court held that the PGA was:

required to allow a competitor with a circulatory disorder to use a golf cart on its tours and in qualifying. The PGA accepted that allowing Martin to use a golf cart was a necessary modification, but contended that it would alter an essential aspect of the game, and was therefore not an adjustment that was required. The Supreme Court held that the adjustment was reasonable, on the basis that there was nothing in the Rules of Golf that required players to walk the course. Golf was a game in which it was impossible to guarantee that all players would play under exactly the same conditions in any event, and Martin endured greater fatigue than his fellow-competitors even using a golf-cart.

(Rose and Weir, 2003: 898[13])

In July 2008 the European Court of Justice upheld an earlier opinion that treating employees less favourably because of their association with a disabled person was unlawful. Sharon Coleman, the mother of a disabled child, was 'forced to resign from her job as a legal secretary, after, she claims, being harassed by her employers and refused flexible working, which was allowed to other employees', and her case was referred back to a tribunal in 2008 (Equality and Human Rights Commission, 2008[14]). As a result of this decision in the European Court of Justice, those caring for elderly relatives are protected under age discrimination regulations (Equality and Human Rights Commission, 2008).

This case was supported by the Equality and Human Rights Commission, whose legal director, John Wadham, has commented:

> This is a very significant case, which has led to new rights for Britain's millions of carers, sixty per cent of whom are women. In this day and age people increasingly have to balance caring responsibilities with work and it is vitally important that they are able to do so without being discriminated against or even forced out of the workforce.
>
> ('Commission supports carer to win rights for millions' at
> www.equalityhumanrights.com, accessed 18 July 2008)

In May 2008 Oscar Pistorius, a South African athlete (a double-amputee) and winner of the Paralympics 400m track event, in 2004, used the Court of Arbitration of Sport Appeal Panel to successfully challenge the IAAF decision to ban him from competing with able bodied athletes in international athletics competitions. The IAAF argued that he allegedly had an unfair advantage, compared to able-bodies athletes, in using his cheetah prosthetics as outlined in Chapter 8 of this text. The CAS decision had limited application (it was only applicable to Oscar Pistorius and only to his cheetah prosthetics). At some point, a similar case could arrive in the civil courts outside 'the family of sport' processes, which tests the laws of disability discrimination on an eligibility matter, in the relevant jurisdiction.

Discrimination on grounds of sexuality

A high profile case in the European Court of Human Rights triggered a change in the law making discrimination on the grounds of sexual orientation unlawful. In the case of *Lustig-Prean and Beckett v the United Kingdom* [1999] ECHR 71; (2000) 29 EHRR 548 ruled that it was contrary to Article 8 of the ECHR to discharge individuals from the Royal Navy on the sole ground that they were homosexuals. 'As a result of this decision it has become impossible for any clubs to argue that discrimination against a gay player is justified by reference to the reaction of his team-mates or the club's supporters' (Welch, 2006: 572). The Framework Directive 2000/78/EC, from the European Council, which requires member states to 'take measures to outlaw discrimination in employment, promotion, access to vocational training and working conditions, on the grounds of religious belief, disability, age and sexual orientation' (Rose and Weir, 2003: 892), was implemented in the United Kingdom in December 2003.

In December 2003, The Employment Equality (Sexual Orientation) Regulations 2003 made it unlawful to discriminate directly or indirectly against a person by less favourable treatment or harassment on the grounds of a person's sexual orientation (see Welch, 2006: 573). It is noted that 'any dismissal on the grounds of sexual orientation would be an unfair dismissal under the Employment Rights Act. A player who resigns in response to being subjected to homophobia at the workplace will succeed in a claim for constructive and wrongful or unfair dismissal' (Welch, 2006: 573). 'The Equality (Sexual Orientation (Regulations) 2007 make it unlawful for a person providing goods, facilities and services to members of the public to discriminate against anyone on the grounds of sexual orientation' (Russell et al., 2008b: 1). This includes discriminating by less favourable treatment of someone not on the grounds of their own sexual orientation but someone else's; for example, towards a parent on the grounds of their son's homosexuality. It also includes treating someone less favourably because of 'perceived sexual orientation' (ibid: 1).

Gender Recognition Act 1999, 2004

The Gender Recognition Act 2004 came into effect on 4 April 2005 and provides for the first time, full legal recognition of transsexual people (Russell et al., 2008e: 1). It enables transsexual people to register and gain full recognition in their acquired gender (surgical intervention is not a prerequisite). Individuals must have lived in an acquired gender for two years to gain a new birth certificate and are entitled to privacy and to marry. Exceptions for sport under s.19 allow prohibition only if the sport is a 'gender affected' one, and the prohibition is on the grounds of fair competition or the safety of competitors. This refers back to the principles in s.44 of the Sex Discrimination Act 1975 and each case is to be judged on its own merit. UK law takes precedence for international events taking place in the United Kingdom. The IOC consensus in May 2004 agreed that sex reassignment before puberty would be recognised for competition.

Sex reassignment after puberty would be recognised for competition if surgical anatomical changes were completed, there was legal recognition of the acquired sex, with appropriate hormonal treatment (verifiable and sufficient length of time), and a minimum period of two years after a gonadectomy (Talbot, 2006: 4). The challenges of the Gender Recognition Act 2004 for sport include a probable return to gender verification, assumptions that only international competition would be affected (see also Donnellan, 2008), effects on goods and services including access to changing rooms, sex/gender conceptual confusion and pre/post-puberty 'advantages' likely to lead to appeals and the whole basis of single-sex competition being open to question, which could affect access (Talbot, 2006: 4).

Harassment

Every individual has the right to be free from harassment. Harassment is variously defined in organisational or institutional policy documents on harassment. Harassment is defined in The Employment Equality (Sexual Orientation) Regulations 2003 as 'where A engages in unwanted conduct which violates B's dignity or creating an intimidating, hostile, degrading, humiliating or offensive environment for B', if it was reasonable for such conduct to be perceived as having that effect, in the circumstances. Policies often include personal harassment, sexual harassment, harassment on the grounds of race, sexuality, gender, or harassment arising out of an employee or member raising an issue of concern in the organisation. Harassment is normally linked to other terms such as bullying, victimisation and discrimination.

The Protection from Harassment Act 1997 was originally drafted to criminalise stalking, which was not covered adequately by existing legislation. It is unlawful under this Act for a person to pursue a course of conduct which amounts to harassment of another and which [he] knows amounts to the harassment of another (s.1). Such harassment includes speech, causing a person alarm or distress, on at least two occasions. Under s.2 a person found guilty of this criminal offence is liable on summary conviction to imprisonment for a term not exceeding six months or a fine or both. Civil remedies can also be sought by the victim, in the county or high court, in terms of damages for, among other things, anxiety caused by harassment or financial loss arising from harassment. If convicted of s.4 offence of pursuing a course of conduct which causes another person to fear, on at least two occasions, that violence will be used against him, a person could face, on indictment, a prison sentence of up to five years, (or a fine) or on summary conviction a term not exceeding six months.

In June 2006 the House of Lords held in the case of *Majrowski v Guys and St Thoma's NHS Trust* [2006] UKHL 34; [2007] 1 AC 224 that the Protection from Harassment Act 1997 applied to bullying and harassment in the workplace. The court heard that the claimant, Mr Majrowski, a researcher at the NHS Trust, was harassed by his line manager on the grounds of his homosexuality. He was awarded damages. In the case of *Conn v Sunderland County Council* [2007] EWCA Civ 1492, the Court of Appeal decided that a judge had 'erred in holding that two incidents of threatening behaviour by one employee of a local authority against another constituted a course of action amounting to harassment under the Protection from Harassment Act 1997, since one of the incidents was not serious enough to amount to harassment' (www.lawtel.com, accessed 19 June 2008). There was no physical threat and the conduct did not meet the threshold for conduct that justified a criminal sanction and could not amount to harassment (see also Addison, 2008; Hogarth, 2005).

EXERCISE 5.11

What are the three ways in which discrimination can occur under the Disability Discrimination Act 1995? What was added to the Disability Discrimination Act in 2005?

EXERCISE 5.12

Explain the legal definition of disability. How has it been revised and why?

EXERCISE 5.13

On what grounds was an Australian Rules football club found by a Tribunal in 1999 to have discriminated against one of its players?

EXERCISE 5.14

What can Olympic Organising Committees learn from the case of *Maguire v Sydney Organising Committee for the Olympic Games* (unreported, 18 October 1999, Human Right and Equal Opportunities Commission, No H 99/115)?

EXERCISE 5.15

Although cases in the United States are not precedents for Anglo-Welsh law or other jurisdictions, the situation and principles of the case of *PGA Tour Inc v Martin* 532 US 661 (2001) could arise in any sport, in other jurisdictions, related to similar statutes on disability discrimination. What were the key legal issues and decision by the Supreme Court in this very high profile golfing case?

EXERCISE 5.16

What did the European Court of Justice decide in July 1998, in relation to discrimination against a carer of a disabled person? Explain your answer with support from a referenced case or source.

EXERCISE 5.17

Does the Protection from Harassment Act 1997 apply to harassment in the workplace? Make up a sport or physical education workplace scenario which would meet the requirements of this Act, drawing on the 1997 Act and relevant case law.

Part two: child protection in sport and recreation

Child abuse

'Defining child abuse is a complex and difficult process and one which causes much professional debate' (Myers and Barrett, 2002: 16). The definitions used by the Department of Health (1999) and the CPSU have been adopted by most organisations in the UK. A child includes anyone under the age of 18, who is suffering or likely to suffer significant harm. 'Child abuse is any form of physical, emotional or sexual mistreatment or lack of care which leads to injury or harm' (CPSU definitions of child abuse). The CPSU, the DOH (1999), Myers and Barrett (2002), and the CCPR identify four main types of child abuse: physical, sexual, emotional and neglect. Physical abuse involves adults or other young people who might physically hurt or injure a child by hitting, shaking, throwing, poisoning, burning, drowning or suffocating.

Sexual abuse involves 'forcing or enticing a child to take part in sexual activities, whether or not they are aware of what is happening' (Myers and Barrett, 2002: 17). This includes rape, incest and all forms of sexual activity involving children, including sexual intercourse, oral sex, anal intercourse, masturbation, fondling, showing children pornography, prostitution or talking to them in a sexually explicit manner (DOH, 1999; CPSU, 2008; Myers and Barrett, 2002). Emotional abuse covers persistent emotional ill-treatment of a child which is likely to cause serious and lasting adverse effects to a child's emotional development (DOH, 1999; Myers and Barrett, 2002; CPSU, 2008). Emotional abuse can include bullying, racist and sexist remarks, isolation or exclusion, the use of sarcasm, being shouted at, threatened or taunted, causing a child to feel frightened or in danger or feel very nervous or withdrawn (CPSU, 2008).

Neglect is a persistent failure by an adult or carer to meet a child's basic physical and/or psychological needs, to an extent it is likely to result in serious impairment of a child's health and development. For example, failing to provide adequate food, shelter and clothing or refusing to give love, affection and attention or protect a child from physical harm or danger or access to medical care (DOH, 1999; Myers and Barrett, 2002; CPSU, 2008). Examples of neglect in sport could include failure to ensure a safe environment, exposure to unreasonable or unnecessary risks, exposure to extreme heat or cold. 'Distinguishing whether bad coaching practice has caused physical injury or emotional harm and should therefore be categorised as an act of abuse rather than an educational issue was and is a particularly difficult area for sport to address' (Myers and Barrett, 2002: 17; see also David, 2004). Brackenridge points out that:

> even though these behaviours may be defined *objectively* it is important to recognise that they may be experienced *subjectively*. Thus the personal and psychological impact of the same behaviour may be vastly different depending on the individual athlete's background and perceptions.
>
> (2001: 28)

Kelly et al. (1995), and Brackenridge (2001) support the use of the concept of 'sexual exploitation' rather than sexual abuse, as an overarching term which includes a range of activities from verbal harassment, sexual harassment, to rape. Having the rules, commitment and culture in a sport organisation to challenge unacceptable behaviour at the lower end of the continuum can prevent or at least alert the officials to the problem before the abuser gains confidence and moves up the sexual exploitation continuum.

Research into sexual exploitation in sport

> Sport is a practice embedded in social and cultural systems (Gruneau 1999) and so there are multiple stakeholders in any sexually exploitative situation [see figure 4.1. in Brackenridge, 2001: 44]. These include not just the athlete and her coach but also sport organisations, the police, child protection and legal agencies, other coaches, peer athletes, siblings and parents. All may contribute to the instigation, continuation or termination of sexually transgressive behaviour in sport and all bear some responsibility for this.
>
> (Brackenridge, 2001: 44)

Which groups are represented in the research or case law? Where are the gaps? What is the nature and extent of the problem? Which participants, in which contexts, are most at risk? What is the profile of the abusers or likely abusers? What is the role and significance of power relations (or perceptions of power), and the subculture of an organisation, sports club or even a group of athletes and their coach? What are the implications of such research for the statutory duties and procedures of risk assessment covered in Chapter 6 of this text, or the framing and application of disciplinary procedures covered in Chapter 8?

Brackenridge (2001; see also for example, Brackenridge et al., 2007; Brackenridge 1997) is the leading authority on sexual exploitation in sport, drawing on over 15 years of research. The text deals with definitions and past research, pioneering primary research with survivors of sexual abuse in sport, theorising around power, masculinity and sexualised subworlds. It develops models around the cycle of sex offending, risk factors for sexual exploitation at the levels of athlete, coach and sports organisation. The critical analysis of official responses leads into the final section (rarely included in research texts) on actually making policy work and the challenges facing sports organisations in addressing sexual exploitation in sport. In 2002 the NSPCC published a report, *In at the Deep End*, which analysed the case files on 78 coaches accused of abuse of children (aged 1–17 years old) over a four-year period, which had been provided by the Amateur Swimming Association in the United Kingdom. The report revealed that:

> In cases of sexual abuse there is a process of grooming swimmers, club officials and parents, conducted by coaches who manipulate the respect they have to gain control, allowing abuse to continue uninterrupted for years. They found that sexual abuse accounted for 68 per cent of the referrals in this study. The risk of abuse appears to increase just before young athletes reach their best performance level. The rationale is that at this stage they have the most to lose and are therefore the most vulnerable. Tolerating violent behaviour of a coach or teacher that produces results can become an acceptable part of the swimming training routine.
>
> (NSPCC, 2002: 1)

Common agreement on the nature and extent of sexual exploitation is affected by variations in definitions, sources of reports, sampling, or the aim of a study. Results can also be affected by going through intermediaries, the method and questions used, the problems of under-reporting, non-response and issues around validity and reliability (Brackenridge, 2001: 49–50). Despite these limitations, research can provide some guidance for risk assessment at an individual and organisational level. Participants in sports where less clothing is worn are not considered to be at a greater risk of sexual exploitation than other sports (for example, Fasting et al., 1999, cited Brackenridge, 2001: 60).

Moving further away from regulated sports or taking part in individual sports or engaging in 'masculine sports' can lead to a greater risk of sexual exploitation or harassment (see, for example, Fasting et al., 2000, cited Brackenridge, 2001, and Myers and Barrett, 2002). Although fewer athletes over the age of 16 report sexual harassment, it is the *level of performance* which appears to indicate a more significant risk of exposure to a range of activities on the sexual exploitation continuum, including sexual abuse. Male or female athletes, at or just about to enter the very highest elite levels of performance (World Championships and Olympic Games), have been found to be at greater risk than those participating at a recreational level (see, for example, Netherlands Olympic Committee, 1997; Cense 1997; Fasting et al., 2000, cited Brackenridge, 2001, and Myers and Barrett, 2002). Brackenridge and Kirkby (1997) suggested that there is 'a particular risk of sexual abuse associated with early-peaking sports amongst those *just below* the top level, especially where this coincides with puberty. They call this the Stage of Imminent Achievement' (cited Brackenridge, 2001: 59). Leahy (2001) found that 'nearly 50 per cent of elite athletes in their study experienced sexual abuse in sport, compared to just over 25 per cent of the club athletes' (cited Myers and Barrett, 2002: 10). This group should be central in the risk management lens of a sport organisation.

Disabled athletes are considered to be at an increased risk (see Westcott, 1993; Morris 1998). This may be partly due their dependency on support needs, where they may learn to comply more readily, which makes them more susceptible to abuse (Kerr, 1999). Such risks reflect research findings in the generic context of residential homes (Westcott and Clement, 1992; Morris, 1998). Studies found that children with disabilities in the US are 3.8 times more likely to be physically abused and 3.1 times more likely to be sexually abused (Sullivan and Knutson, 2000, cited Russell, 2007). Russell (2007: 149) observes that it is worth noting that 'not all disabled people are vulnerable, or perceive themselves to be so, and that not all vulnerable people are disabled . . . as researchers we have to be wary of simply aligning an increase in risk of abuse with a person's dis/ability without first considering the context of the situation'.

Who are the perpetrators in the sport context? Children are more likely to be abused by people they know and trust. Sixty-eight per cent of the abusers on the Myers and Barrett (2002) study in swimming were in the category of club coach or swimming teacher; 85 per cent were male and only 10 per cent were female, supporting the findings of Cawson (2000). There is some 'growing evidence of abuse by females although the prevalence rates are extremely low' and the 'huge majority of abusers are men and prosecutions are almost exclusively of men'[15] (Matthews et al., 1989; Elliott et al., 1995; Lancaster, 1996; Grubin, 1998, cited Brackenridge 2001: 53). Perpetrators in sport can include peer athletes, college or professional athletes, coaches, teachers, community leaders, boys clubs, scout leaders and care workers. There are many theoretical approaches to classifying, labelling, profiling and explaining perpetrators of sexual abuse and over 50 subtypes of rapists alone in the literature (see Kelly, 1988, cited by Brackenridge, 2001).

Research on the profiles of abusers challenges the picture of the socially isolated, 'demon', or stranger and commonly identifies perpetrators in sport contexts as male, holding respected positions of authority, often married. Brackenridge (2001) distinguishes a sexual 'predator' from a 'paedophile'. The 'predator' has a good self-image and personal skills, expects approval or acceptance, seeks a public profile, is assertive, assumes superiority, has sexual confidence, has increased sense of control and self-confidence (see figure 6.3, Brackenridge, 2001: 108; Brackenridge, 1997a). 'Many accounts of sexual exploitation collected by sports researchers indicate that the abusers' feeling of power and control arise from confidence and feelings of superiority, rather than as a response to lack of success and feelings of resentment' (Kirkby and Greaves, 1996; Brackenridge, 1997b; Cense, 1997; Toftegaard, 1998).

> Many of the guys who molested me, are very nice guys, they're successful, they're upstanding citizens in the community, according to male standards, so they don't look sleazy, they don't look like what we think of as a rapist even though they are – it is statutory rape.
>
> (Female survivor of sexual abuse, Brackenridge, 2001: 109)

Some of the most important theoretical lenses which help to understand layers of risk and the lack of action or resistance to sexual exploitation including sexual abuse of children and young people over many years include notions of power, masculinity, grooming, organisational subcultures or 'sub-worlds' (Brackenridge, 2001). Sources of power which can be used by a coach or teacher in sport are wide-ranging and include expert power, referent power, legitimate power, coercive power, charismatic or personal power, positional power, reward power, resource power and relationship power (see French and Raven, 1959; Tomlinson and Strachan, 1996, adapted by Brackenridge, 2001: 83). The same stories and quotes from research interviews regularly illustrate the ways in which sports coaches who abuse children and young people make use of, in particular, reward power, coercive power, legitimate power and charismatic power in interactions with both athlete and parents:

> Drew's success in grooming his victims and their families illustrates the power a coach has.

One coach was actually supported by them against the actions of the statutory bodies, even when examples of the abuse were known. He had been seen to have successfully cultivated the parents' trust to a level where they had unquestioning loyalty to him.

We knew that he had it in his power to give and take away his dream . . . James took advantage of both the child's and parent's wishes for success to fulfil his own sexual desire and fantasies . . . getting into the team was so important that they agreed to do anything that James requested.

(Myers and Barrett, 2002: 21–26)

'People in positions of power with the motivation to abuse will always try to take advantage of a parent/carer's wish for their child to succeed' (Myers and Barrett, 2002: 26). Challenging such notions of the indispensability of such a sports coach, is central to encouraging athletes, peers, other coaches and parents to blow the whistle on child abuse in sport. It may also have resource implications if a sports governing body needs to have a 'reserve' of coaches at each level who can promptly take the place of a coach who might have been suspended or convicted of an offence.

In 1999, in Australia, Brett Sutton, a triathlon coach at elite level, admitted in court to five sexual offences against teenage swimmers in his care, which occurred in the late 1980s.

The judge, despite saying that Sutton had 'interfered with her sexually in a gross and disgraceful way' and 'abused [his] role to an inexcusable degree' passed down a two-year sentence which was suspended because 'a large number of leading athletes will suffer disadvantage from your absence from the scene'.

(Downes, 2002)

Normalising unacceptable behaviour located at any point on the sexual exploitation continuum (Brackenridge, 2001) within the sports club or sports organisational culture can allow the abuser to move his behaviour incrementally to the next level without being challenged by athletes, coaches or parents. The theoretical lens on power, subcultures or 'sub-worlds', the socialisation or normalisation of unacceptable behaviour, covered in Chapter 4 in this text in relation to sports field violence and in Brackenridge (2001, chapters five and six), provide a critical and relevant lens which can provide better risk assessment of sexual exploitation.

Revised risk factors for sexual abuse in sport by Brackenridge (2001: 136) cover the coach, the athlete and the sport (both normative and constitutive organisational culture). A sports governing body can have perfectly constructed and well-publicised child protection/safeguarding policies, or codes of practice. These will have little or no effect as long as there is no understanding of or will to address kinds of power discussed earlier and perceptions of the 'indispensibility' of a sports coach, or the complicity or normalisation of unacceptable behaviour within the club or organisational subculture.

EXERCISE 5.18

What is child abuse? In groups of four, break it down into four main categories and each explain one category. Find out why there has been a move from the use of the term 'child protection' to 'safeguarding children' in the UK, with reference to Brackenridge et al., 2007.

EXERCISE 5.19

Is it useful to use a broader, overarching continuum of 'sexual exploitation' in sport and physical education? Explain your answer with reference to Brackenridge (2001).

EXERCISE 5.20

Critically examine the possible relationship between bad coaching practice and the notion of neglect with reference to the work of Myers and Barrett (2002).

EXERCISE 5.21

With support from relevant research, assess if the following statements are true or false:

1   There is a greater risk of sexual abuse in sports such as swimming or gymnastics as they wear less clothing in training and competition than other sports.
2   Sexual harassment is greater in 'masculine' sports than in those regarded as traditionally feminine with less clothing.
3   The risk of sexual abuse is greatest in athletes in puberty who are just about to enter top level elite sport.
4   Those in individual sports or moving further away from regulated sports are not at a greater risk of sexual exploitation.
5   Disabled athletes are not at a greater risk of sexual abuse than able–bodied athletes.
6   The majority of perpetrators of sexual abuse are female.

EXERCISE 5.22

What is the difference between a 'paedophile' and a 'predator' (Brackenridge 2001)? Explain why the latter is unlikely to be 'in the radar' of the Protection of Children Act 1999.

EXERCISE 5.23

What is meant by the terms *reward power, coercive power, legitimate power* and *charismatic power*? How might these be used by a sports coach or Physical Education teacher or sports leader, along with an organisational or club subculture or subworld, to continue to sexually harass or abuse sports participants without being exposed or challenged?

EXERCISE 5.24

Critically discuss how research into sexual exploitation or child abuse in sport and physical recreation and an appreciation of power and subcultures might inform statutory risk assessment duties covered in Chapter 6.

Criminal offences: overview of relevant statutes and illustrative cases in sport

The NSPCC confirmed that at least 20 British sporting governing bodies are dealing with cases of child abuse. 'We know abuse can occur in any setting where people have access to children' says Kirsty Kinane of the NSPCC. 'The sheer numbers involved in sport in this country means that statistically there are bound to be adults who want to use sport to gain access to children to abuse them.'

(Stephen Downes, 2002)

There have been several high-profile criminal cases in several countries of sports coaches including Paul Hickson, Mike Drew and Matthew Pedrazzini in swimming in England, Derry O'Rourke, in the Republic of Ireland, Graham Jones in ice hockey in Canada, Brett Sutton in triathlon in Australia, Bernard Smith in football, Martin Clarke in tennis, Martin Saunders in archery, Joseph Griffin in karate (see Brackenridge and Williams, 2004).

In 1995 Paul Hickson, a former swimming coach, was jailed for 17 years after a jury found him guilty of 15 charges, including two of raping teenage swimmers under his care, relating to sexual offences committed against swimmers in his Norwich and Swansea squads between 1976 and 1991. 'The story of Hickson's abuse of power over 15 years, including stripping, fondling, whipping and rape of young girls still affects anyone who regularly hands over the care of their child for expert tuition' (Myers and Barrett, 2002: 4). Mike Drew, the former British Team Coach and President of the Association of British Swimming Coaches at the time, made the following comments after Hickson was jailed in 1995. 'The Hickson case did a lot of damage to our profession. Now we have to establish a procedure that will make it easier for suspicions to be dealt with' (cited in Myers and Barrett, 2002: 22).

In June 2001, Mike Drew was sentenced to eight years in prison for ten offences of indecent assault on swimmers between the ages of 13 and 15 over a period of 30 years. These comments above, made by Mike Drew, and his involvement in processes to address child abuse in swimming, following the Paul Hickson case:

are an example of the certainty he felt that his own abusing would not be exposed. His position and condemnation of Hickson made it all the harder for his victims to come forward and make allegations against him . . . the similarities in behaviour and perceived status of the abuser in sport, to those adults who perpetrated the abuse of children in residential care, cannot be ignored.

(Myers and Barrett, 2002: 22)

The last time I saw my old swimming coach, he was on *Crimewatch*.[16] In summer 2001, Mike Drew became the latest high-profile sports coach to be sentenced to a long prison term for sexually abusing children who had been put in his trust. The offences involved five boys, aged between 13 and 15, and ranged back over 30 years.

(Stephen Downes, 2002)

In August 2002, Matthew Pedrazzini, a former Olympic swimming coach, was jailed for 15 months, for one count of indecent assault and four counts of unlawful sexual intercourse with a minor, a 15-year-old swimmer under his care. He had also pleaded guilty to 11 charges of possession of indecent images. Pedrazzini was also placed on the sex offenders list for ten years.

The Sexual Offences (Amendment) Act 2000, among other things, made it an offence for a person aged 18 or over to engage in sexual activity with, or directed towards, a person under that age if he is in a position of trust in relation to that person. Section 3 states that it shall be an offence for a person 18 or over to have sexual intercourse (whether vaginal or anal) with a person under that age or to engage in any other sexual activity with or directed towards such a person, if (in either case) he is in a position of trust in relation to that person (see Brackenridge and Williams, 2004b). In relation to the Sexual Offences Act 1956, the age of consent to homosexual sexual acts in private was reduced to 16 in England and Wales. 'Although the age of consent to sexual activity is 16, in position of trust offences consent cannot be given until the age of 18' (e-mail communication from Yvonne Williams to the author, 19 September 2008). In the consultation process in 2005, Williams argued that:

> any sexual activity between a coach and a 16 or 17 year-old trainee is inappropriate because of the considerable doubts as to whether consent is freely given or not. The reference to 'consensual' sexual activity in q.2. suggests that, regardless of what is said in the *Guidance* (1999), and by those with first hand experience of sexual abuse in sport, for the Government in 2005, sexual activity between a coach and a 16 or 17 year old trainee is 'consensual'.
>
> (2005: 4)

The Sexual Offences Act 2003 includes a wide range of offences such as:

- Rape (s.1)
- Assault by penetration (s.2)
- Sexual assault (s.3) was repealed in this form
- Causing a person to engage in sexual activity without consent (s.4)
- Rape of a child under 13 (s.5)
- Assault of a child under 13 by penetration (s.6)
- Sexual assault of a child under 13 (s.7)
- Causing or inciting a child under 13 to engage in sexual activity (s.8)
- Sexual activity with a child (s.9)
- Engaging in sexual activity in the presence of child (s.11)
- Child sexual offences committed by children or young persons (s.13)
- Meeting a child following sexual grooming (s.15)
- Abuse of position of trust in relation to a range of sexual offences above (s.16–19)
- Positions of trust are covered in s.21.
- Marriage exceptions are covered in s.22, 23
- S.24 covers predating and positions of trust exceptions
- Sexual activity with a child family member (familial child sex offences) (s.25, 26[17])
- Sex with an adult relative (s.64–65)
- A range of similar sexual offences against persons with a mental disorder (s.30–44)
- Indecent photographs of children (s.45, 46)
- Abuse of children through prostitution and pornography (s.47–51).

In November 2007, Clare Lyte, a tennis coach, was found guilty at Liverpool Crown Court, of five counts of sexual activity with a child, under s.9. of the Sexual Offences Act 2003.

The court heard in evidence from the child's mother that she returned home early from a party in October 2005, to find her 13-year-old daughter and her tennis coach naked in bed. Miss Lyte had already received a previous warning from the Lawn Tennis Association about her behaviour towards the girl. The court also heard from the mother in evidence that in August 2006, when her daughter was being dropped off at a motorway services following a tennis tournament, Clare Lyte emerged with 'my daughters clothes. My stomach turned' (Sanderson, 2007). Soon after this the child's mother reported matters to the police. When police searched Clare Lyte's home they found a pink jumper, a jacket and also a pair of pink knickers with the teenager's name tag in them.

Legal frameworks and key guidance documents: child protection/safeguarding children in sport

Child protection policies in sport must 'sit within the legal framework of the key legislative guidance' (Myers and Barrett, 2002: 5). The key document by the DOH (1999), *Working Together to Safeguard Children*, states that 'cultural and leisure services, including organisations involved in sport, should have child protection procedures in place. There should be clear referral when concerns arise' as well as adequate training, working practices and codes of conduct to minimise child abuse. Under The Children Act 1989, local authorities within the UK have a statutory duty to ensure the welfare of children and are responsible for establishing an Area Child Protection Committee. ACPCs (or Area Safeguarding Boards) are expected to take the lead role in ensuring that all local agencies work together to safeguard children and provide local inter-agency guidelines and procedures. Any child protection policies or procedures in sport or physical education need to be compatible with ACPC policies and procedures.

Legislation such as the Protection of Children Act 1999 and the Criminal Justice and Court Services Act 2000 cover the recruitment and vetting of staff (and volunteers) to prevent unsuitable people from working with children. The Protection of Children Act 1999 came into force in 2000. It requires all regulated childcare organisations to refer the names of those individuals who fulfil certain criteria making them unsuitable to work with children for possible inclusion in the PoCA List (List 99). Under this statutory duty they are required to check the names of prospective employees against the list (through a now centralised Criminal Records Bureau[18]) before offering employment (Department for Education and Skills, 2005).

There are, however, many organisations outside the regulated sector including sporting and leisure groups where activities are undertaken by children. The NSPCC and the CPSU advise 'other organisations who organise activities for children, to follow the PoCA 1999 and the Department for Education and Skills (1999) guidance'. In addition, Myers and Barrett (2002: 31) suggested that 'more thought needs to be given to the appropriate use of the PoCA Register by national governing bodies, to prevent unsuitable people moving throughout different sports or even moving countries'.

The Safeguarding Vulnerable Groups Act (2006) Independent Safeguarding Authority will now not be implemented until autumn 2009, due to questions around the reliability of the database, which is being redesigned and tested (e-mail correspondence from Yvonne Williams to author, 19 September 2008). The 2006 Act places a duty on 'Regulated Activity Providers' to check that individuals wishing to engage in regulated activities are registered with the new Independent Safeguarding Authority (ISA) (see www.ccpr.org/ourservices/

childprotection, Williams, 2006; and Welch, 2006). The CCPR advise that some elements of the Act are still under development (see www.isa-gov.org.uk).

Safeguarding children – child protection policies: benchmarks or standards in sport

'It is probably the biggest problem confronting sport today . . . Everyone talks about the perils of doping, but if there were 100 drug cases under investigation in football, or 00 in swimming, and 40 or so in tennis, there would be uproar. Yet that's the scale of the problem with sex abuse today' (Professor Celia Brackenridge, interviewed in Downes, 2002: 2). Brackenridge suggests that 'the Hickson scandal[19] was a defining moment in the history of the abuse of children in sport in the UK because for the first time it required a governing body and the Sports Council to take the matter seriously' (Brackenridge, 2001; Myers and Barrett, 2002: 5). In 1999 an 'estimated half of all governing bodies of sport who received grant aid from Sport England had no child protection policy' (Myers and Barrett, 2002: 5).

Significant changes began in 1999, when following 'two years of lobbying ministers, a special meeting of child protection and sport "experts" was called in June 1999 at the NSPCC Education and Training Centre in Leicester' and were asked to 'work on a national blueprint for child protection in sport' (Brackenridge, 2001: 24). In October 1999, a National Child Protection in Sport Task Force was launched by Sport England and a range of stakeholders drew up an action plan for the Task Force (ibid: 24). In April 2000 the Action Plan for Child Protection in Sport was ratified and the Child Protection in Sport Unit was set up in October 2001 and jointly funded by Sport England and the NSPCC. In April of the same year all sports organisations that receive public funding had to have a child protection policy in place (CPSU, 2008). Although the number of governing bodies with child protection policies in place had risen in England to 55 out of 58 in 2001, there were doubts raised in a number of unpublished studies about the effectiveness of sports governing body policy on child protection practices at local club level (Myers and Barrett, 2002: 5).

The NSPCC and Sport England launched the *Standards for Safeguarding and Protecting Children in Sport* in 2002 to provide a national benchmark of good practice, at all levels in sport in an organised setting, informed by legislation and guidance; evidence from research; and experience of what works, drawing from the field of child protection and sport (CPSU, 2002). There are ten standards:

- Standard 1 : Policy
- Standard 2: Procedures and systems
- Standard 3: Prevention
- Standard 4: Codes of Practice and behaviour
- Standard 5: Equity
- Standard 6: Communication
- Standard 7: Education and Training
- Standard 8: Access to advice and support
- Standard 9: Implementation and monitoring
- Standard 10: Influencing.

Standard 1 expects any organisation providing services for children to have a written child protection policy, which is approved by the relevant management body, is mandatory for all staff and volunteers, and is reviewed every three years or whenever there is a major change in the organisation or relevant legislation. Standard 2 covers procedures and systems for dealing promptly with concerns or complaints about a child's welfare, with a designated person in a child protection role, processes for recording and using information, and clear definitions of abuse and guidance of the use of video and photography at events. Standard 3 deals with prevention through the use of proper processes of recruitment, vetting through the Criminal Records Bureau, supervision, and a whistle-blowing scheme. Standards 4, 5 and 6 cover codes of practice and behaviour, equity and communication.

Codes of practice which provide clear guidance on appropriate standards of behaviour for both children and adults, and a culture of listening and respect for children and young people, form the heart of Standard 4. Standard 5 on equity recognises the 'additional vulnerability of some children and the extra barriers they face in getting help because of their 'race', gender, age, religion, disability, sexual orientation, social background of culture' (CPSU, 2002: 9). Child protection policies need to be communicated in an accessible way and everyone in the organisation should know who is the designated child protection person and how to contact them (Standard 6). Standard 7 expects sports organisations to provide training and development opportunities for all staff and volunteers on the child protection policy, appropriate recruitment procedures, recognising signs of child abuse, and dealing with inappropriate behaviour. In particular, education and training should be provided for those people with special responsibilities for safeguarding children and/or dealing with complaints and disciplinary processes.

Organisations have a duty to make sure that advice and support is available to children and young people, with clearly identified child protection/welfare officers, who themselves need support, advice and supervision in relation to their role in dealing with concerns, or complaints of abuse (Standard 8, CPSU, 2002). In meeting the criteria for Standard 9, sports organisations need to make sure that a statement of intent on safeguarding children is actually implemented, resourced, monitored and evaluated. Anonymised summaries of the number of complaints and incidents of abuse should be kept, as well as arrangements to monitor compliance with child protection and recruitment procedures. Standard 10 on 'Influencing' aims to encourage sports organisations to actively promote safeguarding within all partnership working, where funding and commissioning criteria include a requirement to address safeguarding children and young people. Providing information on the positive stance of a sports organisation on safeguarding along with materials on policies or signposts to resources are expected to be an established part of working within partnerships.

EXERCISE 5.25

What were the charges against Paul Hickson in 1995? Comment on this case in relation to the notion of a 'predator' and the indications from the research of the group or sports participants at highest risk.

EXERCISE 5.26

Which section of the Sexual Offences Act 2003 was used in the case of *R v Lyte* (unreported, November 2007, Liverpool Crown Court, Judge Gilmour)? Why was this case unusual?

EXERCISE 5.27

Explain the duties of local authorities and sports organisations under The Children Act 1989 and The Protection of Children Act 1999.

EXERCISE 5.28

What has been introduced in the United Kingdom by the Safeguarding Vulnerable Groups Act 2006? What will be introduced under the Independent Safeguarding Authority (ISA) in Autumn 2009?

EXERCISE 5.29

Why was the Hickson case considered to be the turning point in taking child protection seriously in sport in the UK? What positive policy developments have taken place between 1998 and 2002 in the United Kingdom?

EXERCISE 5.30

Work in groups of five. Each group take two of the ten NSPCC/Sport England *Standards for Safeguarding and Protecting Children in Sport* (2002). For your two standards summarise the standard, explain its importance and comment on any issues or challenges for implementation.

Summary

Part one

- It is unlawful to discriminate against a person on the grounds of their sex or marital status.
- The discrimination can be direct, indirect or in the form of harassment.
- There are provisions for exceptions in the SDA Act 1975 under s.44, s.19 and in the case of genuine occupational requirements.
- S.44 is a general exception which has been the subject of criticism in relation to gender stereotypical assumptions in sport cases (see Talbot, 1988, 2006; Bradford, 2005).
- A series of legal cases in sport have successfully challenged sex discrimination in relation to qualifications, or the refusal to grant authorisations or licences to compete or officiate in sport competitions.
- It is unlawful to discriminate against a person on the grounds of colour, race, nationality or ethnic or national origins, religion or beliefs.
- Discrimination can be direct, indirect or in the form of harassment.

- Discrimination by way of victimisation occurs when a person is treated less favourably because he or she has raised, or is about to raise, an issue of concern or complaint about sexual or racial discrimination.
- Employers have been taken to a tribunal for discrimination on the grounds of race in relation to conduct such as abusive language, team selection, failure to offer a contract.
- Exposing employees to racist language at an after-dinner speech in a hotel where they worked at a function was held as discriminatory as the employers were seen to have such a degree of control that they should have protected employees from third-party abuse.[20]
- It is unlawful to discriminate against a disabled person by way of less favourable treatment, failure to make reasonable adjustments and by victimisation.
- Cases have been successful in establishing discrimination in sport and recreation contexts where, for example, a failure to make reasonable adjustments in a golf tournament, or a failure to make reasonable adjustments to an Olympics website to allow disabled people access to Olympics reports and purchase of tickets to Olympic events.
- It was held by the European Court of Justice in 2008 that it was unlawful to treat employees less favourably because of their association with a disabled person, leading to new rights for millions of carers.
- It is unlawful to discriminate on the grounds of a person's sexuality. In addition, from April 2005 transsexual peoples have full legal recognition in their new gender.
- The Protection from Harassment Act 1997 was held by the House of Lords in 2006 to be applicable to harassment in the workplace.

Part two

- Child abuse is any form of physical, emotional, or sexual mistreatment or lack of care which leads to injury or harm (NSPCC/CPSU).
- There are four main types of child abuse: physical, sexual, emotional, or neglect.
- It is useful to think of sexual exploitation as an overarching term or continuum on which we can locate a range of behaviours from verbal abuse to rape.
- Research shows that some groups are more at risk than others; for example, athletes at puberty just about to move into the top level, moving away from regulated sports, engaging in individual sports or an increased risk of disabled children in residential care.
- Risk assessment should make use of relevant research on risk as above and risk models which take account of risk at the level of the individual athlete, the coach and the sports organisation.
- Most perpetrators of sexual abuse are male and most are known to the survivor of abuse.
- Research on profiles of abusers challenges pictures of a socially isolated demon or stranger and paints a picture of a 'predator' who often hold positions of authority, are married, with a good self-image and personal skills (Brackenridge, 2001).
- The use of different kinds of power, a grooming process and a subculture or subworld which normalises or tolerates sexual exploitation are important sociological lenses in understanding and challenging sexual exploitation in sport and recreation.
- Charges arising out of the Sexual Offences Act 1957, 1976, or 2003 have been brought against a range of sports coaches or leaders in the UK.
- The conviction and imprisonment of swimming coach Paul Hickson for 17 years in 1995 for 15 sexual offences, including rape of two swimmers, was seen as a turning point

in attitudes towards child protection (safeguarding children) and the commitment to developing appropriate policies in sport in the UK, with the Amateur Swimming Association leading the way in the mid-1990s.

- There are ten national benchmarks or Standards for Safeguarding and Protecting Children in Sport, including procedures, prevention, education and training and access to advice and support (NCPCC and Sport England, 2002).

6 Safe in our hands? Risk management and breaches of health and safety: learning from cases and incidents

Introduction

> Risk is an integral element of sport. Sport without risk would cease to be sport. This unique aspect of sport must be factored into any discussion of risk management within sports facilities, programs and events.
>
> (Corbett, 2002: 1)

> Sport is the act of voluntarily and visibly exposing oneself to the risks of a high standard of performance achievement – for the sake of fun. These risks include the potential for death and permanent disability.
>
> (Clarke, 2005: 11)

This chapter is divided into three sections. Part one will begin with the nature of hazards, risk and risk management in sport and recreation contexts. Why engage in risk management? What kind of hazards and risks might be of relevance to sports organisers, leaders and participants? What are the principles of sensible risk management and risk assessment? Part two will introduce a range of generic statutory duties in health and safety with, among other things, a common theme of formal risk assessment. Part three focuses on criminal cases arising from relevant statutory health and safety duties in sport, local authorities or higher education sport provision. The chapter ends with a leading case in a school context, which has lessons for those concerned with educational visits, including outdoor activities.

Part one: hazards and risks

A hazard is 'anything that may cause harm' such as lightning, heat exhaustion, extreme weather such as flooding, a slippery floor, swimming pool or cleaning chemicals. The risk is 'the chance, high or low, that somebody could be harmed by these and other hazards, together with an indication of how serious the harm could be' (HSE, 2006b). Corbett (2002: 4) defines risk as 'the chance of injury, damage or loss'. In the context of a sports organisation, this could mean 'the chance of injury to your members, damage to your property or property of others, which you may be responsible for, or other loss to your organisation, directors, volunteers, members or to someone else' (ibid: 4). Whitlam uses a formula of:

SEVERITY × LIKELIHOOD = RISK RATING

Significant risks are identified by establishing a risk rating based on a multiplication of the factor for the likely severity of injury from the hazard with the likelihood of injury occurring. Those risks with the highest ratings are addressed first as they are deemed to be the most significant risks.

(2003: 35)

Whitlam (2003) lists hazard severity into five categories:

1 Negligible – near miss or minor injury e.g. abrasion
2 Slight – injury needing medical attention e.g. laceration
3 Moderate – more serious injury causing absence from school
4 Severe – serious injury requiring hospital treatment
5 Very severe – permanent injury or fatality.

The likelihood of occurrence is listed in five categories:

1 Improbable – almost zero
2 Remote – unlikely to occur[1]
3 Possible – could occur
4 Probable – may occur several times – not surprising
5 Near certainty – expected.

(ibid: 35)

TUC (2007: 61) uses a Severity rating of hazards with a value of 1–4.

- Value 1 = Catastrophic, that is, imminent danger exists, and the hazard is capable of causing death and illness on a wide scale.
- Value 2 = Critical, that is, the hazard can result in serious illness, severe injury, property and equipment damage.
- Value 3 = Marginal, that is, the hazard can cause illness, injury or equipment damage, but the results would not be expected to be serious.
- Value 4 = Negligible, that is, the hazard will not result in serious injury or illness and there is a remote possibility of damage requiring any treatment beyond first aid.

Values for rating probability rating of a hazard suggested by the TUC (2007: 61) range from probable to extremely remote:

- Value 1 = Probable, that is, likely to occur immediately or shortly.
- Value 2 = Reasonably probable, that is, probably will occur in time.
- Value 3 = Remote, that is, may occur in time.
- Value 4 = Extremely remote, that is, unlikely to occur.

It is possible to rank risks using 'a simple formula, where risk = severity estimate × probability estimate, although many numerical ranking systems are purely subjective in the numerical values given to each hazard' (TUC, 2007: 61). Although risk is technically a precise statistical concept that defines 'the product of a degree of probability and a degree of consequence' it has 'increasingly turned into a synonym for hazard or danger, linked to a politicised approach to blame' (Hood, 2005, cited in Gaskin, 2005: 2). Gaskin (2005: 2) observes that many definitions of risk emphasise the danger element or risk rather than its potentially enhancing effect, and risk is part of life in businesses, voluntary activities and is an essential part of sport, particularly adventure sports (see Graff, 2003; All Party Parliamentary Group, 2004, cited in Gaskin, 2005: 3). The risk 'must be balanced against the benefits of sport and compared to the risks of everyday life' (Ball, 2005: 58–61, cited in Appenzeller, 2005).

EXERCISE 6.1

Define a hazard. Give examples of six hazards in a sport or recreation context.

EXERCISE 6.2

What are risks? Are risks necessarily only about negative aspects of sport or recreation?

EXERCISE 6.3

Provide examples of six sources of risk which might face a voluntary sports organisation.

EXERCISE 6.4

Identify five risks related to the organisation of major international sports events.

EXERCISE 6.5

Choose one of the models categorising hazards and evaluating risk severity and probability (Whitlam, 2003; TUC, 2007). Apply the chosen model to your own sport or a chosen sport and give examples from that sport from each category of hazards and risks in the model.

EXERCISE 6.6

Using the sport in which you participate or coach or lead, search relevant literature and databases to find out as much as you can about the nature of the risks of that sport. In particular, see if you can find statistics on the nature of risks of injury and deaths, causes of injuries and deaths and any analysis of such matters by sports governing bodies, academics (e.g. sports medicine/sports science, law, sport management) or perhaps, insurers.

EXERCISE 6.7

Select a passage from a sports autobiography which talks about taking risks or rationalising risks. Make notes on this passage and share your example and thoughts with another person in your group.

EXERCISE 6.8

Using media or internet sources and a *Nexis* (or equivalent) media database, find examples of risk-taking behaviour which appears to be celebrated or glorified. Using internet sites such as YouTube, Facebook or MySpace locate examples of individuals who have posted reckless or risk-taking behaviour. Critically discuss the decisions and actions of those individuals and any responses, comments, blogs etc online. Critically analyse such behaviour using any materials from this chapter and Chapter 4 of this text.

EXERCISE 6.9

Read the following material selected from:

Taylor, J 'Don't ban chariot race begs wounded student' *The Mail on Sunday* 29 October 1995: 13. Nine young students were injured in a drunken race, based on the quad race in the film *Chariots of Fire*.[2] One student Tom Sebire, crashed to the ground, carrying a beer bottle and severed an artery, resulting in an operation. The students were taking part in the Great Court Race, a long-standing tradition at the college. Around 100 students were 'trying to complete a circuit of the Great Court before the college clock struck 24 times – a feat celebrated in David Puttman's film about 1920s Olympic heroes Eric Liddell and Harold Abrahams' (Taylor, 1995: 13). The event took place at midnight and the students were wearing dinner jackets and shoes and some were racing round in shopping trolleys. 'Some of the 100 students who took part after a drunken matriculation dinner last weekend were cut by broken glass, others were trampled underfoot and one fell out of a speeding shopping trolley' (ibid: 13).

EXERCISE 6.10

Compare the Great Court Race in the film *Chariots of Fire* with the student Great Court Race of May 1995. Critically discuss the different circumstances and additional risks present in the 1995 student Great Court Race. Should the race be allowed to continue?

What is risk management and risk assessment?

A risk assessment is 'simply a careful examination of what, in your work, could cause harm to people, so that you can weigh up whether you have taken enough precautions or should do more to prevent harm' (HSE, 2006a). The five steps of risk assessment recommended by the British Health and Safety Executive are:

- Step 1: Identify the hazards.
- Step 2: Decide who might be harmed and how.
- Step 3: Evaluate the risks and decide on precautions.
- Step 4: Record your findings and implement them.
- Step 5: Review your assessment and update it necessary (HSE, 2006a: 2).

In the context of outdoor activities such as plunge-pooling it is useful to think about different kinds of risk assessment such as generic risk assessment, event risk assessment, on-site risk assessment and dynamic risk assessment. Generic risk assessment deals with risks in the activity across the employee population. Site-specific risk assessment are particular risks associated with the site; for example, water depth, ease of exit, difficulty of rescue. 'Dynamic' risk assessment focuses attention on the unfolding risks which may emerge as relevant circumstances change – such as changes in staffing, or weather conditions or the fitness of the participants to undertake the activity.[3]

The Royal Society for the Prevention of Accidents (RoSPA) also provides an advice pack for smaller businesses[4] in which Sheet 7 summarises risk assessment at its very simplest and reflects the five steps outlined earlier in the HSE online publication.

> We believe that risk management should be about practical steps to protect people from real harm or suffering – not bureaucratic back covering. If you believe all the stories you hear, health and safety is all about stopping any activity that might possibly lead to harm. That is not our vision of sensible health and safety – we want to save lives not stop them. Our approach is to seek a balance between the unachievable aim of absolute safety and the kind of poor management of risk that damages lives and the economy.
>
> (Bill Callaghan, Chair of the Health and Safety Commission (HSC))[5]

> I am sick and tired of hearing about petty health and safety stopping people doing worthwhile and enjoyable things, when at the same time others are suffering harm and even death due to poor management and complacency. That is why today we are launching a set of principles of risk management.
>
> (Bill Callaghan, Chair of HSC[6])

The HSE launched the set of principles of sensible risk management in 2006. Sensible risk management *is* about:

1 Ensuring that workers and the public are properly protected
2 Providing overall benefit to society by balancing benefits and risks, with a focus on reducing real risks – both those which arise more often and those with serious consequences
3 Enabling innovation and learning not stifling them
4 Ensuring that those who create risks manage them responsibly and understand that failure to manage real risks is likely to lead to robust action
5 Enabling individuals to understand that as well as the right to protection, they also have to exercise responsibility.

Sensible risk management *is not* about:

1 Creating a totally risk free society
2 Generating useless paperwork mountains
3 Scaring people by exaggerating or publicising trivial risks
4 Stopping important recreational and learning activities for individuals where risks are managed
5 Reducing protection of people from real risks that cause real harm and suffering.

(www.hse.gov.uk/risk/principles.htm)

Whitlam (2003: 30) pointed out that:

> every day each teacher makes several decisions, sometimes sub-consciously, about the circumstances under which the children in their care operate – in the classroom,

the playground or in the physical education lesson. This is managing risk. The vast majority of teachers do it well.

Whitlam (2003: 30) argues that managing risk is synonymous with 'good practice' or 'safe practice' and in a school context, involves the 'assessment, and if necessary, further control of any significant risks which may cause harm to pupils or others'. Risk management is 'reducing the chances of injury, damage or loss, by taking steps to identify, measure and control risks' where using common sense, sport organisers or leaders have an organised process of asking the following three questions of their sport provision:

1   What are the possible things that could go wrong (identifying the risks)
2   How likely is it that these things will go wrong and what are the consequences if they do go wrong? (measuring the risks)
3   What can we do to keep things from going wrong? (controlling the risks)

(Corbett et al., 2007: 232)

Gaskin (2005) identified four general strategies in risk management for voluntary organisations – retain, reduce, transfer, or avoid the risks. Risk management might normally seek to avoid or transfer a risk by contract or through buying insurance (Clarke, 2005; Gaskin, 2005). 'The challenge of sport risk management, in contrast, is to control the risk that makes sport, or to at least minimise the unnecessary problems that are known to lie in readiness' (ibid: 13). In the area of risk management sport organisations need to think about their responsibilities to 'provide a safe environment', and 'make decisions fairly' when handling disputes among members and 'properly care for and protect its assets and resources' (Corbett, 2002: 2).

Eve et al. (1998, cited in Severs et al., 2003) developed a risk management model for physical education in the United Kingdom, in which teachers need to think about people, activity and context (see Whitlam, 2003: 31). The activity includes class organisation, teaching style, preparation and progression. The context includes factors such as behaviour or discipline, equipment, procedures or routines and the facility being used (ibid: 31). Corbett (2002: 6) also suggests that there are four sources of risk – facilities, equipment, program (sport activities) and people – and three types of risk – physical injury, wrongful actions, and property loss or damage.

Safeguarding children (child protection[7]) should be a part of mainstream risk management, including formal risk assessment in sport and recreation contexts. The CPSU 2002 *Standards for Safeguarding and Protecting Children in Sport* and the materials on the CPSU and NSPCC websites provide useful briefings and links relevant to risk analysis and risk assessment. A knowledge of relevant statutes (see Chapter 5) and legal duties can be enhanced by an appreciation of relevant research on sexual exploitation, including child sexual abuse. In this area good risk assessment can be informed by information on the nature and prevalence of child abuse, or the groups at higher risk. In addition, it is crucial to develop an appreciation of the use and abuse of different kinds of power, organisational subcultures (or subworlds) and research-informed models of individual and institutional risks (see, for example, Brackenridge, 2001; Williams, 2003, 2006[8]).

Corbett et al. (2007: 230) warns that there is 'no magic formula for risk management'.

> While there are fixed concepts and common approaches there are no black and white rules. One organisation's risk management program will be very different from another, depending on the sport discipline, whether or not the organisation operates a facility, the organisation's structure and mandate, and the organisation's relationship with its members.

Risks connected to the cancellation of a major sports event can include boycotts, a terrorist threat, a health epidemic, a transport breakdown, a national tragedy or sport disaster and a proper risk analysis is needed in advance of drawing up contracts:

> Control of such risks might be through control by contract, including *force majeure* (loss lies where it falls in cases such as 'acts of god' or war), exclusion clauses, warranty and indemnity. Issues of proximate cause, Acts of Terrorism and Acts of War, and ascertainable losses are relevant issues in control by insurance. Finally – control by good management would involve examining the risk matrix and devising contingency plans to deal with those risks.
>
> (Rudgard, 2002: 133)

Risks of physical injury, disease or death can arise from hazards such as the skills and techniques required to participate in the sport; for example, a scrum in rugby or a twisting double somersault in gymnastics. Equally, serious injury or death can arise from the behaviour of players, such as a high tackle or a punch in rugby or ice hockey.[9] Hazards in the sports facilities – for example, a slippery floor or equipment stored close to the edge of a basketball or asbestos being disturbed in the walls of a storage room – can also lead to disease, injury or death. Hazards external to the activity can impact on the sports activity risks, include extreme weather such as floods or heavy rain above a caving area or stream to be used on a school adventure course or educational visit or lightning on a golf course. Other hazards which may lead to physical injury disease or death include taking drugs in sport, HIV/AIDS, heat exhaustion, crowd crush or public order risks, lack of screening or poor first aid provision, a fault in a sports product, or a transport-related incident (see, for example, Nygaard and Boone 1985; Ammon, 1997; Spengler et al., 2006).

Why engage in risk management?

> Managing risk in physical education is important because all children have the right to be taught in a safe and healthy environment.
>
> (Whitlam, 2003: 31)

There is a legal requirement to engage in the more formal risk assessment part of risk management related to the statutes in Anglo-Welsh law which will be discussed in the next part of this chapter. This relates, in particular, to The Management of Health and Safety at Work Regulations (MHSW) 1999. Statutory duties in health and safety are only one source of legal requirement for both organisers of and participants in sport-related activities. Those in sport also owe a duty of care to each other within civil law; for example, the elements of negligence, covered in Chapters 2 and 3 of this text. In addition, operating unfair procedures in disciplinary matters, including matters of, for example, doping, violence, or eligibility in sport, can lead to a legal challenge in the civil courts.

In the United States the law 'expects that sports administrators develop risk management and loss control programmes to ensure a safe environment for all who participate in sport' (Appenzeller, 2005: 9). Risk management should help those in sport to comply with relevant legal duties and 'provide safe programs and enable sport personnel to defend themselves and their programs in the event of a lawsuit' (Baron, 2005: 9). It should also 'effectively reduce costs and enable desirable programs and services to be continued' (Van der Smissen, 1990, cited Appenzeller, 2005: 8). A sound risk management plan and techniques are 'the key to a safe and enjoyable physical education programme' (Halsey, 2005: 151).

It is often assumed that risk management is really a responsibility for sports leaders, officials, event organisers or the owners of facilities. Whitlam (2003: 30) recommends that all teachers should involve children in the management of risk. Nygaard and Boone (1985) advise that comprehensive risk warnings are not only essential in injury prevention, but also build respect for the programme in the minds of participants and parents. It also establishes 'a foundation for implementation of other risk management measures and for educating athletes and parents about their responsibilities for preventing injuries'. Participants, including children, need to learn about risk and their part, along with others, in reducing those risks to an inherent minimum, whilst enjoying all the benefits that sport has to offer.

The Royal Society for the Prevention of Accidents (RoSPA) notes that there is a requirement in the National Curriculum 5–16 years in England and Wales, to 'teach about health and safety' and applies to those subjects where pupils 'carry out practical activities and use tools and equipment. This means in science, design and technology, information and communication technology, art and design and physical education' (McIntire, 2000: 1). This requires children to be taught:

> About hazards, risk and risk control, to recognise hazards, assess consequent risks and take steps to control risks to themselves and others, to use information to assess immediate and cumulative risks, to manage their environment to ensure the health and safety of themselves and others and to explain the steps they take to control risks.
>
> (ibid: 1)

McIntire (2000: 1) suggests that assessing and managing risks is not enough and that safety education in the area of personal and social skills is also about:

> understanding factors which influence attitudes and behaviour to do with safety. Children and young people need skills to deal with pressures and stereotypes that can encourage risk taking. Peer pressure to play 'chicken' on busy roads or media stereotypes about fast driving are examples.

Playing a part in making their own school safer, learning with safety professionals and taking responsibility for social and moral issues, are all seen as part of safety education for pupils in the National Curriculum, particularly in citizenship, personal and social education and career-related learning (ibid.: 2[10]). Children in the UK as young as 11 can, and have been, found liable for contributory negligence. Furthermore, between the ages of 10 and 14 they can be tried like adults in a court of law for crimes such as assault or manslaughter in sport contexts.[11] It would make sense to educate children in physical education or sport, in matters of risk management and their own role and legal responsibilities, from an early age in an appropriate pedagogy, with a common-sense approach. As indicated above by McIntire (2000) this might be part of personal and social education (PSE), cross-curricular moral development, or part of the citizenship curriculum, as well as an appropriate topic in GCSE physical education or the A-level sports studies curriculum.[12]

EXERCISE 6.11

What is risk management? What is 'sensible risk management'? Explain why the British HSE felt the need to introduce ten principles of 'sensible risk management'? Go on the British HSE website and locate a 'Myth of the Month'. Report back to your seminar group.

EXERCISE 6.12

Why engage in risk management in sport and recreation?

EXERCISE 6.13

Identify four strategies of risk management in sport.

EXERCISE 6.14

Risk assessment is part of risk management. Find out further details of the HSE Five Steps to Risk Assessment. Locate and print off the examples for risk assessment forms on the HSE website. Use them hypothetically to risk assess a planned trip taken by, for example, your university or school sports team or on a sport or recreation event which you might be organising as part of a module learning activity or assessment.

EXERCISE 6.15

Do responsibilities in risk management only apply to managers, leaders or organisers of sport or recreation activities? Explain your answer with support from literature and expectations of risk education in schools.

EXERCISE 6.16

Read the CPSU (2002) Standards in Safeguarding and Protecting Children in Sport and the relevant research from Chapter 5. Go onto the CPSU website (see Chapter 1) and learn more about CRB checks and the use of photography at sports events. Put together a two-page briefing paper on which groups are at risk and strategies for reducing risks.

EXERCISE 6.17

Each year, after an evening at the May Ball, many Oxford University undergraduates engage in the traditional activity of jumping 25ft from the Magdalen Bridge into the River Cherwell. There was an unusually dry spring in 2005 leaving only 3ft of water in the river at the time of the May Ball. On 1 May 2005 'more than 30 people were injured yesterday after dozens of Oxford undergraduates misjudged the level of the River Cherwell during a May Day celebration . . . ignoring emergency barriers erected to deter them'. Minor injuries were treated at the scene but '10 were taken to hospital with spinal injuries, broken legs, ankles and ribs. One man had a serious back injury after another jumped on top of him and a Russian woman was impaled on the 6ft fence' (Gianelli, 2005: 1).

'Inspector Justin Archer, head of operations for Thames Valley Police, said that he was disappointed so many had ignored their warnings' (ibid: 1).

Gianelli, M. (2005) 'Thirty Oxford students hurt in May Day leap into shallow river' *The Daily Telegraph* Monday 2 May, p. 1.

EXERCISE 6.18

Working in pairs, critically analyse the magnitude and probability of the risks involved in the above incidents. Should this tradition be banned?

Part two: statutory duties in health and safety

There are a range of generic statutes which place health and safety duties on, among others, employers and employees. Although these are generic and located in the workplace, it is important for all those involved in sport, physical education and recreation, in a professional and voluntary capacity, to be familiar with such statutes and related regulations and codes of practice, which might apply to their particular role or context. This part of the chapter will focus on:

- The Health and Safety at Work Act 1974
- The Management of Health and Safety at Work (MHSWR) 1999
- The Workplace (Health, Safety and Welfare) Regulations 2002
- Control of Substances Hazardous to Health (COSHH) Regulations 1992
- Reporting of Injuries, Diseases and Dangerous Occurrences (RIDDOR) Regulations
- Health and Safety (First Aid) Regulations 1981.

Health and Safety at Work Act (HSWA) 1974

The Health and Safety at Work Act 1974 is an enabling Act under which more detailed health and safety regulations are made.[13] It is written in very general terms and makes employers responsible for people, premises and processes. Management must organise for health and safety, provide people and resources that will make workplaces safe, manage health and safety actively and write a health and safety policy (TUC, 2007: 54). Section 1 covers employers' duties to maintain standards of health, safety and welfare of people at work, protect other people against risks to health and safety arising out of work activities, controlling the storage and use of dangerous substances and controlling certain emissions into the air from certain premises. Section 2 places a general duty on employers to 'ensure, as far as is reasonably practicable, the health, safety and welfare of their employees: to consult with them through recognised trade unions concerning arrangements for joint action on health and safety matters, establish health and safety committees and prepare and publicise their written health and safety policy'. In s.2(2) the Act states that an employer must, as far as is reasonably practicable provide:

- Safe plant, maintenance and systems of work
- Safe use, handling and transport of articles and substances
- Information, instruction, training and supervision
- A safe place of work and safe means of access and egress
- A safe working environment
- Adequate welfare facilities.

Under s.3 employers have a general duty to ensure that their activities do not endanger anybody and, in certain circumstances, to provide information to the public about any potential hazards to health and safety. Section 4 places a duty on employers to ensure that their premises, as well as plant and machinery in them, do not endanger people using them. Section 5 expects controllers of premises to use the best practicable means to prevent emissions into the atmosphere of noxious or offensive substances. Section 6 places duties on those who design or supply articles or substances to be used in the workplace to ensure, as far as it is under their control, that the article or substance is safe when used in accordance with information they supply.

Employees also have obligations to take reasonable care of their own health and safety and inform their employer and other employees of any situation that might be considered a danger to them, as well as making their employer aware of any shortcomings in the employer's safety arrangements. Section 7 places duties on employees to 'take reasonable care to ensure that they do not endanger themselves or anyone else who may be affected by their work activities: and to co-operate with the employer and others in meeting statutory requirements'. Everyone at work has a duty not to misuse anything provided in the interests of health and safety at work under a statutory requirement (s.8 of the HSWA 1974).

The Management of Health and Safety at Work Regulations (MHSW) 1999

The duty to carry out formal risk assessments is centrally located in these regulations, which require all employers to carry out risk assessments of their workers and others affected by what they do. Section 3 requires employers to conduct suitable and sufficient risk assessments and record them where five or more people are employed (TUC, 2007: 59). This will involve identifying the hazards, 'evaluating the extent of the risks identifying measures needed to comply with legal requirements, reviewing risk assessment, recording the assessment (if there are more than five employees) and considering any special factors for young persons' (ibid: 59). Risk assessments should:

> disregard inconsequential and trivial risks, determine the likelihood of injury or harm arising, quantify the severity of the consequences and the numbers of people likely to be affected, take into account existing control measures, identify any specific legal duty or requirement relating to the hazard, remain valid for a reasonable period of time, provide sufficient information to enable the employer to decide upon appropriate control measures and enable the employer to prioritise remedial measures.
>
> (ibid: 60)

The HSE website carries detailed guidance under the Five Steps to Risk Assessment outlined in Part one of this chapter, that is,

1 Identify the hazards
2 Decide who might be harmed and how
3 Evaluate the risks and decide on precautions
4 Record your findings and implement them
5 Review your assessment and update if necessary.

(www.hse.gov.uk/risk/fivesteps.htm)

The risk assessment should ensure that all risks in the workplace are addressed and should cover all groups of employees. Employers with more than five employees must record any significant findings of a risk assessment, which should include a list of major hazards, the existing control measures in place, the extent to which they control the risks and any groups of employees at risk. The MHSW 1999 Regulations also require employers to survey their employees' health, particularly in the following circumstances:

1 Where there is an identifiable disease or adverse condition related to the work concerned.
2 Where valid techniques are available to detect indications of the disease or condition.
3 Where there is a reasonable likelihood that the disease or condition may occur.
4 Where surveillance is likely to improve the protection of the health of the employees.

Employers should consider the risks to particular groups; for example, new or expectant mothers. Employers should carry out risk assessment where 'women of child-bearing age and new and expectant mothers may be at risk from a work process, working conditions or physical, chemical or biological agents, or to medically suspend an employee where it is not reasonable to alter the conditions of work (Regulations 16–18, cited in TUC, 2007: 61). Risk assessments also need to be carried out before young workers (who have not reached 18 years of age) start work. This relates to 'risks to their health and safety as a consequence of lack of experience, or absence of awareness of existing or potential risks or the fact that young persons have not yet fully matured' (Regulation 19, cited in TUC, 2007: 61).

People carrying out risk assessments must be competent to do so. The assessor should 'have an understanding of the workplace, an ability to make sound judgements and have knowledge of the best practicable means to reduce those risks identified' (ibid: 62). They do not have to have a particular level of qualification but may be defined as 'combination of knowledge, skills, experience and personal qualities, including the ability to recognise the extent and limitations of one's own competence' (ibid: 61). Health surveillance is also part of the MHSW Regulations 1999, having regard to the risks to health safety which are identified by the assessment. These now extend beyond exposure to substances hazardous to health.[16] This need arises from:

> any identifiable disease or health condition related to work, where there is a valid technique for its identification, a likelihood that the disease or condition may occur as a result of the work and that the surveillance will protect further the health of the employees.

(ibid: 62)

Practical example

A private company organised courses in leadership and personal development in sport and outdoor activities for corporations and local authorities. It built an army style assault course, and developed a paint balling activity and various team-building challenges. During one of the first bookings by a marketing company, 'Tracy' a female member of staff who was four months pregnant, did not have the strength to weight ratio to climb down a rope from a high platform and fell ten metres to the ground, injuring her legs and hips badly. No risk assessment had been carried out by a competent person on pregnant employees who had to come on the course as part of their staff development.

During the paint balling activity 'Greg' ignored health and safety instructions and failed to wear the required safety goggles. During a very closely fought game, he sustained a serious injury to his eye. During a team-building challenge on the last night, the teams could gain extra points if they engaged in a three mile run followed by a lake crossing. The first person across the lake, 'Jenny' was not a swimmer but did not want to let the team down. She got into difficulties immediately on entering the lake. She was very fatigued from the run and the lake was deeper than she thought and had extensive long weeds in it at this time of year. Eventually she was rescued from the dark water but had sustained brain damage due to lack of oxygen to the brain.

EXERCISE 6.19

What are the four main duties of employers under the Health and Safety at Work Act 1974?

EXERCISE 6.20

How does s.2 of the HSWA 1974 address the involvement of recognised trade unions in matters of health and safety?

EXERCISE 6.21

What does 'as far is reasonably practicable' mean?

EXERCISE 6.22

What six things must an employer provide under s.2 of the HSWA 1974?

EXERCISE 6.23

Explain the duties of employees under the HSWA 1974 and give examples of complying with such duties in your sport activity or workplace.

EXERCISE 6.24

What is the central duty of employers under the Management of Health and Safety at Work Regulations (MHSWR) 1999? Specify the exact nature of s.3 requirements. Must all risks be acted upon? Explain your answer.

EXERCISE 6.25

When does an employer need to record significant findings of risk assessments?

EXERCISE 6.26

Explain why the following groups of people might need separate or special consideration in risk assessments.

- Pregnant women
- Children or young people
- Disabled employees

EXERCISE 6.27

In relation to health and safety law, define a 'child' and a 'young person'.

EXERCISE 6.28

What are the special features of risk assessment which must be taken into account before a 'young person' starts work or begins work experience?

EXERCISE 6.29

What are the restrictions on people under the age of 18 and children under the minimum school leaving age (MSLA)?

EXERCISE 6.30

Locate three references on health and safety guidance related to young people at work.

The Workplace (Health Safety and Welfare) Regulations 1992

Temperature, humidity, ventilation and lighting are all major determinants of comfort in the workplace. Yet conditions in workplaces are often unsatisfactory and result in harmful health effects for workers. In the 2006 TUC representatives' survey, one in three (34 per cent) safety representatives cited high or low temperatures as one of their top concerns.

(TUC, 2007: 262)

Working in the wrong temperature can mean 'loss of concentration, irritability, tiredness, discomfort and increased accident risks. Too much heat can cause fatigue, dehydration, dizziness, fainting, heat stress and ultimately heat stroke'. Cold temperatures 'affect dexterity and mobility and may increase physical and visual strain, fatigue and other problems for people with muscular pain, arthritis, and heart conditions' (ibid: 262).

The Workplace (Health, Safety and Welfare) Regulations 1992 expand on the duties under the Health and Safety at Work Act 1974 and are aimed at 'protecting employees' health from injury or long-term illness; ensuring safety by affording protection from immediate danger and their welfare by providing facilities for personal comfort at work' (Hinde and Kavanagh, 2003: 20). The health aspects expect employers to ensure adequate ventilation, a reasonable temperature (min. 16 degrees centigrade), suitable lighting, clean floors, adequate seating if working sitting down, no undue reaching, bending and stretching when using equipment and machinery and enough space for each person (ibid: 20). 'Suitable and effective provision should be made for enclosed workplaces to be ventilated by a sufficient quantity of fresh or purified air' (Regulation 6, WHSW Regulations 1992).

The Safety section of the 1992 WHSW Regulations expect employers to provide safe premises, floors and stairs, suitably maintained equipment and machinery, space to enter and leave the premises safely. Other examples include fencing off of openings where people are likely to fall, safe storage for all materials and goods, safety glass in windows where appropriate, and control of vehicles where pedestrians are at risk – such as traffic calming procedures (Hinde and Kavanagh, 2003: 20). The welfare part of The Workplace (Health, Safety and Welfare) Regulations covers areas such as sufficient toilets, suitable washing and changing facilities, accessible drinking water, facilities for rest and eating.

These regulations require the employer to make sure that the workplace is in an efficient state; for example, maintained in good working order and kept clean, well lit and ventilated, at an appropriate temperature, with enough space, with adequate supplies of drinking water and suitable and sufficient toilet, washing and drying facilities. Floors should be kept free of obstructions and employers should, as far as is practicable, protect employees from falling a distance likely to cause them personal injury and protect them from being struck by a falling object. Workplaces must also meet the needs of people with disabilities and several of these regulations require, for example, doors, passageways, toilets, wash basins, traffic routes, facilities and workstations, to be suitable for use by workers with disabilities (Regulation, 2(3) and Guidance para 4, cited TUC, 2007: 263).

Control of Substances Hazardous to Health (COSHH) Regulations 2002[15]

These regulations apply to employers who are required to control exposure to hazardous substances to protect employees and others who may be exposed. Hazardous substances include those used directly in work activities (adhesives, paints, cleaning agents), generated during work activities (e.g. fumes from soldering and welding), naturally occurring substances (e.g. grain dust) and biological agents, such as bacteria and other microorganisms.[16] COSHH includes carcinogens (cancer-causing substances) and asthmagens (asthma-causing substances). Substances not covered by the COSHH 2002 Regulations are asbestos, lead, substances which are hazardous only because they are radioactive, at high pressure, at extreme temperatures or have explosive or flammable properties, and biological agents that are outside the employer's control (e.g. catching an infection from a workmate).

Effects of hazardous substances to employees or others can range from skin or eye irritation, asthma as a result of developing an allergy to substances used at work, chronic lung disease, loss of consciousness due to toxic fumes, damage of liver, kidneys or nervous system, cancer, infection from bacterial or other microorganisms, or death (HSE, 2004: 1–2). This may result in 'lost productivity to your business, liable to enforcement action and/or result in civil claims from your employees' (HSE, 2004: 1). Employers are required to:

Step 1: Assess the risks
Step 2: Decide what precautions are needed
Step 3: Prevent or adequately control exposure
Step 4: Ensure that control measures are used and maintained
Step 5: Monitor the exposure
Step 6: Carry out appropriate health surveillance
Step 7: Prepare plans and procedures to deal with accidents, incidents and emergencies
Step 8: Ensure employees are properly informed, trained and supervised

(HSE, 2004: 2–3)

Where there is a risk, employers must monitor the health of employees and retain records for over 40 years. Employers are required to provide employees with suitable and sufficient information, instruction and training which should include names of substances and safety data sheets, main findings of risk assessment, the precautions they should take to protect themselves and other employees, how to use personal protective clothing, results of exposure monitoring and health surveillance, emergency procedures which need to be followed (HSE, 2004: 10). Employees have duties under COSHH to practise safe work habits, use control measures and personal protective equipment (PPE), store equipment and hazardous materials properly, read container labels, report any hazards, take part in training programmes and health surveillance and report any accidents or incidents to managers or supervisors.

Practical example

In a local sport and leisure centre, rotas for lifeguard supervision were extended due to staff shortages, through illness, without consultation with employees or union. The weather in July had been very hot and humid for the last few days. It was hot and humid in the swimming pool, particularly sitting at the top of the elevated lifeguard station. 'Alice' had not had adequate breaks or drinking water and had been sitting at the lifeguard station for over twice the amount of time recommended in the Royal Life Saving Society and local authority code of practice. Late in the afternoon she fainted and fell off the lifeguard station onto the poolside, seriously injuring her back, arm and leg.

Contractors were on site decorating the rooms and halls next to the spa area. 'Rachel' who had recently joined the spa staff and 'Imran' the 17-year-old apprentice, on his first day with the decorating firm, had not been inducted in the COSHH 2002 Regulations. Due to lack of space, decorators and spa staff were using the same storeroom for painting equipment and spa items. 'Rachel' went into the storeroom to replenish the water bowl in the sauna. Ten minutes later, 'Alison' who had been attending the step class, added some water to the coals in the sauna and sustained 50 per cent burns when the coals burst into flames. In the storeroom, bottles of plain water for use in the sauna had been placed next to bottles of white spirit used by the decorators, with inadequate labels or warnings. 'Rachel' had picked up the bottle of white spirit by mistake and put some of it in the bowl in the sauna.

EXERCISE 6.31

What are the three main aims of the Workplace (Health and Safety) Regulations 1992?

EXERCISE 6.32

What are employers expected to do under the 'Health' aspect of the WPHS Regulations 1992?

EXERCISE 6.33

Provide examples of the 'Welfare' section of the WPHS Regulations 1992.

EXERCISE 6.34

Identify the effects of very high or low temperatures on employees and their skills or work competence.

EXERCISE 6.35

Give examples of the categories of hazardous substances covered under the Control of Substances Hazardous to Health (COSHH) Regulations, 1992, 2002.

EXERCISE 6.36

Which substances are excluded or covered by other regulations?

EXERCISE 6.37

What kind of harm or injuries can be caused by exposure to hazardous substances?

EXERCISE 6.38

What steps are employers required to take under COSHH Regulations 2002? How long should records be retained where there is a significant risk? What do employees need to be informed about by the employer?

EXERCISE 6.39

What are the duties of employees under the COSHH Regulations 1992, 2002?

Reporting of Injuries, Diseases and Dangerous Occurrences (RIDDOR) Regulations

> It is essential that ill-health and injuries are reported to the enforcing authorities so that a true picture of the magnitude of the problem is identified and so that lessons can be learned to prevent re-occurrence.
>
> (TUC, 2007: 291[17])

Employers, self-employed people or those occupying premises have a duty to report some accidents and incidents that arise out of or in connection with work, under RIDDOR (Reporting of Injuries, Diseases and Dangerous Occurrences Regulations 1995). These Regulations cover deaths, which must be reported immediately, reportable major injuries, including those resulting from assault/physical violence[18] and injuries where the employee or self-employed person is away from work or normal work for more than three days, which must be reported within ten days.[19] Dangerous occurrences are 'specified events which may not result in a reportable injury, but have the potential to do significant harm' (HSE, 2005a: 1[20]).

> All workplaces with more than 10 employees must have an accident book, where details of all accidents can be recorded. The book should also be used to record any sickness which that was possibly caused or made worse by work, and any dangerous occurrences or 'near misses' in the workplace. Accident book entries must be 'torn off' and stored in compliance with the Data Protection Act 1998. Records should be kept for at least three years after the last entry.
>
> (Hinde and Kavanagh, 2003: 59)

From 31 December 2003, in order to comply with the Data Protection Act 1998, it is essential that all personal details entered into accident books are kept confidential. The new HSE accident book incorporates perforated slips that can be stored securely (ibid: 60[21]).

Health and Safety (First Aid) Regulations 1981

> Sometimes proper first aid can mean the difference between life and death by stopping minor injuries or sudden onset illnesses becoming major problems. The first few minutes after an event are vital, even when an ambulance or a doctor or a nurse has to be called.
>
> (TUC, 2007: 299)

First aid is 'where a person will need help from a medical practitioner or nurse, treatment for the purpose of preserving life and minimising the consequences of injury and illness until such help is obtained' (Regulation 2, Health and Safety (First Aid) Regulations 1981). It also means 'treatment of minor injuries which would otherwise receive no treatment or which do not need treatment by a medical practitioner or nurse' (Regulation 2, HSFA Regulations 1981). Laws which apply to first aid at work include the Health and Safety at Work Act 1974 regarding safe systems of work, information, training, inspection and adequate welfare facilities are all relevant to first aid provision.[22] The Management of Health and Safety at Work Regulations 1999 require suitable and sufficient assessments of risks which includes risk assessment for first aid provision at work. The Safety Representatives and Safety Committee Regulations 1977 require consultation with safety representatives and this includes consultation about first aid requirements (TUC, 2007: 299).

Employers must make a (risk) assessment to decide what first aid facilities are adequate and appropriate in the circumstances and provide adequate equipment and facilities. Factors to consider in an assessment include the workplace hazards and risks, the size of the organisation, the history of accidents, the distribution of the workforce, the needs of travelling, remote or lone workers and the nature of the activities.[23] Under s.3 of the HSFA Regulations 1982, an employer has a duty to provide adequate and appropriate equipment and facilities for enabling first aid to be given to employees (HSFA Regulation 3 (1)). An employer should also provide an adequate and appropriate number of suitable persons who are suitably trained and qualified[24] (Regulation 3.2). In low risk areas such as offices, shops and libraries, for fewer than 50 employees the Guidance Paragraph 47 advises at least one appointed person, for 50–100 employees at least one first aider, and for more than 100 at least one additional first aider for every 100 employed. Remote sites and higher risk areas would need additional first aiders.

If a first aider is absent, in temporary or exceptional circumstances there should be an appointed person to take charge (Regulation 3.3). A first aider must have a valid certificate of competence issued by an organisation whose training and qualifications are approved by the HSE. Under Paragraph 28 of the Approved Code of Practice and Guidance (L74) an employer must ensure that a first aid box, suitably marked and easily accessible, is available in all places where working conditions require it and should be placed, where possible, near hand washing facilities, protect first aid items from dust and damp, and only be stocked with items useful for giving first aid (TUC, 2007: 302). Minimum and additional first aid box contents are listed in Guidance Paragraphs 31, 34–36, with Paragraph 37 covering travelling first aid kits and Paragraph 38 and 40–41 on the requirements of first aid rooms. Guidance Paragraphs 56–57 recommend that employers provide first aiders and appointed persons with a book to record incidents which would include the date and time of the incident, name and job of the injured person, details of the injury or illness for which first aid was given, action taken immediately afterwards and name and signature of the first aider or person dealing with the incident (ibid: 303[25].

Practical example

A pioneering initiative to provide sport in the community in an inner-city area involved young men who had been excluded from school or had been in a young offender institutions accessing leadership in the outdoors sessions, culminating in a residential outdoor activities week in the Scottish mountains. The scheme was going very well, with the exception of a number of physical assaults on staff by one or two participants, which resulted in four days absence from work on two or three occasions. No records were kept or reports made under the RIDDOR 1995 Regulations, as the employer did not realise such incidents were covered by the RIDDOR 1995 Regulations. Other staff on the scheme were concerned about the behaviour of 'Andy' one of the participants on the scheme, who was involved in these incidents and did not want him to go on the residential. The staff most closely involved with him, however, felt he would benefit and learn from the valuable residential experience.

During the residential weekend, three staff were due to go away with the participants but one phoned in sick the day before and a less experienced replacement, 'Annie', was called in, who was not qualified in first aid. On the day of the overnight exercise on the mountain, the first aider had not arrived back at the centre as the minibus had broken down. 'Annie' joined the group leader, 'John' (who was a first aider) on the overnight exercise, where they stayed in the climbing hut in a remote part of the mountainous area. During the night in the climbing hut, an argument between two participants led to a fight. When the group leader (and first aider) tried to intervene, he was assaulted by 'Andy' and seriously injured by a knife wound to the stomach and lost consciousness. 'Annie' who was not qualified in first aid, tried to find the first aid kit but, in the rush, it had been left in the minibus. She did not know what to do to stem the flow of blood and 'John' died shortly afterwards. There had been no risk assessment of revised first aid provision after the staff member had called in sick the day before.

EXERCISE 6.40

Give two reasons for the Reporting Injuries, Diseases and Dangerous Occurrences (RIDDOR) Regulations 1995.

EXERCISE 6.41

Explain the three categories of reportable matters under RIDDOR.

EXERCISE 6.42

Is it only actual harm or injury which needs to be reported? Explain your answer.

Which workplaces require an accident book?

Who reports under RIDDOR 1995, how and to whom?

EXERCISE 6.43

What is first aid? Although circumstances will vary, what normally would be provided in a first aid kit?

EXERCISE 6.44

Explain the links between the Health and Safety (First Aid) Regulations 1981, the HSWA 1974 and the MHSW Regulations 1999.

EXERCISE 6.45

Identify five factors to consider when risk assessing first aid provision.

EXERCISE 6.46

What must an employer provide under the HSWFA Regulations 1981 s.3 and Regulation 3.2?

EXERCISE 6.47

How many first aiders are recommended in the HSE Guidance for 50–100 employees in a 'low risk' setting such as offices or libraries?

EXERCISE 6.48

Identify situations in sport or recreation where you would consider providing travelling first aid kits. What would be recorded in a first aid book following a first aid incident?

Part three: case law – breaches of statutory duties in sport and recreation

Michael and Stuart Ely, operators of Lake Estates Water Sports Centre, were charged with breaches of the Health and Safety at Work Act 1974, following the death of a visitor in a jet skiing accident at the centre. In August 1997:

a novice jet skier, Anthony Gee, with his niece riding pillion, crossed the line of buoys from the jet ski zone into the water-skiing area. Faye was knocked into the water and was run over by one of the water ski power boats. She was fatally injured by the propeller of the powerboat.

(Jamieson, 2003: 86)

The prosecution presented documents based upon expert witness opinion, which, they argued, 'demonstrated that good industry practice [standard and approved practice] dictated proper separation between areas of the lake for personal watercraft (e.g. jet skis) and for water skiing'.[26] The prosecution case was based mainly on the failure to ensure an effective form of division between the two activities or use a neutral buffer zone.[27] The defendants were convicted of the breaches of health and safety in November 1999, but the Court of Appeal, on 19 July 2002, concluded that all three convictions were unsafe. The appeal was around the process by which the opinions of expert witnesses was accessed and accepted as evidence in trial. Questionnaires had been:

completed by local authority officials after approaching operators for information. After disclosing the questionnaire to the defence prior to trial, it was on the basis that it would not be used in evidence. During the trial the Crown changed its mind and despite objections from the defence counsel, the trial judge ruled that this evidence was admissible.

(ibid: 87)

The key questions for the Court of Appeal were 'was the judge correct? If not, did such an error make the convictions unsafe?' The Court of Appeal concluded that this was an error and it did make the convictions unsafe. The water-based activity operators who were expert witnesses did not personally visit the site of the accident, and when there was a dispute over the evidence, there was therefore no opportunity, during the trial, to challenge the expert evidence (ibid: 87). Jamieson (2003: 88) reminded readers that the Health and Safety at Work Act 1974 imposes 'onerous duties to risk assess activities, implement proper precautions and carry out effective supervision and monitoring'. In her opinion if fair notice had been given regarding submitting the questionnaire as evidence with the 'opportunity to cross-examine on accuracy of the information contained in them, the document would have been admissible and the convictions would have been upheld'.

Leeds City Council were charged with two counts of breaching health and safety regulations by:

failing to prevent, as far as is reasonably practicable, people outside their employment, being exposed to health and safety risks, on a river walk, during a residential course at Stainforth Beck in North Yorkshire, in October 2000, as well as a failure to complete an adequate risk assessment in relation to this river walking activity.

(Herbert, 2002)

The council was convicted of the health and safety offences for 'failure to carry out a risk assessment for river walking activities run by Royds School in Stainforth Beck' and were fined £30,000, with £50,000 costs awarded to the Yorkshire and Humberside HSE (see case no. 2012944, HSE Public Register of Convictions[28]). Fifteen pupils and two teachers had walked about 70 metres up Stainforth Beck near Settle, when pupils Rochelle Cauvet, aged 14 and Hannah Black, 13, were swept to their deaths, during their annual outdoor activities residential, which had run since 1987. In August 2001, the Crown Prosecution Service (CPS) decided that there was not enough evidence to support a realistic chance of a manslaughter conviction or lesser offence against the teachers or other school staff or local education authority officials (Herbert, 2002).

The HSE investigation concluded that it was the local authority which was to blame and not the teachers for 'failing to provide them with the right preparation' (ibid. 2002). An inquest jury returned a verdict of accidental death. A verdict of unlawful killing by gross negligence was not offered because it 'did not meet the criteria' (see Jeffery, 2002). In a statement the parents of the two girls who died stated: 'Hannah and Rochelle were swept away and drowned while river walking in treacherous conditions without proper supervision and with minimal safety equipment. Anyone with any common sense at all would never have gone near the river' (ibid, 2002).

On 20 July 2002 Gameli Akuklu and William Kadame attended a summer school organised by the Metropolitan Police and Barnet Council, at the Pell Centre, Hendon. They were both reported to be strong swimmers but they drowned during a swimming pool session, after banging heads/hands when jumping off the diving board and were later discovered lying at the bottom of the pool. PC Danny Philips, the only lifeguard on duty at the time, was acquitted of charges of manslaughter by gross negligence and breaches of health and safety law in June 2006 (Dutta, 2006). The council pleaded guilty to the health and safety charges because it 'did not make a formal risk assessment or a formal register of the swimming abilities of those on placement, though both were done formally on the day' (Barnet Council Leader Mike Freer, quoted in Dutta, 2006).

The University of East Anglia, Norwich, was convicted of health and safety offences relating to risk assessment failures at one of their swimming pools, used by members of the public. In September 2002 a member of the public using the UEA Sports park swimming pool was 'found on the bottom of the pool, by another swimmer, who alerted the lifeguard. The lifeguard rescued the swimmer but the casualty died a few days later in hospital. The case was brought by the HSE because the risk assessment, which indicated that only one lifeguard was required, was not suitable and sufficient. At least two lifeguards were recommended for a 50m pool. This deficiency may have contributed to the death of the swimmer' (HSE Prosecutions Area, case no. 2013535[29]).

Caerphilly Unitary Authority in Wales was found guilty of breaches of health and safety under s.3 (1) of the 1974 Health and Safety at Work Act after a student drowned in a flooded river during a student field trip with Ystrad Mynach College. 'No risk assessment was completed for the trip and the lecturer was unaware of the health and safety policy of the college' (HSE Public Register of Convictions, case no 2016631[30]). The Jewish Senior Boys' School in Salford, England, was fined £3,500 and ordered to pay HSE costs of £400, for failure by the school:

> to give sufficient consideration to the health and safety precautions regarding their duties under s.3 (1) of the HSWA 1974. An adult teacher, in sole charge of 15 children, had become separated from the group as they were stranded in challenging terrain on an open hillside, when poor weather conditions descended. The teacher and seven children were injured. One child slipped on a scree and boulder covered slope and sustained a serious head injury. The children had to be airlifted from a variety of dangerous positions on the slope by an RAF helicopter.
>
> (HSE Public Register of Convictions, case no 2014925[31])

In *R v Gullivers World Theme Park Ltd* (unreported, 22 November 2006, Chester Crown Court), the theme park was fined £80,000 for breaching health and safety laws relating to the death of a teenager Salma Saleem on a Ferris wheel at the theme park in 2002. Chester Crown Court heard, in November 2006, that the 15 year old, who had Down's

Syndrome, wanted to ride alongside her mother, but the attendant felt she was too large and directed her to a different gondola. Her mother tried to protest, but neither she nor Salma spoke fluent English. Salma fell about 21ft (6m) from the ride (BBC News online, 22 November, 2006). Although the HSE lawyer advised the court that there was no evidence that Salma's death was caused by health and safety breaches, several safety failures were found which 'could have caused similar accidents' (ibid[32]).

The case of *R v Beckingham* (unreported, July 2006, Preston Crown Court, Burnton J), *R v Barrow Borough Council* (unreported, March 2005, Preston Crown Court, Poole J) is covered in relation to the manslaughter charges and trial in Chapter 7 of this text, this incident also resulted in charges relating to breaching health and safety laws. It illustrates the importance of maintenance issues and the impact of management behaviour within a public leisure/arts centre on the health and well-being of members of the public who have not even entered the premises. In the summer of 2002, in Barrow, Cumbria, England, an ageing air-conditioning unit on the wall of the Forum 28 Arts Centre became infected with legionnaires disease. It released water droplets into the atmosphere, infecting people who were just walking along the street past the centre. Some 180 people fell ill with legionnaires disease and seven people died from the disease.

The council pleaded guilty to breaching health and safety laws. In the case against Gillian Beckingham, an architect and Head of Design Services Group at Barrow Council and allegedly responsible for maintaining the air-conditioning unit, a jury found her guilty of breaches of health and safety.

> The case clearly highlighted the importance of taking adequate precautions to protect people from legionnaires disease. There were several lapses in the duty of care by Barrow Council as the employer and by Gillian Beckingham, the Council's Design Services Manager. There is a clear lesson for all those who are responsible for installations that carry a risk from legionella. You should check your management arrangements and your control measures regularly and you should oversee the work that contractors do on your behalf. There is no room for assumptions that systems are working as they should, and no room for ignoring personal roles and responsibilities at any level of management.
>
> (HSE statement on Barrow Legionnella, 31 July, 2006: 1)

A Great Yarmouth leisure firm was fined £90,000 after admitting they had failed to protect 57 employees and thousands of night clubbers and children at risk from asbestos contamination at their Atlantis Arena (previously the Tower Ballroom). The directors of Towering Leisure:

> knew of the risks as they had been given a report on the asbestos in 2004. Norwich Crown Court heard that there must be a substantial risk to health of employees and this was a case of dealing with profit over safety.
>
> (Recorder Guy Ayes, to the directors,
> when fining them, bbc.co.uk cited on asbestostech.com[33])

Wear Valley District Council in Co. Durham was fined £18,000 after it admitted six breaches of health and safety law. The council was warned about the presence of asbestos in the plant room of Woodhouse Close Leisure Complex in Bishop Auckland in 2001, but inspection reports were ignored until 2006 when an employee made an official complaint against the council. At least three men known to have worked full time in the boiler room during that five-year period have been warned that 'the exposure will pose a significant risk to their health, but because no official monitoring records were kept, it is unclear how many people have been affected' (McFarlane, 2007).

EXERCISE 6.49

Outline the events of August 1997 at Lake Estates Water Sports Centre which led to the prosecution of Michael Ely, Stuart Ely and Lake Estates Ltd. Briefly summarise the HSE prosecution case for breaches of health and safety and the outcome of the criminal trial in *R v Ely and Lake Estates Watersports Ltd* (unreported, November 1999, Northampton Crown Court).

EXERCISE 6.50

Explain why the Court of Appeal made all three convictions 'unsafe'? Despite this, what does Jamieson (2003) point out in relation to the application of the risk assessment duties under the HSWA 1974, if the circumstances of accessing expert testimony were different?

EXERCISE 6.51

Leeds City Council, West Yorkshire, England, were convicted of health and safety offences in relation to a school trip to Stainforth Beck, Yorkshire in 2000. What were the circumstances of the Stainforth Beck school trip which led to the deaths of Rochelle Cauvert (aged 14) and Hannah Black (aged 13)?

EXERCISE 6.52

Explain the two counts of breaches of health and safety against Leeds City Council under the specific sections of the HSWA 1974 and the MHSW Regulations 1999. What was the outcome of the inquest and the manslaughter investigation following the events at Stainforth Beck?

EXERCISE 6.53

Search the media databases for information and commentary on the Stainforth Beck school trip noting critical commentary and outcomes of the various legal processes – HSE case, inquest (for example, LexisNexis Executive for print and online media, BBC news archives, HSE Register of convictions). Make notes on what you find and contribute an article and your comments to your seminar group. What is your opinion of the events at Stainforth Beck? What have you learnt about risk assessment from this case?

EXERCISE 6.54

In the case of *R v Barnet Council* (unreported, 13 July 2006, Central Criminal Court, Bean J) explain why the defendants were found guilty of breaches of health and safety following the deaths of Gameli Akuklu and William Kadame during a summer school in July 2002.

EXERCISE 6.55

In the case of *R v University of East Anglia* (unreported, 2002, Norwich Magistrates' Court) explain why the risk assessment by the defendant was not 'suitable and sufficient' under s.3 of the Management of Health and Safety at Work Regulations 1999 and s.3 of the Health and Safety at Work Act 1974.

EXERCISE 6.56

Do people have to actually enter a sport/leisure/arts facility to be damaged or killed by the acts or omissions of those managing or maintaining the facility? Explain the evidence in the HSE prosecution in *R v Beckingham* (unreported, July 2006, Preston Crown Court, Burnton J) and *R v Barrow Borough Council* (unreported, March 2005, Preston Crown Court, Poole J). What was the outcome of the criminal case brought by the HSE? What is the lesson for all who are responsible for installations that carry a risk from legionella (HSE, 2006)?

Key case: Glenridding Beck – learning lessons from the death of 10-year-old Max Palmer

Introduction

In October 2002, three staff from a Lancashire high school took a party of 12 Year 8 pupils to Glenridding, Cumbria, for an activity weekend. The party also contained three primary school age children, including the deceased, Max Palmer. The deceased's mother was one of the adults accompanying the visit. On the Sunday morning the party went to a pool in Glenridding Beck to do an activity called 'plunge pooling'. 'Max was washed over the weir at the exit of the pool. He was pulled from the beck approximately 150 metres below the pool, but was pronounced dead at the scene' (HSE, 2005c: 1). In September 2003 the teacher leading the visit pleaded guilty to manslaughter and was jailed for one year. In July 2004 the HSE announced that, following a lengthy and detailed investigation of the role of the Local Education Authority, Lancashire County Council (LCC) it would not prosecute LCC (HSE, 2005d: 3).

Main findings of the police HSE/police investigation

The report summarises the very detailed investigation by the HSE and Cumbria Police into the tragedy at Glenridding Beck.[34] It shows that 'the chain of events leading to the tragedy began long before the fateful weekend'. It also shows how:

> compliance with existing guidelines and good practice prevents such chains developing. The report emphasised having effective health and safety management systems and guarding against individual and institutional complacency. It also demonstrates the importance of pupil involvement in organising safe and successful educational visits.
>
> (HSE, 2005c: 1)

The investigation identified two main issues:

* The wholly inappropriate actions of the party leader before and during the incident.
* The shortcomings of the management systems which allowed an unsuitable leader to be in charge of a party of schoolchildren in a high-hazard environment.

The main lessons are:

* Leaders need to be competent, diligent and always put safety and the best interests of the young people at the top of their agenda. They should always follow published guidance.
* Schools and providers of outdoor education/adventure activities need to have effective management systems to prevent unsuitable leaders taking young people into hazardous environments. Effective arrangements for assessing and ensuring competence and for monitoring are particularly important (HSE, 2005c: 1).

Preparation and planning

The investigation examined the history of past school visits to Glenridding going through the leader's background, the nature of Glenridding visits and the supervision of pupils. The visit leader joined the school in 1998 and in his application form made 'a number of claims relating to a mountain leadership qualifications. He had attended part of a Mountain Leadership Award (Summer), but had not completed the required logbook or assessment. Therefore, he did not hold that qualification' (HSE, 2005c: 8). The leader had experience organising outdoor visits at another centre and soon after joining the school started organising 'activity trips' (p. 8). The HSE commented that no checks on qualifications or subsequent assessment of technical competence were made before he began organising visits to Glenridding. There was a 'lack of clarity at the school about who was responsible for checking qualifications' and no risk assessment of a proposed new activity (p. 8).

In addition, the LCC required at least one of the supervisory staff to hold a first aid certificate and carry a first aid kit. The leader had a certificate for 'Emergency First Aid' and did not qualify him as a 'first aider', which the HSE suggested may be a common misunderstanding. The LCC procedures required supervision by staff holding the relevant RLSS qualification if swimming, water play or water-based activities took place. This was not followed. The visits to Glenridding included activities such as walking, ghyll scrambling and rock climbing and photographs of the plunge-pool activity on display at the school. There had been concerns raised in 2000 about the level of supervision in the evening on previous visits but this was seen as a 'personality clash' between teachers at a school meeting held in October 2000. The HSE recommended that supervision on school visits 'needs to be 24 hours per day 7 days per week, the precise arrangements being based on risk assessment and that schools and LEAs need clear procedures for dealing with any concerns about unsafe practice' (p. 9).

In planning and preparing for the visit the leader had sent out a brief letter to parents, but no consent/medical information form and no requests to clarify if pupils could swim. There was no parents' meeting and the leader was unfamiliar with the LCC Guidelines, which had been brought to his attention at the school meeting in October 2000 (p. 15). No prior consent from parents was sought for swimming activities on the visit (p. 17). The visit did not have clearly defined educational objectives and although the leader asked another teacher and Max's mother to help him with the visit, neither had any significant experience or formal qualifications in outdoor activities. This meant that although the child:adult ratio was 5:1, the ratio of novice:experienced participants was 17:1. The 12 Year 8 children from the school were accompanied by three primary school children, including Max Palmer, aged ten (p. 16).[35]

The events at Glenridding Beck Sunday 26 October 2002

The HSE investigation examined the environmental conditions, the decision to do the activity, the ignored warning, the jump into the pool, the failed rescue attempt and the recovery of casualties. It had been wet for much of the week and rained heavily en route to Glenridding on the Friday night. When the next day was cold, wet and windy, the leader dismissed the idea of doing anything in the Glenridding area and went instead to Ambleside and Keswick. The leader did not check the local weather forecasts displayed in the Tourist Information Centre. The HSE commented that 'interpretation of the current and past forecasts would indicate that any rainwater running off the fells into Glenridding Beck would be very cold. This would be important information for a *dynamic* risk assessment' (HSE, 2005c: 20).

The pupils kept asking when they could do the plunge pool activity in the afternoon and in the evening the leader said that they would do it the following day. 'The leader was under pressure to do the activity because of the pupil expectation that had been created. Leaders need to be careful not to create unrealistic expectations and should not allow participant pressure to cloud their judgement' (HSE comments for educational visits, p. 20). There was no rain on Sunday morning and the leader decided to go ahead with the plunge pool activity as he had 'looked at the beck and took the view that it had gone down' (p. 20). The party left the hostel at 10.30 am and those who did not want to participate had to walk up anyway. Pupils who were going to jump in were told to 'put on shorts (or swimming kit), T-shirts and trainers and to take a towel' (p. 20).

Teachers leading a school party from a neighbouring hostel visited the plunge pool on that Sunday and decided not to use the pool because of the weather and water conditions, but 'to take the children up anyway and show them why it was too dangerous'. This party walked back from the pool and on the way down met Max's school party and 'told the leader that he thought the pool was too dangerous and that they would not let the children jump. The leader replied that he had a rope and continued towards the pool' (p. 21). On arriving at the plunge pool, the leader jumped from the platform, got out quickly and said that it was fine.

The other teacher went down to the exit point while the leader and Max's mother stayed at the jumping point. When it was Max's turn to jump, the leader asked him if he could swim and if he wanted to go in. Max replied 'yes' to both questions. The leader directed him where to jump and Max entered the pool. As soon as he surfaced, it was evident that he was in trouble and panicking.

(p. 21)

The leader jumped in a number of times to try to rescue Max but:

the boy was so panic-stricken that he kept pushing the leader under the water. Max's mother then jumped in to try to save her son. Shortly afterwards, the leader realised that he was succumbing to the cold and went to the exit point where the teacher helped him out. He was by now so cold that he was unable to contribute anything further to the rescue. There was an attempt to use a string of towels as a substitute rope, but they sank. Eventually Max's mother was also overcome by the cold. At some point when Max's mother was in the water, the teacher told some boys to get the rope. They ran to the hostel. Some fetched the rope while others raised the alarm. Three staff from the other school ran towards the scene with rescue and survival equipment.

(p. 22)

A pupil went into the water and tried to rescue Max, but Max was washed out of the exit to the pool and down the beck. The same pupil found Max's mother and with assistance from a teacher pulled her from the water. The pupil was by now very cold and Mrs Palmer was semi-conscious.

The children with the rope arrived back at the pool at about the time Max was washed over the weir. The teachers from the other school arrived soon after. They put Mrs Palmer in a sleeping bag to keep her warm until the mountain rescue arrived. Max was pulled from the beck further downstream by some pupils. He was pronounced dead at the scene. His mother and the pupil who saved her were flown to hospital and treated for hypothermia.

(p. 22)

Keeping risks and benefits in perspective: the value of educational visits involving outdoor activities

The publicity surrounding the incident and the subsequent jailing for manslaughter of the teacher who led the trip has led to a lot of concern about the safe running of school visits. This was reflected in a recent report from the Commons Select Committee. To put the Glenridding tragedy in context, however, it has been estimated that, in England, there are 7–10 million pupil visits per year, which involve educational or recreational activity. The overwhelming majority of these visits are carried out safely and responsibly by teachers who take the time and effort to get things right. The benefits to children of these trips is immense.

(HSE, 2005c: 1)

The HSE believes that school trips are 'a vital part of a child's education' and do not want 'misplaced risk aversion to deprive them of such opportunities' as adventure activities provide 'the ideal opportunity to make children "risk aware" by involving them in practical decision-making in challenging environments' (p. 1).

It has never been our belief that school trips should cease as a result of Max's death. We have always maintained that they form an important part of a child's development and education. However, it is crucial that all the necessary safety and supervision measures should be in place and should be strictly adhered to.

(Mr and Mrs Palmer in HSE, 2005d: 1)

HSE, DfES and LCC have a very clear view that:

- adventure activities are an essential option within the PE and sports part of the curriculum, not least because of the opportunity to learn about the management of risk
- such activities must be properly planned and managed
- most teachers are careful and professional. If the small numbers of less careful teachers learn lessons from this report and undertake proportionate risk assessment then that will be a purpose served
- people who follow the available guidance should have nothing to fear, those who ignore it may be asking for trouble.

(HSE, 2005c: 6)

At a conference for the Girls' Schools Association in Leeds, Robert McKenzie Johnson, headteacher of Queen Mary's School for Girls in North Yorkshire, 'gave a 15 minute speech about his stimulating approach to outdoor learning at his school' (Bearsdall, 2008: 32).

Children and staff exposed to low level risks he thinks are better for it, and he tackles the Health and Safety Executive (HSE) – the public body responsible for the encouragement, regulation and enforcement of workplace health, safety and welfare – head on. 'It wasn't set up to stop schools doing things or as a reason not to do something. I use it as a check to do it safely' he says. 'Too many schools worry about secondary risk – what happens to the school if a child is injured. That's irrelevant. Schools are insured. Occasionally, children do break arms. Accidents should not stop us – only if we found we were negligent would it affect what we do in the future. It is the primary risk – the risk to the child – that matters'. During term time at Queen Mary's every child from the age of nine takes part in organised outdoor learning activities as part of the curriculum.

(ibid: 32)

The above article, 'Double Dare' written by Bearsdall in the *Daily Telegraph* on 13 September 2008, is very supportive of the value of risk-taking and outdoor learning in the school curriculum. The direct quotes in the paragraph above, from the headteacher, Robert McKenzie Johnson, clearly illustrate that he is taking the approach outlined earlier in this chapter in the HSE (2006) Ten principles of Risk Assessment, and supports the comments on outdoor learning by the HSE, DFES and LCC following the HSE investigation into the death of Max Palmer. Yet the commentary by the feature writer contradicts Johnson by stating that the headteacher is tackling the HSE head-on. Bearsdall (2008: 32) introduces the article with the statement:

Bumps and scrapes were once part of growing up, but that was before the advent of the Health and Safety Executive and today's compensation culture. At some schools, though, a certain amount of risk remains an essential part of the curriculum.

The chair of the HSE, Judith Hackitt, OBE, responded to this article in a letter to the editor of *The Daily Telegraph*, pointing out, among other things that:

I enjoyed your article on children experiencing risk through adventurous activities. What a pity we were sat, incorrectly, as opponents rather than supporters. The Health and Safety Executive (HSE) agrees completely with Headmaster Robert McKenzie Johnston's comment that 'it was not set up to stop schools doing things or as a reason not to do something'. HSE does not advocate wrapping children in cotton wool; we are here to save lives, not to stop people from living them. Adventurous activities, in the playground or elsewhere, provide ideal opportunities to make children 'risk aware' by involving them in practical decision-making in challenging environments.

(Letter from Judith Hackitt, chair, Health and Safety Executive, to editor of *The Daily Telegraph*, 16 September, 2008)

This reponse by Judith Hackitt is in line with the HSE Ten Principles of Risk Assessment covered earlier in this chapter and the HSE and DfES statements earlier, following the HSE and police investigation into the death of Max Palmer at Glenridding Beck, published in 2005.

EXERCISE 6.57

Briefly outline the circumstances on the 26 October 2002 at Glenridding Beck. What were the outcomes of any criminal investigations into statutory duties and manslaughter in relation to this tragedy?

EXERCISE 6.58

The investigation by the Health and Safety Executive (HSE) and Cumbria police identified two main issues. What were they?

EXERCISE 6.59

Explain accurately the issues around leader qualification and competence, and child/adult ratios included in the HSE/Police 2005 report. Which kind of qualifications might be suitable for leading an activity such as 'plunge-pooling'?

EXERCISE 6.60

Imagine that you were a teacher who was asked to arrive on the Sunday morning to help with the latter part of the school visit to Glenridding Beck. You decide to conduct a 'dynamic' risk assessment on the morning of 26 October 2002. What would you include, particularly in relation to the weather conditions?

EXERCISE 6.61

What warnings were given to the leader on the day of the tragedy by teachers from another party? What was the response from the leader of Max's school party?

EXERCISE 6.62

Critically discuss the rescue provision including the rope, seeking assistance, and the possibility of a panicking casualty, using the HSE 2005 web report.

EXERCISE 6.63

Explain the significance, for risk assessment, of the expectations of the pupils and the importance of having an alternative plan.

EXERCISE 6.64

Divide into two groups. One group argue for the continuing inclusion of educational visits including outdoor activities and one group argue to exclude such activities from the school curriculum. Both groups should use relevant information from the HSE 2005 web report into the Glenridding Beck 2002 tragedy but also search for other relevant sources and commentaries.

EXERCISE 6.65

Get into groups of four. Each group locate one of the guidance documents listed below. Summarise the contents of the document on one page of A4 and explain the connection to the Glenridding Beck HSE 2005 report.

DfES 1999 *Health and Safety of Pupils on Educational Visits* (HASPEV at www.teachernet.gov.uk/ wholeschool/healthandsafety/visits/)
BAALPE 2004 *Safe Practice in Physical Education*. Leeds: Coachwise (section on outdoor activities)
AALA Collective Interpretation for combined water/rock activities at www.aala.org/guidance.html
HSE Information Sheet *Combined Water and Rock Activities: Guidance for Providers* at www.hse.gov.uk/pubns/etis13.pdf

Summary

- Some hazards and risks are an integral part of the challenge of sport.
- A hazard is anything that might cause harm.
- A risk is the magnitude of the harm and the probability of it materialising.
- Risk assessment is a careful examination of what could cause harm to people and weighing up if the precautions are appropriate (adapted from HSE, 2006: 2).
- Risk assessments can be generic, at or for, an event, on-site or 'dynamic' (ongoing).
- Sensible risk management is about ensuring that people are properly protected, providing an overall benefit by balancing risks with a focus on reducing real risks, enabling innovation and learning, taking risk management seriously and understanding that as well as the right to protection, people also have exercise responsibility (ibid: 2).
- Sensible risk management is *not* about creating a totally risk-free society, generating paperwork, scaring or exaggerating or publicising trivial risks, stopping important recreational and learning activities where risks are managed or reducing protection from real risks that cause real harm and suffering (ibid: 2).
- Risk management is important as, among other things, it is a legal requirement, and it should help those in sport to comply with such duties.
- Children and adults have the right to be taught or coached sport in a safe environment, and can learn about risk education by being involved in risk management.
- Risk management helps keeps risks to a minimum and keep sport enjoyable.
- Risk education should be part of the school curriculum in the areas of personal and social education (PSE), physical education, citizenship, science, design technology information and communication technology, art, and design in England and Wales.
- Engaging in risk education and personal responsibility in physical education and other school subjects can help children and young people apply such lessons to their own engagement in informal leisure and physical recreation outside school.
- There are a range of statutes and EC Directives which deal with health and safety duties in a work environment.
- Local authorities who run sport or leisure centres, universities, theme parks, and county councils, as well as a range of corporations have been the subject of criminal investigations and/or prosecutions for breaches of health and safety in the criminal law.

7 Causing and investigating death: an overview of selected manslaughter cases

Introduction

Sports carry an element of risk of injury or even death. That may be part of their appeal and challenge. Chapter 4 was restricted to a socio-legal view of sports violence and non-fatal assaults under the statute Offences Against the Person Act 1861 and The Criminal Justice Act 1988. This chapter deals exclusively with some aspects of manslaughter. It begins with a generic overview of the two categories of involuntary manslaughter – constructive (unlawful act) manslaughter and manslaughter by gross negligence. It moves on to a summary of the challenges of applying common law manslaughter to a corporation. The ad hoc development of the law in this area and the appropriateness of the test of corporate manslaughter for large and complex organisations have been illustrated by the failures of the law to respond to, in particular, major disasters in the UK. This led to a lengthy process of legal reform which began in 1995 and, at the time of writing, saw the implementation of the Corporate Manslaughter and Corporate Homicide Act which came into effect on 6 April 2008.

It is important for sports organisations and individuals to appreciate the very fine line between causing death in sport and being found liable for negligence, a civil matter, and causing death and being charged with manslaughter – a criminal offence.[1] It is often assumed that manslaughter charges are mainly brought against managers or organisers of sport facilities or events. The second half of this chapter hopes to illustrate the wide range of defendants to date, in a sport or physical recreation context, who have already been investigated or charged with manslaughter. These include players, competitors, sports leaders, fans, parents, facility managers, local council maintenance officers, an officer on a commercial ferry, and even children as young as ten or 11 (at the time of an alleged offence). The final section of the chapter focuses on the Lyme Bay canoe tragedy of 1993, in which four teenage pupils lost their lives during a residential outdoor activities week. The evidence heard in the trial of the centre manager and the managing director of the company in November 1993 provides important lessons for all those involved in sport and physical recreation and not just 'adventure' activities.

Involuntary manslaughter: generic principles and cases

Involuntary manslaughter is used for those unlawful killings or homicides where the defendant has caused the death of the victim but does not have the necessary mental element (*mens rea*) for murder. For example, a defendant 'D might punch P in the face, intending to do P actual bodily harm. If by some mischance P should suffer a brain haemorrhage and die as a result of this attack, D would be charged with manslaughter' (Molan et al., 2003: 198). There are two main kinds of involuntary manslaughter – constructive (or unlawful act) manslaughter and manslaughter by gross negligence. Nearly all the cases in this chapter fall into the second category, manslaughter by gross negligence.

Constructive (unlawful act) manslaughter requires the defendant to commit an unlawful act, which is dangerous and caused the death. The dangerous element of this category of manslaughter really means that 'all sober and reasonable people would inevitably recognise' that such an act 'must subject the other person to, at least the risk of some physical harm', even if it is not serious harm (Dobson, 2005: 105[2]). In the case of *Director of Public Prosecutions v Newbury and Jones* [1977] AC 500 two 15-year-olds had stood on the parapet of a bridge which straddled a railway line. As a train approached they pushed a paving stone over the bridge. It crashed through the front window of the cab, killing a guard. The defendants appealed on the grounds that they 'had not foreseen any harm as a likely result of their actions' (ibid: 105). They lost their appeal in the House of Lords who followed the ruling in *R v Church* [1966] 1 QB 59.

Lord Salmon expressed the view in *Newbury* that an accused was 'guilty of manslaughter if it was proved that he intentionally did an act, which was unlawful and dangerous, and that act inadvertently caused death. It was, he said, unnecessary to prove that the accused knew that the act was unlawful or dangerous' (Molan et al., 2003: 198–199[3]). In *R v Cato* [1976] 1 All ER 260, two drug addicts were unlawfully in possession of heroin. They each filled up their own syringes with heroin and water, and injected each other. One of the drug addicts died. The jury convicted the survivor of two offences (1) unlawfully and maliciously administering a noxious substance, contrary to the Offences Against the Person Act 1861, s.23 and (2) manslaughter. On appeal, it was held that it was an unlawful act as, at the time of the injection, the mixture of heroin and water had been unlawfully taken into his possession by the defendant, for the purposes of the injection (see Molan et al., 2003; Dobson, 2005).

Manslaughter by gross negligence requires a duty of care owed by the accused or defendant to the victim, a breach of duty which causes the death of the victim(s). The negligence must be so gross as to go beyond a matter of civil law negligence such that it warrants criminal liability. There is no need to show that the defendant engaged in a criminal act when he caused the death of the victim. The principle in this category of manslaughter is that the defendant was performing an otherwise lawful act in such a negligent manner, causing death that he/she deserves to be charged with the crime of manslaughter. Such lawful acts can include medical treatment, maintenance work, or the organisation of or participation in sport or recreation events.

The case of *R v Bateman* [1925] 94 LJ ICB 791, involved a defendant, a doctor, being charged with manslaughter arising out of the death of a patient, whom he was attending at a home birth. It was alleged that he was 'guilty of two aspects of medical negligence, and he had delayed too long in having the patient removed to hospital' (Dobson, 2005: 108). He appealed successfully against his conviction.

> in order to establish criminal liability the facts must be such that, in the opinion of the jury, the negligence or incompetence of the accused went far beyond a mere matter of compensation between two subjects and showed such disregard for the life and safety of others as to amount to a crime against the State and conduct deserving punishment.
>
> (Lord Hewart CJ, in *Bateman*, cited Molan et al., 2003: 203)

Although it does establish that conduct sufficient only to establish civil law negligence is not enough for manslaughter in criminal law, it has been criticised for leaving matters to the jury (Molan et al., 2003). In December 1989 Norman Holt, company director of Holt Plastics, was 'prosecuted for manslaughter over the death of an employee, George

Kenyon. He was given a one-year term of imprisonment, but it was suspended for two years. The leniency of the sentence caused an outcry locally' (Dalton, 1998: 35).

The medical cases of *Sullman*[4] in 1993 and *Adomako* in 1994, reinforced the return to manslaughter by gross negligence, after some cases in the 1980s which characterised a period of confusion around 'reckless' manslaughter (see Hartley 2001b: 94–96). *Adomako* was an anaesthetist who failed to notice that an endotracheal tube had become disconnected from the ventilator, starving the patient of oxygen, for around six minutes, leading to a cardiac arrest and death. He failed in his appeal against a manslaughter conviction. Their Lordships overruled their own decision in *Seymour* (1983) now deciding that Caldwell's recklessness had no part in the test of liability for manslaughter.[5] The test in *Adomako* was one of gross negligence (Dobson, 2005: 109). Lord Mackay identified key steps for the prosecution to prove in establishing liability. These were:

1 A duty of care owed by D to P
2 A breach of that duty of care in circumstances where D's act or omission created a risk of death
3 That the breach of duty caused the death of P and
4 Negligence on the part of D that was so culpable it warranted being labelled as criminal.

(Lord Mackay in *Adomako* HL 1994)

The Court of Appeal case of *R v Misra and another* 8 October 2004 tested the question of any conflict between the ingredients of the offence of manslaughter by gross negligence, in *Adomako* and Article 7 of the European Convention on Human Rights. The Court of Appeal dismissed their appeal and decided that 'the definition of the crime was not incompatible with the ECHR Art.7, which required the law to be certain' (Dobson, 2005: 109). After this journey through key cases, what is manslaughter in 2008? The Law Commission 2008 guide to the present law and proposed changes to murder and manslaughter summarises the kinds of manslaughter you are reading about in this chapter. Reckless manslaughter is 'when someone does something really stupid that they knew might kill or badly hurt another person' (ibid: 24). Unlawful Act Manslaughter is 'when someone does something against the law which leads to the death of another person' (Law Commission, 2008: 24). Gross Negligence manslaughter is 'when someone does something stupid that puts another person at risk which then leads to them dying' (ibid: 24).

EXERCISE 7.1

Explain the meaning of i. unlawful act manslaughter, ii. manslaughter by gross negligence, and iii. reckless manslaughter, with reference to relevant cases and literature.

EXERCISE 7.2

Go back and check Chapter 2 on the elements of civil law negligence. What are the similarities and differences between civil law negligence which causes death and (involuntary) manslaughter by gross negligence? Is this a fine line? Write a hypothetical scenario which involves an individual player engaging in gross negligent conduct which results in death. It should be so culpable it should be labelled as criminal, demonstrating a very serious deviation from the expected standards and/or relevant sport codes of practice.

EXERCISE 7.3 HYPOTHETICAL

'Nicola' a nutritionist advising a team of elite endurance cyclists, gains access to a stock of illegally obtained designer steroids and human growth hormone. She offers them to the team. Most of the team decline the offer as they are aware that it is unlawful possession and they are worried about the safety issues as the source is not regulated. Two of the team meet up one night at a 'Mike's' house, one of the players. 'Mike' and 'Pete' inject each other with both the steroids and the human growth hormone. 'Mike' is fine but 'Pete' suffers an adverse reaction which affects his brain and liver and he dies a week later. Could 'Mike' or 'Nicola' be charged with manslaughter? If so, would it be unlawful act manslaughter or manslaughter by gross negligence? Refer to relevant literature and case law in support of your decision. What would the police/prosecution need to find out from medical experts in relation to chains of causation leading to death?

EXERCISE 7.4 HYPOTHETICAL

In 2008, a university rugby club of male players hosts an evening of initiation rites for new members of the club. They wanted to go one better than the previous year and made the initiation tasks particularly challenging. Each team captain was in charged of a group of first-year students. 'Richard' set his group two tasks. First they had to run five miles with a rucksack on their backs at 2 pm in the heat of an August afternoon. On returning to the campus at 3 pm the group were then instructed to dress up in sweat suits and do press-ups for five hours in the sports centre sauna. Some students completed the first running task and about half an hour of the sauna task. 'Oliver' a first-year student was told he had to continue or he would face an alternative task which was worse than the sauna task. 'Oliver' continued with the press-ups in the sauna, intermittently, for around three hours. At around 6 pm he collapsed and had a cardiac arrest. An ambulance was called and resuscitation was started at the scene and continued in the emergency department of the local hospital.[6] 'Oliver' died at 6.45 pm. Imagine you are a CPS lawyer making a decision on the nature of any manslaughter charges. Would you bring manslaughter charges against 'Richard' and/or the university student union sports club? Give reasons for your decision.

Personally reflect on your involvement in or witnessing of, any pranks, drunken antics or initiation rites in a sport or leisure context which, if you were honest, could have foreseeably led to serious injury or death. Share this with others in the group without identifying those involved in any incidents. How easy is it to cross the line from causing injury to causing death?

The perfect crime? Corporate manslaughter

'Did you ever expect a corporation to have a conscience when it has no soul to be damned and no body to be kicked?' (Edward Thurlow, Lord Chancellor, 1731–1806, cited Crainer, 1993: 132). Corporate manslaughter has been described by critical commentators as the 'perfect crime' as charges are rarely brought and convictions are extremely rare and by 1993 it had only once resulted in the conviction and imprisonment of a managing director[7] (Bergman, 1993).

> Murder and manslaughter are . . . common law offences developed to reflect the fact that, historically, the concern of the law has been with individuals who cause death. Corporate identity is a relatively new phenomenon in legal terms, hence the difficulties the courts have encountered in attempting to apply the principles of homicide (developed to deal with the thoughts and actions of real people) to the actions of corporate bodies.
>
> (Molan et al., 2003: 211)

There have been various criminal offences such as breaching health and safety laws which can be applied to a corporation. A crime such as manslaughter is different 'not only because it requires direct human intervention to cause a result, but also because it requires proof of degree of fault' (ibid: 211). Where an offence requires a mental element, for example, a *mens rea*, a corporation cannot be held vicariously liable, so the doctrine of identification or alter ego was adapted from civil law (Hartley, 2001b: 97). This doctrine of identification was established in the case of *HL Bolton Engineering v TJ Graham Ltd* when Lord Denning described a company having a nerve centre that controls what it does and servants or hands that carry out its will. Some are mere servants who are:

> nothing more than the hands that do the work and cannot be said to represent the mind and will. Others are directors and managers who represent the directing mind and will of the company, and control what it does. The state of mind of these managers is the state of mind of the company and is treated by the law as such.
>
> (*per* Lord Denning [1957] 1 QB 159: 172)

The principle of the controlling mind of a company was further reinforced in *Tesco v Natrass* (1972) when Lord Reid spoke of a controlling mind:

> Acting as the company and his mind which directs his acts is the mind of the company. There is no question of the company being vicariously liable . . . he is the embodiment of the company . . . his mind is the mind of the company. If it is a guilty mind then that guilt is the guilt of the company.
>
> (*per* Lord Reid [1972] AC 153: 170E–F)

This means that it is necessary to prove that the controlling officers or directing minds of a company are guilty of manslaughter in order that the company itself can be found guilty of corporate manslaughter. The doctrine of identification, the failure of the law to aggregate the faults of individual officers to make a collective corporate mind, can serve as a barrier to prosecutions and convictions for corporate manslaughter (see Jefferson, 2000; Parsons 2003; Sheikh, 2007). The weaknesses of the law of Anglo-Welsh corporate manslaughter and the marginalisation of corporate crime causing death have been severely criticised by academic commentators and campaigners alike (see Wells, 1993, 1995; Field and Jorg, 1991; Bergman, 1991, 1993, 1997, 1999; Slapper and Toombs, 1999; Hartley, 2001b).

Prior to the prosecution which followed the sinking of the *Herald of Free Enterprise* in 1990, there had only been two previous prosecutions of both a director and a company. The first was *R v Cory* Brothers (1927) and the second case was at Glamorgan Assizes in 1965, when the company was also acquitted.[8] The high profile manslaughter case of *R v P &O European Ferries (Dover) Ltd* (1991) 93 Cr App R 72, reinforced the principle that a company could be prosecuted for manslaughter whilst at the same time clearly illustrated the failures of Anglo-Welsh corporate manslaughter laws (Crainer, 1993; Wells, 1993a; Hartley, 2001b). On 6 March 1987 the *Herald of Free Enterprise* roll-on, roll-off ferry capsized in shallow water at Zeebrugge. The immediate cause of the disaster was water flooding the car deck through the bow doors, which had been left open by a junior member of the crew (Crainer, 1993).

The public inquiry into the disaster chaired by Sheen J concluded that:

> The underlying cardinal faults lay higher up the company . . . all concerned with management . . . who were guilty of fault in that it must be regarded as sharing responsibility for the failure of management. From top to bottom the body corporate was infected with a disease of sloppiness.
>
> (Sheen J 1987, para 14.1[9])

On 22 June 1989, a summons was issued, by the Director of Public Prosecutions (DPP), alleging reckless manslaughter by seven defendants, from the assistant bosun, who left the bow doors open, to shore-based director level. The company itself, P&O European Ferries, was also charged with corporate manslaughter. LJ Bingham accepted that a company could be charged with manslaughter, not based on vicarious liability but on the doctrine of identification, of those who were the embodiment of the company itself, but he rejected the principle of aggregating the faults of individual defendants to make up the collective corporate mind and will (see Hartley, 2001b: 103). 'There is no doubt this is an untested part of the law' (Crown Prosecution Service spokesperson, at the time of the summons, 22 June, 1989, cited Crainer, 1993: 96). The criminal trial for individual and corporate manslaughter began on 10 September 1990 at the Old Bailey and was only the third in legal history.[10]

The prosecution had to show that 'the recklessness of one or more individual defendants was in either not recognising or disregarding an obvious and serious risk that a ferry would sail with its bow doors open' (Crainer, 1993: 98–99). In a legal ruling, in the absence of the jury, Turner J concluded:

> There is no evidence that reasonably prudent marine superintendents, chief super-intendents, or naval architects, would or should have recognised that the system gave rise to an obvious and serious risk of open-door sailing.
>
> (cited in Crainer, 1993: 101)

The prosecution tried to continue its case but, after only 66 out of the 138 prosecution witnesses had been heard, the judge, Turner J directed the jury to acquit P&O European Ferries and the other defendants except the first officer, Leslie Sabel, and the assistant bosun, Mark Stanley.

> I have come to the very clear conclusion there is at this stage, no evidence which would justify it being left to the jury to find that there was obvious and serious risk.
>
> (Turner J *R v Stanley and others* October 1990, The Old Bailey)

The issues around the awareness of a serious and obvious risk by the key defendants, who were the directing minds of the company, related to a series of complex questions.

These included different definitions of the term 'obvious' [risk], and the poor internal communications of the company which may have resulted in a lack of awareness by the directors. In addition, witnesses reported that the industry operated in much the same way in relation to sailing with the bow doors open. There was a lack of previous ferry disasters of this kind. There were no clear criminal regulatory breaches and the findings of Sheen J public inquiry could not be used. All of these factors, among other things, presented challenges to the prosecution (see Crainer, 1993; Hartley, 2001b). Following the acquittal of the other defendants, the cases against Mark Stanley and Leslie Sabel were dropped by the prosecution, as it was considered not in the public interest to proceed solely against these two defendants. The judge then directed the jury to find them not guilty too.

The verdict was seen to emphasise 'the need for a review of the law as it relates to individual and collective liability' (Robert Adley, Vice-Chair of the Conservative back-bench Transport Committee, cited in Crainer, 1993: 102). 'If the law is such that you cannot prove a case, which appears, to the ordinary human being, to be absolutely apparent, then the law should be changed' (Greville Janner MP, at the end of the P&O trial, cited Crainer, 1993: 102).

EXERCISE 7.5

Can a corporation be charged with manslaughter? Explain your answer.

EXERCISE 7.6

Critically discuss the challenges facing any prosecution of a large company for corporate man-slaughter in relation to the doctrine of identification, the awareness of a serious and obvious risk and the failure of the law to allow aggregation of the faults of several individuals to support a collective corporate manslaughter case. Illustrate these difficulties in relation to the case of *R v Stanley and others* October 1990, arising out of the sinking of the *Herald of Free Enterprise* off Zeebrugge harbour in March 1987.

EXERCISE 7.7

The Lyme Bay canoe tragedy occurred in March 1993. In advance of studying the case of *R v Kite, R v Stoddart, R v OLL Ltd* (unreported, 9 December 1994, Winchester Crown Court, Ognall J) as the key corporate manslaughter case in sport, check the legal dates of the case law on involuntary manslaughter by an individual officer and a corporation itself. What is the test for individual and corporate manslaughter applicable in March 1993? Keep notes of your response and use it in the exercises on *R v Kite and others* later in this chapter.

EXERCISE 7.8

In 2008, 'Bardsley' a rugby union team, in an incorporated club, was up against one of their closest rivals 'Tramdon'. Their past matches had been characterised by niggling violence and high tackles from the 'Tramden' players. The 'Bardsley' captain and coach wanted to make sure they had the upper hand psychologically and felt that it was important to make it clear from the outset that they were not going to be intimidated by the 'Tramdon' team. They decided, along with the 'Bardsley' team, that at the first sign of trouble (any high tackles or punching), there would be a coded call ('13') from the captain. On this call '13' all 'Bardsley' players had to start punching their opposite number, with all the force they could muster, regardless of the response of the referee to the original incident. This strategy was agreed by all the 'Bardsley' team, and approved by the coach and senior management, who were used to such tactics in their days as team players. Within ten minutes of the start of the match, one of the 'Tramdon' players delivered a dangerously high tackle to one of the 'Bardsley' players. Code '13' was implemented and the whole team started punching. A well-built player on the 'Bardsley' team punched a much smaller player on the 'Tramdon' team. The 'Tramdon' player collapsed on the pitch and died two days later from a brain injury. Apply the test of the Corporate Manslaughter and Corporate Homicide Act 2007 to these circumstances. Should charges of corporate manslaughter be brought against the incorporated 'Bardsley' rugby union club?

Manslaughter: illustrative cases in sport, recreation and schools

Players and participants

R v Bradshaw (1878) 14 Cox CC 83

> In this case in football the defendant had 'charged the deceased after the ball had been played. The deceased died from internal injuries caused by the defendant's knees catching him in the stomach and rupturing his intestines' (as *per* Bramwell LJ in *R v Bradshaw*. The defendant clearly caused the death but was the causative conduct an unlawful act?

>> No rules of practice of any game whatever can make lawful that which is unlawful by the law of the land; and the law of the land says that you shall not do that which is likely to cause the death of another.

> After introducing the issues in this way LJ Bramwell advised the jury not to be concerned with the rules of football. However,

>> if a man is playing according to the rules and practices of the game and is not going beyond it, it may reasonable to infer that he is not actuated by any malicious motive or intention and that he is not acting in a manner which he knows will be likely to be productive of death of injury.

>> (*per* LJ Bramwell in *R v Bradshaw* cited James, 2001: 654)

R v Moore (1898) 14 TLR 229

> The goalkeeper in a football match was in the process of clearing the ball when the defendant jumped, with his knees up, against the back of the victim, which threw him

violently towards the knee of the goalkeeper. The victim died a few days later from his internal injuries. In summing up, the judge said that the rules of the game were quite immaterial and it did not matter whether the defendant broke the rules of the game or not. Football was a lawful game but it was a rough one and persons who played it must be careful not to do bodily harm to another person. No-one had the right to use force which was likely to injure another and if he did use such force and death resulted the crime of manslaughter had been committed. A verdict of guilty was returned.

(*R v Moore*, cited James, 2001: 663)

James (2001: 662) observes that these two cases demonstrate how difficult it is to predict the outcome of an action for participator violence. In *Moore* the defendant was convicted on the basis that his body charge was an unlawful assault beyond the scope of the game, whereas *Bradshaw* was acquitted for a similar move that was found not to be an assault, but 'an inherent part of the game' (ibid: 663).

R v Hardy (unreported, 24 July 1994, Central Criminal Court)

In March 1993, Seamus Lavelle was 'felled by a punch while playing rugby [union]. He suffered severe swelling of the brain and was placed on a life support machine. He died two days later' (Cleary, 1995). In July 1994, Hardy, the Centaurs hooker from that game, stood in the dock at The Old Bailey, charged with manslaughter.[11] During the early days of the criminal investigation, the police took some time to establish that it was indeed Hardy, the defendant, who threw the punch which led to Lavelle's death, because so many players on the pitch were punching.[12] The court in *R v Hardy* heard evidence from Hardy, regarding the ill-tempered match, where he 'saw one of his side punched and kicked by three Hendon forwards'. He said 'I told them to leave it out and play rugby. But one of their players came towards me looking menacing. I thought he was going to hit me'. The defendant claimed that,

> after seeing team mates hit and after receiving at least two blows to the back of his head, he had struck out at his assailant in self defence. He had lashed out at whoever was attacking him from behind, but for his own protection.

(*R v Hardy*, cited James, 2001: 675)

As Hardy 'squared up he was hit from behind by two punches from Lavelle, and this caused the hooker [Hardy] to "lash out blindly"' (Hardy in evidence to The Old Bailey, *R v Hardy*). When it was suggested in court that he was not acting in self-defence Mr Hardy replied, 'No Sir. I hit out because I was going to be hit some more . . . whether or not you call that self-defence, I don't know.' Hardy was acquitted of the charge of manslaughter on the grounds of self-defence.[13] However, the Rugby Football Union imposed a retrospective ban on him for violent conduct. Any punch is against the rules of rugby, even if thrown in self-defence (James, 2001: 655, 675).

R v Warren (unreported, 21 September 2004, Preston Crown Court, Judge Openshaw)

Adrian Warren, an international sand yacht pilot with 30 years' experience, was taking part in an international competition on St Annes Beach, in Lancashire, England, on 19 August 2002, organised by Fylde International Sand Yacht Club. There was one weathered sign on the beach which stated 'Caution – sand yacht racing – you are advised to keep clear of the course' (Roberts, 2002a: 16). On the day of the race, Carole Cruz, a 38-year-old teaching assistant from Burnley, Lancashire, was walking across the beach from the sea to the sand dunes, with her two sons, aged 14 and 12. As she crossed the beach she was hit by Adrian Warren's sand yacht at a speed of 45mph, breaking her back and nearly severing her legs. The sand yacht narrowly missed one of her sons. Paramedics were called but Mrs Cruz later died in hospital. Fylde Council suspended the licence of Fylde International Sand Yachting Club following the accident (2002b: 20).

Adrian Warren was charged with manslaughter. No charges were brought against the sand yacht club which organised the event. In September 2004, the court heard Leighton Davies QC, prosecuting, question:

> whether the race organisers had put adequate safety measures in place, but added that 'ultimate and real responsibility for the death of Carole Cruz lies with the defendant. The reality is that [Mr Warren] was so preoccupied with racing and with speed that it just didn't occur to him to give any proper thought to members of the public who were on the beach.
>
> (BBC News online, 21 September 2004)[14]

Ironically the very points raised by the prosecution could also be seen to be relevant to arguments by the defence in this case. Sand yacht pilots normally travel at 45mph with speeds possible up to 70mph. The design of the sand yacht means that the pilot is lying back, very close to the ground, with his/her visibility restricted by the sail. The focus of a pilot is to race as fast as possible along the length of the course. The competitors would not be responsible for the safety of the course or of restricting access by the public to what is effectively a competitive racing circuit for an international event. At the end of the trial Adrian Warren was cleared of manslaughter. He 'accepted that his actions were a significant cause of Mrs Cruz's death but said as a competitor he was not responsible for safety considerations' (ibid).

R v Hubble (unreported, February 2007, Winchester Crown Court)

On 20 August 2006, Jason Downer, Rupert Saunders and James Meaby were on board the sailing yacht *Ouzo* which had left Bembridge on the Isle of Wight, bound for Dartmouth Regatta in Devon. The 27ft sailing sloop and the crew vanished and the bodies of three sailors were found in the sea between 20 and 23 August. The P&O *Pride of Bilbao* was in the area at the time, and the officer of the watch on the vessel, Michael Hubble, was arrested on 2 September 2006, and appeared before Portsmouth Magistrates' Court. In February 2007 he appeared at a brief hearing at Winchester Crown Court, where he was facing charges of manslaughter by gross negligence and granted unconditional bail.[15] He was acquitted of manslaughter at a later hearing in March 2008.

EXERCISE 7.9

In the 1880s would it be safe to say that even if a soccer player caused the death of another player he/she would probably not be convicted of manslaughter if he/she followed the rules of the game? Explain your answer and critically comment on the verdicts in *R v Moore* (1898) 14 TLR 229 and *R v Bradshaw* (1878) 14 Cox CC 83.

EXERCISE 7.10

Summarise the evidence in *R v Hardy* (unreported, 24 July 1994, Central Criminal Court). Consider the following two questions and discuss them together. i. The sport of rugby union is regarded as a lawful, valuable and entertaining activity in society. Should punching in a rugby union match be regarded as a lawful activity? ii. If a punch leads to death, which kind of manslaughter offence might be applicable – unlawful act manslaughter or manslaughter by gross negligence? Give reasons for your answer with reference to the elements of each offence and relevant case law.

EXERCISE 7.11

Hardy was acquitted on the grounds of self-defence. Critically comment on the evidence and verdict and if typical, the picture it paints of the modern game of English amateur rugby union. Reflect on the question of whether or not reading this case and Chapter 4, has changed your view of punching on the rugby field.

EXERCISE 7.12

In the case of *R v Warren* (unreported, 21 September 2004, Preston Crown Court, Judge Openshaw) explain the successful defence by the sand yachting competitor. In a hypothetical scenario imagine you are the Crown Prosecution Service lawyer advising on the matter of any charges which might be brought in relation to the *R v Warren* sand yachting manslaughter case. Which kind of manslaughter offence would you recommend? Who would you charge with that offence? Give reasons for your answer.

Sports coaches, leaders or teachers

R v May (unreported, 11 July 2002, Winchester Crown Court, Turner J)

In August 2000 a group of young footballers from Charlton Athletic FC attended a physical training residential course at the Aldershot Army School of Physical Training. The group had already completed a 40-minute endurance run when their instructor, Sergeant Dean May, told them to 'cross a weed-infested pond' where Pierre Bolangi, one of the young footballers, got into difficulty. Although Dean May tried to save Pierre, he could not find him when he disappeared under the water and Pierre drowned in the pond.[16] Dean May admitted breaching health and safety rules but denied manslaughter. He also argued in the case that the Ministry of Defence was keen to develop courses for external clients as it generated income.

Sergeant May felt that he was not appropriately trained to deal with this new area of provision. The judge commented in the case 'I am satisfied that you had insufficient appreciation of risk because of the manner in which you had been trained or not trained as the case was' (Turner J in *R v May*, BBC News Friday 12 July, 2002 online). He also said that he 'believed that the Army had made him a scapegoat for its own failures to take adequate health and safety precautions'[17] (Turner J 11 July 2002, BBC News Friday 12 July 2002).

R v Doubtfire (unreported, 14 January 2004, Swansea Crown Court, Evans J)

Kevin Sharman, a 17-year-old army recruit and a non-swimmer, travelled to the *Porth-yr-Ogol* cave formation in Powys, on a five-day adventure training course, with other recruits from the Army's Technical Foundation College in Berkshire, in July 2002. Matthew Doubtfire, 33, civilian instructor, employed by the Ministry of Defence, had opted to lead the group of 11 army recruits into the *Porth-yr-Ogof* cave complex in the Neath Valley, Mid-Wales. This group was:

> larger than usual because a colleague was absent due to illness. He opted to lead the group alone but later told police he had taken the wrong entrance but failed to discover his mistake immediately. Doubtfire singled out Sharman as a non-swimmer and instructed him to walk directly behind him.
>
> (prosecution case in *R v Doubtfire* cited in
> *The Western Mail* 15 January 2004, p. 9)

When they reached a deep water resurgence pool, Kevin Sharman began to panic, as he:

> struggled to keep up with Doubtfire as the water level rose. He was going under the water and was splashing a lot from side to side. The defendant got hold of Mr Sharman and started to move through to the exit of the Resurgence pool. Doubtfire lost his grip and Mr Sharman went under the water. When he surfaced he grabbed hold of the recruit behind him and they both went under. The recruit tried in vain to help him when he surfaced but he was forced to let go and Mr Sharman went under again.
>
> (prosecution witnesses in *R v Doubtfire*,
> Swansea Crown Court, cited *The Western Mail*
> 15 January 2004, p. 9)

He was flown to hospital by Swansea air ambulance, but was pronounced dead on arrival (BBC News, online, 25 February, 2003[18]). On Friday 20 July 2007, a jury at Swansea Crown Court cleared Matthew Doubtfire of manslaughter through gross negligence. 'He hopes that the outcome of this trial will encourage the Ministry of Defence to review its training prodecure, especially in relation to recruits sent on external leadership courses, despite having failed a military swimming test'.

> (Mr Doubtfire's defence team after the court decision,
> BBC News, 22 July 2007[19])

R v Ellis (unreported, 23 September 2003, Manchester Crown Court, Morland J)

'Ten-year-old Max Palmer drowned in an icy pool during a school trip to the Lake District on 26 May 2002. Although Max was at primary school, he had been allowed to join an adventure weekend at Glenridding in the Lake District with pupils at Fleetwood High School, Lancashire, where his mum worked as a teaching assistant' (Christie, 2003[20]). Rain and low temperatures had prevented much of the planned programme taking place and it was alleged that the geography teacher in charge, Paul Ellis, 'was keen to do some form of activity to prevent a complete washout' (ibid). The pool was around eight degrees centigrade and swollen by heavy rain. That morning an RAF Adventure Training Team had checked the pool and decided that it was too dangerous for them to use (ibid).

Having watched a video film of the river at the time of the rescue of Max's mother it struck me as unbelievably foolhardy and negligent that anyone would venture into that beck when it was in a state of full spate. And that any teacher or leader of an adventure group would allow any child to enter that beck or plunge into the pool below.

(Morland J in *R v Ellis* (BBC News, 23 September 2003[21]))

After being given permission by Mr Ellis, Max Palmer, who was much younger than the other boys on the trip, plunged into the river pool. After he struggled in the icy water, the defendant, Paul Ellis, jumped into the water to try to save Max. Mr Ellis was dragged from the water and then Mrs Palmer also tried to rescue her son. She 'grabbed Max and managed to hold his head above the water, but found the current too strong . . . she then became very cold to the extent that she had trouble breathing . . . Max by this time was probably beyond help' (Mr Alistair Webster QC, prosecuting, *R v Ellis*). The group had no flotation aids and safety ropes had been left in the minibus. Max slipped under the water and later resuscitation attempts by a mountain rescue team on exercise failed and he died.

The teacher, Paul Ellis, had already pleaded guilty to a health and safety offence of failing to take effective measures to prevent physical injury, in February 2003. He pleaded guilty to manslaughter and was sentenced to one year in prison by Mr J Morland. Paul Ellis was the first teacher to plead guilty to manslaughter and be imprisoned for a child's death during a school trip. In July 2004, the Health and Safety Executive reported that the role played by the school and local authority had been investigated and that there would be no further prosecutions in relation to the death of Max Palmer (*The Birmingham Post* 16 July 2004[22]).

In June 1999, 13-year-old Gemma Carter went on a trip to Le Touqet, France, with other pupils from Cockburn High School Leeds. Leeds Coroner's Court heard that her mother had written to the school a few days before the trip warning them that Gemma could not swim, but the headteacher advised the inquest that the school never received the letter. The pupils were told by their French teacher, Mr Duckworth, 'not to swim but to paddle close to the shoreline' and 'as the children returned to the beach from the water to the beach, Gemma was not present' (Keely, 2003).

Mr Duckworth assumed that Gemma had 'got out of the water and gone back to the hotel to get dry, (ibid). After a thorough search of the hotel and the beach, Mr Duckworth called the emergency services, but when they still had not responded half-an hour later he rang them again, was told somebody would come but nobody did (ibid). Mr Duckworth, the French teacher, was found guilty of negligent homicide in a French court, but was later acquitted on appeal (Robinson, 2003).

EXERCISE 7.13

Apply the elements of (involuntary) manslaughter by gross negligence to the circumstances of *R v May* (unreported, 11 July 2002, Winchester Crown Court, Turner J). What was unusual about the punishment in this manslaughter case? Hypothetically, if you had been the CPS lawyer advising on the case, would you have considered a charge of corporate manslaughter against the Ministry of Defence? If yes, what difficulties might you face in relation to the requirements of the offence and immunity from prosecution?

EXERCISE 7.14

Compare and contrast the evidence, circumstances and verdicts in *R v May* (unreported, 11 July 2002, Winchester Crown Court, Turner J) and *R v Doubtfire* (unreported, 14 January 2004, Swansea Crown Court, Evans J).

EXERCISE 7.15

In the case of *R v Ellis* (unreported, 23 September 2003, Manchester Crown Court, Morland J) apply the elements of (involuntary) manslaughter by gross negligence to the evidence, drawing on the comments by the judge. In particular, examine the risks of death and the deviation from the expected standard of care – enough to make it criminal.

Spectators or parents

R v Still, R v McAllister (unreported, 26 May 1994, Cardiff Crown Court, Schiemann J)

In November 1993, two brothers, who were soccer fans, attended an international soccer match between Wales and Romania at Cardiff Arms Park. Prior to the match, Andrew McAllister and Kerry Still had consumed alcohol and had purchased a powerful distress flare rocket, believing it to be a hand-held flare, took it into the ground with them and pointed it horizontally, across the stadium towards the north stand and fired it. The rocket was still accelerating when it hit Mr Hill, sitting in the north stand.[23] He died in the arms of his son, who was in the stand with him. McAllister and Still had pleaded not guilty to murder but admitted manslaughter.

Schiemann J said that it was 'important that the courts severely punished "mindless and crass stupidity" at public events'. It was 'totally predictable' that such a powerful device would cause serious injury in a crowded stadium. He said that the brothers had not bothered to read the instructions which clearly identified what the rocket was – "probably because you were too merry from alcohol to care about anyone else" (*The Guardian* 27 May 1994). The conduct of the defendants was described as 'the ultimate act of football hooliganism' by Patrick Harrington, QC, prosecuting (*R v McAllister, R v Still*). Andrew McAllister and Kerry Still were convicted of manslaughter and sentenced to three years in prison.

Massachusetts v Junta (unreported, January 2002, Middlesex Superior Court, Judge Grabau)

Although this is a manslaughter case in the United States and is not precedent setting in Anglo-Welsh law, it is an important, high-profile case and serves as a warning to all spectators or parents of what can happen if there is a failure of anger management and self-discipline by those on the sidelines of training sessions or competitive sports.

The problem of parents becoming aggressive at their children's sports games is growing in the US.

(Kay, 2002)

The manslaughter case has focused national attention on the growing problem of parental violence at children's sports games. There have been many reports of fights and shouting matches breaking out between overzealous and over-competitive mothers and fathers, but no case has matched this one for sheer bloodiness.

(Usborne, 2002)

In July 2000, Thomas Junta, 43, was watching an ice hockey practice game, in which his son was playing, alongside other young boys 10 to 15 years of age, at the Burbank Ice Arena in Reading, just north of Boston, Massachusetts, in the USA. Michael Costin, 40, was coaching the session, in which his son was also participating. Mr Junta was 'angered by the hitting, fighting and slashing'[24] during his son's practice and said that during the argument afterwards Mr Costin the hockey coach, 'shoved his chest into the defendant and slashed his shins with the blades of his skates' (Mr Thomas Orlandi, defence lawyer, *Massachusetts v Junta* (cited Usborne, 2002). Thomas Junta was accused of:

> pushing the coach, Michael Costin, to the ground by the edge of the ice and repeatedly pounding his head on the floor in full view of the children who had been in the practice game, most of them aged between 10 and 15. Mr Costin died the next day in hospital.[25]

(Usborne, 2002)

The judge sentenced Thomas Junta to six to ten years in a state prison. During sentencing Michael Costin, the victim's son, said that he 'should not be allowed to go free to ruin another family's life' (Kay, 2002: 18). The jury had opted for 'involuntary manslaughter' which is less serious than the US equivalent of unlawful act (constructive) manslaughter, the latter carrying a possible sentence of up to 20 years in prison[26] (CNN.com law 25 January 2002[27]). The courts hope that 'this conviction will send a strong message to all sports parents of the consequences of violent behaviour' (Herbert, 2002: 59).

Manslaughter charges against children

Civil cases covered in Chapter 3, included children as young as 11 being held as contributorily negligent by the civil courts, in relation to their injuries. This led to a proportional reduction in the compensation paid to them by the defendants found liable for negligence. Children as young a ten can and have been charged with criminal assault including on the sports field and sent to young offenders institutions. Five children, as young as ten at the time of the incident, stoned a father with bricks and sticks as he was playing a game of cricket with his teenage son in the grounds of a leisure centre in London in February 2006. Two of the bricks hit Ernest Norton on his head and cheek, causing a head injury and a broken cheek bone. He immediately collapsed and died of a heart attack. Mr Norton had undergone a triple heart bypass operation in 1977, but had been fit and active since then. 'Five boys, one aged 12, sobbed at the Old Bailey after they were found guilty of killing a pensioner who they spat at and pelted with stones' (*The Guardian* online, 31 August, p. 1[28]). The boys were convicted of manslaughter in October 2007, and retained in a Young Offenders Institution.[29]

EXERCISE 7.16

Argue the case for the prosecution in *R v McAllister, R v Still* (unreported, 26 May 1994, Cardiff Crown Court, Schiemann J) with reference to the elements of manslaughter. What is the difference between hand-held candles used by fans at Italian football matches and the flare used by the defendants in this case? Critically comment on the ability of the defendants to take such dangerous items into a public soccer match in a large city stadium.

EXERCISE 7.17

Explain the names of the parties in *Massachusetts v Junta* (unreported, January 2002, Middlesex Superior Court, Judge Grabau). In contrast to Anglo-Welsh legal systems, the jury had a choice regarding the offence of manslaughter. Critically comment on the jury's choice of offence and the unusual decision regarding the length of the sentence.

EXERCISE 7.18

What lessons could and should be learnt from *Massachusetts v Junta* (unreported, January 2002, Middlesex Superior Court, Judge Grabau) on both sides of the Atlantic? Have you or your peers experienced any examples of parental or spectator aggression at children's sport competitions or training events? If yes, how was this issue addressed, if at all? The National Coaching Foundation (NCF), now Sports Coach UK, used to publish a leaflet called *Fair Play – Children in Sport* covering shared values and behaviour expected by various groups of spectators at children's sport events – including parents, officials, media etc. Imagine you are writing such a publication in 2007 in the UK. Which groups of spectators would you include? What kind of behaviour would you want to avoid? What kind of behaviour would you expect? Who might disseminate and educate parents and other spectators on such matters?

Sport and recreation event organizers and facility managers[30]

R v Aitkenhead, R v Wicks (unreported, May 7 2004, Bristol Crown Court, Hallet J)

On 24 November 2002, Kostadino Yankov, a 19-year-old Oxford University student, travelled to Somerset, alongside other members of the dangerous sports club known as the 'Oxford Stunt Factory'. They each paid to experience a 'human catapult'.[31] David Aitkenhead and Richard Wicks designed, set up and operated the contraption, which they had taken three years and £3,000 to develop. Four participants using the catapult prior to Mr Yankov, landed safely in the net. However, Mr Yankov 'appeared to go higher than the other participants before clipping the edge of the safety net and hitting the ground' (Morgan, 2004). He suffered serious head and spinal injuries and was airlifted to the Frenchay Hospital in Bristol, where he was pronounced dead. David Aitkenhead and Richard Wicks were charged with the manslaughter of Kostadino Yankov and appeared before Hallet J in Bristol Crown Court in May 2004, where they denied the charge.

The court heard that a new sling was being used on the day of the accident and Philip Mott, QC for the prosecution, said that the new sling 'was crucial to the cause of the accident. It was clearly reckless to assume that the performance of the two slings would be the same. This is not just careless and negligent, but grossly negligent, perhaps even reckless.' At the end of the second week of the trial, the judge directed the jury to return 'not guilty' verdicts as there was 'insufficient evidence to convict the two men of unlawfully killing Kostadino Yankov by being grossly negligent in their care of him' (Hallet J Bristol Crown Court, 7 May 2004, cited in Morgan, 2004).[32]

R v Beckingham, R v Barrow Borough Council

The conduct of those who manage or maintain sport, leisure, arts or school facilities can adversely impact on members of the public who have not even set foot on the premises. This is exactly what happened in the summer of 2002 in Barrow, Cumbria. An ageing air-conditioning unit on the wall of the Forum 28 Arts Centre became infected with legionnaires disease. It released water droplets into the atmosphere, infecting people who were just walking along the street past the arts complex. Some 180 people were seriously ill with legionnaires disease and seven people died from the disease.

> The decision by the Crown Prosecution Service to charge Barrow Borough Council for the manslaughter of seven people who died of legionnaires disease in 2002 is the first time a council has been charged with manslaughter. This is a landmark decision. It does not reflect a change in the law, but a change in the way work-related deaths are investigated. Since the introduction of new police procedures in 1998 (which were revised last year) work-related deaths now tend to be the subject of manslaughter investigations by the police. Prior to the introduction of these procedures such deaths may not even have been investigated by the police.
>
> (David Bergman, chief executive, Centre for Corporate Accountability,
> Press Release, 12 February 2004[33])

In March 2005 the judge, Poole J at Preston Crown Court, directed the jury to find Barrow Borough Council not guilty of all seven manslaughter charges. The council had already pleaded guilty to breaching health and safety laws. The case continued against Gillian Beckingham, an architect and head of Design Services Group at Barrow Council (her employers, and the owners of the building). It was alleged that Gillian Beckingham was responsible for the maintenance of the air-conditioning unit, and a few months earlier had cancelled the contract, which ensured the unit was kept clean and safe.

The court heard from Alistair Webster, prosecuting, that 'Mrs Beckingham failed to maintain the system and that she was the "prime cause of the tragedy which unfolded" (BBC News online, 11 March, 2005[34]). However, when asked by the defence counsel, Peter Borkett QC, if maintenance contracts were her responsibility, she said 'no'. She said it was 'down to building managers and added that she sometimes offered advice on maintenance contracts when asked' (BBC News, online, 6 April, 2005). The jury found Gillian Beckingham (and Barrow County Council) guilty of health and safety breaches, that is, 'failing to take reasonable care of the health and safety of members of the public, thereby exposing them to the risk of legionnaires disease' (Basnett, 2005: 1).

> This case has clearly highlighted the importance of taking adequate precautions to protect people from legionnaire's disease. There were several lapses in the duty of care by Barrow Council as the employer and by Gillian Beckingham, the Council's Design Services Manager. There is a clear lesson for all those who are responsible for installations that carry a risk from legionnella. You should check your management

arrangements and your control measures regularly and you should oversee the work that contractors do on your behalf. There is no room for assumptions that systems are working as they should, and no room for ignoring personal roles and responsibilities at any level of management.

(HSE Statement on Barrow Legionnella, 31 July 2006: 1[35])

EXERCISE 7.19

List a range of activities which would be classified as 'dangerous' or 'extreme sports'. Are they all lawful, recognised sports? If not, why not? Explain the nature of the human catapult activity in the case of *R v Aitken* [1992] 1 WLR 1006, *R v Wicks* (unreported, May 7 2004, Bristol Crown Court, Hallet J) in comparison to a sport such as bungee jumping. Do you think that participants would have consented to the normal inherent risks of this activity? (See Chapter 3 on inherent risks.) Consider the verdict in this case and try to explain this outcome in relation to proving the elements of manslaughter by gross negligence.

EXERCISE 7.20

Outline the events in the summer or 2002 at the Forum 28 Arts Centre in Barrow in Cumbria in relation to the outbreak of legionnaires disease and the resulting charges against Barrow County Council and Gillian Beckingham.

EXERCISE 7.21

What was the outcome of the manslaughter charges and the health and safety breaches against Barrow Council and Gillian Beckingham in Preston Crown court in March 2005?

Involuntary (reckless[36]) Manslaughter: land mark case in a sport and education context

The Lyme Bay Canoe Tragedy 1993

R v Kite, R v Stoddart, R v OLL Ltd (unreported, 9 December 1994, Winchester Crown Court, Ognall J)

In March 1993, a party of eight sixth-form pupils and their teacher, Norman Pointer, from Southway Comprehensive School, Plymouth, attended a week-long outward-bound course at St Albans Centre, Lyme Regis, Dorset. The centre was managed by Joseph Stoddart and owned by Active Learning and Leisure, whose managing director was Peter Kite. On 22 March, at 10.00am, this group set off on a canoe trip, across Lyme Bay to Charmouth, about three miles away, with two of the centre's instructors, Karen Gardner, 21, and Thomas Mann, 27. Members of the group got into difficulty soon after setting off and began to capsize. By around 12.30 they had all capsized and some had drifted off-course. After spending over four hours in the ten degrees centigrade water, with an increasing swell and an offshore wind of force 3–4, there was no sign of a rescue. Some pupils were losing consciousness and others tried to swim for the shore. Eventually, between 5.00pm and 6.45pm all were rescued by helicopter or lifeboat and taken to Weymouth District Hospital. However, four pupils in the school party eventually died due to the effects of hypothermia.

Peter Kite and Joseph Stoddart were charged with the unlawful killing – manslaughter by gross negligence – of Simon Dunne, Clare Langley and Rachel Walker, all 16, and Dean Sayer, 17 (Randall, 1993). After three months studying the report of the Dorset Police investigation, criminal proceedings were approved by the Crown Prosecution Service. In addition to charges of individual manslaughter against Kite and Stoddart, charges of corporate manslaughter were brought against the company which owned the outdoor activity centre, Active Learning and Leisure (ALL) Ltd. 'No company had been successfully prosecuted for manslaughter under English law' (ibid).[37] The case was heard at Winchester Crown Court in November 1994.

What follows is a detailed account of the circumstances and context of the Lyme Bay canoe tragedy, using evidence presented to the court in *R v Kite and others* and referenced commentaries on the case and the campaign for private outdoor activity centres to be registered and regulated. The St Albans outdoor activity centre began operating in 1992 and had plans for expansion in 1993. In May 1992, the year before the tragedy, Joy Cawthorne and Richard Retallick, qualified instructors, began working at the centre. There was supposed to be an in-house training programme but they only had a one-hour drill on canoe capsizes (*The Guardian* 25 November, 1994: 14[38]). Soon after, Joy Cawthorne took part in supervising a group of children near The Cob, at Lyme Regis, alongside another instructor, whose ability she described to the court as "limited" (ibid: 14).

In evidence to the court they outlined their concerns about safety matters and the way in which the centre was organised. They reported that safety requirements there were virtually non-existent and a very, very low standard. Although Mr Stoddart did accept some of the criticisms they raised, around, for example, the lack of provision of first aid kits, flares, hooded waterproofs and tow ropes, he trivialised such matters and his standard excuse was that the centre was in its first year of opening. When asked by Neil Butterfield QC, how Joseph Stoddart appeared to be coping with running the centre, Joy Cawthorne replied 'like a headless chicken' describing him as 'disorganised, trying all the time to keep up. Things were happening and he never seemed to catch up' (ibid: 14). When giving evidence to the court regarding 1992, Mr Kite, managing director of OLL Ltd, acknowledged that 'by the summer of 1992' he had begun to realise that Mr Stoddart was overworked' but he believed that the problem 'only related to the peak of the summer season' (*The Guardian* 1 December, 1994: 6[39]).

After only working at the centre, Joy Cawthorne and Richard Rettallick resigned. 'Our ethics got the better of us. We are both professionals. We felt we could not make it any better. I did not want to be involved with working in a place which was going to lose somebody' (ibid: 6). They wrote a letter to Peter Kite in June 1992 including concerns about breaching guidelines on class sizes, as well as non-swimmers instructing on raft-building sessions.

> There is most definitely not one person here on this site technically qualified to instruct, or instructors to deal with the activities you offer. Youngsters have been literally thrown in at the deep end without even a guided tour of the site by a supposed senior member of staff.
>
> (Evidence presented to the court in *R v Kite and others*,
> cited in *The Guardian* 25 November, 1994: 14)

The letter concluded:

> Having seen your 1993 brochure and planned expansions, we think you should have a
> careful look at your standards of safety. Otherwise you might find yourselves trying to
> explain why someone's son or daughter might not be coming home. No one wants this
> to happen, but it will, sooner or later.
>
> (Evidence presented to the court in *R v Kite and others*,
> *The Daily Telegraph* 16 November, 1994: 3)

The court heard that Peter Kite responded and advised them that the 'vast majority' of the
points raised had either been resolved or sorted out. He told the court 'essentially I agreed
with a lot of the points made in the letter' and 'I felt that we probably could aspire to a
higher standard of instructor training and qualifications' (*The Guardian* 1 December 1994:
6[40]). The activity centre had been inspected by the British Adventure Holiday Association
(BAHA) and abided by its guidelines.[41] In 1993 the company, OLL Ltd, intended to
'upgrade its safety standards to conform to the more rigorous regulations [standards] of
the British Canoe Union' (BCU) (*The Guardian* 1 December, 1994: 6). The 1993 St Albans
Centre brochure indicated that the centre employed qualified staff. It was one of the
centres listed by Devonshire County Council, and staff from Southway School, Plymouth,
had visited the centre in advance of their 1993 school outdoor activity week.

On the day of the Lyme Bay canoe tragedy, there were two qualified instructors at the
St Albans Centre. However, one was 'supervising sailing, whilst a second was in charge
of a trip to Dartmoor' (*Western Morning News* 18 December, 1994: 5[42]). The rescue boat
was also deployed elsewhere on a dinghy sailing course. Two other employees, Karen
Gardner, 23, and Simon Mann, 25, were allocated to the Southway Comprehensive
School sea canoe trip of 22 March 1993, by centre manager, Joseph Stoddart. Following
an in-house training course run at the centre by BCU canoe instructor, Stephen Gynes,
Karen Gardner and Simon Mann gained the one-star BCU personal proficiency award,
a very basic award which could be passed by eight-year-olds. Of the 20 staff involved
in the basic canoe training, they were not among the four instructors deemed suitable
by Stephen Gynes, to go on to canoe instructor training, a point which was made
clear to Joseph Stoddart (expert evidence given by Stephen Gynes, in *R v Kite and others*,
ibid: 5).

Karen Gardner had personal experience in waterskiing, but before coming to St Albans
worked as a cleaner at another centre. The expedition with Southway comprehensive on
22 March was her first-ever sea canoe trip. Simon Mann had received no training in taking
people out to sea, and was given no information about tides and currents, but had been
taught to get people back into capsized canoes.

> Mr Mann and Miss Gardner were barely sufficiently competent to undertake the
> journey themselves let alone instruct others. It was nothing short of utter folly on the
> part of Mr Stoddart, to allocate Mr Mann and Miss Gardner, to supervise and expedition
> such as this.
>
> (Noel Butterfield, QC, prosecuting, *R v Kite and others*,
> *The Guardian* Wednesday 16 November 1994: 6)

Another expert witness in canoeing, Martin Melling, a BCU senior officer, with 28 years'
experience in sea kayaking, told the court that these two supervisors allocated to this trip
at St Albans were 'totally inappropriate to lead it' (*The Guardian* Saturday 26 November,
1994: 3[43]). In his opinion the group should have been led by 'a senior sea [canoe] instructor
aided by a second instructor with moderate proficiency' (ibid: 3). When asked if the trip

was appropriate for such staff and pupils, this expert witness said 'I am just staggered. I cannot believe anyone would contemplate taking a group of absolute and complete beginners on a trip like this' (ibid: 3). When asked if a properly qualified instructor would have embarked on such a trip he answered 'Absolutely not' (ibid: 3).

According to BCU guidelines the upper limit for those with this level of a one-star personal proficiency award would be a force 4 wind, which was predicted on the day of the trip on 22 March 1993. Although the weather forecast had predicted force 4 onshore winds, with a mounting swell on exposed waters, Simon Mann told the court that he had not checked the weather forecast, but if he had, he would have considered that those conditions were not suitable for novices.[44] The route of the planned expedition would take the group across the bay from Lyme Regis to Charmouth. In evidence to Winchester Crown Court, on 30 November 1994, Peter Kite reported that he thought the group would be hugging the beach and staying close to the estuary. He would 'not have permitted novices to go anywhere other than close to the harbour area and near the beach' (*The Guardian* Thursday 1 December, 1994: 6[45]).

Peter Kite admitted, when cross-examined by Neil Butterfield QC, that 'the expedition had been reckless' and 'in breach of every safety requirement he had put in place' (ibid: 6). However, he considered it to be Joseph 'Stoddart's overall responsibility that the novice canoeists were out on that day', but the instructor in charge was 'potentially capable of making the decision to abandon the trip before it started if he had correctly assessed the weather conditions' (ibid; *The Guardian* 2 December 1994: 4[46]). The court heard evidence about other issues relating to equipment and clothing. When they set out from Lyme Regis that morning the instructors had no distress flares or a two-way radio, only the instructors actually had spray decks on their canoes, the pupils had no gloves, head gear or footwear and were not wearing bright colours (*The Independent* 9 December, 1994: 6). Although the pupils were wearing life jackets they were not inflated when they entered the water.

Peter Kite told the court that he 'had been told that mini flares were available and assumed they would be taken on expeditions, where necessary' (*The Guardian* Thursday December 1, 1994: 6[47]). One of the two instructors, Karen Gardner, reported in evidence that she 'had never been given flares to carry but knew that they were available' (ibid: 6). On previous occasions Simon Mann, one of the instructors, had raised the issue of the lack of spray decks for canoes with Joseph Stoddart and was told to 'treat them like beginners'. 'A kayak without a spray deck is like a boat with a big hole in it' (Martin Melling, BCU senior officer, giving expert evidence in *R v Kite and others*, *Western Morning News*, 26 November 1994: 2[48]).

Despite all of the issues above in relation to qualifications, planning, equipment and weather, the party of eight six-formers, their teacher Norman Pointer, set off on this fated canoe trip in the care of Karen Gardner and Simon Mann, at 10.00am on 22 March 1993. 'The serious risks should have been glaringly obvious to anyone of experience who gave the matter a moment's thought' (Mr Neil Butterworth QC, for the prosecution, in *R v Kite and others*, 15 November, 1994). The coastguard and the harbourmaster were not informed of the trip by the staff at the activity centre. The group was due to arrive in Charmouth about three miles down the coast, at around 12.00 midday.

The pupils and the teacher could not steer straight and kept going round in circles. After only a few minutes Simon Dunne's canoe capsized. Then Mr Pointer, a beginner, who had been given an unsteady laser 350 kayak, repeatedly capsized and Mr Mann, one of the instructors, kept trying to help him back into his canoe. Soon Mr Mann and Mr Pointer became separated from Miss Gardner and the eight pupils. Karen Gardner fought bravely to keep the two boys and six girls together and afloat. She encouraged them to put their canoes together in a raft, but the group drifted further away. None of them could stay upright for long and gradually, by 12.30 all but Samantha Stansby lost their canoes. They all tried to hold onto hers for about half an hour. The swell was increasing and the force 4 winds continued to blow them offshore well away from their route to Charmouth. They tried to attract the attention of boats using their whistles but this failed and they had no distress flares or two-way radios. Karen Gardner assumed that someone would raise the alarm when they failed to return by their deadline.

Meanwhile, back in Lyme Regis, Glyn Upham, who ran the centre's safety boat, set out:

> to look for the canoeists when they failed to return. The boat had no radio or mobile phone. Hugging the coastline about 20 yards offshore, he motored to Charmouth, but found no sign of them. Instead of calling the coastguard he returned to the centre and told its manager, Joseph Stoddart, they were missing.
>
> (*The Guardian* 9 December, 1994: 3[49])

Joseph Stoddart did not ring the coastguard at this point. He took a boat out to look for them, in vain, returning at 1.30pm. He then 'drove along the coast, looking for canoes drifting inshore. The party was, by then, two hours overdue' (*The Independent* 9 December, 1994: 6[50]). At 2.40pm a local fishing boat, *Spanish Eyes*, spotted an empty canoe some miles off Charmouth and radioed the coastguard at Weymouth, but details of the location were not recorded at the time. At 3.07pm at the suggestion of the Lyme Regis harbourmaster, Joseph Stoddart finally alerted the coastguard. He indicated to coastguard officer Anthony Day that the group was due in Charmouth at 1pm and that 'the guy in charge has got a first aid kit, flares and that stuff in a water-proof container' (*The Daily Mail* Wednesday November 23, 1994: 30[51]). The party was due in Charmouth at 12.00 midday and they had no distress flares with them.

At 3.25pm the coastguard centre at Portland had to contact the fishing vessel *Spanish Eyes* to get details of the exact location of the upturned canoe reported to them at 2.40pm. The court heard that there was no clear chain of command at the Portland Maritime Rescue Centre (*The Guardian* 9 December, 1994: 3[52]). In addition, shipping was not alerted when the group went missing and the Portland Centre had a weather report giving the wind as onshore. At 3.32pm after speaking to the fishing vessel *Spanish Eyes*, coastguard Anthony Day told the court that, at this point, they realised that the weather report was wrong and that the wind that day was in fact a north westerly offshore. At this point nothing was done to launch the helicopter and lifeboat. Twenty minutes was wasted following up a report that some canoes had been found at Exmouth. Coastguards investigated to see if they were the missing ones (*The Guardian* 23 November, 1994: 3[53]).

A call was made 20 minutes later to Plymouth, asking for a helicopter. At 3.56pm the first helicopter was scrambled. It arrived on scene at 4.09pm.

> The helicopter was asked to make a search from the point where the empty canoe was found. At this stage Mr Day realised there was a high probability that the party was out at sea. He was asked to explain why, in that case, the helicopter, which arrived at the scene at 16.09 was asked to make a trip up and down the coast, and said he was not aware that the instructions to the pilot had been changed by someone else in his office.
>
> (ibid: 3)

Mr Day, in evidence to the court, admitted that having no chain of command at Portland Maritime Rescue Centre, failing to alert shipping in the area of the missing group, the delays in the rescue due to having the wrong wind direction, were all 'serious breaches of rescue rules' (ibid: 3). At 4.24pm the Lyme Regis lifeboat was launched. At 5pm two more helicopters were scrambled and another, 20 minutes later. At 5.30pm Mr Mann and Mr Pointer were rescued by the lifeboat and taken to Weymouth hospital. What of the main party of Karen Gardner and eight pupils since they all ended up in the water at around 12.30 and had now been in the sea water of a temperature of ten degrees centigrade for five hours? On entering the water the pupils were wearing life jackets but they were not fully inflated. 'Life jackets do not function as life jackets unless they are inflated . . . these children had effectively entered the water not wearing life jackets and no action was taken to convert them into life jackets' (Expert witness Royal Navy Surgeon Commander Edward Oakley, giving evidence in *R v Kite and others*[54]).

Commander Oakley told the court 'an order should have been given to inflate the life jackets as soon as the children entered the water' (ibid: 3) When asked by Jonathan Barnes, prosecuting, 'if the lifejackets had been inflated throughout, is there a probability that the four would have survived?' Commander Oakley replied 'yes' (*Daily Mail* 26 November, 1994: 3). Between 12.30 and 5.40pm the party had lost all their canoes, faced an increasing swell and an offshore wind blowing them out to sea, and become increasingly sick and cold in sea temperatures of ten degrees centigrade. Karen Gardner instructed them to 'link arms but they were treading water in only partially inflated lifejackets' (*The Guardian* 9 December, 1994: 3[55]).

'The sea conditions deteriorated and it was exhausting to paddle' Karen Gardner, the instructor with the pupils, told the court. 'We seemed to be drifting faster and the waves were getting higher . . . when the waves came everybody lifted their heads. I saw Claire was not lifting her head anymore. She was blinking but she didn't speak. She started spitting phlegm and speaking like a baby' (written evidence from Samatha Stansby, survivor, from this group, read to the court by Neil Butterfield QC, 17 December 1994[56]). Finally, with permission from Karen Gardner, two of the group, Samantha Stansby and Emma Hartley, decided to try to swim for the shore. Emma started to fall behind and Samantha saw a grey helicopter going along the coast. She waved her arms, but it did not see her.

Ten minutes later, another helicopter saw her this time and at around 6.40pm, after nearly six hours in the water, Samantha Stansby and Emma Hartley were rescued. The rest of their party had been rescued at around 5.40pm. All of them were taken to Weymouth hospital. All were suffering from hypothermia. Four of them, Simon Dunne, Claire Langley, Dean Sayer and Rachel Walker, could not be revived and died. In summary, there were basically several areas where things went wrong:

1 Two inexperienced and untrained instructors.
2 Novice canoeists who should have not been on the sea.
3 Incorrect weather report giving the wrong wind direction.
4 Lifejackets were not properly inflated.
5 Students not told to wear brightly coloured clothing.
6 The pupils did not have spray decks on their canoes.
7 Teenagers should have worn warm headgear.
8 The coastguards were given no prior details of the trip.
9 The safety boat was otherwise engaged.
10 The party had no distress flares or two-way radios.[57]

After nine hours of deliberating, the jury returned a majority verdict on Peter Kite of guilty of [gross negligence] manslaughter. He was sentenced to three years in prison.[58] The judge in his comments said that Peter Kite was 'more interested in sales than in safety'. He added 'The parents and the teachers trusted you . . . and you betrayed that trust' (Ognall J, *R v Kite and others*, *The Independent* 9 December, 1994: 1[59]). It was also very clear that the warning letter to Peter Kite was highly significant in the conviction. Mr J Ognall told Peter Kite that he 'had ignored a "chillingly clear" warning of the risks he was running in a letter sent to him by two instructors the previous year' and that he had 'a duty to enforce safety procedures' (*The Guardian* 9 December, 1994: 1[60]). In the case of Joseph Stoddart, the centre manager, the jury could not reach a verdict and eventually he was found not guilty of manslaughter at the direction of the judge. The company OLL Ltd was found guilty of corporate manslaughter and fined £60,000.

> In the Lyme Bay case, as the company was small, it was easy to find the 'controlling mind'. The risks to which the children were exposed were serious and obvious. The director(s) could not claim ignorance of them because, some eight months prior to the accident, they had received a letter signed by two former instructors at the activity centre that safety standards must be improved. If they weren't, the Directors would have to explain to parents, why their son or daughter was not coming home.
>
> (Barbor, 1995: 44)

This ruling on OLL Ltd made legal history as it was the first time a company had been convicted of corporate manslaughter and 'opens the way for more prosecutions of companies whose gross negligence kills employees or users of their services' (*The Guardian* 9 December, 1994: 3[61]). 'The jury's decision to convict OLL Ltd is a warning to organisations, directors, senior executives and shareholders that they bear the ultimate responsibility for the safety of people passing through their care' (*The Independent* 9 December, 1994: 1[62]). Mr J Ognall announced to the court that he would be 'sending a transcript of the trial to the Department of Transport over criticisms made of the coastguard's role that day' (*The Guardian* 9 December, 1994: 1[63]). He would be passing the details of the tragedy to ministers for their 'immediate appraisal' adding 'the potential for injury and death is too obvious for safety procedures to be left to the inadequate vagaries of self-regulation' (*The Independent* 9 December 1994: 1[64]).

This referred to 'the Government's reluctance to introduce statutory registration of private outdoor activity centres' although reports variously refer to 'mandatory safety inspection', 'statutory registration' or demands for 'mandatory accreditation and inspection of outdoor centres' (*The Guardian* 9 December, 1994: 1; *The Independent* 9 December, 1994: 1).

> Since the tragedy on March 22, 1993, the Department for Education had consistently resisted demands for mandatory accreditation and inspection of outdoor centres. Instead it promulgated new guidelines for teachers and arranged a two-year pro-gramme of inspections by Health and Safety Executive officials.
>
> (*The Guardian* 9 December 1994: 1)

> I don't see how anyone having listened to the evidence could not conclude that there must be statutory regulation. There has to be statutory regulation. There has to be a compulsory register of activity centres. Section three of the national curriculum even mentions canoeing.
>
> (Norman Pointer, German language teacher from Southway Comprehensive School, a survivor of the Lyme Bay tragedy, speaking after the conclusion of the manslaughter trial, *The Guardian* 9 December 1994: 3[65])

Following the deaths of their children in the Lyme Bay canoe tragedy, the parents began a campaign for statutory regulation of outdoor activity centres 'with Devon County Council and their MP David Jamieson, Labour MP for Plymouth, Devonport' (*The Independent* 9 December, 1994: 18[66]). In May 1993 the families of those who died in the tragedy, met with John Patten, Secretary of State for Education, as they had received information regarding the warning letter sent by Joy Cawthorne and Richard Rettallick to Peter Kite in 1992. On 29 July 1993 a Devon County Council internal inquiry into the Lyme Bay canoe tragedy called for a national register to regulate outdoor activity centres. The inquiry regarded such a registration system as 'inevitable' and 'should be developed as soon as possible' (*The Guardian* 30 July, 1993: 3[67]). In November 1993, John Patten issued a four-point set of:

> guidelines to schools and asked the Health and Safety Executive to carry out a random sample of more than 200 centres to see if further regulation is necessary. HSE's advice was that centres are covered by existing legislation, including the 1974 Health and Safety at Work Act 1974.
>
> (*The Independent* 9 December, 1994: 18)

The guidelines to schools on school trips, 'reminded school governors of their legal duties to ensure the safety of children in their care' (ibid. 1994: 18). It is not clear how this improves matters after the Lyme Bay tragedy. Southway Comprehensive had used the approved list of activity centres provided by the B.A.H.A. (who had approved St Alban's activity centre in 1992. The school had checked the brochure, which listed appropriately qualified staff, and they conducted a site visit prior to the school trip.[68]

Ian Jenkins, who published a study on 121 activity centres in Wales in 1993, found that the industry was 'unregulated, staffed by unqualified instructors with little emphasis on accident prevention' (ibid: 18). 'If you are going to regulate an industry on a voluntary basis you are always to leave room for cowboys, and it's usually cowboys that kill people and destroy the industry' (Ian Jenkins, Swansea Institute of Higher Education, cited, Midgley, 1994: 18). In January 1995, The House of Commons Select Committee met to consider safety of outdoor activity centres and David Jamieson MP was in the queue to present a Private Member's Bill which would make regulation mandatory.

> The privately run centres have no obligation to register their existence with anyone . . . the activity centre industry estimates that about ten per cent of centres are sub-standard. As around a million children pass through the centres each year, this suggests that tens of thousands are being exposed to cut-price instruction and safety standards.
>
> (David Jamieson MP, cited in *The Independent* 9 December, 1994: 18)

The Activity Centres (Young Persons' Safety) Act 1995 c.15 made provision for the regulation of centres and providers of facilities where children and young persons under the age of 18 engage in adventure activities, including provision for the imposition of requirements relating to safety. These regulations covered the circumstances for holding a licence, safety requirements for a licence, conditions for a licence (including inspections), renewal, transfer and revocation of licences by the licensing authority. It also covered complaints, investigations of complaints, and appeals. Anyone convicted of operating without a licence could be liable to summary conviction, carrying a two-year prison sentence, fines or both. The 1995 Act allows for provisions in the regulations similar to those in the 1974 Health and Safety at Work Act. The Adventure Activities Licensing Authority (AALA) was set up (see www.aala.org). The powers of this authority were transferred from the Tourism Quality Services (TQS) to the Health and Safety Executive (HSE) on 1 April, 2007.[69]

EXERCISE 7.22

Outline the charges brought against Peter Kite, Joseph Stoddart and OLL Ltd in 1994, arising out of the 1993 Lyme Bay canoe tragedy.

EXERCISE 7.23

Outline the concerns of Joy Cawthorne and Richard Rettalick in their letter to Peter Kite in 1992. Explain the legal significance of this letter in the manslaughter case against Peter Kite and the company OLL Ltd. What was the response of Peter Kite? Did he truly appreciate the pressures on Joseph Stoddart the centre manager, as the outdoor activities centre went ahead with the planned expansions? Explain your answer with referenced support.

EXERCISE 7.24

At the time of the Lyme Bay canoe tragedy were private outdoor activity centres regulated, registered, accredited or approved?

EXERCISE 7.25

What steps did Southway Comprehensive School in Plymouth take to assure themselves that the centre was suitable for an outdoor activities week for their pupils and staff? What did they find out?

EXERCISE 7.26

Critically discuss the appropriateness of the following quote. 'As indicated in their brochure, St Albans Centre did have qualified staff and a rescue boat in the centre. The problem lay partly with the rate of expansion of the centre activities and the deployment of those staff in areas other than the Southway Comprehensive sea canoe trip on 22 March 1993'.

EXERCISE 7.27

Outline with referenced support the canoeing qualifications of the two instructors Karen Gardner and Simon Mann and their appropriateness or otherwise for a sea canoe trip with novices. What did the court hear about the competence of the school pupils and their teacher? Identify expert witness support in the court case on these matters.

EXERCISE 7.28

Using such instructors was described by the prosecution as 'utter folly'. The 'serious risks [of such a trip] should have been glaringly obvious to anyone of experience who gave the matter a moment's thought'. The sea canoe trip on 22 March 1993 was described by the prosecution as 'reckless' and 'in breach of every safety requirement he had put in place'. Explain why these quotes from the prosecution are legally relevant to proving the offence of manslaughter applied at the time of the tragedy in 1993.

EXERCISE 7.29

Explain why the pupils and the teacher got into difficulties very quickly. Was this predictable?

EXERCISE 7.30

Outline the evidence to Winchester Crown Court around the delays by the St Albans Centre in notifying the coastguard of the missing canoeists. Who first alerted the coastguard that canoeists may be missing and when?

EXERCISE 7.31

A rescue helicopter was not scrambled until 3.56pm on the day of the canoe tragedy. Why was this and how did some of the intervening events constitute a 'serious breach of rescue rules' by the Portland Maritime Rescue Centre?

EXERCISE 7.32

Critically comment on the lack of equipment and clothing taken on the sea canoe trip.

EXERCISE 7.33

There were ten areas basically where things went wrong. Locate these ten areas and put them in rank order of risk in their role in causing death. Give reasons for your decisions. (You also have a hypothetical risk assessment exercise in Chapter 6 applied to the situation at St Albans Activity Centre in 1993.)

EXERCISE 7.34

Report accurately the verdicts on the manslaughter charges against Peter Kite, Joseph Stoddart and OLL Ltd. Go on one of the legal databases such as Westlaw UK or Lawtel and find out the reasons for decision to reduce Peter Kite's sentence to two years on appeal. (See *R v Kite*, unreported 8 February, 1996, Court of Appeal.)

EXERCISE 7.35

Why do you think the case of corporate manslaughter was successful against OLL Ltd bearing in mind commentaries on the challenges of bringing such cases?

EXERCISE 7.36

Why was this guilty verdict against OLL Ltd so legally significant?

EXERCISE 7.37

What action did Mr J Ognall take in relation to the conduct of HM Coastguard? OLL Ltd brought a civil case against HM Coastguard in relation to their conduct on 22 March 1993. Search the legal databases for the civil case of *OLL Ltd v Secretary of State for Transport* [1997] 3 All ER 897 and accurately report the outcome of that case.

EXERCISE 7.38

What was the view of the judge on the lack of regulation of private outdoor activity centres in the UK? What action did he take?

EXERCISE 7.39

What action did the government take in 1993 following the Lyme Bay Canoe tragedy and calls to regulate the industry? Was this adequate? Following the comments of the judge in *R v Kite, R v Stoddart, R v OLL Ltd* (unreported, 9 December 1994, Winchester Crown Court, Ognall J), outline what led to the Adventure Centres (Young People's Safety) Act 1995 and the areas it covers. Do some research and briefly provide a literature review on the effectiveness of the 1995 Act.

EXERCISE 7.40

Reflect on what you have learnt about a) the accumulation of risk b) the relevance of good internal communication and listening to the concerns of staff c) the nature of corporate manslaughter.

Summary

- Involuntary manslaughter is divided into two categories: a. constructive (or unlawful act) manslaughter, and b. manslaughter by gross negligence.
- 'The courts have encountered difficulties in attempting to apply the principles of homicide . . . to the actions of corporate bodies' (Molan et al., 2003: 211).
- The case of *R v Stanley and others* October 1990, arising from the sinking of the *Herald of Free Enterprise* in Zeebrugge harbour in 1987, clearly highlighted the failings of the Anglo-Welsh laws of corporate manslaughter. This case led to a Law Commission consultation on Involuntary Manslaughter in 1995, followed by draft government proposals in 2000 and 2003. In April 2008 the new Corporate Manslaughter and Corporate Homicide Act was implemented.
- The first manslaughter cases involving individuals in a sport or recreation context were in the 1880s, both against football players.
- In July 1994 an amateur rugby union player was acquitted of manslaughter at the Old Bailey (Central Criminal Court) London.
- Manslaughter cases in sport and recreation contexts have been brought against players, competitors, sports coaches and leaders, teachers in schools, organisers of school trips in the UK and abroad, organisers of 'dangerous sports society' activities, spectators, fans, parents, facility managers, and a first officer of a commercial ferry which collided with a small yacht, leading to the deaths of three young men.
- Children as young as 11 or 12 have also been charged with manslaughter.
- The Lyme Bay canoe tragedy in 1993, in which four teenagers died during a school trip to an outdoor activities centre in Dorset, led to the high-profile case of *R v Kite and others*, Winchester Crown Court. It made legal history with the first conviction of a company for corporate manslaughter. The managing director of the company, Peter Kite, was convicted of manslaughter and imprisoned for three years. The manager of the outdoor activities centre was found not guilty.
- The Department for Education introduced new guidelines for teachers and a two-year programme of inspections by the Health and Safety Executive in 1994.

- The Activities Centres (Young Persons' Safety) Act 1995 c.15 made provision for the regulation of centres and providers of facilities where children and young people under the age of 18 engage in adventure activities, including the imposition of requirements relating to safety.
- The Adventure Activities Licensing Authority (AALA) was set up on 1 April 2007. The powers of this authority were transferred from the Tourism Quality Services (TQS) to the Health and Safety Executive (HSE).

8 Natural justice principles, sport disciplinary processes and key doping cases

Introduction

The conduct of individuals and organisations in sport and recreation can often launch participants and governing bodies into a range of quasi-legal and legal processes which can be lengthy, traumatic and costly to all parties. These processes may include disciplinary processes, appeals, employment tribunals, civil lawsuits, criminal cases and legal challenges to sports governing body rules and penalties with reference to human rights legislation or, for example, European Community laws or treaties. Disciplinary and civil cases in sport cover a range of issues including eligibility,[1] doping,[2] violence,[3] sexism,[4] racism,[5] and the broader category of 'bringing the sport into disrepute' or 'not acting in the interests of the sport'. Civil cases have been brought against sports governing bodies in relation to, among other things, a failure to follow correct procedures,[6] access to relevant evidence,[7] refusing legal representation at a hearing, allegations of apparent bias by members of a panel,[8] or refusing an appeal.

This chapter will focus on sports disciplinary processes and legal challenges in the civil courts in a domestic and international context. What are the expectations of sports governing bodies in conducting disciplinary processes? What are the rules of natural justice and how can they be unpacked into a set of rights and duties? A range of cases from Anglo-Welsh law will be used to illustrate areas where sports governing bodies have been challenged in relation to the rules of natural justice. Following this a range of structural arrangements will be introduced from an informal grievance right up to international sport arbitration services provided by the Court for Arbitration for Sport (CAS).

The second part of this chapter will provide an overview of the justification and criticisms of the strict liability rules and penalties for doping offences followed by an illustration of the harsh reality of such rules for athletes through the case of Alain Baxter, an Olympic skier. National and international sport governing bodies have to negotiate a complex range of sports rules, codes, European, International Federation and Olympic rules as well as domestic and international laws. What kind of issues can this present in relation to clarity, inconsistencies and conflicts? Is there a need for harmonisation, particularly in doping and international sport? Does the strict liability rule conflict with certain domestic or international laws or with human rights? Will the courts view sports rules, particularly strict liability, as compliant with the Human Rights Act 1998? Finally, the chapter will end with the Diane Modahl doping case as it provides a clear illustration of the issues in this chapter.

Ethical and policy context

Deontologists see ethics as a set of rights and duties such as welfare, do no harm, respect autonomy, and treat people in an equal, fair and just manner. These are regarded as incontestable, universal and arising out of the characteristics of 'being' (ontological) (see Thompson, 2006). We bring such values *to* sport and traditionally claim that there are a set of values *in* sport competition, which inform our practices and rules – including fair play, shared aims or goals, and a voluntary contract to compete (see McNamee and Parry, 1998; Hartley, 1998; McFee, 2004).

Article 7 of the 1989 Anti-Doping Convention states that Convention countries must encourage their sports organisations to harmonise 'disciplinary procedures, applying recognized international principles of natural justice and ensuring respect for the fundamental rights of the suspected sportsmen and sports women' (cited in Wise, 1996: 79).

> Sports related organisations have a responsibility to publish clear guidelines on what is considered ethical or unethical behaviour and ensure that consistent and appropriate incentives are applied.
>
> (European Code of Sports Ethics, 1992,
> Council of Europe, cited Wearmouth, 1995: 31)

Criteria for recognition by sports authorities such as the Central Council for Physical Recreation and the UK Sports Council, include evidence of a properly constituted, democratic organisation, with stable membership, rules and officials, good risk management and insurance, audited accounts and responsible planning, as well as clear disciplinary processes (see Wearmouth, 1995). The CCPR Fair Play Charter makes it clear that its expectations of fair play go beyond the game to all matters of the individuals' or sports governing bodies' conduct, as does the International Committee for Fair Play (CIFP). Disciplinary guidelines should be available to all members of a sports club or organisation and be clearly understood by all, particularly coaches and officials. The law expects sports governing bodies to conduct their disciplinary procedures in accordance with the 'rules of natural justice' (see Parpworth, 1996; Grayson, 2000; Boyes, 2006).

> Sporting disciplinary bodies, like other domestic tribunals, are not required to conduct themselves as if they were amateur courts of law. They are not bound by strict rules of procedure and evidence . . . except to the extent that their rules provide. However, they must not misinterpret the rules they are applying; nor must they conduct themselves other than in conformity with well recognised *principles of fairness* (emphasis added).
>
> (Beloff et al., 1999: 173–174)

What does natural justice mean?

'Natural justice' does not mean that justice will or should happen naturally in relation to sport disciplinaries. The rules of natural justice are so-called because 'they are rules every ordinary, reasonable man would consider fair' (Collins, 1984: 74). They are:

> not a prescriptive set of rules as such, more a set of principles whose flexibility enables them to demand procedural fairness in the decision-making process, but then defines what is fair according to the particular circumstances of the case.
>
> (Parpworth, 1996: 5)

They are really minimum standards of fair decision-making. Sports governing bodies are expected to be fair, reasonable and impartial in the ways in which they conduct their disciplinary proceedings (Hartley, 2001). There are two main rules of natural justice (see Parpworth, 1996; Grayson, 2000; Boyes, 2006). The first is that no man shall judge his own cause (*nemo judex causa sua*). This is also known as a rule against bias, which 'requires an adjudicator to be free from an interest in the case. This can be financial, which automatically disqualifies the adjudicator, or where there is a likelihood of or the appearance of bias' (Boyes, 2006: 198).

The second rule is that no man shall be condemned unheard (*audi alteram partem*). This is the right to have the case heard. It would not be fair to decide a sport disciplinary matter without hearing the side of the accused. An accused sports participant facing a disciplinary charge can:

> rightly expect a hearing before an impartial body, the right to independent legal representation, prior notice of the charge and disclosure of its material particulars, clearly identified evidential rules . . . and the right of appeal.
>
> (McCutcheon, 2000: 121)

Beloff et al. (1999) provide examples of unlawful conduct in the course of disciplinary proceedings. These include finding fault on the basis of a defective charge, mis-construction or misapplication of the disciplinary rule, making a finding on fact which is unsupported by any evidence, acting in bad faith, deciding a disciplinary without hearing the accused or with insufficient time to prepare a defence (Beloff et al., 1999). Also categorised as unlawful would be a panel which has an interest, financial or otherwise, which may give rise to a real danger of bias, or one which imposes a penalty outside the range of sanctions open to the panel (ibid: 174).

These examples are reinforced by the checklist for sports governing bodies to conform with a duty to act fairly provided by Grayson (1994, cited Felix, 1998). This checklist covers things such as avoiding a risk of prejudice or likelihood of bias, clear notification of any charges or assertions needing a reply, and, preferably in writing, any date for a hearing, acting *intra vires* (within the rules), and, in complex cases, carefully considering any request for legal representation (Grayson, 1994, 2000; Felix 1998). The courts 'have not been shy of interfering where the allegation is of a breach of the rules of natural justice' and in sport the 'general rules of natural justice are adapted to the special elements of the matter in question' (Beloff, 2001: 53).

Natural justice: principles and cases

Welch and Wearmouth (1994) and Wearmouth (1995) suggest that the principles of natural justice can be translated into practical guidelines, under general themes of rights and duties relating to the following themes:

- correct procedure
- evidence
- fair and reasonable
- impartial and thorough
- conclusions.

The World Anti-Doping Code (2007) Article 8 sets out a set of principles to be respected when a person who has allegedly committed an anti-doping rule violation faces a disciplinary hearing. These include a right to a timely hearing, a fair and impartial hearing body, the right to be represented by counsel, the right to be informed of and respond to the asserted anti-doping violation, the right of each party to present evidence, question and call witnesses, the right to an interpreter and a timely, written decision (Article 8, WADA Code 2007).

Following correct procedure supports the second rule of natural justice, *audi alteram partem* the right to have the case heard. A person has the right to be given notice of the charge and a reasonable chance of answering it; be clear which rule or code has allegedly been breached; be given an opportunity to state their case and notice of a disciplinary hearing where relevant. In *Keighley RFC v Cunningham* (unreported, 1960), Mr Holmes, a rugby player, was:

> sent off during a cup tie on 13 February 1960. On the following day, 14 February, the referee submitted his report to the appropriate disciplinary committee in accordance with the rules. On 15 February the committee met to hear the case and suspended the player. Neither the club nor the player had been notified that the case was going to be heard.

> Mr Justice Dankwerts held that:
> On the grounds of natural justice it was the duty of a body like this to hear the player and it should be the onus of the committee to notify him that the case would be heard on a certain day.

> (Grayson, 1994: 298)

A person accused of a breach of rules or codes has the right to be assisted or represented by someone of their choice at any hearing. Wearmouth (1995: 33) suggests that:

> the role of this person should be clarified; they should not be someone who will play a part in the decisions in the case and will be subject to the rules of the association relating to the handling of disciplinaries and appeals.

In the early 1970s, a decision by a governing body to refuse legal representation was upheld by the courts. However, Grayson (1994: 305) advises that 'in cases of difficulty or complexity, consider carefully any request for legal representation'.

> It is useful to have someone to advise and or speak on behalf of the accused or complainant. They can monitor procedure, clarify points, speak on behalf of that person, during a traumatic and disorientating process.

> (Wearmouth, 1995: 33)

In conducting the hearing the procedure should be explained to all parties in advance of the hearing and procedures standardised for all cases (Welch and Wearmouth, 1994). Matters of evidence often create problems for both governing bodies and accused persons or complainants. A person charged has the right to be given access to the evidence, respond to the evidence, know the names of persons giving evidence and for the evidence to be presented systematically and thoroughly (ibid). The Diane Modahl doping case, covered towards the end of this chapter, clearly illustrates problems around lack of access to, and cross-examination of, relevant evidence regarding storage of a urine sample, the need for published research and scientific experiments to support any challenge of a positive doping result. The burden of proof ('beyond reasonable doubt' or 'on the balance of probabilities') should be clearly stated in the rules relating to sports disciplinaries.

A sports governing body should have clear and reasonable instructions on submitting evidence to a disciplinary hearing. Is hearsay evidence accepted or should all evidence submitted be individually attributable? What are the deadlines for submitting evidence? What happens if new evidence comes to light? The evidence presented might be written, oral and, increasingly, video evidence, although there are reasons for viewing the introduction of video evidence with some caution. In 1993 John Fashanu was disciplined by the FA for an incident in which his elbow shattered the cheekbone of Gary Mabutt. It highlighted the difficulties of a referee making a decision, in the game, not to send players off – then when confronted with slow-motion, then frame by frame video pictures of the incidents, feeling under pressure to alter his/her view of the incident. In McIllvaney's opinion, the referee's 'original opinion appears to have been eroded by repeated viewing of video evidence' (McIllvaney, 1993: 3).

In an unusual case in rugby league in 1990, Andy Currier was sent off, allegedly, for a high tackle. However, a video recording revealed that it was 'nothing of the sort, more of a shoulder charge in fact. The opponent on the receiving end didn't think Currier should have been sent off and gave evidence at the hearing. More importantly, the referee who sent him off, admitted he had made an error' (Corrigan, 1990). However, in a High Court hearing, when Currier appealed against a two-year suspension from his professional work, the judge rejected his appeal, commenting on the need for the integrity of the sports contest and the fair and proper proceedings of the governing body (Corrigan, 1990; Wearmouth, 1995: 34).

In 1998 Mark Bosnich, a soccer player, was given a yellow card for wasting time during Aston Villa's UEFA cup quarter final match against Athletico-Madrid. The referee was unaware that Bosnich was being pelted with objects and thought he was just standing there wasting time. Video evidence supported Bosnich's explanation, yet, because the referee did not include that in his match report, Bosnich was unable to include it in his appeal (Holt, 1998). Following an alleged violent incident on the field, a rugby player's legal representative was not allowed to discuss or challenge the videotape evidence during the disciplinary hearing. It was discussed in private by the panel[9] (Rose and Albertini, 1997; Felix, 1998).

The third practical guideline relates to the duty to be fair and reasonable (Welch and Wearmouth, 1994) under which a disciplinary panel is expected to conduct the affairs of the sport 'fairly and reasonably, in line with the constitution and rules of the association' (Wearmouth, 1995: 34). A panel must act on good faith, deal with cases consistently and fairly, by standardised procedures making their decision on evidence relevant to the case, disregarding extraneous considerations (ibid: 34). The fourth practical guideline covers the duty to be impartial and thorough, relating to the first rule of natural justice *nemo judex causa sua* – no man shall judge his own cause. Parties to any disciplinary hearing should be notified of the panel membership, well in advance of the hearing, to allow opportunities for any challenge on the grounds of impartiality.

In the case of *Revie v the FA* [1979] the protests of the England team manager, regarding the 'constitution of the disciplinary tribunal, imposing a ten-year ban, because of members' adverse attitudes personally expressed to him by tribunal members' were upheld by the court and described to him as 'contrary to natural justice because of the likelihood of bias which is among tribunal members' (Grayson, 1994: 308). This was despite the fact that Mr Justice Cantley called Don Revie 'greedy, deceitful and selfish' and that it was 'reasonable for the FA to be satisfied that his conduct brought the sport into disrepute' (Bitel, 1995: 7). It is not necessary to prove actual bias, only the likelihood of bias and conduct indicative of such apparent bias need not be restricted to the formal hearing itself.

EXERCISE 8.1

Explain why sports governing bodies or clubs should have codes of conduct and disciplinary procedures.

EXERCISE 8.2

What does 'natural justice' mean? Explain the two main rules of natural justice with referenced support.

EXERCISE 8.3

Outline the rights of an accused sports participant in relation to the following practical guidelines for natural justice (Welch and Wearmouth 1994; Wearmouth 1995): correct procedure, matters of evidence, and impartial and thorough procedures. For each of these themes illustrate that theme with an example from this chapter and an additional example or case supported by referenced literature or appropriate databases.

EXERCISE 8.4

Should the decisions of referees on the field be considered in disciplinary hearing arising from an allegedly violent incident on the sports field? (Make reference to relevant cases and incidents.)

EXERCISE 8.5

Find a disciplinary case in a sport or recreation context and comment on the evidence and the findings in relation to following or breaching any rules of natural justice.

EXERCISE 8.6

Explain how *Keighley RFC v Cunningham* (unreported, 1960) breached the rules of natural justice in their disciplinary action against Mr Holmes.

EXERCISE 8.7

Is it advisable, these days, to refuse an accused player legal representation at a disciplinary hearing? Support your answer with reference to relevant literature

EXERCISE 8.8

'An accused player who alleges bias by any member of a disciplinary panel must provide evidence of actual bias'. True or False?

EXERCISE 8.9

Locate a referenced example of an incident or disciplinary issue or legal case in sport or recreation for each of the following themes using any part of this text or other relevant literature or databases:

- sexist conduct
- discrimination – direct or indirect
- racist conduct
- violence
- dissent or lack of respect towards an official
- slander
- bringing the sport into disrepute
- negligence
- a breach of a statutory health and safety duty
- doping in sport
- sponsorship issue
- fraud
- contractual matters.

Summarise the evidence and comment on the application of the relevant sport rules, rules of natural justice or domestic laws which were broken or alleged to have been broken.

A range of disciplinary processes

A range of hearings, both within and beyond sport disciplinary processes, can follow an incident, accusation or disagreement. These include:

1 Informal grievance
2 Disciplinary hearing or tribunal
3 Appeal
4 Sports Resolutions UK (formerly national UK sport resolution panel)
5 Court of Arbitration for Sport (CAS) ordinary or appeal hearing
6 CAS advisory decision
7 CAS mediation process

8 Civil case (private writ)

9 Criminal case (brought by the state or private prosecution by an individual/group).

Numbers one to seven above are disciplinary processes within national or international sport governing bodies. It is important to clearly distinguish between those processes and numbers eight and nine, which are legal cases brought by an individual sportsperson/ organisation or by the state. This chapter will mainly focus on a range of processes from one to eight above.

An 'informal grievance' can take the form of an informal meeting and/or written communication, where the complainant outlines the problem, with specific names and dates, in the presence of an official from the club or organisation, who acts as a mediator.[10] The complainant should identify the rule to which it relates and the detrimental effect on both the individual and the aims or mission statement of the organisation or club. It does not have the status of a formal disciplinary hearing but can help to highlight and resolve any misunderstandings or miscommunications between the complainant and 'accused' person. Warnings or requests to refrain from the identified behaviour may hopefully prove successful, and this is usually monitored by a relatively short 'trial' or 'monitoring' period. An informal grievance can remind participants of their ethical obligations and what they value in their sport, framed in their aims or mission statement, as well as trying to address issues in the early stages, before they get out of hand and parties become entrenched (see Welch and Wearmouth, 1994: 8). However, there is a tension between the advantages of settling matters as soon as they arise and the lack of human resources and training of club officials who may have to implement such a processes at a local level.[11]

Most sports governing bodies have a 'disciplinary hearing' or 'tribunal', relating to the second rule of natural justice *audi alteram partem*, the right to have a case heard. In processing and managing a disciplinary hearing, correct procedures should be carefully followed. Information to members should clearly state the procedures to be followed. A person has the right to be given notice of the charge or complaint, the rule or code which has allegedly been breached, an opportunity to state their case and be given reasonable notice of a disciplinary hearing, if one is to take place. Deadlines for exchange of written evidence, any rules or expectations of behaviour or engagement[12] and any costs incurred in submitting a complaint or going through a disciplinary process should be made very clear. In conducting the hearing the procedures and rules of etiquette should be explained to all parties in advance of the hearing and standardised as far as possible for all hearings. An accurate record should be made by someone in an official capacity who will not have to take part in the decision making. The panel members should seek information and clarification on relevant matters and should refrain from making judgmental comments or advising the complainant or accused parties (Hartley, 2001a).

The parties have no right of access to the deliberations of the panel. The punishments should fit the case, follow the relevant national or international sports rules and be applied consistently across disciplinary panels.[13] In disciplinary matters, the right of appeal should always exist and the grounds for an appeal made clear to all members. Normally an appeal is allowed for two reasons. First, if new evidence comes to light, which was not available to the original panel and could have an impact on the original findings. Second, if it could be argued that, for example, the disciplinary panel or administrators were unfair, displayed apparent bias or did not follow correct procedures or deviated from the rules or codes. Normally there is a financial charge for an appeal and a time limit on submitting an appeal to the secretary of the organisation. An officer or chairperson of the original panel would normally prepare documents for the appeal panel on the original alleged offence or complaint. A panel of three people, who were not connected to the original panel or related incident, would hear the appeal (see Welch and Wearmouth, 1994; Wearmouth 1995; Hartley 2001a).

Although an appeal is the last process within an individual sports governing body, a person or group can make use of organisations and processes beyond the governing body and hopefully avoid pursuing a private and costly writ (legal challenge) in the civil courts. Arbitration and mediation processes are available at national and international levels. There are dispute resolution services available at domestic levels, for example the Sport Dispute Resolution Panel (Sport Resolutions UK[14]), established in January 2000, and modelled on the Court of Arbitration for Sport (CAS). It provides arbitration, mediation and dispute guidance. The new National Anti-Doping Panel, launched in 2008, will be administrated by Sport Resolutions UK and will hear anti-doping cases on behalf of national governing bodies, providing a 'totally independent Tribunal service implementing the WADA code in a consistent and fair way' (Peter Leaver QC, speaking at a sports law breakfast at Bird and Bird Solicitors in London, 25 September 2008, NADP, 2008)

Disputes in sport can, among other things, drain resources, tarnish the image of sport, strain relationships, and detract from the enjoyment of sport (Siddall, 2004, cited in Blackshaw 2006a: 249). 'Growing commercialisation, the greater risk of legal challenge and litigation, and the need for sport to regulate itself in a modern and businesslike manner, all combine to emphasise the merits of effective dispute resolution in sport . . .' (ibid). In the first four years of operation, approximately 25 sports made use of the UK SDRP, covering a 'wide range of issues, including discipline, selection, eligibility, doping, exclusion from membership, funding, contractual rights, employment, discrimination and child welfare' (ibid). Domestic sport dispute resolution processes also operate in other countries and sport law literature provides updates and commentaries on such processes (see for example Doyle, 2000; Findlay and Corbett, 2002).

At an international level, the Court for Arbitration in Sport (CAS) was established in 1984, by the IOC, to provide a 'central, specialised authority' for resolving disputes related to international sports (Nafziger, 2004a: 40).

> This litigation tactic is a serious threat to international athletic co-operation. It undermines the very purpose of international procedures for resolving athletic eligibility disputes that is free from any perceived national bias.
>
> (Gulland, 1995: 10[15])

The aim of the CAS was to 'create a specialized authority capable of settling disputes and offering a flexible, quick and inexpensive procedure' (Reeb, 2000: 10). 'Sports persons and bodies prefer not to "wash their dirty linen in public" but settle their disputes "within the family of sport". In other words, in private and amongst others who understand what makes sport special' (Blackshaw, 2006d: 1). Lengthy, expensive litigation is 'not suited to this area of law', with 'technical, highly specialised disputes, with cross-border juris-dictional issues' requiring a settlement 'in days and weeks, rather than years' (Nicholson, 2004: 3).

In the first ten years CAS was funded by the IOC, who had the power to appoint the members, approve the budget, and modify the CAS Statute (Blackshaw, 2003: 64). In 1992, a horse rider named Elmar Grundel lodged an appeal with CAS, challenging a decision by the Federation Equestre Internationale (FEI) to disqualify, fine and suspend him following a horse doping case (see Reeb, 2000; Blackshaw, 2003, 2006c). Although the Swiss Federation Tribunal recognised the CAS as 'a true court of arbitration that had acted independently of an International Federation (IF) – in the case in point' the SFT observed that the numerous links between the CAS and the IOC, both organisationally and financially. It called into question the independence of CAS if the IOC was a party to CAS arbitration (Reeb, 2000; Blackshaw, 2003; Nafziger, 2004a: 43). Following the Grundel case, the International Council of Arbitration for Sport (ICAS) was formed to organise and finance the CAS entirely independently of the IOC, appoint arbitrators and approve budgets, and make any changes to the new Code of Sports Related Arbitration, only at a full ICAS meeting (see Reeb, 2000; Nafziger, 2004a).

'Proceedings are generally heard before a tribunal of three, made up of a President and one Arbiter chosen by each party from the list published by CAS' (Nicholson, 2004: 4). The CAS generally hears 'three kinds of disputes: disciplinary, eligibility-related, and commercial' (Nafziger, 2004a: 41). In 1996 ICAS created two central offices, in Sydney, Australia and New York, still attached to the court office in Lausanne, Switzerland. Ordinary arbitration considers 'disputes between parties' and in the appeals arbitration the CAS considers 'appeals from final decisions of sports federations, whose statutes provide for appeal to the CAS' (Nicholson, 2004: 3). Also in 1996 a CAS ad hoc division, of two co-presidents and 12 arbitrators, was created to settle disputes within the Atlanta Summer Olympic Games, within 24 hours of them being lodged (see Beloff, 1996[16]). In 1998, two new ad hoc divisions were set up – for the 1998 Winter Olympic Games in Nagano[17] and the 1998 Commonwealth Games in Kuala Lumpur, Malaysia. The AHD panels have continued to operate at the Summer and Winter Olympics,[18] the Commonwealth Games, and more recently, the 2000 European Football Championships and the FIFA World Cup in 2006.[19]

The CAS also provides advisory opinions, known as 'Consultation Proceedings' and, since 1999, a mediation service. The CAS Advisory Opinion was used to consider a decision by FINA to 'approve the use of full-body ("long john") swimsuits' less than a year before the 2000 Olympic Games (Nafziger, 2004b[20]). Oscar Pistorius, a South African athlete, was born without fibula bones in both legs and as a baby had both legs amputated below the knee. He took up athletics in 2004 and in the same year, won the 200m sprint event at the Athens Paralympic Games. He competed against able-bodied athletes in South Africa but he really wanted to compete with able-bodied athletes in the international arena. Oscar Pistorius wore Ossur Cheetah Fox-Foot prosthetics to compete in track events and 'was regarded with deep suspicion by the authorities who questioned whether they gave him an unfair advantage' (The Times 17 May 2008[21]). The International Amateur Athletics Federation, commissioned a scientific study in Germany in December 2007, and held an IAAF Council Hearing in January 2008.

The IAAF ruled Oscar Pistorius ineligible to compete against able-bodied athletes at the summer Olympics in Beijing. 2008. The Council decided that the Cheetah blades were 'technical aids' and in contravention of IAAF Rule 144.2 (e) that 'provides the user with an advantage over an athlete not using such a device' (CAS Press Release 30 April 2008[22]).The IAAF Council concluded that:

> an athlete using the 'cheetah' prosthetic is able to run at the same speed as an able-bodied athlete with lower energy consumption. Running with prosthetic blades leads to less vertical motion combined with less mechanical work for lifting the body. As well as this the energy loss in the blade is significantly lower than in the human ankle joints at maximum speed. An athlete using the prosthetic blade has a demonstrable mechanical advantage (more than 30 per cent) when compared to someone not using the blade.
>
> (The Times online, 14 January 2008[23])

Oscar Pistorius immediately filed an appeal with CAS in February 2008. On 16 May 2008 the CAS Panel were critical of the IAAF scientific tests and upheld his appeal revoking the IAAF ban with immediate effect.

> The IAAF did not meet its burden of proof that Rule 144.2 (e) is contravened by Oscar Pistorius. On the basis of evidence brought by experts called by both parties, the Panel was not persuaded that there was sufficient evidence of any metabolic advantage in favour of the double-amputee using Cheetah Flex-Foot. Furthermore, the CAS Panel has considered that the IAAF did not prove that the biomechanical effects of using this particular prosthetic device gives Oscar Pistorius an advantage over other athletes not using the device.
>
> (CAS Press Release, 16 May, 2008[24])

The CAS Panel emphasised that the scope of the application of their decision is limited to Oscar Pistorius only and only to his prosthesis at issue in this appeal.

The CAS Mediation Service is a 'non-binding and informal procedure' where each party:

> undertakes to attempt in good faith to negotiate with the other party, and with the assistance of a CAS mediator, with a view to settling a sports-related dispute.
>
> (Blackshaw, 2003: 70)

CAS mediation excludes doping cases, but Blackshaw (2003: 71) argues that it is:

> very appropriate for settling commercial and financial issues and consequences . . . which often follow from a doping case, particularly where a sports person concerned was wrongly accused of being a drugs cheat. For example, Diane Modahl would have been better advised to try to settle her claims for compensation against the British Athletics Federation through mediation rather than through the courts.[25]

Reeb (2005) expected cases to rise, especially after 2002 when FIFA appeals were included, but 'rather than a linear increase the number of cases has exploded – 271 in 2004, compared to 109 in 2003', partly due to the inclusion of commercial disputes (cited Blackshaw, 2006d: 1). 'As of 2004, the CAS has received over 500 requests for arbitration and decided some 250 of them' with such rapid growth being supported by the agreements between CAS and International Federations to accede to the compulsory jurisdiction of CAS (Nafziger, 2004a: 44[26]). An Arbitral award by CAS is:

> final and binding and can be enforced according to the usual rules of private law and, in particular, with the provisions of the New York Convention on the Recognition and Enforcement of Foreign Arbitral Awards
>
> (Blackshaw, 2003: 81)

CAS is the last dispute process where disputes are resolved within the family of sport. Sports participants or organisations may still use the courts in a private writ, where they might sue the sports governing body in a domestic court of law.[27] In addition, incidents which lead to disciplinary processes within a sport governing body may also lead to criminal charges, such as those related to Offences Against the Person Act 1861 – different kinds of assault, covered in Chapter 4, or those causing death, such as manslaughter, covered in Chapter 7. In relation to doping, it is one thing to ingest or purchase banned substances for individual use – and even personal use of a drug may lead to criminal prosecutions in the country which hosts a sports event, whose domestic laws ban that substance.[28] It is quite another to distribute or supply such a substance, for example, anabolic steroids, to others.

In June 2003, it was discovered that BALCO [the Bay Area Laboratory Co-operative in San Francisco, California] was in possession of a designer steroid called THG. A syringe of THG was anonymously sent to the United States Anti-Doping Agency (USADA). This action allowed chemists to unmask a previously undetectable substance. The discovery sparked an extensive United States grand jury investigation in October 2003. The American sprinter Kelli White was the first athlete suspended based on information from the BALCO investigation. Soon after, Dwain Chambers, a British sprinter tested positive for THG and was suspended for two years.

(McClaren, 2004: 176–177)

On 12 February 2004, 71-year-old Remi Korchemny, the Ukrainian coach of Dwain Chambers, was charged, along with four other men, in California, with running an illegal drugs distribution operation, at BALCO. Korchemny had coached British athlete Dwain Chambers since 2001, who was one of the five athletes who tested positive for a designer steroid, tetrahydrogestrinone (THG) in 2003 (Knight, 2004: 1).[29]

EXERCISE 8.10

What is an informal grievance process? Explain the advantages and challenges of including such a process in the policies of a sports organisation at a local level.

EXERCISE 8.11

To which rule of natural justice does the provision of a sport disciplinary tribunal relate? Outline the work to be done in advance of, during and after a sport disciplinary tribunal.

EXERCISE 8.12

Discuss what you might do in the following hypothetical situation. Give reasons for your answer. An accused coach is provided with a date for a disciplinary hearing by the sports governing body three times and he advises that he is unable to attend any of the dates as he has a) a funeral b) a date for an operation which has already been delayed twice by the hospital and c) a cup final which he cannot miss or rearrange. As the general secretary organising the disciplinary hearing, what would you advise in this situation, bearing in mind *audi alteram partem*?

EXERCISE 8.13

What are the usual grounds for appeal against the findings of a sport disciplinary panel? Why is it good practice to have clear grounds for an appeal and an accompanying fee?

EXERCISE 8.14

Identify the training and resources challenges facing a small voluntary sports governing body in providing a range of disciplinary and appeal panels.

EXERCISE 8.15

Prior to the UK and CAS services, what route might an athlete or club take if they were unhappy with a disciplinary and appeal process within their sport?

EXERCISE 8.16

Find out what you can about Sport Resolutions UK (formerly the UK Sport Dispute Resolution Panel – UKSDRP). When was it formed and revised? How does it operate? What kind of cases have come to the UKSDRP in the past?

EXERCISE 8.17

Find, download and share with your seminar group, one referenced source or case from the Canadian or the Australian Sports Dispute Resolution Service.

EXERCISE 8.18

Explore the reasons for setting up the Court for Arbitration for Sport (the CAS). Evaluate the impartiality of the CAS and its capacity to operate independently of the International Olympic Committee (IOC).

EXERCISE 8.19

What are the four kinds of services of the CAS? How is a CAS tribunal constituted?

EXERCISE 8.20

The CAS deals with three main categories of cases. What are they? Give an example of each with a brief summary supported by referenced sources.

EXERCISE 8.21

What are the ad hoc divisions – the AHDs of the CAS? Why were they introduced? Explain why the world swimming sports governing body FINA, sought a CAS advisory opinion prior to the 2000 Summer Olympics in Sydney, Australia. What was the outcome?

EXERCISE 8.22

Get into groups of five or ten. Number yourselves 1–5 or 1–10 until you all have a number. Find the case which matches your number below and report it to the group using referenced sources. Provide a concise summary of the evidence, decision and implications of the case:

1   The *Andrade* (Cape Verde) case at the 1996 Summer Olympics in Atlanta.
2   The *Smith* case at the 1996 Summer Olympic Olympic Games in Atlanta.
3   The *Sachenbacher-Stehle* case at the 2006 Winter Olympic Games in Turin, Italy.
4   *Bernhard v ITU* (unreported, 9 August 1999, Court of Arbitration for Sport, CAS 1998/222).
5   *USA Shooting and Quigley v IUT* (unreported, 13 May 1995, Court of Arbitration for Sport, CAS 94/129).
6   *Aanes v FINA* (unreported, 9 July 2001, Court of Arbitration for Sport, CAS 2001/A/317A).
7   The *Raducan* case at the 2000 Summer Olympics in Sydney, Australia.
8   The *Rebagliati* case at the 1998 Winter Olympics in Nagano, Japan.
9   The *Koorneev* and *Bouliev* cases at the 1996 Summer Olympic Games in Atlanta.
10 The unusual cases of two Greek sprinters *Kostadinos Kenteris* and *Ekaterina Thanou* 24 hours before the opening ceremony of the 2004 Summer Olympics in Athens, Greece (see McLaren, 2004 and other relevant sources and databases).

EXERCISE 8.23

Do you anticipate an increase in the demand for the CAS services? Explain and support your answer with referenced sources.

EXERCISE 8.24

Find out what you can about the 'BALCO' [Bay Area Laboratory Co-operative] drug scandal, which allegedly involved company management and a range of athletes, coaches and professional sports players. In particular investigate the allegations against Remi Korchemny and Dwain Chambers. What was the outcome?

Doping and the strict liability rule

> The offence of doping takes place when either (i) a prohibited substance is found to be present in an athlete's body or tissue fluids or (ii) an athlete uses or takes advantage of a prohibited technique.
>
> (IAAF handbook, 1992–3, Rule 55, cited Houlihan, 2002: 197)

> Doping is the presence in the body of a prohibited substance, whether or not intentional or negligent, and can affect the results of the event so that the presence of the substance is sufficient to find a doping violation.
>
> (Article 2.2 of Chapter II of the Olympic Movement Anti-Doping Code OMAC)

> Doping is defined as the occurrence of one or more of the anti-doping rule violations set forth in Article 2.1 through to Article 2.8 of the [WADA] Code.
>
> It is each athlete's personal duty to ensure that no Prohibited Substances or its metabolites or markers[30] are found to be present in their bodily specimens. Accordingly, it is not necessary that intent, fault negligent or knowing Use on the Athlete's part be demonstrated in order to establish an anti-doping violation under Article 2.1.
>
> (Article 2.1. WADA Code, 2007)

> Refusing or failing without compelling justification, to submit to sample collection, after notification as authorized in applicable anti-doping rules or otherwise evading sample collection.
>
> (WADA Code Article 2.3)

> Failure or refusal to submit to sample collection after notification is prohibited in almost all existing anti-doping rules.
>
> (WADA Code comment on Article 2.3, p. 10)

A doping rule of strict liability means that a competitor or person subject to the jurisdiction of a sports governing body can be found guilty of a doping offence 'without the sports governing body proving culpable intent, knowledge or fault, or without the possibility of the accused being allowed to show that she had no culpable intent, knowledge and/or was faultless' (Wise, 1996: 70). Even where a sportsperson can provide evidence of unknowing, inadvertent consumption of a prohibited substance 'this evidence will be treated as irrelevant by the sporting association' (Sithamparanathan and Schillings, 2003: 140[31]). However, Article 10.5 of the WADA Code provides for the period of ineligibility to be reduced or eliminated if the athlete can show that 'he/she bears no fault or negligence for the violation' but must 'establish how the prohibited substance entered his/her system' (WADA Code 2007: 30[32]). More recently, Article 10.5 of the WADA Code provides that the two-year standard penalty for doping offences may be reduced if the athlete may show no, or no significant fault or negligence[33] (Sithamparanathan and Schillings, 2003: 140; Hooper, 2006). The WADA Code and list was updated in January 2009. 'Lessened sanctions are possible where the athlete can establish that the substance involved was not intended to enhance performance' (Kirkup and Solly, 2008).

The following examples following a positive 'B' test result would be captured within the strict liability rule:

1   Someone spikes an athlete's drink with a banned substance, unbeknown to the athlete, who later fails an official doping control test. (Although Article 10 of the

WADA Code 2003 provides for a reduction in or elimination of a sanction in certain circumstances.)
2 A coach, team doctor or nutritionist supplies a natural supplement, which unbeknown to any party, contains a concentrated form of a banned substance.
3 An athlete buys a nasal decongestant whilst at an international competition, which is not the same as the legal product he has used before at home. It contains a banned substance unbeknown to him and he fails a doping control test.
4 An athlete who has asthma fails to register this condition to the appropriate authorities under the therapeutic use exemption clause and subsequently fails a doping test for a banned substance used in asthma medication.
5 An athlete whose drug-free urine sample is stored inappropriately in unrefridgerated conditions, leading to bacterial degradation and a 'false' positive test.

It has to be recognised that most athletes, who return a positive test, given the chance, will protest their 'innocence' and deny the deliberate ingestion of any banned substance. Equally, any governing authority is unlikely to be in a position to prove exactly how the banned substance came to be in the athlete's body. Thus many rules include a provision for strict liability: an athlete has charge of his own body and must accept responsibility for what is found in it.

(Griffith-Jones, 2002: 2)

The nature of a doping offence, whether or not it should be a strict or absolute liability offence and the length of penalties, are among the recurring controversies in drugs in sport (Opie, 2002: 133). Strict liability doping rules are acknowledged as 'draconian', necessary in the fight against doping, legally established but naturally problematic (see Beloff, 2001; Sithamparanathan and Schillings, 2003; Hooper, 2006). Why have a strict liability rule? A doping rule which required a sports governing body to prove fault (or intention) would be 'unfair to competitors in the tainted event' and would 'probably be too difficult to prove and therefore would open the floodgates to cheats' and 'be too expensive to prove' (CAS panel in *USA Shooting and Quigley v IUT* (unreported, 13 May 1995, Court of Arbitration for Sport, CAS 94/129), cited in Flint et al., 2003: 950).

It appears to be 'a laudable policy objective not to repair an accidental unfairness to the whole body of other competitors. This is what could happen if banned performance-enhancing substances were tolerated when absorbed inadvertently' (WADA Code 2007: 8). Strict liability is regarded as 'indispensable for an effective fight against doping in sport and for the protection of fairness towards all competitors and of their health and well-being (*Bernhard v ITU* (unreported, 9 August 1999, Court of Arbitration for Sport, CAS 1998/222), cited in Flint et al., 2003: 951). The high objectives and 'practical necessities of the fight against doping amply justify the application of a strict liability standard' and 'performance-enhancing drugs confer an unfair advantage even if taken accidentally or without intent to gain an unfair advantage' (*Quigley*, para 14, cited in Beloff, 2001: 46).

If the rule required fault liability it would 'impose a burden which it could not easily discharge, and lead to protracted and bitter and ultimately inconclusive hearings' and 'the fight against doping would become virtually impossible' (ibid: 44). Michelle Verokken reported that not only was the life ban from the British Olympic Association recommended by the athletes' commission, but that athletes were 'the strongest promoters of a strict liability approach to doping' (see Kelham, 2004: 138[34]). Dick Pound QC, the president of WADA, argued at a British Association for Sport Seminar in 2004 that the Code is:

to protect athletes who do not cheat and that it is a welcome move away from previous systems which appeared to do everything to allow cheaters to keep cheating and strict liability was essential . . . if every banned substance was included in the prohibited substances list by name, the list would be five inches thick.

He observed that a two-year ban was the norm and could be reduced in deserving circumstances and did not agree with the argument that there should be evidence that a substance is performance enhancing on a particular day as 'athletes know that, if a substance is on the banned list, they must not take it' (Dick Pound QC, cited in Kelham, 2004: 139).

Criticisms of the strict liability doping rule include:

1 It does not follow the established legal principle of innocent until proven guilty.
2 It has fixed, mandatory penalties, which can impact on an athlete's livelihood, a 'restraint of trade' (see Beloff, 2001; Hooper, 2006).
3 It does not take into consideration the circumstances of the individual case (see Bitel, 1995).
4 The circumstances for the chance to mitigate against the length of the ban, where there has been no, or no significant fault are confusing and difficult to follow. Does Article 10 really allow a defence?
5 The public policy reasons given by J Scott in *Gasser v Stinson and Another* (unreported, 15 June 1988, Queen's Bench Division, Scott J), for strict liability such as stopping the floodgates opening and making attempts to prevent doping futile, are not as persuasive as, for example, other circumstances outside sport where strict liability offences are provided for in the criminal law such as the protection of the public (see Sithamparanathan and Schillings, 2003; Hooper, 2006).
6 Such rules and mandatory penalties could be seen to be non-compliant with Article 6 of the Human Rights Act 1998.[35]
7 The use of an analogue or mimic is banned as well as the list itself. So how does an athlete know if they have taken a mimic or analogue if it not on the list?
8 It appears to disregard the principles of necessity and proportionality (see Griffith-Jones, 2002).
9 The strict liability rule does not even require the sports governing body to prove that the banned substance enhances performance unfairly.
10 Strict liability drug rules 'have as their purpose to catch the majority of "guilty" parties while sacrificing a few "innocent" ones: a concept incompatible with the basic legal tenets of civilised societies' (Wise, 1996: 80).

EXERCISE 8.25

Make sure that you have completed the task from Chapter 1 which requires you to locate and download the *current* WADA Code and list of Prohibited Substances from 1 January this year.

EXERCISE 8.26

Give an example of a fault liability doping rule. Identify the problems of such a rule.

EXERCISE 8.27

Give an example of a strict liability doping rule. Provide a detailed account of the reasons for introducing a strict liability doping rule.

EXERCISE 8.28

Provide three brief examples of the application of the strict liability rule to a positive 'B' sample test in sport.

EXERCISE 8.29

Divide the seminar group into two groups. Group A research arguments and cases which support a strict liability rule. Group B research areas of concern about a strict liability rule. In each group make detailed notes and arguments using relevant literature and cases.

EXERCISE 8.30

What is the penalty for a first doping violation? What is the penalty for a second doping violation? Critically discuss these penalties.

EXERCISE 8.31

Are there any circumstances where an athlete's penalty can be reduced or even eliminated? Give a detailed explanation, well supported with referenced sources and examples.

EXERCISE 8.32

Are there Articles in the WADA Code which allow an athlete to raise the issue of the incompetence of the accredited laboratory? If yes, provide details.

EXERCISE 8.33

Look up the doping case of *Poll v FINA* (unreported, 31 January 2003, Court of Arbitration for Sport, CAS 2002/A/399) . What substance was found in her sample? What was the penalty? What issues did Claudia Poll raise in this case around the burden of proof in relation to the sampling procedure. What was the outcome of the appeal to CAS?

EXERCISE 8.34

Having read and discussed the arguments and issues thus far, what are your first impressions of the introduction of the strict liability doping rule?

An example of a CAS doping case: the wrong inhaler – the Alain Baxter story

On 23 February, 2002, Alain Baxter thought he had secured a place in history by becoming the first British Olympian to secure a podium position in a downhill ski-ing event, having finished third in the Men's Alpine Slalom at Salt Lake City 2002.

(Nicholson, 2004: 4)

He tested positive for a banned substance, methamphetamine, was found guilty of a doping offence and stripped of his bronze medal and later banned from competing for three months.[36] Mr Baxter had a well-documented, long-standing nasal condition, for which he had used a non-prescription, 'Vicks Vapour Inhaler', for many years, normally buying the British version of the product, which contained no banned substances according to the UK Sports Council (Reeb, 2005: 303). When a different Vicks product, recommended by the British team doctor was unsatisfactory, Mr Baxter purchased a Vicks inhaler, for sale in a local store, 'he did not consult with the team doctor because, he said, it appeared to be the same product as the one he had used regularly in the United Kingdom' (ibid: 304). Unfortunately, the nasal decongestant Mr Baxter innocently used in the United States:

contained an additional substance to the same branded substance in the UK. The first issue was whether that additional substance itself, was a prohibited substance, and Baxter argued that it was not.

(Flint et al., 2003: 955)

The panel concluded that the OMAC list:

prohibits either use of methamphetamine, including levmetamphetamine, so that Mr Baxter's urine contained a prohibited substance. The IOC has not established any threshold level for methamphetamine. As a result, any level of methamphetamine, including the quantity found in Mr Baxter's urine, constitutes a violation.

(Reeb, 2005: 309)

Mr Baxter argued that the disqualification was a 'disproportionate remedy in violation of Swiss law, general principles of law and the European Convention on Human Rights' (ibid:

309). This was rejected by the CAS panel. Mr Baxter also argued that there was 'no lawful basis to disqualify him where not only had he acted innocently but there was no basis on which the substance could have enhanced his performance.[37] Baxter's interpretation of acting innocently means that his conduct was not intentional as he has no idea of the distinction between the UK and USA version of the Vicks inhaler and inadvertently ingested a banned substance. However, it is reasonable for the IOC to have determined that it may not always be possible to prove or disprove fault or performance enhancing effect, but that in order to ensure the integrity of the results, 'the mere presence of a prohibited substance requires disqualification' (Reeb, 2005: 310[38]).

Whether or not an athlete had acted entirely innocently (without intent, or fault) 'the other athletes against whom he competed must be protected against him having enjoyed an advantage' (Flint et al., 2003: 955[39]).

> The panel is not without sympathy for Mr Baxter, who appears to be a sincere and honest man who did not intend to obtain a competitive advantage in the race. It is unfortunate that, for whatever reason, he did not see the term levmetamphetamine on the package he bought or did not understand its import, and that he did not consult with his team doctor before taking the medication. Nevertheless, because Mr Baxter took the medication, at the time of his slalom race his body contained a prohibited substance. The consequence for this doping violation must be disqualification and the loss of his bronze medal.
>
> (*Baxter v IOC* (unreported, 15 October 2002, Court of Arbitration for Sport, CAS 2002/A/376) in Reeb, 2005: 310)

This particular CAS panel was only addressing the matter of disqualification from the Games and loss of the bronze medal. There was also the matter of the FIS rules providing for a penalty of 'suspension from participation in all international ski competitions for three months' (Nicholson, 2004: 4). However, if the FIS had simply applied their own rules and implemented the three-month ban Baxter would only have missed the southern hemisphere season, in which he would not have competed anyway. In implementing the ban from 23 February 2002, the FIS gave:

> an effective sanction of almost ten calendar months, of which seven or so arose in either the 2001/2002 international ski competitive season or 2002/2003 international ski competitive season. Baxter appealed the decision of the FIS to CAS.
>
> (ibid: 4)

CAS understood the need for international federations to apply effective sanctions in response to doping offences but 'such effectiveness must be sought by observing the regulations in force' (ibid: 5[40]). Parker (1995) observed that sports governing bodies often do not apply their own rules in relation to disciplinaries. Nicholson (2004: 5) observes that in relation to the Baxter case:

> The message was and is clear: sports federations and governing bodies must apply their rules as they are drafted and not as they choose or as they understood to mean by those applying them. Consequently, unless disciplinary bodies administer their powers having regard to a narrow, consistent, purposive and proportionate construction and application of their rules, their decisions will be open to challenge and they may find themselves on appeal to CAS.

EXERCISE 8.35

Explain the circumstances of the positive doping test result for the sample given by the British skier, Alain Baxter at the 2000 Winter Olympic Games in Salt Lake City, Utah, USA.

EXERCISE 8.36

In relation to the disqualification from the 2000 Winter Olympics and loss of the bronze medal, was metamphetamine actually a banned substance?

EXERCISE 8.37

Alain Baxter argued that his disqualification was disproportionate and that he had acted innocently (that is, without intent). Explain the response of the CAS panel on these two points.

EXERCISE 8.38

The manufacturers of the *Vicks* inhaler, Proctor and Gamble, provided written evidence to the panel that the product was not performance-enhancing. Did this, and indeed *should* this, help Alain Baxter in his case?

EXERCISE 8.39

In relation to the separate ban by the Federation of International Skiing (FIS), learn about their approach to what was effectively a ten-month ban (see Parker, 1995; Nicholson, 2004).

EXERCISE 8.40

The Alain Baxter case is a good illustration of the reality of the strict liability rule in action and its impact on the life of an athlete. What have you learnt from the Alain Baxter doping case?

Harmonisation or conflict? Sport rules, human rights and domestic laws

> Of the many disputes prevalent in the industry at the moment many can be put down to the governing bodies' inability to uphold and enforce their own rules and regulations.
>
> (Parker, 1995: 3)

Sport is a rule-governed activity. Within the sports themselves, at a domestic level, there is a need to engage with technical rules, rules of conduct and etiquette and disciplinary rules, as well as the constitution, codes and various doping rules. At international level governing bodies need to consider the sports rules of European, World and Olympic bodies, including the doping rules of the World Anti-Doping Agency (WADA). Beyond the sport governing bodies themselves, there are domestic laws of the land, including statutory duties (health and safety, discrimination, harassment etc), international treaties, codes and Human Rights Conventions, Acts, or in the USA, a Constitutional Bill of Rights. Club secretaries and chief executive officers of sports governing bodies are advised to keep up to date with and disseminate all relevant rules. It is also important to make sure that if a code (such as the WADA code) is adopted, then it is formally incorporated into the governing body constitution.[41]

> Harmonisation is an attempt to achieve broad agreement between different legal systems, whether codified or common law variety so that, for example, the penalties meted out to individual competitors for infringements are treated in a similar fashion – as such it is the opposite of conflict.
>
> (Stinson, 1995: 180)

Houlihan (2002: 184) suggests that harmonisation needed to include technical uniformity, proximity, compatibility, and shared values on the application of natural justice. Advantages of vertical and lateral harmonisation within sports rules and between sports rules and domestic or international laws include increased fairness, a resisting the intrusion of the civil courts, assisting sports governing bodies when a precedent is established through the widespread adoption of standardised policies (Vrijman, 2000: 13). Reservations about harmonising rules and laws include making it difficult for SGBs to take into account special circumstances in a particular sport, the possibility of countries losing autonomy and amateur/professional or Olympic and non-Olympic sports may not wish to be treated in the same way (ibid).

> There is in my opinion, a grave danger that a major conflict could develop between the laws of a country which is sympathetic to restraint of trade arguments and the rules of sport which may well be more severe.
>
> (Stinson, 1995: 182)

If a country has a restraint of trade rule, this may be in conflict with a sport rule such as the International Olympic Committee or more recently WADA strict liability doping rules, which have mandatory sentences or penalties ranging from a three-month ban, to two years, four years or a life ban for repeat offences (see Stinson, 1995; Findlay, 1998; Beloff, 2001). 'Can a sport organisation stop, or limit a coach or athlete from earning a living through sport? This is the essence of the legal doctrine known as "restraint of trade"' (Findlay, 1998: 1). In the High Court case of *Gasser v Stinson and Another*, Scott J decided that the restraint of trade doctrine was applicable to sporting rules, including international bodies. The test was whether or not the restraint of trade was unreasonable and Scott J decided that there were reasonable considerations for applying a strict liability test with a range of penalties (Sithamparanathan and Schillings, 2003: 141).[42]

Beloff (2001: 45) suggests that the factors which appear to have influenced his decision were:

> First, the difficulty of determining the validity of an explanation that the drug was ingested unknowingly; secondly, the importance to world athletics, both in the public interest and in the interests of athletes themselves, that the practice of doping should be firmly dealt with; and, thirdly, the slowness with which the courts should interfere with the manner in which an association governing a particular branch of the sport administers the sport.

Would a *Gasser* case be treated differently in 2008, after the Human Rights Act 1998? Perhaps not if *Edwards v British Athletic Federation and International Amateur Athletic Federation* [1998] 2 CMLR 363; [1997] EuLR 721 (Ch) was an indicator of the current climate (see note 16). More recently in the case of *Meca-Medina and Majcen v Commission of European Communities*, two long-distance swimmers, David Meca-Medina and Igor Majcen, argued that the IOC rules on doping control 'violated the European Community Rules on competition' (Dios Crespo, 2006: 116). The IOC and the European Commission had argued that such rules were purely sporting in nature and:

> were not subject to Community Law, even if they restrained the economic freedom of certain professional or semi-professional athletes. As a consequence, it was not for the European Court of Justice (ECJ) to assess whether or not such rules (and the resulting sanctions) were disproportionate with regard to the objectives pursued. In its landmark judgement, the ECJ reversed the position of the IOC and the European Commission and considered that even anti-doping rules . . . are subject to Community law and that it must be shown on a case by case basis that the restrictions they cause are inherent and proportionate with regard to the sporting objectives pursued. This is revolutionary for the relationship between sport and Community law.
>
> (ibid: 118)

This is a landmark case in which the European Court of Justice has rejected all the arguments of the international sports federations that European Community Rules or treaties do not apply because of the 'sporting exception' principle. They did, however, accept that anti-doping rules were necessary and in this case proportional for the proper administration of sport. Dios Crespo (2006: 118) argues that this 'very important change will finally force federations to demonstrate self-restraint and moderation' in both adopting and applying their rules, particularly doping rules. In 2003, Dwain Chambers, a British 100m athlete, was suspended from athletic competition for two years for taking the designer steroid THG (part of the BALCO scandal in the United States which involved several athletes). A bylaw of the British Olympic Association (BOA) does not allow an athlete, guilty of a doping offence, to compete for Team GB in the Olympic Games – effectively a life ban. Chambers wanted to compete in the 2008 Beijing Olympics and sought a temporary injunction in the High Court in July 2008 to allow him to compete in the 2008 Olympics.

He claimed he represented the UK's best chance of a medal in the 100m and his counsel, Jonathan Crystal, argued that the bylaw was 'unfair, contrary to competition law and an unreasonable restraint of trade' and that 'redemption and rehabilitation should be recognised' (Williams, 2008). Mr J Mackay rejected all arguments against the BOA bylaw. He thought that allowing the challenge 'would upset the harmony and management of the British Team and undermine its orderly administration' (ibid). He was also concerned about the effects of these last-minute proceedings[43] on other athletes and the BOA and would probably have refused the injunction for that reason alone (ibid). Including him on Team GB at the expense of others would have been unfair. In the judge's view Chambers' 'right to work was not a good enough reason to overturn the ban' and although many people both inside and outside sport would see this bylaw as 'unlawful' the claimant needed a much better case to persuade the judge to overturn the status quo at this stage and compel his selection for the games (BBC News 'Chambers loses Olympic ban case' 18 July 2008 at http://newsvote.bbc.co.uk/). The case was disposed of on procedural grounds and the merits of the case itself are not due to be heard until Spring 2009.

It could be argued that strict liability doping rules are not compliant with Article 6 of the Human Rights Act 1998 – the right to a fair and public hearing in criminal and civil trials, although it does not appear that this includes *internal* sport *disciplinary* processes. The strict liability doping rule may be in conflict with the legal principle of innocent until proven guilty, as well as facing challenges in relation to mandatory punishments and proportionality (see Hooper, 2007; Sithamparanathan and Schillings 2003). The WADA Code (2007: 30) argues that the approach in Article 10.5, which allows for the possibility of reduction or elimination of the ineligibility sanction only is 'consistent with basic principles of human rights'.

Even if the strict liability rule is seen as draconian, the courts repeatedly use a 'policy lens' to justify and condone its use in sport competition. For example:

> Strict liability was indispensable for an effective fight against doping in sport, and the protection of fairness towards all competitors and of their health and well being.
>
> (*Bernhard v ITU*, in Flint et al., 2003: 951)

> the interests of the athlete concerned in not being punished without being guilty, must give way to the fundamental principle that all competitors must have equal chances.
>
> (*Aanes v FINA* CAS 2001/A/317A 9 July, 2001: 16–17)

Legal commentators often raise questions about the potential conflict between strict liability or blood tests as part of doping control and the HRA 1998 Article 6 and 8 respectively, then conclude that the courts will still regard such rules and tests as HRA compliant:

> I believe that, in all likelihood, strict liability is human rights compliant and that, under Article 6, the yielding to the common good of the right to be presumed innocent until proved guilty, would be justified as both necessary and proportionate, in the circumstances.
>
> (Griffith-Jones, 2002: 2)

> there seems a persuasive argument that the genuine and pressing concerns of sports governing bodies world-wide, in defeating, deterring and detecting drug use in athletes, and in preserving the integrity of sport as a whole will outweigh any individual concerns, presented by compulsory blood-testing policies.
>
> (Hiscox, 2004: 16)

Despite these examples above, Griffith-Jones (2002: 2) warns of complacency by sports governing bodies regarding the imposition of mandatory minimum punishments as 'in an atmosphere generated by the HRA the position is ripe for reconsideration'. Soek (2006) concludes from his PhD research that the strict liability principle, which involves a basic presumption of guilt, is incompatible with the European Convention on Human Rights, particularly Article 6 and that the ECHR should take precedence over strict liability doping rules (Blackshaw, 2006c: 127).

In relation to therapeutic use exemptions (TUEs) in doping rules, Opie (2002: 138) observes that 'if there was no alternative effective therapy not prohibited under the anti-doping rules, it would be unreasonable and therefore discriminatory for a sports body to require the athlete not to take the drug'. Furthermore, a sport which 'does not adopt a therapeutic use exemption . . . risks breaching the Disability Act (with reference to Australia) or corresponding state legislation and there needs to be harmonisation between domestic and international sports governing and doping bodies' (ibid: 136–137).

It is not only between doping rules and human rights where there might be a lack of harmonisation. Approaches to penalties for doping violations appear to vary between sports, with cycling and soccer having a reputation for being lenient, compared to weight-lifting or track and field athletics, which are regarded as more harsh on their competitors (see Bitel, 1995; Griffith-Jones, 2002).

> A primary argument in favour of harmonisation is that it is simply not right that two athletes from the same country test positive for the same Prohibited Substance under similar circumstances should receive different sanctions only because they participate in different sports.
>
> (WADA Code 2007: 26)

Furthermore, lack of harmonisation of sanctions has led to 'juridictional conflicts between international federations and national anti-doping organisations' (ibid: 26). The reversal by the IAAF of the dismissal by UK Athletics of doping cases against British athletes Walker, Cadogan, Christie and Richardson, and two-year suspensions imposed on all of them, indicates a lack of harmonisation between national and international sports federations (Griffith-Jones, 2002: 2).

Vrijman (2000) found many inconsistencies in relation to doping rules across, for example, definitions, policies and penalties. Of the 34 International Federations investigated, nine had adopted a strict liability rule, whilst the rest, in Vrijman's opinion, had adopted definitions of doping which, to some extent could be viewed 'indefensible, weak, vague, or contradictory' (ibid: 14). Thirty out of 34 had adopted the IOC list of banned substances but only 21 had adopted provisions for out-of-competition doping control, the remainder being 'unable to provide an effective deterrent for anabolic steroids' (ibid: 14). As far back as 1995, Stinson regarded the international harmonisation of penalties as a matter of urgency.

In March 2003 over 1,000 participants and over 70 sports governing bodies welcomed the World Anti-Doping Code, in Denmark, with UNESCO adopting a convention on the Code in 2005. Seventy-three national governments supported the declaration for the formal adoption of the WADA Code. The World Anti-doping Code is described as 'miracle of co-operation between sports federations, sports agencies and public bodies' by the president of WADA, Dick Pound QC, who emphasised the need for 'consistency in doping sanctions throughout all sports' (see Kelham, 2004: 136). The Code is accompanied by the banned list of substances and methods, which was applied to the 2004 Summer Olympic Games in Athens and replaces the IOC doping code and list.

Among other things, the WADA Code introduced a uniform two-year suspension period for any performer caught using illegal substances. In addition:

> National federations will be fined $100,000 and the person in charge banned for two years, where four or more of its athletes test positive for drugs in 12 months or less.

WADA would also keep a database on all athletes' whereabouts, which may be passed on to other anti-doping agencies.[44]

(Cairns, 2003: 118)

It is not only in cross-referencing the definition and application of rules, but the timescale and jurisdiction of both sport disciplinary and legal, particularly criminal, processes which need to be considered by sports governing bodies. Greenburg and Gray (1994) clearly show the difficulties facing the various skating governing bodies, after a member of their national team, Nancy Kerrigan, was assaulted with an iron bar at a US skating competition, on 6 January, just a month away from the 1994 Winter Olympics, threatening her eligibility (for the Olympic Team).

The complicity of her rival, Tonya Harding, became front-page news. On February 5, 1994, the United States Figure Skating Association (USFSA) concluded that there was reason to believe Harding had violated the Olympic code of fair play because of her role in the assault and its aftermath.[45]

The United States Olympic Committee (USOC) announced plans to hold a disciplinary hearing, which would have been conducted by the Games Administration Board, held in Norway as the Winter Olympics were soon to be held there, with the decision subject only to approval by the IOC (Nafziger 2004a: 83). A criminal investigation was also ongoing but the outcome would not be known until after the 1994 Winter Olympics. Issues around harmonisation of rules and laws include:

1 Would Harding's due process rights under the United States Constitution and the Amateur Sports Act (1978) be satisfied by proceedings conducted in a foreign country? (Nafziger, 2004a: 83)
2 Can the USOC Administrative Board eliminate the arbitration appeal process as provided in the Amateur Sports Act 1978, in order to make a quick decision at the Olympic Games? (Greenburg and Gray, 1994)
3 Can and should the USOC ban Harding from competing at the 1994 Olympic Games if a disciplinary hearing, appeal or criminal investigation will not be completed prior to the US Olympic Team departing for the Games?

After filing a $25 million lawsuit against the USFSA for breach of contract, Harding sought an injunction against a disciplinary hearing in Norway. Soon after the parties:

reach an agreement whereby Harding would compete in the Winter Olympics but appear at the USFSA disciplinary hearing in the United States whose dates would be determined by the parties after conclusion of the Games. She then competed in the Games but did not win a medal. Afterwards, in the face of a possible criminal indictment for her role in the assault, Harding pleaded guilty to a lesser felony charge of hindering the prosecution and was placed on three years' supervised probation with a fine and other conditions, including resigning from the USFSA.[46]

(Nafziger, 2004a: 83)

EXERCISE 8.41

Give three reasons for the harmonisation of sport rules, domestic and international laws.

EXERCISE 8.42

Explain Stinson's (1995) concerns around the conflict between doping rules or penalties and the restraint of trade of an athlete.

EXERCISE 8.43

Discuss the following statement. 'When athletes sign on the dotted line to become eligible for competition, they willingly subject themselves to all relevant rules, disciplinary processes and sanctions. If they test positive for prohibited substances, they should reasonably expect to receive the appropriate penalty even if it means they lose their "trade" for two years or for life.'

EXERCISE 8.44

How did the British athlete Paul Edwards argue against a four-year ban for doping? What was the decision of Lightman J in *Edwards v British Athletic Federation and International Amateur Athletic Federation* [1998] 2 CMLR 363; [1997] EuLR 721 (Ch)?

EXERCISE 8.45

Explain why *Meca-Medina and Majcen v Commission of European Communities* [2006] ECR I-6991 is a landmark case. Which long-established policy was challenged in this case?

EXERCISE 8.46

Are strict liability doping rules compliant with the Human Rights Act 1998 and criminal justice principles in relation to:

a) Innocent until proven guilty.
b) Blood tests in doping control and Article 8, the right to personal family life and privacy.

EXERCISE 8.47

Explain the potential conflict between the Therapeutic Use Exemptions (TUEs) and relevant Disability Acts (see Opie, 2002).

EXERCISE 8.48

Give an example of each of the following:

a) a lack of harmonisation between the doping rules of the same sports in different countries.
b) a lack of harmonisation between the application of doping rules or penalties in different sports. Are some sports more lenient than others?

EXERCISE 8.49

Locate and discuss the research by Vrijman (2000, 2001) on the lack of harmonisation in doping policies, rules and penalties in the areas of:

a) use of the strict liability rule.
b) out of competition testing.

EXERCISE 8.50

Choose one sport or the sport in which you are most involved. Is the sport governing body signed up to the WADA Code? If yes, is the WADA Code formally incorporated into the constitution and rules? Critically examine your relevant lists for any areas of inconsistency, contradiction or lack of clarity. To whom might you address any queries relating to such matters in this sport?

EXERCISE 8.51

Why was the World Anti-Doping Agency (WADA) created? Is it working? Research relevant literature and using referenced sources, critically comment on the success or otherwise of WADA.

EXERCISE 8.52

Describe the incident which was the springboard for the Tonya Harding skating controversy.

EXERCISE 8.53

Imagine that you are the press officer for the United States Olympic Committee (USOC) and the United States Figure Skating Association (USFSA). Prepare an informed press release which responds to the following hypothetical criticism: 'How can these two sports governing bodies even think of allowing Tonya Harding to get on a plane to the 1994 Winter Olympics and be part of the same USA Olympic skating team as Nancy Kerrigan? Surely this can only bring the sport into disrepute and damage team morale so close to the Games?'

An innocent abroad: the Diane Modahl doping case 1994–2001

> In short, strict liability drug rules have as their purpose to catch the majority of 'guilty' parties while sacrificing a few 'innocent' ones: a concept incompatible with the basic legal tenets of civilized societies.
>
> (Wise, 1996: 80)

A high-profile doping case, involving the British 800m athlete, Diane Modahl, progressed through the sport disciplinary processes and the courts from 1994 until 2001. In 1994, at the time of the alleged doping offence, the IAAF. 'Control of Drug Abuse' rule 55.2 (i) stated that 'the offence of doping takes place when a prohibited substance is found to be present within an athlete's body tissue or fluids'. This is a rule of 'strict liability'.

The competition, the sample and the suspension

This very high-profile doping case really began on 18 June 1994, when a urine sample provided by Diane Modahl, a British 800m athlete, at an international athletics competition, in San Antonio, Portugal, tested positive for testosterone, present at a ratio of 42:1. So here was a British athlete, taking part in a European Amateur Athletics Association (EAAA) competition, under International Amateur Athletics Federation (IAAF) rules, organised by the Portuguese Athletics Federation (PAF), with urine samples being tested by a Lisbon laboratory, which was accredited by the International Olympic Committee (IOC). On 28 August, Diane Modahl asked for access to the remainder of the samples. This has never been granted. In September 1994 the 'B' test was completed.

However, representatives for Diane Modahl, argued that the test should not proceed, since the sample was invalid on the grounds that the 'pH' reading and the absence of metabolites (normally present if testosterone is taken by an athlete), did not fit with a positive test result. They also argued that there were no 'chain of custody' documents, contemporaneous with the collection of the urine sample on 18 June. The 'B' test went ahead, producing the same positive result as the 'A' test. On 6 September 1994, the BAF suspended Diane Modahl, pending a disciplinary hearing. On 23 September 1994, the IAAF refused Diane Modahl access to the remaining samples. On 27 September 1994, she requested the testing of her samples at another laboratory.

BAF Disciplinary Panel, 13–14 December 1994, London

The BAF disciplinary hearing took place at the Savoy Hotel in London, on 13 and 14 December 1994 (within the three-month deadline). The BAF panel appeared to have a very logical membership, comprising ex-athletes, police officer/coach, EAA member, GP and ex-athlete, and a solicitor, with a mixture relating to gender, race and age of the panel. This is quite difficult to achieve, when one considers the voluntary nature of governing body membership, resources, as well as the availability of all the members all in one time and place, outside their jobs and the busy athletics calendar.

The expert witness for Diane Modahl, Dr Honour, put forward a theory that if a urine sample is allowed to bacterially degrade, as a result of incorrect storage, for example, it can convert a perfectly innocent sample of urine to one which contains high levels of testosterone, without the testosterone ever having passed through the athlete's body. At this point in time, there was no empirical, experimental research presented to prove this *probably* happened. Three expert witnesses for the BAF argued that the environment of a urine sample was 'too hostile' for such a process to take place. The Modahl legal team were unable to question the director of the LABD in Lisbon, or have access to any documentation relating to the custody and testing of Diane Modahl's urine sample.

The BAF deliberated and announced their decision to the world press outside the venue on 14 December.

> Having heard all the evidence and read all the documents, the committee was satisfied, unanimously, beyond reasonable doubt, that a doping offence had been committed by Mrs Modahl. Accordingly, she is ineligible to compete in the UK and abroad for four years, from 18 June, 1994.
>
> (Announcement of decision to press and media, by Dr Martyn Lucking, chair of the
> BAF Disciplinary Panel, 14 December, 1994)

On 15 December Diane Modahl gave notice of appeal to the BAF. Between January and June 1995, the IAAF refused a request from the BAF to have further tests done at the Lisbon laboratory. Then the IAAF announced that they would take place on 22 June. On 20 June the AAAF abandoned the test, citing lack of co-operation from Lisbon.

Independent Appeal Panel (IAP) 24/25 July 1995, London

The Independent Appeal Panel was constituted under BAF rules and took place on 24 and 25 July 1995, chaired by Robert Reid QC. This panel of three considered documents which were presented to the BAF disciplinary panel, as well as further documents and oral evidence. Reid (1995: 6) listed the key issues for the IAP:

1) Were they satisfied, as to the chain of custody relating to the sample, from the time it was given by Mrs Modahl to its final analysis?
2) Was the laboratory at which the analysis took place properly accredited, and were its procedures acceptable and staff competent?
3) Were the 'A' and 'B' samples analysed (or tested) those given by Mrs. Modahl and, if so, should they have been analysed?
4) Were the tests properly carried out in accordance with relevant guidelines, and what ratio of testosterone to epitestosterone did they reveal?
5) Could the degradation of the sample have given rise to a false result?

The panel found that, although there were unsatisfactory features relating to the chain of custody documents and the laboratory personnel were 'less than frank' at the 'B' test, they were satisfied that the sample was sealed and was that of Mrs Modahl. On the issue of accreditation, despite the laboratory moving premises as rebuilding work took place on the original premises, the accreditation was for the institution, rather than a particular address. There were 'departures from best practice' [e.g. failure to take pH readings at the 'B' test] but on the whole the procedures were acceptable and the staff were competent (Reid, 1995: 6–7). However, the most significant evidence related to the storage of the sample and the new scientific evidence presented to the IAP.

The sample 'had been stored for a period between the 18 and 20 June, unrefrigerated in the office of the Sports Medicine Centre in the Estadio Universitario' (ibid: 7). In addition, although it is good practice in normal laboratory work not to analyse such samples, due to the remarkably high pH levels and odour (raised by Modahl's representatives and reinforced by expert medical testimony at the IAP), the panel found that the duty imposed on the laboratory was to go ahead and analyse the samples. The important thing was the status of the results. The panel accepted that the low levels of metabolites pointed out by Modhal's representatives, at the 'B' sample, were not consistent with the presence of *administered* testosterone. (There should have been higher levels.)

The IAP expressed disappointment that the remaining sample was not available, despite requests to the Lisbon laboratory, as 'that analysis might (on the evidence we have heard) have answered definitively, some of the questions we have had to consider' (ibid: 7) New scientific evidence, in the form of experiments carried out by the expert witnesses for Diane Modahl, showed that 'bacterial degradation, such as existed in Mrs Modahl's urine, could affect the levels of testosterone in the urine sample' (ibid: 7). Professor Gaskell's team had treated the urine samples of two clean female athletes to the same storage conditions as those alleged to have applied in Lisbon to Diane Modahl's sample. The result was bacterial degradation leading to a vast increase in testosterone. This was crucial. What had been a theoretical possibility presented to the BAF hearing had now become scientific support for the explanation of the Modahl team, of the 42:1 test result.

> The only basis for the decision at the [IAP] in the claimant's favour was the new material giving support to what had previously merely been an assertion as to the possibility that bacterial contamination could have affected the testosterone reading.
> (Latham LJ, *Modahl v British Athletics Federation Ltd* [2001] EWCA Civ 1447;
> [2002] 1 WLR 1192)

The IAP concluded that Diane Modahl was entitled to succeed in her appeal. They could not be sure, beyond reasonable doubt, that she was guilty of a doping offence. Considering all the evidence presented, they had to acknowledge the possibility that the doping test result in Portugal was '*not caused by any testosterone being administered*', but 'by the samples *becoming degraded, owing to them being stored in unrefrigerated conditions*, and that bacterial action had resulted in an increase in the amount of testosterone in the samples' (emphasis added, Reid, 1995: 8). On 6 February, Diane Modahl served a writ against the BAF Ltd for compensation for legal and medical costs and loss of earnings.

On 25 March, 1996, the IAAF abandoned arbitration, stating that Lisbon laboratory analytical data were not satisfactory, and further analysis was impossible. There was serious concern regarding the way in which analysis was handled in the Lisbon laboratory. The IAAF announced in March that it would not be challenging the IAP's decision. Finally, Diane Modahl was cleared of all allegations and could compete again in athletics at international level. The IOC withdrew accreditation status from LABD in Lisbon, Portugal.

Modahl v British Athletics Federation Ltd [1999] UKHL 37 (Lords Irvine LC, Nicholls, Hoffmann, Clyde and Millet)

Now that the matter of the reinstatement of the athlete was resolved within the sports disciplinary process, Diane Modahl and her legal team now turned to the matter of financial compensation for loss of earnings. The HL noted that the IAAF's procedural guidelines 'required the BAF to act upon notification of a positive doping result from a foreign country' (para 3, p.5, *per* Lord Hoffmann). The BAF was not 'making a "finding" but deciding, on the evidence it had been given, that there was evidence that a doping offence had taken place' (*Sports Law Bulletin* September/October, 1999b: 6). The HL held that the claim had no reasonable cause and was bound to fail on the grounds submitted and was struck out under Rules of the Supreme Court Order 18 and 19. However, Modahl was still able to proceed on only two grounds, those of an implied contract between Modahl and the BAF and alleged bias on the part of two members of the original panel, which imposed the four-year ban (ibid: 6).

Modahl v British Athletics Federation Ltd (unreported, 14 December 2000, Queen's Bench Division, Brown J)

Diane Modahl proceeded to the High Court in December 2000 on these two issues, by which time BAF Ltd were 'in administration'. The issues facing the High Court in December 2000 were:

1 Was there a contract between Mrs Modahl and the BAF?
2 If there was a contract was there a duty to act fairly?
3 If there was a contract, with a duty to act fairly, was that duty breached?
4 If there were breaches in the implied term, did these cause loss?

The crucial issue was the contract (Farrell, 2001: 110). Several cases were considered but the treatment of earlier cases was far from straightforward, as there were issues of interpretation and relevance. Brown J:

> pointed to the exhortations of Lord Denning MR in *Nagle v Fielden* [1966] 2 QB 633 and Scott J in *Gasser v Stinson* not to create fictitious contracts, and concluded that it was quite artificial to identify a contract between the athlete and the BAF out of either her membership of Sale Harriers, her participation in other meetings organised by the governing bodies or her submission to doping control at a different event abroad run by a different organisation.
>
> (Lewis et al., 2003: 164)

Brown J concluded that no contract existed. This finding:

> was sufficient to dispose of Modahl's case. However, at the invitation of the parties the court would deal with the other issues, which had been argued. For that purpose the court was prepared to assume that the BAF was under a duty to act fairly throughout the entire disciplinary process.
>
> (*Sports Law Bulletin*, January/February, 2001: 3)

It was alleged that two members of the original disciplinary panel, Dr Martyn Lucking and Alan Guy, were biased, as was Arthur Gold in his selection of the members of the disciplinary panel. Modahl's case was that Martyn Lucking had allegedly made comments to an athlete, Linford Christie, at an athletics competition in Gateshead, in 1990, that 'all athletes were guilty until proved innocent'.

> It is more probable than not that in the heat of an argument, Dr Lucking did say that 'all athletes were guilty until proven innocent'. He continued: 'I also accept his evidence that if he did say that it did not represent his view, which was that all athletes are under suspicion of taking drugs and that was why the testing procedure was in place'. The judge regarded Dr Lucking as a responsible and sensible man 'rather careless in his phraseology at times, who did not carry into the Disciplinary Committee, a belief that all athletes were guilty until proved innocent.
>
> (Brown J 14 December, unreported, cited, Farrell, 2001: 21)

It was Alan Guy's involvement, in an official capacity in relation to the EAA's doping control, which was cited by counsel for Modahl as 'disqualifying him from sitting on the

Disciplinary Committee, because to do so would entail him sitting as a judge in his own cause' (Farrell, 2001: 114). Arthur Gold was alleged to be biased in his choice of members of the Disciplinary Committee. The claims of bias were not upheld and Brown J concluded that 'the constitution of the disciplinary committee was carefully and fairly chosen to give a balance of skills and representation and provide Mrs Modahl with a trial by at least some of her peers', and after all, she won her appeal through an Independent Appeal Tribunal provided by the BAF processes (*Sports Law Bulletin* January/February, 2001: 3).

Modahl v British Athletics Federation Ltd [2001] EWCA Civ 1447; [2002] 1 WLR 1192 (Mance, Latham, Parker LJJ)

On 22 February 2001 Diane Modahl won the right to take her claim for damages of £1 million to the Court of Appeal. The CA, on 12 October, 2001, upheld the HC ruling of Brown J that there was no contract and no bias and even if there was, the decision of the disciplinary committee was unaffected and no damages could follow.

Obligations to carry out disciplinary tribunals fairly were accepted by the defendants (BAF) even in the absence of a contract. Latham LJ and Parker LJ agreed. Mance LJ agreed, but made an interesting comment on rules, contract and bias:

> the rules of the defendant clearly created contractual obligations between the parties and doubted that the chairman of the panel should have been regarded as free from apparent bias, as opposed to actual bias. However, the appeal should be dismissed on the basis that any other tribunal acting without bias, would not have come to any different conclusion.
>
> ([2002] 1 WLR 1192 report by Ken Mydeen, barrister)

On 18 October 2001, in a paper presented to the Annual Conference of the British Association for Sport and Law, Anthony Morton-Hooper, Diane Modahl's lawyer, commented on Mance LJ's opinion that the submission to jurisdiction of the federation rules was a 'consensual one', and 'the framework of rights and duties' were 'of sufficient certainty to give contractual effect, with regard to the athlete's entitlement and ability to compete'.

This case highlights issues, which are still relevant today, around the 'strict liability' rule in doping, the structural arrangements and power relations of the international and national athletics bodies, and the difficulties of using the law of contract in such a case. In addition, it illustrates the application of natural justice principles relating to procedure, in the areas of relevant evidence, apparent bias and the right to appeal. One of the defining features of this case is the central role played by sports science, as well as the significant financial costs to both the plaintiff and the national sports governing body.

EXERCISE 8.54

Work in pairs and draw a diagram of all the sports governing bodies and individuals involved in the Diane Modahl doping case and identify their powers and roles.

EXERCISE 8.55

What substance was found and in what ratio in the 'A' sample in June 1994 in Lisbon?

EXERCISE 8.56

Locate the relevant athletics governing body doping rule applicable in June 1994. Was it a fault liability or strict liability rule? Give reasons for your answer.

EXERCISE 8.57

Outline the questions raised by Diane Modahl's representatives regarding the validity of going ahead with the 'B' test in Lisbon in September 1994.

EXERCISE 8.58

Does and should an athlete have access to their remaining urine sample used in doping control? Compare this with a defendant's rights in their own experts accessing relevant forensic evidence in a criminal case.

EXERCISE 8.59

Describe and comment on the membership of the British Athletics Federation (BAF) disciplinary panel in December 1994.

EXERCISE 8.60

Briefly outline the theory put forward by Dr Honour to explain the positive doping result. What was the response of the BAF panel?

EXERCISE 8.61

Critically comment on the absence from the disciplinary hearing of the Director of the LABD or any relevant documents, in relation to natural justice. Do you think it is fair to expect the national sports governing body to handle a disciplinary case like this without the power to make relevant witnesses attend from the internationally accredited laboratory, where the problems of incorrect sample storage arose? Give reasons for your answer. What was the conclusion of the disciplinary panel?

EXERCISE 8.62

Was the Independent Appeal Panel satisfied that the urine samples A and B were those of Diane Modahl?

EXERCISE 8.63

Outline, with referenced support, the crucial scientific evidence which formed the basis of this successful appeal. Was the positive test cause by *administered* testosterone?

EXERCISE 8.64

Explain the differences between the fight to be reinstated as a competitive athlete and the legal case for compensation in relation to:

a) Aim and outcome b) processes c) legal terminology d) costs.

EXERCISE 8.65

The House of Lords (HL) in July 1999 allowed Diane Modahl to proceed with her legal case for compensation on two grounds only. What were they?

EXERCISE 8.66

The CAS mediation service was launched in 1999. 'Diane Modahl would have been better advised trying to settle her claims for compensation against the BAF through [CAS] mediation, rather than through the courts' (Blackshaw, 2003: 71). Discuss.

EXERCISE 8.67

What were the key questions and evidence regarding a contractual relationship and apparent bias? Report and comment on the decisions of the courts in *Modahl v BAF Ltd.*

Summary

- The conduct of individual athletes and sports governing bodies can often land them in serious trouble in a range of quasi-legal and legal processes. These include sports disciplinary processes, employment tribunals, CAS appeals, civil cases, criminal charges as well as a dose of bad publicity and escalating costs.
- Deontological rights and duties which we inherit as human beings, alongside the values in the sport community, make equitable and fair practices in sports disciplinaries a non-negotiable requirement.
- Sports governing bodies are expected to conduct their sports disciplinary processes according to the rules of natural justice. There are two main rules: no person shall judge his or her own case, and the right to be heard. In general it involves a duty to be fair, reasonable and impartial in all aspects of conducting sports disciplinary processes.
- Challenges to the conduct of disciplinary processes can arise from failures to follow correct procedures, take care in matters of evidence, or through unfair, unreasonable or partial practices and failure to follow the SGB's own rules.
- Processes range from informal grievances, to a civil or criminal case, or a challenge in the European Court, on a matter of a breach of human rights.
- There should be a right of appeal with clear grounds, deadlines for submission and costs of an appeal.
- The Court of Arbitration for Sport (CAS) is based in Lausanne, with offices in New York, Colorado and Sydney. It also has ad hoc divisions (AHDs) in the summer and winter Olympics and Paralympics as well as some international soccer events.
- CAS provides appeals panels of three people, a president and an arbitrator chosen by each party from a list published by CAS. They hear appeals mainly in the categories of doping, eligibility and commercial disputes, although from 1999 a mediation service was introduced by CAS which was suitable for commercial disputes.
- CAS also provides 'advisory opinions' on, for example, technical matters, such as the use of the 'long john' swim suits, prior to the Sydney summer Olympics and Paralympics in 2000.
- The strict liability principle in doping does not require any proof of fault or intent. The presence in the B sample of a banned substance or the use of a banned method would be enough for the instigation of disciplinary hearing, within three months of a positive 'B' sample.
- Traditionally, the principle of strict liability and related rules are seen as harsh, but necessary, in the fight against doping in sport and have been viewed by the courts through a 'policy' lens, which tends to give the sports doping authorities quite a bit of leeway in their important role in looking after the welfare of the sport contest and the participants.
- There are many critical commentaries on the rationale and systems of doping control, including the principle of strict liability.
- There is potential for a lack of harmonisation between sports rules, domestic laws, international treaties, restraint of trade principles and human rights.
- The key doping cases of Alain Baxter and Diane Modahl clearly illustrate the reality of the strict liability principle and mounting a legal challenge as well as the links between sport science, law and ethics.

Introduction

In Chapters 4 and 5 of this text, sociologists cast a critical eye on a range of behaviours in sport and recreation using a theoretical lens of hegemonic masculinity, power and masculine or sport-specific subcultures (or subworlds). Conduct coming under scrutiny in Chapter 4 included: violence on and off the ball, on and off the field, punishments given to team players, assault charges and defences, violent incidents and responses from the sport community, normalisation of unacceptable conduct – from the sports field to the law courts. The focus was on the law as it stands on common assault and the OAPA 1861. In Chapter 5, child abuse was located on a continuum of sexual exploitation in sport. Research on a range of issues informed both risk assessment and the development of child protection (safeguarding policies). Illustrative criminal cases arising out of the Sexual Offences Act were followed by legal and policy developments in child protection in sport and recreation. Prior to this, statutory frameworks and illustrative cases of discrimination and harassment were introduced.

In Chapter 7, the complex law of manslaughter by individuals and corporations made a journey through principles, generic cases, illustrative cases in sport and recreation, leading to the landmark cases of *R v Stanley and others 1990* and *R v Kite and others*. This chapter seeks to revisit the themes of Chapter 4 and Chapter 7. It will begin with offences against the person and the start of the legal reform process which followed the landmark case of *R v Brown* in 1994. It will follow the LCCP 1995 review of offences against the person, and the implications for sports and games – in particular boxing, martial arts, horseplay and secondary liability for violence. Although the LCCP made some generic recommendations to parliament in 1998–99, the area of sports and games remains 'unfinished business'. Yet the questions and issues at the heart of the original LCCP proposals in 1995 are still very current and relevant for sports and games – illustrated by a very brief examination of such activities as 'hazing' and 'cage-fighting'. In the final section, the developments in the legal reform of corporate manslaughter, since the time of the cases covered in Chapter 7 will be reported. At the time of writing, the very recent Law Commission 2008 proposals on murder and manslaughter have just been made public and are included in a very short summary.

Sado-masochism and sport: reviewing the law on criminal assault

R v Brown [1994] AC 212

In the landmark case of *R v Brown* a majority of three Law Lords decided that 'the intentional infliction of injuries during sado-masochistic,[1] homosexual acts, by consenting adults, in private, can give rise to convictions for assault and unlawful wounding. The fact that the victims consented to being injured is not a defence to criminal charges' (Herbert, 1993: 7). The Crown alleged that the activities of the defendants 'amounted to either an assault occasioning actual bodily harm, contrary to s 47 of the Offences Against the Person Act 1861, or to unlawful wounding contrary to s 20 of that Act' (McArdle, 1995: 4).

The majority ruling was based on the following considerations:

1 Their Lordships were not prepared to invent a defence for acts which 'bred and glorified cruelty'.
2 It was a matter of public interest. It was not in the public interest for such activities to be held lawful, being a risk to public health and morals (enough reason to intervene).
3 There was a risk of physical danger, cruelty and degradation.
4 It was only good luck, rather than good judgment which prevented serious injury (unlike sport there were no rules or officials to control the risk).
5 Consent was a matter for the judge and was not to be left to the jury.

The dissenting Law Lords (Mustill and Slyn) expressed the view that:

> Private, consensual, homosexual acts, involving violence, were outside the criminal law unless Parliament specifically amended the statutes. If society took the view that this kind of behaviour should be brought within the criminal law, then it was for legislature to decide. It was not for the courts, in the interest of paternalism, or in order to protect people from themselves, to introduce into an existing statutory crime, relating to offences 'against' the person, concepts which did not properly fit there. If Parliament considered that the appellant's behaviour should be made specifically criminal, then it should amend the statutes.
>
> (Lord Slyn in *R v Brown* cited in Herbert 1993: 7)

> It is the essence of assault that it is done without the consent of the victim. But there are some acts to which the victims' consent will not be a defence. The decision in *Brown* is simply the latest in what has been called a long line of decisions penalising private passion.
>
> (Pannick, 1992, cited in Padfield, 1992)

The *Brown* case raised significant outrage and debate. Should the state interfere in private sexual matters which involve consenting adults? Lord Mustill, dissenting, thought that the 'wrong law was being used to prosecute the men involved, arguing that the 1861 Act was designed to deal with public outbreaks of unruly violence and was not the proper vehicle to deal with sexual relationships between consenting adults' (McArdle, 1995: 6). The *Brown* case was described as a 'homophobic escapade' (ibid). Comparisons were made between private sado-masochistic activities and public sport contests.

Jaggard, one of the defendants in *Brown*, pointed out that 'in our case there was no harm done, unlike some sports – no medical treatment was required' (*R v Brown*). 'If consent here calls for closer investigation, then so does consent given by boxers, who run huge risks for what are usually rather paltry financial rewards' (Hedley, 1993: 196). The question may be asked following *Brown* 'to what extent should the courts intervene in the case of injuries inflicted in the course of sporting activities?' (McArdle, 1995: 1). Bibbings and Allridge (1993) note the significance of *Brown* beyond the world of sado-masochists such as plastic surgery, body piercing or alteration, tattooing or scarification.

Following *Brown* the Law Commission held two consultations in 1994 and 1995 on *Consent and the Criminal Law* relating to offences against the person. The LCCP proposals took a more liberal view of sado-masochistic activities than that taken by the majority in *Brown*. The law 'should be changed to decriminalise sado-masochistic acts where the participants consent and are likely to suffer no lasting harm, the Law Commission suggests today' (Dyer, 1994). The Law Commission suggested that the line should be drawn at serious bodily harm. In the second consultation paper of December (1995) the Law Commission proposed the general principle that 'a person with capacity should be able to give a legally effective consent to any injury up to a level which we will describe as "serious disabling injury"' (Omerod and Gunn, 1996: 694).

'If the present "very restrictive" law is retained, it says, special rules will be needed to exempt ritual circumcision, ear-piercing and tattooing from criminal liability' (Dyer, 1994 on the first LCCP consultation paper). In the second consultation paper the Law Commission included Class II exceptions – activities such as tattooing, circumcision, branding, scarring, dangerous exhibitions, and undisciplined horseplay, *but not serious disabling injury* will be permitted (Omerod and Gunn, 1996: 703). The Law Commission recognised the need to revisit other activities, such as sports, games, boxing, martial arts, recognition criteria, fighting and public order, horseplay, and reasonable chastisements. Special considerations apply for public interest reasons to make it possible to continue to play 'contact' sports without attracting criminal liability.

Class II exceptions include recognised sports and games. The LCCP provisionally proposed that 'a person should not be guilty of an offence of causing injury if he/she caused the injury in the course of playing or practising a recognised sport, in accordance with its rules' (LCCP, 1995: para 12.68). This includes playing or practising in informal settings. This will not give rise to criminal liability for a serious disabling injury unless a defendant is 'acting outside the rules designed to ensure safety' so a footballer 'would not be denied the defence just because he was off-side. There would have to be a breach of a safety rule, such as "foot up" or elbow usage' (Omerod and Gunn, 1996: 704). The intentional infliction of injury will always be criminal (LCCP, 1995: 67, para 45.1). Causing injury by an act of subjective recklessness will only be criminal[2] in sport if three conditions are satisfied:

1 That the player in question was aware of the risk of serious disabling injury;
2 That the risk was not a reasonable one for him or her to take, having regard to all the circumstances known to him or her (including the consent of the other participants to the risk inherent in playing according to the rules in question);
3 The injury resulted in permanent bodily injury, permanent disfigurement etc.

(Farrell, 1996: 6–7)

Secondary liability

The notion of secondary liability is not new to the sports arena. In 1994 the Sports Council reviewed its doping rules and made it a breach of such regulations for anyone to 'aid, abet, counsel or procure the commission of an offence'. In addition the IAAF handbook 1996–7 rule 56 states 'any person assisting or inciting others to use prohibited substances or prohibited techniques, shall have committed a doping offence.

(O'Leary, 1998, cited in Hartley, 1998: 50)

Could sports officials and/or governing bodies be held criminally liable for intentional and reckless behaviour on the field of play?

The violent sportsman or sportswoman [the principal] who inflicts injury on another player may not be the only person to incur criminal liability. It is possible that those who 'aid, abet, counsel or procure the commission of an offence' may also face liability as 'secondary parties'.[3]

(Law Commission, 1995: 17, para 12.52)

The Law Commission (1995) identified two areas of secondary liability relating to sport contexts:

1 The presence of spectators and others, at the scene of a sports event where an offence is committed.
2 Failure by coaches and sports administrators to exercise control over-violent players.

The leading case on presence at the scene of an offence is *R v Coney* (1882) 8 QBD 534, which emphasised that mere presence was not sufficient. It had to be proved that 'the spectator's presence *did* encourage the commission of a violent offence, and, secondly he/she *intended* his/her presence to encourage the principals' (Farrell, 1996: 10).

> The organisation of an unrecognised event in which intentional or reckless infliction of injury is likely to occur, will represent a positive act of encouragement to unlawful activity and is likely to lead to the *organisers* personally incurring liability in respect of any offences that may be committed by participants.[4]
>
> (Law Commission, 1995: 172, para 12.56)

Mr Edward Grayson suggested that 'the selection, by team managers of players known to be violent on the sports field may provide evidence of encouragement by them in relation to any offences committed by those players in the course of a match' (Law Commission, 1995: 172, para 12.57). This situation was viewed as likely to create problems in establishing the requisite *mens rea* (or mental element), if, for example, the manager selects the violent player in advance but is not actually present when he or she commits an offence (Law Commission, 1995: 172, para 12.57; Farrell, 1996: 10).

> If the accessory is not present at the scene, but merely assists in advance, a requirement of knowledge of a particular offence in the future may not only be logically unsound, since one cannot 'know' the future, but also unduly limiting from the point of view of enforcement.
>
> (Law Commission, 1995: 172, para 12.57)

Failure to exercise control (over-violent players)

> The team manager who fails to withdraw from the field, a player who is known to be violent, may face secondary liability for a failure to control the actions of that player, if the latter commits a violent offence in the course of the match.
>
> (Law Commission, 1995: 172–173, para 12.58)

Farrell (1996: 10) observes that the 'dividing line between selecting a player who is known to be violent and failing to control the actions of that player on the field can, at times, be a thin one'. He advises that managers 'should be aware of their responsibilities' and be careful in choosing the right moment to withdraw a player who may have even been provoked into violent conduct.

Boxing, casual fighting and horseplay

In the first consultation paper in 1994, the Law Commission viewed boxing as lawful·

not through any application of principle, or by reference to legal rules applying to other sports, but simply because it was not prize-fighting that was declared unlawful, on the grounds a much related to public order as to the law of offences against the person, in *R v Coney* (1882) 8 QBD 534.

(LCCP, 1995: 166, para 12.36)[5]

The 1994 LCCP noted that the 'only explanation for the immunity of boxing from the criminal law was that it was so firmly embedded in the law that only special legislation could change that position' (Farrell, 1994b: 3). The Law Commission was 'impressed by the safety provisions in force which was contrasted with the situation obtaining in full contact, unrecognised martial arts' with both amateur and professional boxing regarded as having 'adequate controls' (Farrell, 1996: 8).

They concluded, in 1995, that the criminal law should 'continue to afford protection to those who cause injuries in the course of fights, even if the injured party agreed to take part in the fight, except in the context of recognised sports' (LCCP, 1995: 188, para 14.16). They proposed that an 'exception to this rule should continue to be available where, any injury, other than a serious disabling injury, is caused in the course of undisciplined horseplay' (ibid: 190–191, para 14.20). This was consistent with the defence in common law to rough undisciplined horseplay where there is no anger and no intention to cause bodily harm.

Their Lordships in *Brown* and the Law Commission both referred to the case of *R v Jones* (1986) 83 Cr App R 375 where:

> half a dozen boys had seized two others and thrown them some 9 or 10 feet into the air during the course of what was described in court as 'rough and undisciplined horseplay'. The protests of the victims were ignored and they suffered a ruptured spleen and a broken arm, respectively in the course of the attack.[6]

(McArdle, 1995: 11)

In the opinion of one respondent to the Law Commission 1995 consultation, the horseplay defence was:

> placing some culturally acceptable forms of dangerous behaviour beyond the criminal law [such as playground thuggery] and that violence between masters and pupils in public schools, was being legally sanctioned.

(Law Commission, 1995: 187, para 14.9)

In the case of *R v Aitken* [1992] 1 WLR 1006, the court heard that drunken colleagues poured white spirit on an RAF officer and lit a match to it at the end of an evening's celebrations, causing life-threatening burns on 35 per cent of his body.

> The Court of Appeal said that in the absence of any intent to cause injury, if the victim consented to take part in rough and undisciplined mess games involving the use of force towards those involved, no offence was committed by any defendant whose participation extended only to taking part in such an activity.

(pp. 184–5, para 14.30)

The Law Commission was concerned about the decision in *Aitken* in the 1994 consultation paper and suggested that 'the present special category of horseplay should be abolished even if a special list of exceptions was retained in the unreformed criminal law' (p. 188, para 14.12). Legal responses from the Armed Services supported this proposal, commenting on the difficulties the general horseplay defence created when trying to deal with cases of bullying, abuse of rank and drunken behaviour. How was it in the public interest for consent to amount to a defence in horseplay where there was a risk of serious injury? Several respondents supported the abolition of the general defence of horseplay but suggested retaining, as exceptions, genuine childish horseplay and minor struggles (p. 188, para 14.13). In contrast the Crown Prosecution Service (CPS) was concerned that 'if this defence was abolished almost all levels of horseplay, including rough playground games, would become illegal and far too much discretion would be left in the hands of the prosecutors' (p. 188, para 14.14).

EXERCISE 9.1

What was the legal significance of the *R v Brown* [1994] AC 212 case in relation to criminal assault and consent?

EXERCISE 9.2

Divide into two groups for a debate. One group take the majority view of the Law Lords in *Brown* and one group take the dissenting (minority) views of Lords Mustill and Slyn. Argue your case as a group. After this debate, reflect on and share with others, in a sensitive manner, your own personal view on this matter.

EXERCISE 9.3

The defendants in *Brown*, along with academic commentators, were critical of the decision in *Brown* and made comparisons with public sport contests. Identify and explain those criticisms and connections, particularly in relation to control of risk, consent and attitudes towards homosexuality. What do you think?

EXERCISE 9.4

The Law Commission in their first consultation paper in 1994 took a more liberal view than the majority in *R v Brown* [1994] AC 212. What was different about their approach?

EXERCISE 9.5

Summarise and critically comment on the LCCP 1995 proposals of exemption from criminal liability for sports and games and the three conditions proposed for attracting criminal liability in sports and games.

EXERCISE 9.6

Should managers or sports governing body officers be held *criminally* liable for intentional and reckless behaviour on the field of play? Critically evaluate the two criteria proposed by the LCCP in 1995 for addressing this kind of secondary (criminal) liability for intentional and reckless behaviour by their players on the field.

EXERCISE 9.7

What are the two legal mechanisms for dealing with casual fighting?

EXERCISE 9.8

What was the Law Commission's view in 1995 of the safety provisions in boxing compared with *full contact* martial arts? What is your own view of this?

EXERCISE 9.9

Why does the case of *R v Aitken* [1992] 1 WLR 1006 raise concerns about the general defence of horseplay? What did the LCCP propose in 1995 on this matter? Can you think of a hypothetical scenario of horseplay which is too dangerous and harmful to be covered by such a defence? Should the general defence of horseplay be retained?

Hazing and punishments in sport and recreation

Hazing activities have been defined as 'any activity expected of someone joining a group that humiliates, degrades, abuses or endangers, regardless of the person's willingness to participate' (Hoover, 1999, cited Tinmouth, 2004: 3).

Any act whether physical, mental, emotional or psychological, which subjects another person voluntarily or involuntarily to any thing that might abuse, mistreat, degrade, humiliate, harass, or intimidate him/her, or which may, in any fashion, compromise [a persons] inherent dignity as a person.

(University of Vermont 2000, cited Tinmouth 2004: 3)

Are initiation rites the same as hazing? In principle, at a conceptual level, initiation rites are supposed to be a team building, low risk, fun activity, testing loyalty and commitment to a group. Horseplay, a defence to assault might form part of a range of activities which also allegedly assist in team bonding. In reality, hazing activities have in many, but not all instances, developed into something much more dangerous, and arguably unlawful. Activities labelled as hazing, or similar to hazing might not always be located at the time of someone joining a group or a course or a sports team or club. In institutions such as the military, or police, such activities may be a regular occurrence or even normalised as part of the training.[7] They may also be common in informal groups of (usually) young men engaging in physical recreation or leisure and not particularly located at the point where a new member joins the group.[8]

Punishments regarded as 'reasonable chastisements' by the courts, may also act as a defence against charges of criminal assault, except in the case of adults punishing children as outlined in the Children Act 2004. What would make a chastisement or punishment 'unreasonable'? Research by sport sociologists such as Coakley and Hughes (1991) and Young (1993) found severe punishments given by sports teams to their own team members, such as 'suicide drills' or playing for hours in the Oklahoma sun without drinking water. What would the law make of such conduct? Would it be regarded as 'reasonable' chastisement, an act as defence to assault, if it resulted in serious injury?

Hazing has been part of the high school and university traditions in the United States for many years, although bullying and hazing are universal issues and are not limited to male athletes (Doleschal, 2000: 16). They are well established in sports teams or clubs, as well as male-dominated institutions such as the military and the police (see, for example, Scraton, 2000; Burnham, 2003; Jackson, 2006). In the United States, hazing activities include 'humiliation, excessive consumption of alcohol, dangerous or illegal acts performed under cover of darkness, or agonizing sexual acts such as sodomy with a broom handle' (Dolescahl, 2000: 16). Research and policy initiatives often follow a near-fatal hazing incident or negative publicity. Tinmouth (2004) conducted research and developed an initiation rites policy at Southampton University following a near-fatal initiation incident involving a sports club. He reported a range of common activities such as being forced to consume unpleasant concoctions, ritualised nudity, task performance, physical and psychological abuse, and consumption of unpleasant or 'dirty pints'.

Task performance can involve trespassing and engaging in criminal damage within and beyond the university campus. In the Southampton University survey, 22 per cent reported physical abuse including 'beatings with items such as hockey studs, cricket bats or studded boots' and 14 per cent reported sexual abuse (see Tinmouth, 2004: 10). In the United States, Hoover found a range of similar practices from:

> being yelled at or being asked to embarrass oneself publicly, to incidents of substance abuse, during which students were asked to drink alcohol until they passed out. At the far end of the spectrum were acts of dangerous hazing, which required initiates to perform illegal acts of vandalism, being beaten up, or being exposed to extreme cold or heat.
>
> (Hoover, 1999, cited in Doleschal, 2000: 16)

'Between 1978 and 1997, 70 college students died in hazing related incidents' (Goose, 1997). Hollaman (2002: 1) noted that 'hazing-related deaths had tripled in the past 20 years to about 18 deaths a year'. The landmark study by Hoover (1999) at Alfred University, on hazing in athletics in the United States, was 'the result of a 1998 hospitalization for alcohol poisoning of five freshman football players, who had been forced to drink large quantities of alcohol and water at an off-campus party' (Suggs, 1999, cited Burnham, 2003: 1).

Challenges facing schools, authorities and law enforcement is the 'cloak of secrecy and tradition' and the viewing of hazing as a rite of passage, building team spirit, or individual courage or loyalty (Doleschal, 2000: 16). 'Such rituals of interpersonal bonding have long been recognised as rooted in the social and psychological need to belong to a group, and for the group to feel assured that its members are committed to and deserving of membership' or bonds shared by team mates or friends which are not shared by others (Tinmouth, 2004: 6). Only 89 per cent of athletes in one study believed that initiation ceremonies humiliated freshers while only 17.65 per cent believed that they promote team bonding (ibid: 6).

University athletic unions or sports teams have had to deal with negative press coverage in relation to drunken antics, injury or death of students in general and more specifically in relation to sports club initiation rites in the United Kingdom, the United States and Australia (see for example Paine, 1994, cited Boucher, 2002). Under present Anglo-Welsh law, it is possible, at first glance, to identify several areas of criminal and civil law which could be applied to the conduct of individuals, aged ten years old and above, and relevant institutions or organisations who engage in hazing.

Criminal law

1 Drunk and disorderly conduct or causing an affray or other public order offences.
2 Buying or attempting to buy alcohol for a drunken person.
3 Common assault and battery, assault under s.47, s.20 or s.18 of the Offences Against the Person Act 1861 (as outlined in Chapter 4) if a horseplay defence is not used or accepted.
4 Criminal damage or trespassing on property (see for example, Bayer, 2003).
5 Indecent or sexual assault under the Sexual Offences Act 1976, 2003.
6 Indecent exposure, vagrancy, and outraging public decency.
7 In the case of deaths arising out of hazing or generally drunken behaviour leading to death of an individual, charges of unlawful act manslaughter or gross negligent manslaughter (as outlined in Chapter 7 of this text) could be applied, at both individual and organisational level.
8 Statutory breaches of health and safety in relation to, for example, s.3 of The Management of Health and Safety Regulations 1999, failure to conduct suitable and sufficient risk assessments, and s.2 and s.3 duties under the Health and Safety at Work Act 1974 in relation to both employees and non-employees (as outlined in Chapter 6 in this text).
9 Negligence claims for physical or psychological harm (against those athletes who organised the initiation rites or hazing activities or the school or authority) which must meet the criteria for negligence covered in Chapter 3 of this text.

State law responses to hazing in the United States (Criminal law)

In the United States 'forty-two of the fifty states have statutes which classify hazing as a crime', where individuals who 'participate in hazing rituals or initiation rites can be charged with violation of the particular state hazing law' (Doleschal, 2000: 16). Curry (1989) observed that 'the states' rush to adopt anti-hazing legislation reflects a shift in society's view of hazing' (cited in Boucher, 2002: 4). Although there are some variations in state laws on hazing, definitions are similar and mostly include physical harm, classify hazing as a misdemeanour and in most states consent by the pledge or new member is not a defence (ibid: 4–5). As in England and Wales, individuals who sodomise an initiate with a broom handle, or require a sexual act to be performed as part of the hazing ritual, may be charged with 'additional crimes including sexual assault or assault and battery' (Doleschal, 2000: 16[9]).

Civil law

Civil remedies in England and Wales include trespass to the person or the tort of negligence (covered in Chapters 2 and 3 of this text). Negligence is also a possible legal response in the US to harm caused in the course of hazing (see, for example, Nygaard and Boone, 1985). The plaintiff's attorney 'must prove that a coach or other school official, breached a duty to the plaintiff and that breach of duty caused harm' usually linked to failure to supervise, or knowledge of the hazing and failure to prevent it occurring, by a coach or school official' (Doleschal, 2000: 16). 'Students may have reached the age of adulthood', yet 'their lack of emotional maturity may make them more susceptible to hazing' (Boucher, 2002: 1). The courts in the United States have engaged in contradictory discussions and decisions, ranging from *in loco parentis* doctrine, to 'no duty' trends or exceptions (Boucher, 2002; see also McGlone and Shaefer, 2008).

Recent hazing case law 'predicts that the trend towards institutional liability with regard to hazing will continue' (Boucher, 2002: 7–8). Doleschal (2000: 16) suggests that if it is not feasible to utilise any of the above legal approaches, attorneys in the US can 'allege a violation of a student's United States constitutional rights' or apply child protection laws in European Union countries or Canada, New Zealand or Australia. In addition to the possible application of horseplay defences to criminal assault, 'reasonable chastisement' (punishment) is also a defence against assault between adults. Research by Coakley and Hughes (1991), Young (1993) and Messner (1992, 2002), for example, reported quite extreme punishments given to athletes by their team mates – such as suicide drills in American Football and training for hours in the Oklahoma heat without water, in response to poor performance.

Under the Children's Act 2004, the defence to assault of 'reasonable chastisement' was removed in relation to an adult punishing a child. Aside from the criminal and civil law, sports clubs, sports organisations, sports governing bodies and educational institutions, should have at their disposal a range of options when dealing with activities such as hazing or unreasonable punishments. These include codes of conduct and ethics, disciplinary and grievance procedures, harassment policies and more generic rules such as 'bringing the sport or organisation into disrepute'.

EXERCISE 9.10

Explain what is meant by hazing? Is it the same as team bonding or initiation ceremonies? Where does hazing or punishment take place outside sport and recreation contexts?

EXERCISE 9.11

What reasons are given for continuing hazing within sports teams or clubs? Explain why masculinity, organisational or club subcultures may throw a critical, theoretical light on the perpetuation of athletic hazing in schools and university teams (or in other institutions). Do women take part in hazing?

EXERCISE 9.12

Summarise the hazards and risks of hazing for both individuals and institutions?

EXERCISE 9.13

Get into groups of eight. Each person should find one area of the criminal law and explain how it might be applied to hazing in the UK.

EXERCISE 9.14

Which areas of civil law have been applied to hazing in the United States? Could the same civil law principles be applied in UK or to your country of residence or study?

EXERCISE 9.15

In 2002 how many of the United States had passed anti-hazing laws which made hazing a misdemeanour?

EXERCISE 9.16

What are the most common characteristics of hazing used in state laws, according to Boucher (2002)? Is consent a defence to a hazing misdemeanour? Should it be a defence?

EXERCISE 9.17

Apply the tort of negligence to harm caused by hazing in a hypothetical incident. What must the claimant or plaintiff prove?

EXERCISE 9.18

Summarise the 'contradictory discussions and decisions' (Boucher, 2002) in relation to the possible legal responsibilities of universities towards students who might be harmed through hazing in university sports. Identify and discuss any relevant differences in the university contexts in your country of residence or study.

Recognition scheme for sports and martial arts

One of the problems concerning the Law Commission in 1995 was the apparent lack of any machinery for determining a 'lawful' sport or even an agreement on a definition of 'sport' in the United Kingdom (see Farrell, 1996: 11). One definition of sport was included in the 1994 and 1995 Law Commission Consultation Papers:

> All forms of physical activity which, through casual or organised participation, aim at expressing or improving physical fitness and mutual well-being, forming social relationships or obtaining results in competition at all levels.
>
> (Law Commission, 1995: 177)

These problems are no surprise since 'sport' or 'sport contest' are regarded as essentially contested concepts. Hartley adapted Fraleigh (1984) and proposed the following conception of recognised sport or sport contest in her response to the Law Commission 1995 consultation paper:

> A voluntary activity, where one or more human opponents opposes at least one human other, to seek mutual appraisal of relative abilities of all participants, to move mass in time and space, which involve the exhibition of an agreed physical skill, effort, or challenge, which is justified in its various contexts or levels, within a broader moral/social policy framework to the satisfaction of the appropriate recognising authorities.
>
> (Hartley, 1997, 1998: 39)

The Law Commission felt that there was a need for formal machinery to examine the rules and organisation of all sports and martial arts activities where there was a risk of physical injury. The Law Commission 1995 considered that if an expert recognition body, through a lawful recognised sport, permitted the intentional infliction of injury or reckless infliction of serious disabling injury on the sports field, the criminal law should sanction it. This would be dependent upon the court having access to 'the rules of the sport which had been approved by the appropriate recognition body when determining if the risk of causing the injury was reasonable' (Law Commission, 1995: 177–178; Farrell, 1996: 11).

'First, a sporting activity itself is recognised; second, the organisation responsible for that activity may be recognised as the governing body for that sport' (Farrell, 1996: 11). For an activity to be a recognised as a lawful sport for the purposes of the criminal law, the Law Commission proposed the use of the ten key points used by the Sports Council, with a primary focus on 'safety and the steps that are necessary to contain the risk of avoidable injury' and procedures for handling injuries (Law Commission, 1995: 179–180). The ten key points used as a basis for discussing whether an activity should be recognised are:

1 *Physical Skills.* Does the activity involve physical skills? Are physical skills important for successful participation? Can they be developed or are they inherent to the individual?

2 *Physical Effort.* Does the activity involve physical effort? Is it important for successful participation? How important are any mechanical or other aids in comparison to skills and physical effort?

3 *Accessibility.* Is participation available to all sections of the community and not overly restricted for reasons of cost, gender or any other grounds?

4 *Rules and Organisation.* Is there an established structure to the activity with rules and where appropriate, organised competitions nationally or internationally?

5 *Strategies and Tactics.* Are the strategies and tactics within the framework of the rules? Is developing and employing awareness of them important for successful participation?

6 *Essential Purpose.* What is the essential purpose of the activity? Is it some form of physical recreation or is physical recreation a means to another more basic purpose?

7 *Physical Challenge.* Does the activity present a physical and/or mental challenge to the participant whether against himself/herself, others or the environment?

8 *Risk.* Does the activity involve any degree of risk? Is this level acceptable? What safeguards are employed by those taking part to minimise any risk?

9 *Uniqueness.* Is this a unique activity or is it a variation of another, more similar activity that is already recognised?

10 *Other considerations.* Are there any other political, moral or other ethical considerations which might prohibit the Sports Council from recognising the activity?[10] (Sports Council, Recognition of Activities and Governing Bodies, Sports Council Paper SC (93) 68, para 4.3, cited Law Commission, 1995: 179–180[11]).

The Law Commission felt that 'boxing should continue to be treated as a lawful sport for the purposes of the criminal law unless and until Parliament decides otherwise' (Law Commission, 1995: 181). The other activities which drew comments of concern around the intentional infliction of extremely serious injuries are martial arts. Martial arts activities which 'were not presently recognised by the Sports Council would be *prima facie* unlawful if our present proposals were to be implemented unless the activity and a recognisable governing body qualified for recognition' (ibid: 181). Martial arts activities which are presently recognised by the Sports Council at the time of the second consultation paper in 1995, include aikido, jujitsu, karate, kung fu and taekwondo. The martial arts activities which do not have recognition include knockdown sport budo, full-contact karate, knockdown karate, semi-contact karate and Thai boxing and kick-boxing (see Appendix D Martial Arts in Law Commission, 1995: 283–290). Following the case of *R v (Mark) Barnes* what status would these unrecognised martial arts have now in 2008? Would they be protected from criminal liability arising out of serious bodily harm, caused during the course of such sporting activities?

Since the Law Commission made limited recommendations to parliament in 1999 on the more generic aspects of the LCCP 1995 paper and the areas of sports, martial arts and recognition remain, at the time of writing, without any recommendations to parliament, the law at present on criminal liability for serious injuries caused intentionally or recklessly in the course of sport still relies on the OAPA 1861 and the Court of Appeal Case of *R v (Mark) Barnes* outlined in Chapter 4.

Cage fighting

> This bloody spectacle of two men colliding like rams and sometimes entwining but inevitably pounding, kicking and punching each other into oblivion. So what does it mean when cage fighting, an exhibition of men battling within a chain link fence enclosure, begins popping up on our television screens and in our arenas?
>
> (West, 2007, cited in Timmins, 2007: i)

Cage fighting or mixed martial arts or ultimate fighting contests arrived in the United States in 1993 and was introduced as 'cage rage' in the United Kingdom in 2003. This activity is 'styled after the popular *Vale Tudo* (Portuguese for 'anything goes') matches in Brazil' (Peligro, 2003, cited in Timmins, 2007) and in the Ukraine it is known as *boi bez pravil* (battle without rules). These early Ultimate Fighting Contests (UFC) were 'marketed as brutal, no-holds-barred tournaments with no time limits, no weight classes and few rules' (Hamilton, 1995, cited in Timmins, 2007: 1). Mixed Martial Arts (MMA) is a general term used to describe 'the convergence of striking, grappling, and submission techniques into one forum, whereby fighters can submit to their opponents' (Gentry, 2002, cited in Timmins, 2007: viii). It takes place in an octagon, an engineered fence 30 feet in diameter and stands 5 feet 6 inches high.

Various techniques, including finger manipulations and up to 11 chokes and locks can be used, but the most dangerous techniques are the chokes and strangleholds (Timmins, 2007: 46). There are four different kinds of chokes including one which is 'caused by the biceps [and] the opponent's own shoulders . . . closing off the carotid artery on both sides' (ibid: 46). The cage fighters interviewed by Timmins (2007) perceived cage fighting to be no more dangerous than boxing. Their perceptions appeared to be supported by research completed by medics at Johns Hopkins Medical Centre in the United States, where Bledsoe et al. found that:

> the overall injury rate in MMA competitions is now similar to other combat sports including boxing. Knockout rates are lower in MMA competitions than in boxing. This suggests a reduced risk of traumatic brain injury (TBI) in MMA competitions when compared to other events involving striking.[12]
>
> (Bledsoe et al., 2006, cited in Timmins, 2007)

Bledsoe et al. (2006) aimed to determine the incidence of injury in professional MMA fighters between September 2001 and December 2004 using data obtained from the Nevada Athletic Commission. Around 82 per cent of injuries were to the face, hands, nose and ears and eyes. Of these facial lacerations accounted for 47.9 per cent of all injuries, with hand injuries at 13.5 per cent, nose and ear injuries at 10.4 per cent and eye injuries at 8.3 per cent. Most of the cage fighters interviewed by Timmins (2007) knew that they were not insured and would have great difficulty getting insurance for injuries or loss of earnings arising out of cage fighting. Timmins' own enquiries by letter to insurance companies confirmed that insurance was not available for cage fighters (ibid). Spectators, fighters and promoters are often of the opinion that cage fighting is already accepted as a lawful, recognised sport. In fact, although it might be a physical activity which is licensed entertainment, it is not a recognised sport.

If someone intentionally or recklessly caused a serious injury to another cage fighter during a cage fight, there would appear to be no protection or exemption accorded, under Class II exemptions proposed by the LCCP in 1995. Since the green book of provisional proposals by the Law Commission on Consent and Offences Against the Person (Criminal Law) 1995 has yet to progress to a 'red book' of proposals to parliament, even in 2009, the law as it stands under the OAPA 1861 and the lead CA case in *R v (Mark) Barnes* remain the only legal guidance or sources applied to all sports and activities such as cage fighting. The UK Sports Council criteria for recognition remain unchanged and as reported in the LCCP 1995 document, Thai kick-boxing, full-contact karate remain classified as 'unrecognised' sports.

Strictly Baby Fight Club

On Thursday 24 April 2008, a television documentary called *Strictly Baby Fight Club* was aired on Channel Four in the United Kingdom. The trailers for the programme were reported as including:

> A blonde-haired girl with her hands strapped into boxing gloves sobs at the side of the ring. In another image her twin brother takes a direct hit in the face from a sparring partner. Miah and Kian Flannagan are just five years old.
> The opponents – some of them barely old enough to be at school – kick and punch in chilling scenes, while parents shout impassioned advice from the sidelines. Incredibly parental 'advice' includes encouragement to 'come on Princess, go forward, kick 'em, kick 'em'.
>
> (Hale, 2008, following the selective trailers for the programme)

Another child featured is Thai Barlow, already a veteran fighter at ten and named after his parents' burning passion for Thai boxing

> on top of school and homework, a normal week for Thai consists of running over 2 km, doing 400 sit ups, and at least 10 hours on the bags and sparring.
>
> (Hale, 2008)

The documentary then screened on 24 April at 9.00 pm on Channel Four, included the examples above, as well as, in the view of some viewers and critics, a 'more balanced view of Thai boxing and what it offers to children' and with the exception of the above

> the youngsters featured appeared to enjoy the sport. And with contestants swathed in protective gear, and no blows to the head allowed, it looked a lot safer than traditional boxing. That said, the sight of nine and ten-year-olds kicking each other for sport was unpleasant.
>
> (O'Donovan, 2008)

There were very contrasting responses to Gerard O'Donovan's article, illustrated in the blogs posted on *The Telegraph* website the day after the screening of the programme:

> Who is taking responsibility for safeguarding these children, it should be the parents, but where they are failing to do so, the Local Authorities, where these children live should be exercising their safeguarding responsibilities. If I knew the authorities I would make a referral to social care for them to undertake statutory duties. Tagging sport to this activity does not make this alleged sport Ok. It is child abuse.
>
> (Online blog in response to O'Donovan, 2008,
> posted by Chrissy Williams, 25 April, 2008 7: 19 pm)

There were also mixed responses from those who have experience of martial arts.

> I watched *Strictly Baby Fight Club* and I too thought it was a balanced documentary. I think it's a bit strong to suggest that civilisation has taken a backwards step because children compete in the sport. I started Thai boxing at 11 and had my first fight

4 weeks later and loved the sport so much that I trained 3 times per week until I was 23.

> (Blog posted by Joanne (qualified social worker)
> on *The Telegraph* online, 25 April 2008, 9.26 am)

As an avid martial arts student and being married to a professional cage fighter I was simply horrified by this programme last night. Whilst I agreed that competition fighting is a key part of any martial art, there is a good reason why no UK organisation will allow full contact, no protection kicks, punches, knees and elbows to the head, so I am appalled that the parents of Thai see fit to take him to Thailand to ensure that he can participate in such extreme events.

> (Blog posted by Catharine Shubrook,
> on *The Telegraph* online, 25 April, 2008, 8.51 am[13])

The National Society for the Prevention of Cruelty to Children (NSPCC) in the United Kingdom received a significant number of enquiries in response to this television documentary, from a wide range of individuals and organisations around the 'appropriateness of the activity', the 'serious risks' and the 'need for intervention to protect their safety and welfare'. Steve Boocock, the CPSU Director, posted a letter on the CPSU website in response to these concerns, providing some guidance, clarification and seeking further information about local reactions to the Channel Four programme. The letter confirmed that Thai kick-boxing was not recognised as a sport by any of the UK Sport Councils or the Department of Culture, Media and Sport. Steve Boocock recommended local intervention in response to this example of unregulated sports and recreation involving children and young people, perhaps drawing on, among others, the Clubmark model of best practice for club accreditation.[14]

The letter pointed out that 'Local Education and Welfare Services have a responsibility under the Children and Young Persons Act 1937, 1963 and the Children (Performances) Regulation 1968, to investigate and monitor employment undertaken by young people of compulsory school age'. Steve Boocock noted clear examples, of 'children participating in a "professional" fight, to which this legislation could apply'. The Licensing Act (2003) requires Local Licensing Committees to 'grant licenses for provision of regulated entertainment of facilities. The applicant must demonstrate promotion of the four objectives of the Act, which include the protection of children from harm'. Boocock noted examples of children 'exposed to unnecessary risk of harm' which could be grounds for refusing or withdrawing a license under the 2003 regulations. Steve Boocock also suggested that when non-affiliated or unregulated sports apply to hire local leisure, sport, or local authority facilities, Local Authorities can require minimum standards in relation to safeguarding children and young people.

In relation to the LCCP 1995 document, the activity of Thai kick-boxing, in an octagonal fight cage, involving children and young people, taking place as public entertainment, is unlikely to be included in Class II exemptions from criminal liability under the Offences Against the Person Act 1861. It follows that any intentionally or recklessly caused serious injury, in such an activity, which is not a lawful, recognised sport, could result in criminal charges being brought under the OAPA 1861 against any participant as young as ten years old. What influence, if any, does *Barnes* have on such an issue?

EXERCISE 9.19

What are the ten criteria for a recognised sport in the UK? Try to think of reasons for each criteria. Which criterion was of most interest to the Law Commission in 1995? Apply the criteria to the following activities and see if, in your opinion, all ten criteria are met. Give reasons for your decision:

1 soccer or rugby
2 darts or chess
3 cage fighting
4 'parkour' ('city running').

EXERCISE 9.20

What are the three criteria for a recognised sports governing body?

EXERCISE 9.21

Are boxing and martial arts viewed in the same way by the LCCP 1995? If not, why not?

EXERCISE 9.22

Which martial arts are recognised by the UK Sports Councils? Which martial arts remain unrecognised in 1995 according to the LCCP 1995? What are the legal implications in relation to Class II exemptions from criminal liability for an unrecognised martial art? What is the situation today?

EXERCISE 9.23

What is cage fighting (or mixed martial arts or ultimate fighting)? What are its origins? Where does it take place? What techniques can be used?

EXERCISE 9.24

What are the main injuries in US cage fighting according to Bledsoe et al. (2006)? How do the risks of traumatic brain injury in cage fighting compare to boxing?

EXERCISE 9.25

Is cage fighting a recognised sport in the UK? Please give reasons for your answer. Do you think it should be a recognised sport in the UK? Please give reasons for your answer.

EXERCISE 9.26

Explain why the Channel Four television documentary *Strictly Baby Fight Club* screened in the UK on 24 April 2008 led to controversy and criticisms as well as enquiries of concern to the NSPCC Child Protection in Sport Unit in the UK. Summarise the guidance given by the CPSU Director on i. the status of the activities in the programme as a recognised sport and ii. the possible responses using legislation or policy relating to child protection.

Corporate manslaughter

The need for reform was recognised as long ago as 1990 due to the collapse of the trial against P&O European Ferries for the manslaughter of those who died when the *Herald of Free Enterprise* capsized off the coast of Zeebrugge. People were shocked that *the company* was able to escape conviction simply because the *individual directors and senior managers* were acquitted. This was because the law only allowed companies to be convicted of manslaughter if a senior manager was convicted of manslaughter [the identification doctrine].

(Centre for Corporate Accountability, 2008: 9)

Following the collapse of the P&O trial for manslaughter, covered in Chapter 7 of this text, the Law Commission Consultation Paper 1995, on Involuntary Manslaughter, included a new offence of corporate killing if a 'management failure by a corporation is the cause or one of the causes of a person's death and that failure constitutes conduct falling far below what can reasonably be expected of the corporation in the circumstances' (LCCP 1995, 1996, cited in Molan et al., 2003: 216).

Government proposals for consultation followed in 2000 and 2003, and were followed by an examination of the 2005 Corporate Manslaughter Bill, by a House of Commons Select Committee in 2005/6.[15] A wide range of written evidence to the Select Committee included concerns around the issues of the exclusion of deaths in custody and human rights, the fault of senior manager, the duty of care and the range of punishments (see CCA, 2005; Disaster Action, 2005; Hartley, 2005).[16] The HOC Select Committees recommended, among other things, the application of the offence to deaths in police or prison custody.

The government released the Bill without these changes in the summer of 2006. In February 2007, the House of Lords voted against the Corporate Manslaughter and Corporate Homicide Bill 2006, due to the exemption from prosecution of those individuals or organisations that cause deaths in police or prison custody. The Corporate Manslaughter and Corporate Homicide Bill 2006 went to the House of Lords for the second and probably the last time on 17 July 2007. 'Unless either the Lords vote in favour of the Commons amendment or the Government makes a concession to the Lords on the Bill's application in relation to deaths in custody the Bill is likely to fall' (CCA, 16 July 2007[17]).

On 18 July 2007, the government tabled a new amendment 'allowing the new offence to apply to deaths in prison and police custody. This is a direct concession to the House of Lords that has refused to pass this bill unless it applied to such deaths' (CCA, 18 July, 2007[18]). The Bill was then passed by the House of Lords. The Corporate Manslaughter and Corporate Homicide Act became law on 6 April 2008. Lord McKenzie suggested that this Act 'will provide important new enforcement options in cases where a fatality results from serious management failures' used where 'organizations fall far short of what the law requires' (CCA 2008: 5). Events or conduct which might be used as evidence for such an offence must have occurred before 6 April 2008.

It identifies the offence as follows:

S.1. An organisation to which this section applies is guilty of an offence if the way in which its activities are managed or organised

(a) causes a person's death, and
(b) amounts to a gross breach of the relevant duty of care owed by the organisation to the deceased.

A breach of the relevant duty of care (owed by an organisation under the law of negligence) is:

S (1) (b) A 'gross' breach if the conduct alleged to amount to a breach of that duty falls far below what can reasonably be expected of the organisation in the circumstances; S (1) (c) 'senior management' in relation to an organisation, means the persons who play significant roles in –

(i) the making of decisions about how the whole or a substantial part of its activities are to be managed or organised, or
(ii) the actual managing or organising of the whole or a substantial part of those activities.

(Corporate Manslaughter and Corporate
Homicide Bill 2006–7 session, S (1) parts (b) and (c), 10 July 2007[19])

Under s.8(2) a jury will have to decide if there has been a gross breach of duty. To assist them in this task, a jury will consider if the evidence shows that the organisation has failed to comply with any health and safety legislation that relates to alleged breach. If it has, then the questions 'how serious was that breach?' and 'how much of a risk of death did it pose?' will be assessed by a jury. If evidence shows that 'attitudes, policies, systems, or accepted practices within the organization' were present and shown by the evidence to be likely to have encouraged or produced tolerance of any such failures in s.8 (2) then the jury can consider this. These principles recognise the impact on health and safety of organisational culture, leadership and the mindset of the board or executive team.

A jury can also have regard to any health and safety guidance that relates to the breach.[20] Such guidance could include the HSE (2004) *Management Standards on Work-related stress* and the voluntary guidance *Leading Health and Safety at Work*. The latter voluntary guidance was launched by the IOD and the HSE on 29 October 2007:

The starting point for any Board of Directors is effective corporate governance – central to that corporate governance is the leadership on health and safety. Effective control of business risks is linked with effective leadership in health and safety risks, that is, the health and safety risks of the workforce . . . failure to address health and safety can cause significant damage to the workforce, as well as serious damage to the reputation of the corporation or organization.

> (Lord McKenzie, Minister for Health and Safety, presentation at Launch of *Leading Health and Safety at Work: Leadership Actions for Directors* by IOD/HSE, London, 29 October 2007)

Health and safety is a key area of Directors' duties. Directors, Board of Directors set the tone and set the scene for everyone, and should be engaging with employees, including listening to the concerns of employees.

> (Lord McKenzie, ibid)

There are key differences between the new statutory offence and the old common law offence. This single offence for England, Wales, Scotland and Northern Ireland is applicable to Crown bodies, partnerships and other unincorporated organisations (as long as they employ staff). Under the new offence 'the prosecution of a director or senior manager is no longer necessary. Instead, there is now an 'entirely new test to assess the guilt of the company that rests upon whether there has been serious management failure within the organisation' (Centre for Corporate Accountability, 2008: 13). The test for 'gross negligence' is clearer with guidelines for the jury as outlined above. In addition to fines 'the court has the power to make a "remedial order" that requires the company to remedy the breach of the Act, and to make a "publicity order" that requires the organisation to publicise any conviction' (ibid: 13).

The new Act should make it easier to prosecute large and medium-sized organisations, but the CCA (2008: 17) asks will prosecutions have a real impact in terms of the size of the fines and the impact on companies? 'The penalty imposed needs to be significant indeed in its punitive and deterrent impact' (p. 17). It is recognised that there are 'clear benefits with the offence opening up to partnerships, police forces and crown bodies' (p. 17).

> In relation to many activities of these public bodies – law enforcement, emergency services, military operations, child protection issues, probation and statutory inspections – gross failures will only be able to result in prosecution of a public body where the death was a gross failure in its responsibilities as an employer and occupier, not in relation to its responsibilities as a provider of services and how this impacts on members of the public.[21]

> (pp. 17–18)

Parent company immunity has not been addressed and the Act will not apply to any death unless the failures necessary to prove that offence take place after that date. In addition, the new Act does not apply to any harm resulting in death that takes place outside the UK and there is no provision for an individual offence or imprisonment of individuals (p. 19).

Degrees of murder? The 2008 Law Commission proposals on murder and manslaughter

At the time of writing, another relevant area of legal reform has been ongoing for at least 18 months. Murder and manslaughter is being reviewed in two stages. In stage one the Law Commission Project on murder and manslaughter led by Professor Jeremy Horder reported on 29 November 2006.[22] Their recommendations included a three-tier law of homicide first degree murder, second degree murder, manslaughter. Some kinds of manslaughter, such as the worst kinds of killing by recklessness and killing under provocation or diminished responsibility, will become second degree murder, not manslaughter.[23] In stage two, the Law Commission's findings of November 2006 were being studied by the Home Office Review Team, who took over the review of this area of law in 2007 and will be 'consulting on broader issues of public policy and sentencing' (Law Commission, 2006[24]).

In August 2008 the Law Commission Report recommended a system of first and second degree murder and a more limited version of manslaughter. 'The foundation of the proposed framework was that the mandatory life sentence should be confined to cases where the offender intended to kill . . . taking a risk, even a high risk, of killing someone is recklessness and is very serious, but it is not the same as the deliberate taking of life' (BBC News 2008: 1[25]). First degree murder under these proposals would embrace intent to kill, unless a defendant has a partial defence. This would carry a mandatory life sentence. Second degree murder covers:

1 intention to cause serious harm (currently murder). Here someone means to badly hurt another person but did not realise it could kill them. For example, if someone punched someone and the victim then fell down on say, frozen or hard ground and banged their head and died. This would not carry a mandatory life sentence.
2 Killing through reckless indifference to causing death (currently manslaughter).
3 Intentional killing where a partial defence applied (currently manslaughter). This would include cases where killers were provoked, suffered diminished responsibility or were under duress.

Manslaughter would be used for someone who killed by gross negligence or deaths caused by intentionally or recklessly causing harm.

EXERCISE 9.27

In Chapter 7 of this text, you read about the challenges of bringing a charge of corporate manslaughter against a company which is not a person (or 'has no soul to be damned'). You also read about the collapse of the trial in the case of *R v Stanley and others* October 1990, arising from the sinking of the *Herald of Free Enterprise* near Zeebrugge in March 1987. Why did the law need to be reformed in this area? Outline the processes of legal reform in this area between 1995 and 2008.

EXERCISE 9.28

Outline the offence of corporate manslaughter in the Corporate Manslaughter and Corporate Homicide Act which became law in England and Wales on 6 April 2008. Critically discuss: does it address the matter of the doctrine of identification and other issues, which were highlighted in the collapse of the trial in *R v Stanley and others* in October 1990?

EXERCISE 9.29

How does the jury decide if there has been a gross breach of duty? What does this have to do with codes of practice, guidance, or statutory breaches in health and safety? Give examples to support your answer.

EXERCISE 9.30

In addition to reading this chapter and Chapters 4 and 7 of this text, go on the Law Commission website and Lexis newspapers search facility and see what you can find on the Law Commission proposals on Murder and Manslaughter from 4 August 2008. See if the easy read version of the proposals is still on the Law Commission website. Outline the main changes to present law. What is first degree murder? What is second degree murder? What is manslaughter? If you were taking part in the consultation in 2008, what feedback would you give to the Law Commission?

EXERCISE 9.31

Imagine a rugby player throws a punch on the rugby field and the victim receives serious head injuries, prompting a police investigation under s.18 of the OAPA 1861 (see Chapter 4 in this text). Two days later the victim dies. Imagine you are a CPS lawyer and the Law Commission 2008 proposals are the law. Would you bring criminal charges? If so, which offence would you select?

EXERCISE 9.32

Go back to Chapter 7 of this text. Select the following hypothetical:

Exercise 7.4 (Hypothetical). The university rugby club initiation rites. Imagine if the University Sport Executive Committee and the university senior executive team were fully aware of these practices and failed to act or intervene. Apply a. the Law Commission 2008 proposals for murder and manslaughter to this hypothetical scenario, considering both the individual captain 'Richard' and the rugby club, b. the Corporate Manslaughter and Corporate Homicide Act 2008.

EXERCISE 9.33

Go back to Exercise 7.8 Hypothetical in Chapter 7 of this text – the 'Bardsley' rugby union team. Apply a. the Corporate Manslaughter and Corporate Homicide Act 2008 to this scenario, b. the Law Commission proposals on murder and manslaughter of August 2008 and imagine they are the law. Discuss which offence might be applied to the conduct of the individual who threw the fatal punch, the team captain and the senior management of the club.

EXERCISE 9.34

Choose any of the manslaughter cases in sport and recreation in Part two of Chapter 7 of this text. Read through the Law Commission proposals of August 2008 on degrees of murder and manslaughter. Hypothetically identify which of these new offences you might apply to your chosen case. Give reasons for your choice.

> **EXERCISE 9.35**
>
> Get into groups of three. Each person should write their own hypothetical scenario from sport or recreation which would match each of the three proposed categories of second degree murder, from the Law Commission proposals of August 2008. Explain it to the others in the group.

Summary

- In the landmark case of *R v Brown* the majority of the Law Lords held 'that the intentional infliction of injuries during sado-masochistic, homosexual acts, by consenting adults in private can give rise to convictions for assault and unlawful wounding. The fact that the victims consented is not a defence to criminal charges' (Herbert, 1993: 7).
- The *Brown* case raised significant outrage and debate and led to the Law Commission Consultation on Consent and Offences against the Person in 1994 and 1995.
- It made proposals on exceptions to criminal liability for recognised sports and games, and covered, among other things, secondary liability, boxing, casual fighting and horseplay.
- Hazing and unreasonable punishments raise serious ethical, legal and policy issues for sports clubs, universities and other institutions such as the armed services.
- The present criminal law on assault and the failure of the Law Commission to make any formal recommendations to parliament after 1995, regarding sports and games, raises some interesting issues for a range of activities including 'cage fighting', or unrecognised martial arts such as Thai (kick) boxing in the UK.
- The LCCP 1995 consultation on involuntary manslaughter, the 2000 and 2003 government proposals, the HOC Select Committee Report on the Corporate Manslaughter Bill 2005, led to the Corporate Manslaughter and Corporate Homicide Bill 2006. The House of Lords voted against the Bill due to the exclusion of deaths in custody. In July 2007 the government tabled a new amendment and in 6 April 2008 the revised Bill was enacted.
- The voluntary code of practice *Leading Health and Safety at Work: Leadership Actions for Directors* IOD/HSE was launched on 29 October 2007.
- The House of Commons (Select) Work and Pensions Committee examined the Role of the Health and Safety Commission and the Health and Safety Executive in regulating workplace safety in February 2008, taking oral and written evidence. They published their reports in February, April and July 2008 making a range of recommendations to parliament (see HOC, 2008a, 2008b, 2008c).
- The Law Commission published its proposals on murder and manslaughter in August 2008. These included the introduction of first and second degree murder, a more limited offence of manslaughter and related changes in sentencing.

Personal reflections of a book journey: opportunities for applied teaching of legal aspects of sport and physical recreation

In this final section I am going to reflect back on my journey through writing the chapters for this book. Finally I shall try to draw out some common themes which have emerged which may be of interest in our approaches to teaching this wonderful subject. These include opportunities for multi-disciplinary enquiry, interrogating sports rules and procedures, young people and popular culture, and some final comments on risk education.

Chapter 1 grew out of quite a bit of trial and error, working with undergraduate students studying law on sports-related courses. In addition to orientating them to the more traditional legal sources and resources, I have found it useful and motivating for students to broaden their understanding of what can support the study of legal aspects of sport and physical recreation. One of the most important resources is the individual student. We all have personal biographies as participants, observers, leaders, officials, coaches or as avid readers of sports autobiographies. Drawing on their 'contextual' and experiential knowledge very early on in an applied law module helps to build up their confidence and appreciate, at the outset, the kinds of materials they can already contribute to shared learning.

Out of around 150 hours of module time, perhaps one-fifth may be in lectures of seminars. Students need to be committed to their responsibilities in the independent learning time – searching, investigating, using and sharing a wide range of print, electronic, media and website resources. It takes time to learn and practise such search and investigation skills. The materials used in Chapter 1 were used most effectively in a library orientation session run jointly by academic and library staff, which was specifically designed for the sport, recreation and law modules. The search exercises in Chapter 1 can be used in this way in advance of or at the start of a module – or as directed learning during a module. All materials in the orientation or pre-module sessions are normally located on the X-stream (or Web CT) with links already established to key legal databases or sport and law websites.

Chapter 2 introduced the three elements of negligence. Duty of care relationships nearly always exist in sport and recreation contexts. It is the duty of care relationships with other professionals such as coastguards, police, or ambulance service, for example, which may be less clear, as shown in Chapter 2. Causation is a very complicated matter, with intervening causes and individual histories able to complicate matters in a claim for negligence. In teaching this subject most attention is usually paid to the second element, a breach of duty. Grouping the cases into practical themes from rule breaking to failure to provide a safe environment in sport and recreation helps students to unpack the notion of a breach of duty. Learning lessons out of cases was a common thread through my teaching and this book. The case of *Watson v the BBBC* taught us that a standard and approved practice of a sports governing body is not sacrosanct and can come under severe scrutiny by the courts.

Chapter 3 continued the theme of negligence, examining initially two neglected areas of law and sport – *volenti non fit injuria* and contributory negligence. It is very important for students and sports practitioners to understand and interrogate each logical condition of *volenti* and analyse the application to their particular sport. Not any risks will do for *volenti*. It is important to distinguish between inherent risks and extraneous or unacceptable risks. Students are often completely unaware that the courts can reduce compensation for negligence according to any negligent contribution to the injury by the claimant or plaintiff. They are particularly surprised by the courts applying contributory negligence to children as young as 11.

The Occupier's Liability Acts of 1957 and 1984 made us think about some very interesting and current issues such as the duty of care owed to trespassers. In an age where drunken antics and reckless conduct by trespassers (including teenagers or students) often lead to serious injury or death, we are likely to see more cases like *Ratcliffe* in the future. We should not be waiting until the courts have to deal with some of the possible negligence cases arising out of injuries during 'urban physical recreation' activities such as 'Parkour' or 'City Running'. These activities are not part of a codified, institutionalised sport and as participants seek greater physical challenges, this activity may at times involve trespassing. The *Smoldon* and *Vowles* key negligence cases at the end of Chapter 3 showed the standard of care in sport being examined by the courts when dealing with the duty of a referee, rather than players or organisers of sport competitions. Aside from the issues raised in these cases by judges and lawyers, I have tried to encourage sports students to think about:

- The significance of safety rules – introducing and disseminating changes in safety rules and the difference between hearing about them and actually understanding and applying them.
- The subculture and institutionalised practices and values which discouraged abandoning a rugby match when facing problems with scrummaging or encouraged adult players to carry on playing with an unsuitable substitute in the front row following an injury. The courts were not interested in common practice – they focused on the formal sports rules or rugby 'laws'.
- The atmosphere of the matches, the responsibilities of players, captains and coaches as well as referees.
- The possible application of *Smoldon* and *Vowles* to other sports.

In Chapter 4, a socio-legal lens was applied to sports violence and criminal liability for assault on a sports field. This very interesting and relevant topic is more than a journey through the technicalities of s.47, s.20 and s.18 of the Offences Against the Person Act 1861. What we identify and label as violence, or criminality, and how we deal with other contested concepts such as assertion, intimidation and aggression are far more than preliminary 'word games'. The key cases of *Cey*, *Ciccarelli* and *Barnes* established a set of 'objective' criteria to assist the courts. Ninety-nine per cent of the criminal assault cases from the Anglo-Welsh courts arise from 'off-the-ball' incidents, clearly not part of the game, although defendants often tried to argue otherwise. Amateur soccer and rugby union were well represented in these criminal cases.

The critical sociological lens used hegemonic masculinity, masculine or sports-specific subcultures and power to scrutinise socialisation processes which normalised, celebrated or encouraged violence on the sports field. The influence of such socialisation into male athletic identity (Messner 1990, 1992, 2002) can be observed all the way from the sports field to the law courts, through sports disciplinary processes and the opinions expressed by expert witnesses in criminal assault cases in sport (see Hartley, 1998, 2001a; James, 2006).

Chapter 5 brought together three areas which can be seen on a continuum – discrimination, harassment and child protection (safeguarding children) in sport. Again, the importance of interrogating contested concepts such as sex, gender, 'race', disability, was evident. The sociological lens was present in the scrutiny of, for example, gender stereotypes and medico-legal discourse highlighted in the cases of *Bennet v the Football Association, Couch v BBBC* and the much later but more positive *Taylor* case against the Australian Ruloo Football Association (see Talbot, 1988, 2006; Felix, 1998; McArdle, 2000; Bradford, 2005). Conceptual challenges on the nature of child abuse affect research outcomes and risk assessment. The very brief overview of the nature and prevalence of child abuse and research into groups at risk, also made us aware of a critical sociological lens, which identified the use of power, subcultures or subworlds as key factors in, again, the normalisation, tolerance and lack of resistance to sexual exploitation including child abuse and sexual harassment.

All of this research needs to be centrally placed in informing policies on child protection/ safeguarding children in sport and recreation, as well as legal duties in risk assessment. Joined up thinking, which understands the link between research on child protection policies, grievances and disciplinaries, codes of practice and notions of power, needs to go further than merely identifying risks. Sports governing bodies need to use such research to inform risk assessment and use grievances and disciplinaries to challenge unacceptable conduct lower down the continuum of exploitation or abuse. Perceptions of the power and 'indispensibility' of a sports coach have implications for risk management and also for resourcing, especially at the high-risk 'stage of imminent achievement' (see Brackenridge, 2001).

In Chapter 6 it was argued that learning about hazards, risks and risk management was not just for sports managers or event managers but should feature in risk education for school pupils in personal and social education, physical education and citizenship. Incidents such as tombstoning, or after dinner activities including bridge jumping or a midnight race round a university quad, can introduce students to risk analysis and risk decisions which are located in informal physical recreation, rather than institutionalised sport settings. Myths and fears about risk assessment were challenged making reference to the HSE ten principles of sensible risk assessment (HSE, 2006). A range of statutory health and safety duties in the workplace were introduced, followed by examples of prosecutions for breaches of health and safety brought against individuals and organisations in sport, education and recreation contexts. The accessibility to the HSE/police investigation into the Glenridding School adventure weekend in Cumbria in 2002, provided on the British HSE website, allows students and practitioners to learn many lessons on the broader context of risk assessment from the circumstances surrounding the death of 10-year-old Max Palmer in October 2002.

Manslaughter is a complex area of law which has developed in an 'ad hoc' manner and does not often feature centrally in sport, recreation and law modules at undergraduate level. Yet there can be a very fine line separating causing death and being found liable for negligence and causing death and being charged with manslaughter by gross negligence. Equally if someone throws a punch to the head of another player in a game of rugby and the victim hits his head on, say, frozen ground and dies a few days later from such injuries, what was initially a police investigation into a s.18 offence under the OAPA 1861 can become a manslaughter investigation or, in the future, possibly second degree murder.

The public inquiry by Mr J Sheen in 1987 into the sinking of the *Herald of Free Enterprise* outside Zeebrugge harbour in March 1987, and the collapse of the subsequent trial of the individuals and the company in *R v Stanley and Others* in October 1990 contain crucial lessons for structures, cultures and risk management in organisational settings as well as a clear illustration of the need for legal reform of the law of corporate manslaughter (see Sheen J, 1987; Bergman 1993; Crainer, 1993; Hartley, 2001b). The landmark man-slaughter case of *R v Kite and others* provided a graphic illustration of the application of this area of law to a very small company running an outdoor activities centre in England in the early 1990s. All those who run such activities and those who seek to regulate them have much to learn from this case. For students it can be used for learning about, among other things, manslaughter, organisational risk, risk assessment, and the rate of expansion of a new enterprise in an outdoor activities context.

In Chapter 8 students were introduced to natural justice principles and a range of disciplinary processes in sport from an informal grievance to international CAS panels as well as civil or criminal cases. Doping cases illustrated the harsh reality of the strict liability rule in anti-doping articles. Despite what some perceive as a very harsh rule which might be in conflict with some domestic or international laws, the courts continue to use a policy lens to view strict liability favourably and do not intervene, as sports governing bodies engage in the valuable task of protecting the welfare of sport competition through anti-doping rules.

The reality of the strict liability rule for athletes was illustrated very clearly by the Diane Modahl doping case in Chapter 8, and to a lesser extent by the Alain Baxter CAS case arising out of the 2002 Winter Olympics in Salt Lake City. I have found that students actively engage in collecting and contributing to module materials on the themes of Chapter 8 (and Chapter 4) as every week they study this topic on a sport and law module – an individual or organisation in sport usually gets into trouble in some way in an incident or disciplinary process. As I was nearing the completion of my journey writing this book, the high-profile cases of Oscar Pistorius and Dwain Chambers reached the CAS panel and the English courts.

Unfinished business in the form of the 1995 consultation of the Law Commission of England and Wales on consent and offences against the person dominates the first part of Chapter 9. I engaged students in the process of discussing and providing feedback to what I consider was one of the most important consultations on legal reform affecting sport and leisure activities in the history of Anglo-Welsh law. Such activity can be a real-life experience in citizenship and being a critical advocate for sport and recreation. The 1995 consultation was an excellent example of an inclusive process which had to address the fall-out of the *Brown* case for sports, games and dangerous exhibitions, among other things.

In 1996 at a BASL seminar on this topic in London, one of the Law Commissioners advised that the Law Commission consultation on consent and offences against the person would be cross-referenced or co-ordinated with the LCCP on Involuntary Manslaughter 1995, which included corporate manslaughter. The long-awaited legal reform on involuntary manslaughter went ahead with the enactment of the Corporate Manslaughter and Corporate Homicide Act 2008 in April 2008. Unfortunately, apart from some limited recommendations to parliament in the generic areas of the document in 1999, there have been no recommendations made to parliament on sports, games and dangerous exhibitions. The examination in Chapter 9 of recognised and unrecognised sports, casual fighting, horseplay and secondary liability from the 1995 Law Commission consultation on offences against the person, highlights a need for this consultation to be resurrected and completed.

Recent activities such as cage fighting and Thai kick-boxing public exhibitions in 2008 involving children and young people in England provided a salutary reminder of the importance of revisiting issues such as recognition criteria and their relationship to exemption from criminal liability, as well as testing the policies and procedures on child protection or safeguarding children, covered in Chapter 5. The activities of hazing, horseplay, punishments in sports teams not only highlight the very important debates in the LCCP 1995 consultation, but also provide interesting and current examples for students to use the sociological lens to critically analyse, yet again, the operation of power, subcultures and traditions which normalise, tolerate, and perpetuate hazing.

Collaborations in the curriculum: opportunities for multi-disciplinary enquiry

The study of law applied to sport and physical recreation has been linked with other disciplines at several points in the journey through this book. Law worked with science–medicine and epidemiology, in Chapter 2, in proving causation in the third element of negligence and the assessment of any damages awarded by the courts. In Chapter 3 changes to safety rules in rugby union were informed by orthopaedic research into spinal injuries in the U19 age group. Psychologists, philosophers and sociologists contributed to the analysis of sports violence, criminal liability, masculinity and consent in Chapter 4. In Chapter 5, the medico-legal discourse was central to discrimination legislation and key cases involving sex discrimination in sport and physical recreation.

The sociological critique was ever present, challenging assumptions, including gender stereotypes, embedded in the medico-legal discourse of expert witnesses or the legislation itself. Law, social work, psychology and sociology were needed to meet the challenges of defining and researching the nature, prevalence, risk and perpetuation of sexual exploitation, including child abuse, in sport and recreation. In Chapter 6 the analysis of risk drew on statistical data, insurance expertise, risk and hazards formulae, as well as empirical data on deaths and injuries. In Chapter 8 sports science played a key role in the Independent Appeal Panel of 1995, during the Diane Modahl doping case and is seen as essential in mounting a legal challenge against a positive doping result. Biomechanics and physiology were at the heart of the decision of the CAS panel, in May 2008, to uphold the appeal by Oscar Pistorius against the IAAF decision to ban him from competing against able-bodied athletes, using his cheetah prosthetic limbs.

There have been several points in this book, for example, in Chapters 4, 5 and 9, where the socio-legal lens has thrown a critical light on stereotypes, assumptions, power, masculinity and subcultures or subworlds in sport and recreation. It can assist students in their understanding of the perpetuation, tolerance, or lack of resistance or action against unacceptable or unlawful conduct such as sports violence and criminal assault, sexual exploitation including child abuse, participation in high-risk activities, or activities such as hazing, punishments and horseplay leading to serious injury or death. The socio-legal lens can be enhanced through collaboration with philosophy. For example, in the study of the legal treatment of acts of violence or doping in sport, philosophy can contribute a critical and practical approach. Conceptual analysis of the nature of a sport competition, the core and contingent aims, the contract to compete, violent acts and acts of violence, can be used to challenge attempts by players or managers to normalise 'acts of violence' merely by common practice or by reference to the norms and values of the sports team or club.

Philosophy of sports science can be a useful tool in challenging assumptions and stereotypes in sex and race discrimination legislation and cases. I have used ethical theories with students from level one to analyse and challenge conduct which ignores the law or common sense. In addition, students have worked well with the application of deontology and virtue ethics to natural justice principles, arguments for and against doping control, and the norms and values of a sports team who seek to normalise acts of violence. There may be opportunities to broaden the teaching base on sport and law modules using other disciplines, or in some cases explore possible combinations for joint honours degree courses.

Rules, disciplinary processes and laws: harmonisation or conflict?

Sports rules and procedures have received significant attention from the law in many of the themes explored in this book. Sports rules and, in particular, *safety* rules have played a key role in judicial decisions and academic analysis. Deviation from formal rules has in some cases, but not others, supported a successful claim for negligence in sport. Changes to a safety rule and the dissemination and application of that rule was at the centre of the key case of *Smoldon* in Chapter 3. Rule changes like this one often rely on input from other disciplines such as medicine, sports medicine, physiology or biomechanics. We saw that the courts use the failure to follow the written sport rule, rather than institutionalised practices or working culture in both the *Smoldon* and the *Vowles* rugby cases in Chapter 3.

Failure to follow sports rules and procedures in disciplinaries and doping control were significant in Chapter 8. The International Skiing Federation did not follow its own rules on penalties when it attempted to impose a longer ban on Alain Baxter. The law expects sports governing bodies and clubs to follow the Rules of Natural Justice in relation to the conduct of their disciplinary processes. Rules and technical procedures for doping control must be followed. Failure to do so can lead to serious consequences such as a false positive as in the case of Diane Modahl in Chapter 8. Sports rules were revisited in criminal cases for assault on the sports field, although there is further work to be done viewing rule-breaking and 'legitimate sport' as highlighted in the case of *R v (Mark) Barnes* in Chapter 4. The potential conflict between sports rules, domestic laws, international laws and human rights included in Chapter 8 is likely to continue to occupy the courts and academics.

Young people and popular culture: opportunities in teaching legal aspects of sport and physical recreation

Partly as a result of encouraging students to contribute and discuss a wide range of resources from their daily lives, I have increasingly introduced materials which bring together law and popular culture, alongside young people and students at work, study and informal recreation. The development of 'City Running' or 'Parkour' activities in this country is a site ripe for socio-legal analysis of law and popular culture. An informal urban, physical recreation activity which goes beyond traditional sport venues and is not (yet) a codified, recognised sport raises some interesting issues for teaching and research. If a sports governing body provides sessions on Parkour skills, are they potentially liable for any injuries? Will urban planners work with participants to design urban Parkour routes or would that ruin the nature and appeal of the activity? How might the courts deal with Parkour or City Running if a negligence case came to court under the OLA 1984? In Chapter 6, the smuggling of 'sport contest skills' into a leisure or entertainment environment such as the Cambridge quad race or the traditional May ball bridge jumps helps to raise points of reflection and discussion on risk taking versus valuable traditions.

It has been useful to dip into popular culture in several areas of my teaching, for example:

- Films such as *Erin Brockovich* or *A Few Good Men* in relation to causation in a class action and illustrating subcultures, power and causation.
- *Jackass* or *You've been Framed* or similar materials can be used in thinking about risk, masculinity, consent, reasonable foreseeability of harm or injury.
- Students never cease to amaze me in their enthusiasm and support for this topic and their use of sources such as *YouTube*, or blogs or discussion sites to identify examples of celebration of various risk-taking or rule-breaking conduct such as tombstoning off cliffs or a guide to ball-tampering in cricket.
- Documentary television programmes or news items can report or comment on new trends in popular culture are useful for sport, recreation and law modules.

Risk education

There are significant challenges which need to be addressed for sports practitioners and students alike in the area of risk perception and risk education. Perceptions abound in sport and schools about a compensation culture, mountains of risk assessment paperwork, fears about being charged with manslaughter and the adverse effects on school trips or adventure activities have featured in my reading for this book. I have found nothing to support such fears, but plenty to challenge them. Cross-curricular risk education in schools and universities should involve pupils and students in risk-assessment methods, risk taking and personal, legal responsibilities. At several points in this book we have seen the teenagers and children as young as ten or eleven facing criminal charges, such as manslaughter, or being evaluated for contributory negligence or for their horseplay activities. Subjects such as citizenship, personal and social education, physical education and science have a role to play in risk education. The law does not expect perfection but a reasonable standard and approved practice, under the guidance of our own professional associations and sports governing bodies. We need to use the law to inform, support and protect our positive endeavours in sport and physical recreation and to identify, resist and challenge those seeking to harm or threaten, in any way, those who participate and enjoy what sport has to offer.

Notes

1 Legal sources, databases and organisations

1 The material and exercises in this chapter have been piloted with significant success with several undergraduate and post-graduate student groups at Leeds Metropolitan University, where academic staff have worked with library staff in induction and directed learning support sessions for modules which apply law to sport, physical education, or leisure contexts.

2 However, as Elliot and Quinn (2006: 1) point out, 'there is not always agreement on what kinds of conduct should be considered criminal' and types of criminal conduct can vary from society to society and over time; for example, homosexuality is no longer a crime, nor is a man raping his wife.

3 The exception to this rule is a group of offences known as strict liability, such as health and safety offences under the Health and Safety at Work Act 1974, or The Management of Health and Safety Regulations 1999 and other relevant legislation.

4 See for example the appeal cases of *R v (Mark) Barnes* [2004] EWCA Crim 3246; [2005] 1 WLR 910 or *R v Ahmed* [2002] EWCA Crim 779 in Chapter 4.

5 In 2009, the new Supreme Court will replace the House of Lords Appellate Committee as a result of the Constitutional Reform Act 2005, which, among other things, aims to remove 'obvious breaches of the separation of powers and to seek judicial independence required by Article 6 of the European Convention on Human Rights' (Darbyshire, 2007: 4).

6 See this sport doping case in Chapter 8.

7 See the European Court of Justice at http://curia.eu.int/en/. See European Court of Human Rights at www.echr.coe.int.

8 See for example *R v Barnes*, The Times, January 10, 2005: 54.

9 The author acknowledges the use of Leeds Metropolitan. University Learning and Information Services 'Law: case law' guide Edition 2a, September 2005 in relation to this list and accessing law reports above.

10 See www.legislation.hmso.gov.uk.

11 See www.butterworths.co.uk.

12 The material in this CSL handbook series, along with others in the series, has been incorporated into Corbett, R., Findlay, H. and Lech, D., (2007) *Legal Issues in Sport* Toronto: Montgomery.

13 See BASL website for details. I recommend that students join the BASL as student members at a reduced rate, and also access the Hospitality, Leisure, Sport and Tourism Subject Network website, introduced later in this chapter and use the *Sport and Law: Learning Resource Guide* (Hartley, 2009).

14 You may also be interested in the Higher Education Academy United Kingdom Centre for Legal Education (UKCLE) based at the University of Warwick, Coventry, CV4 7AL. It has events, a newsletter, teaching resource notes. See website at www.ukcle.ac.uk.

15 In relation to the topics covered in this text, see handbooks on *Managing Risks:*

A Handbook for Recreation and Sport Professionals; Your Risk Management Programme; Negligence and Liability: A Guide for Recreation and Sport Organisation; Rights and Obligations: A Handbook for Athletes and Sport Organisations. The CSL website advises (in August 2007) that a forthcoming CLS book Legal Issues in Sport: Tools and Techniques for the Sport Manager by Rachel Corbett, Hilary Findlay and David Lech, will 'consolidate and update the ten-volume handbook series' and will also 'incorporate abundant new materials' (CSL Newletter 'What's new' section, accessed 21 August 2007).

16 Formerly 'The Society for the Study of Legal Aspects of Sport and Physical Activity'.
17 For example, the IASL collaborated with the National Sports Law Institute at Marquette University Law School in Milwaukee, Wisconsin, to organise the International Sport Business and Law in the 21st Century international conference in September 2003, at Marquette University Law School, Wisconsin.
18 See Reeb, M. Digest of CAS Awards 1986–1998, 1998–2000, 2001–2003.
19 See www.1st4sport.com which includes the Running Sport Guides, coaching aids, physical education, sports management and development, sports medicine, long-term athlete development and sports officiating.
20 See www.sportengland.org.
21 This incident is briefly covered in Chapter 7 in the manslaughter case of R v Ellis (unreported, 23 September 2003, Manchester Crown Court, Morland J) and is used in Chapter 6 in relation to risk assessment.
22 See websites for examples.
23 See http://news.bbc.co.uk/
24 See www.cnn.com and also www.cnn.com/LAW or www.fox.com.
25 If you are using these or similar sites, it is important to follow carefully all guidance on good practice, personal safety and the prevention of identity fraud, which is normally provided on those sites.

2 Principles of negligence

1 Bermingham (2005: 34) explains that 'although no duty is owed to the public at large to respond to a call for help, once a 999 call has been accepted, the ambulance service assumes responsibility and has an obligation to provide the service for a named individual at a specified address'.
2 See a more detailed case analysis of this adult rugby union case of Vowles v Evans [2003] EWCA Civ 318; [2003] 1 WLR 1607 in Chapter 3.
3 See Williams v Eady (1893) 10 TLR 41 and Lyes v Middlesex County Council (1962) 61 LGR 443 cited in BAALPE (2004).
4 See Condon v Basi [1985] 1 WLR 866; [1985] 2 All ER 543 (CA).
5 See Elliott v Saunders and Liverpool Football Club Ltd (1994) unreported, in James (2001: 699). See Gardiner and Felix (1994).
6 See Watson v British Boxing Board of Control [2001] QB 1134 later in this chapter.
7 Chapter 3 includes a brief discussion of the standard of care in sport. Is it 'failure to take reasonable care to prevent reasonably foreseeable harm in all the relevant circumstances' or does it require a defendant to show 'reckless disregard for the health and safety of others'? See McArdle (2005).
8 The court considered the previous cases of Staples v West Dorset DC [1995] PIQR 439, CLY 473 and Wilson v Best Travel Ltd [1993] 1 All ER 353.
9 Under the umbrella of the remoteness criterion see the 'direct consequence' test in

Polemis v Furness, Withy and Co, Re [1921] 3 KB 560, and the 'reasonable foreseeability' test in *Overseas Tank Ship (UK) Ltd. v Morts Dock & Engineering Co (The Wagon Mound (No 1))* [1961] AC 388 (PC) in Cooke (2003: 138–129) and Harpwood (2003: 151–152).

10 This case relates to relevant duties under the Occupier's Liability Act 1957, s.2 covered in Chapter 3 and considered and applied the cases of *Staples v West Dorset DC* [1995] PIQR p 345 [1995] CLY 473; *South Australia Asset Management Corporation v York Montague Ltd* [1997] AC 191, [1996] CLY 4519.

11 The *Tremain* case has attracted significant criticism 'partly because the evidence which was accepted about the unusual nature of the disease which the claimant suffered was doubtful' partly because of the case requiring 'too precise a degree of foresight' and was 'probably wrong on this point' (Harpwood, 2003: 153; Jones, 2002: 270). The decision in *Tremain* seems quite harsh compared to the decision in *Bradford*. The latter case is regarded as a 'more accurate reflection of the current tendency to adopt a more liberal approach to this issue' (Bermingham, 2005: 50). In *Tomlinson v Congleton Borough Council* [2003] UKHL 47; [2004] 1 AC 46 the HL moved towards a recognition of the autonomous risk-taking and did not impose liability on the defendants.

12 Weil's disease is an illness which can often be confused with flu as its symptoms are very similar. If left undiagnosed and untreated, it can lead to death within a short time. Members of the British Canoe Union (BCU.) can carry a card with them which advises that if this person falls ill with the following symptoms etc, please send blood to the BCU which gets it tested for Weil's disease. The risk of catching Weil's disease from rats' urine may be increased if canoeing, for example, in stagnant water, with the additional risk of doing so with any break in the skin or an open wound.

13 Bristol Crown Court, March, 1996, Rougier J decided allocation of compensation payments between parties. See Weaver (1996).

14 For example in the manslaughter case of *R v P&O European Ferries (Dover) Ltd* (1991) 93 Cr App R 72, although the case eventually collapsed against both the individual defendants and the company, it was established that even though it was common industrial/professional practice to leave port with the bow doors open, it was regarded as folly and negligent to do so (see Hartley, 2001a; Turner 2003: 30).

15 A soccer case covered in Chapter 3 under 'the standard of care in sport'.

16 Although ordinary cleaning had taken place the special systematic and chemical cleaning prescribed by the manufacturers was not followed and the court heard evidence of previous complaints to the swimming pool staff that had gone unheeded. The plaintiff was not a swimmer but a visitor who was walking round the pool 'wearing suitable shoes and walking in a sensible manner' (*Taylor v Bath and North East Somerset District Council* (unreported, 27 January 1999, Judge Chambers) in 'Legal precedents in a "slipping accident" and an introduction to PE which you may not wish to know about!' Information sheet, Ref. 183: 19/99 Institute of Sport and Recreation Management (www.isrm.co.uk)).

17 See *McCracken v Melbourne Storm Rugby League Football Club and Others* [2005] NSWSC 107.

18 See the section in Chapter 3 on 'contributory negligence' and the 'Occupiers Liability Act 1957'.

19 See also *The Times Law Report* 9 February 1984 and Grayson (1986).

20 In contrast to the Anglo-Welsh court hierarchy, the High Court of Australia (HCA) is the highest court, beyond the individual territorial courts.

21 Zurich Municipal Court Circular, cited Whitlam (2005: 147–148).

22 In addition all boxers were to undergo head CT scans at certain times, where any irregularities could lead to the BBBC exerting its power to take whatever steps it deems necessary in the interest of the health and safety of the boxer.

23 On this issue Kennedy J cited the previous decisions in *McGhee v National Coal Board* [1972] 1 WLR 1 (HL) and *Hotson v East Berkshire Area Health Authority* [1987] 1 AC 750 (cited Thompson, 2000: 7).

3 Defences against negligence

1 See also McArdle and James (2005: 193) which discusses why *volenti* is rarely relevant to sports cases after the case of *Caldwell v Maguire and Fitzgerald* [2001] EWCA Civ 1054; [2001] PIQR 45.

2 This is based on a real, tragic incident in July 2005, where a 19-year-old cricketer who was batting, collapsed and died from a cardiac arrest after being hit directly on the heart from a lawful ball, hit within the rules of the game. See *The Liverpool Post & Echo Ltd Daily Post* Monday 11 July 2005; *The Guardian* (London) Tuesday 11 July 2005. In another incident, a cricketer was struck by lightning in a match in Eastern Australia, causing him to collapse and die. (See *The Independent* (London) Monday 26 January 2004).

3 See Chapter 6.

4 See Chapter 4.

5 See Chapter 7.

6 However, this can be contrasted with *Klyne v Bellegarde* (1978) 6 WWR 743, a Canadian case, where the claimant, an ice hockey spectator, in the first instance, recovered damages for an injury suffered when being hit by the puck whilst standing in the aisle. The defendants 'failed to reasonably protect spectators' as there were no protective guards above the sideboards (Griffith-Jones, 2003: 1058). This was reversed on appeal.

7 See *Froom v Butcher* (1976) QB 286 (CA), where guidelines of 'a reduction of 25 per cent where the injuries could have been avoided altogether, and 15 per cent in respect of those which could have been less severe' (Bermingham, 2005: 58).

8 See *O'Connell v Jackson* [1972] 1 QB 270.

9 See *Owens v Brimmell* [1977] QB 859.

10 See *Fowles v Bedfordshire County Council* [1996] ELR 51 (CA). See also Chapter 2 where this case was outlined in relation to the subtheme of 'supervision'.

11 In this case the defendants had appealed against a decision in Middlesbrough County Court, by Briggs J on 5 March 1998, which found the defendants liable for negligence because of poor visibility of the edge of the pool and murkiness of the water, with no finding of contributory negligence on the part of the claimant. See *Greening v Stockton-on-Tees Borough Council* [1998] EWCA Civ 1704; Simon Brown, LJ, Mantell LJ. 6/11/98, Lawtel 7/18/03.

12 See a detailed account of this case and other negligence cases in skiing in Maxlow-Tomlinson (1995).

13 The judge in the first instance considered that they were equally to blame and held the defendant liable with 50 per cent contributory negligence by the plaintiff (Jones, 2002: 214).

14 See also *Jepson v MOD* [2000] 1 WLR 2055, where a drunken guard returning from a night out with a group of soldiers, organised by their company commander, tried to climb on top of the roof of the lorry transporting him, and fell, sustaining serious injury.

The MOD was held 25 per cent liable as the transport package was not reasonably safe and it was reasonably foreseeable that the claimant would be drunk. The claimant was held 75 per cent responsible for contributory negligence, being largely responsible for his own misfortune with actions which were foolish and dangerous in the extreme. See also *Martens v Thomson Holidays Ltd* (unreported, 20 February 2001, Mayors and City of London County Court). Here a drunken tourist, on a package holiday in Goa, wandered off a campsite to find firewood and fell down an unguarded well, after drinking 22 bacardis with his partner. The claimant was held 60 per cent responsible for contributory negligence and the defendants 40 per cent liable as there was no clear indication to tourists that they were actually leaving the boundary of the campsite.

15 See also other cases brought in a sport or recreation context under the 1957 Act, for example *Simms v Leigh RFC Ltd* [1969] 2 All ER 923, *Gillmore v London County Council* [1938] 4 All ER 331, *Evans v Waitemata District Pony Club* [1972] NZLR 773 at 775, *Murray and Another v Harringay Arena* [1951] 2 KB 529, *Harrison v Vincent* (1982) RTR 8 (CA).

16 See also *Bottomley v Todmorden Cricket Club* [2003] EWCA Civ 1575 where a volunteer assistant at a pyrotechnics display, organised by an independent contractor (allowed by the defendant), suffered severe burns and other injuries. Although not about risk and the state of the premises under the 1957 Act, both the independent contractor and the defendants were held liable in common law negligence (see Bermingham, 2005: 88).

17 See *Wheat v Lacon and Co Ltd* [1966] AC 552 where it was made clear that, where there are two or more occupiers, the nature of the duty may rest on those with the greater degree of control (Bermingham, 2005: 81).

18 See for example, *O'Shea v Royal Borough of Kingston upon Thames* [1995] PIQR 208.

19 In the first instance, educational institutions viewed with concern the judge's decision to hold McConnell Agricultural College liable for the student's spinal injuries, as the college knew that the warnings were regularly flouted. The claimant at that stage of the case was held to be contributorily negligent in relation to his own injuries. As the HC decision was reversed in the Court of Appeal in 1999, and *volenti* accepted, contributory negligence was no longer an issue.

20 See *Scott and Swainger v Associated British Ports* (unreported, 18 March 1999, Queen's Bench Division, Deputy Judge Rafferty) affirmed by *Scott and Swainger v Associated British Ports* (unreported, 22 November 2000, Court of Appeal) (on *Westlaw UK* 1741511, p.1, 26/12/01).

21 Please note that this hypothetical is adapted from the real experience of a young English soccer player who went to work at a soccer camp in the USA. He went out to celebrate with his friends, had a few drinks, trespassed on the disused bridge, fell onto the road below and sustained serious spinal injuries, leading to a lengthy stay in hospital. His insurance was invalidated for two reasons.

22 This principle is taken from *Nabozny v Barnhill* 334 NE 2d 258 (Ill App Ct 1975).

23 Felix (1996: 35) also identifies the same weakness in the Australian case of *Johnston v Frazer* (1990) 21 NSWLR 89.

24 See *Wilks v Cheltenham Homeguard Motor Cycle and Light Car Club* [1971] 1 WLR 668.

25 See *Harrison v Vincent* (1982) RTR 8 (CA).

26 As outlined in the negligence cases of *Bolton v Stone* [1951] AC 850; [1951] 1 All ER 1078; *Gillan v Chief Constable Strathclyde Police and Airdrie Football Club* 1996 RepLR 165.

27 Considering the fact that five or six was considered, by expert witnesses in *Smoldon*, to be 'normal' and 25 to be 'abnormal', it is surprising this issue did not receive much more attention and discussion in the courts or in commentaries on the case.

28 In the professional game, is a front row forward likely to be better trained, fitter and have more specialist techniques, as well as having available sufficient substitutes to replace a front row forward who is injured or sent off? (See Colley and Gordon, 2002.)

29 Law 3 (12) is a safety rule and when a prop is injured and leaves the field, requires the referee to confer with the captain of his team to determine whether another player is suitably trained or experienced to take his position.

4 Sports violence and criminal assault

1 Mr Steve Barker, defence lawyer, quoted in 'Let Sport Deal with Discipline' BBC News online reporting of the CPS Crime in Sport Conference 3 June 2005 at http://news.bbc.co.uk/1/hi/uk/4607153.stm.

2 This case is covered in more detail later in this chapter and, alongside the Offences Against the Person Act 1861, *R v Cey* (1989) 48 CCC (3d) 480, and *R v Ciccarelli* (1989) 54 CCC (3d) 121 on the objective criteria for the boundaries of consent, provides the current guidance on criminal assault on the sports field (with the current situation summarised at the end of *R v (Mark) Barnes* [2004] EWCA Crim 3246; [2005] 1 WLR 910 later in this chapter).

3 Dr Mark James (senior lecturer in law at Manchester Metropolitan University, now at Salford Law school) in a post-graduate lecture to the students on the M.A. in Sport, Leisure and Equity course, core module in 'Socio-Legal Issues in Sport and Leisure', Carnegie Faculty of Sport and Education, Leeds Metropolitan University, March 2005.

4 See *R v Ciccarelli* (1989) 54 CCC (3d) 121.

5 See *R v Cey* (1989) 48 CCC (3d) 480.

6 See *R v Leclerc* (1991) 67 CCC (3d) 563 (CA). This case involved a non-contact recreational hockey league. Following a collision on the boards as two players tried to retrieve the puck, the defendant, Leclerc, hit the other player in the back with his hockey stick. The victim was permanently paralysed from the neck down (Centre for Sport Law, 2002: 2).

7 This took place in a professional hockey game, and as James (2006a: 610) reports there was no injury caused. If this was the case, then there appears to be a lack of *actus reus* (resulting harm) caused by the defendant.

8 Steve Barker quoted in 'Bowyer lawyer condemns court case' BBC News online, 8 June 2005 at http://news.bbc.co.uk/1/hi/england/tyne/4074814.stm.

9 BBC News online at http://news.bbc.co.uk/1/hi/uk/40607153.stm 'Let Sport Deal with Discipline' Crown Prosecution Service Conference on Crime in Sport 3 June 2005.

10 Under s.115 of the Magistrates Court Act 1980 and the Justices of the Peace Act 1361.

11 See *Butcher v Jessop* 1989 SLT 593.

12 See *R v Chan Fook* [1993] EWCA Crim 1; [1994] 1 WLR 689 in Dobson (2005: 79).

13 The authority case for this principle is *R v Savage; R v Parmenter* 1991; [1992] 1 AC 699, two separate appeal cases heard together in the House of Lords. The case involving a s.47 offence, *R v Savage*, was set in a leisure context, and involved a defendant who 'threw a glass of beer at her victim. In the process D lost her grip of the glass itself and cut the victim's wrist' (Dobson, 2005: 81). On appeal the conviction for assault under s.20 was reduced to a s.47 offence, then the defendant appealed

to the House of Lords on the s.47 conviction, saying that she had 'not foreseen that her action might cause any bodily harm' (ibid: 81). The House of Lords dismissed the appeal, and held that for a s.47 offence the prosecution does 'not have to prove that the defendant foresaw the risk of causing some bodily harm' (ibid: 81).

14 See *R v Lincoln* (1990) 12 Cr App R (S) 250.

15 Ibid: 2. The Court of Appeal was also asked to take into account imprisonment already imposed, the effects on his young family and employment and his one year suspension from local league football and the fact that he may have to pay compensation (Westlaw UK, 2004: 2).

16 See *R v Davies* [1991] Crim LR 70.

17 Ibid: 2.

18 Evidence was also heard that Mr Davies 'looked to make sure that the referee was not watching in that direction and therefore would not see it' *R v Davies* [1991] Crim LR 70, Westlaw UK, 2004: 2.

19 See *R v Davies* [1991] Crim LR 70, Westlaw UK, 2004: 3.

20 See *R v Moss* [2000] 1 Cr App R (S) 64, Lawtel, 9/6/2004.

21 See *R v Ahmed* [2002] EWCA Crim 779, Westlaw UK, 2004: 2.

22 See note 9.

23 The EWCA heard that, in relation to the present incident, Mr Ahmed had been banned for five years and fined £500 by the Football Association.

24 See *R v Johnson* (1986) 8 Cr App R (S) 343, WL 406739, p. 1.

25 Ibid: 2.

26 See also [2005] 1 WLR 910 CA Crim Div.

27 After a four-day trial at Canterbury Crown Court (Van Der Bijl J.). Barnes was sentenced on 12 December 2003. He was given a Community Punishment Order for 240 hours and ordered to pay compensation in the sum of £2,609 to the victim, at £20 per week, commencing on 2 January 2004.

28 See *R v (Mark) Barnes* [2004] EWCA Crim 3246; [2005] 1 WLR 910, page 2 of 7.

29 See p. 1. in Case Comment: *R v Barnes* [2004] EWCA Crim 3246 in *International Sports Law Review* (ISLR) 2 (May), 2005, SLR 53–57.

30 *R v (Mark) Barnes* [2004] EWCA Crim 3246; [2005] 1 WLR 910.

31 Ibid: 4, para 21.

32 See p. 5, para 25. Case Comment: *R v Barnes* [2004] EWCA Crim 3246; [2005] 1 WLR 910, CA Crim) in *International Sports Law Review* (ISLR), 2 (May) 2005, 53–57.

33 Ibid: 5, para 28.

34 Ibid: 5, para 30.

35 *R v Brown* [1994] 1 AC 212.

36 *R v McSorley* (unreported, 6 October 2000, British Columbia Provincial Court Criminal Division, Judge William Kitchen) 166 at para 9. See full judgment at www.provincial court.bc.ca/judgments/pc/2000/01/p00_0116.htm.

37 Ibid. *R v McSorley*, cited in 'Violence in sports backgrounder' *Law Connection: Current Issues in Law*. At www.lawconnection.ca/ accessed 14/3/02.

38 This would have quite an impact as both players would normally regularly play each other at the highest level in the National Hockey League.

39 As in the case of *R v Blisset* (1992) The Independent, 4 December earlier in this chapter.

40 This chapter is mainly focusing on charges of assault contrary to s.47, s.20 and s.18 of the Offences Against the Person Act 1861. Chapter 7 will provide an overview of some cases of manslaughter in sport and physical recreation contexts.

5 Discrimination, harassment and child protection

1 See also the Sex Discrimination (Indirect Discrimination Burden of Proof) Regulations 2001, and Sex Discrimination Act 1975 (Amendment) Regulations 2003.

2 For example, everyone in an organisation normally working late on a Friday evening may have a detrimental effect on a young female member of staff with young children (Russell et al., 2008).

3 See for example *Price v Civil Service Commission* [1978] ICR 27.

4 Applied in the case of *Bennet v Football Association* (unreported, 1978, Court of Appeal.

5 Section 42 Sex Discrimination Act 1984, s.66 (1), Equal Opportunity Act 1995 and other anti-discrimination legislation (see Bradford, 2005).

6 See Section 66 (1) of the Equal Opportunity Act 1995 (Victoria). This exception does not apply to sporting activities for children under the age of 12.

7 See Talbot (1988) and McArdle (2000) and McArdle (1996) on the *Bennet* case, among others. Also see in Australia, the cases of *South v Royal Victorian Bowls Association Inc* [2001] VCAT 207; *Ferneley v Boxing Authority of New South Wales* [2001] FCA 1740; *Robertson v Australian Ice Hockey Federation* [1998] VADT 112, cited Bradford (2005: 79).

8 In Australia, s.44 was seen 'not to exempt a rule restricting access to affiliation for a female bowler who wished to play in men-only competitions. This section of the SDA 1975 has been heavily criticised and there have been numerous calls for its repeal' *South v Royal Victoria Bowling Association* [2001] VCAT 207 (see for example, McArdle, 1988; Pannick, 1983, cited Rose and Weir, 2003: 905).

9 A female pool player also won a sex discrimination case in 1991, arising out of the refusal by the Professional Pool Players' Association to 'grant her membership of the PPPA, where membership amounted to the grant of a professional status' (*Thompson v Professional Pool Players' Organisation* (unreported, 1992, Employment Appeal Tribunal, EAT Nos 15898/91 and 47323/91) cited Rose and Weir, 2003: 901).

10 See s.1 (1) of the RRA; read with s.3 (1)–(3) (Rose and Weir, 2003: 896). Welch (2006: 558) notes that the new definition of 'racial group', applied to employees only under s.1 (1A), excludes colour and nationality.

11 Mr Sterling also succeeded in claims of 'victimisation against the club, its managing director and its chief executive on the basis that they had failed properly to investigate his complaint of race discrimination' (Rose and Weir, 2003: 901).

12 Rose and Weir (2003: 898) note that 'progressive conditions such as HIV and cancer may also be covered' whilst some conditions are expressly excluded such as hayfever.

13 Unreported decision of the US Supreme Court of 29 May 2001 (Scalia and Thomas JJ dissenting).

14 See Equality and Human Rights Commission (2008) 'Britain's six million carers get new rights after mother's legal victory in Europe' news section at www.equalityhuman rights.com/en/newsandcomment/Pages/legalvictoryinEurope.aspx, accessed 5/12/08.

15 The case of *R v Lyte* (unreported, November 2007, Liverpool Crown Court, Judge Gilmour), later in this chapter, is very rare.

16 A BBC 1 television programme which reports ongoing cases and seeks assistance from viewers to locate those suspected of criminal offences highlighted in the programme.

17 See Brackenridge and Williams (2004) *New Law Journal* vol. 154, no. 7114: 179–180,

who discuss whether the provisions under the Sexual Offences Act 2003 on, for example, familial child sex offences (s.25–26) should extend to the relationship between sports coaches and child athletes and the nature of familial relationships and living in the same household.

18   The Criminal Records Bureau was set up in 1998.

19   See earlier in this chapter *R v Hickson* (unreported, 27 September 1995, Cardiff Crown Court, Judge Prosser), the former Olympic Games swimming coach who was jailed for 17 years after a jury found him guilty of 15 charges including two of raping teenage swimmers under his charge between 1976 and 1991 (Myers and Barrett, 2002).

20   This decision was later disapproved in a decision where it was held that third-party liability for harassment required the failure to protect the employee to be racially motivated (Welch, 2006: 70).

6 Risk management and breaches of health and safety

1   It may be that remote should go first with the phrase 'almost zero' and improbable is better placed second on the list, with the phrase 'unlikely to occur'.

2   In the film *Chariots of Fire* two elite athletes, who had trained for the event, knew the rules, had not been drinking alcohol and were wearing appropriate attire and shoes, raced around the quad at 12 noon. A sports official was present monitoring and timing the event. Spectators were kept out of the way of the route taken by the two athletes.

3   See, for example, the HSE 2005 investigation into the death of 10-year-old Max Palmer in October 2002 in the final section of this chapter.

4   See RoSPA (2007) *Learning, Sharing and Moving Forwards: Advice Pack for Smaller Firms* Sheets 1–7 available online at www.rospa.com/occupationalsafety/smallfirms/.

5   See HSE press release, 'Principles of sensible risk management' at www.hse.gov.uk/risk/principles.htm, accessed 29/8/07.

6   See 'HSC tells health and safety pedants to "get a life"' statement by Bill Callaghan, Chair of Health and Safety Commission at www.hse.gov.uk/risk/statement.htm. This statement followed a series of stories which claimed that health and safety requirements were stifling various activities and drawing attention away from serious health and safety issues. The HSE website now has examples of the 'Myth of the Month'. These include myths such as 'workers banned from putting up decorations' (November 2007), 'Kids must wear goggles to play conkers' (September 2007), 'Egg boxes banned in craft lessons' (August 2007) and 'HSE has banned stepladders' (April 2007) see www.hse.gov.uk/myth/index.htm (accessed 6/1/08).

7   See Brackenridge et al. 2007 on the changing use of such terms in a broader historical and policy context.

8   See the section on safeguarding children (child protection) in Chapter 5 of this text.

9   See, for example, criminal assault cases in Chapter 4 and manslaughter cases involving players in Chapter 7 of this text.

10 See also QCA 1999 *The National Curriculum Handbook for Primary Teachers in England and Wales, The National Curriculum Handbook for Secondary Teachers in England and Wales, The National Curriculum* website at www.nc.uk.net.

11 See Chapter 3 and Chapter 7 on defences against negligence and manslaughter respectively.

12 See, for example, the research into risk education programmes in schools and universities at www.hse.gov.uk/education/index.htm and the safety education

materials from aged three upwards on the Royal Society for the Prevention of Accidents (RoSPA) website.

13   Some of these are also related to European Health and Safety Directives.

14   Health surveillance might include, for example, 'vibration white finger', forms of work-related upper limb disorder, and work-related stress linked to physical conditions and diseases (see HSE (2004) Management Standards on Work Related Stress).

15   These regulations have been amended by the COSHH (Amendment) Regulations 2004. See *The Control of Substances Hazardous to Health Regulations* (as amended); *Approved Code of Practice and Guidance L5* 5th edn, HSE Books, 2005, ISBN 0 7176 2981 3. See also *COSHH Essentials: Easy Steps to Control Chemicals. Control of Substances Hazardous to Health Regulations* HSG 193 2nd edn, HSE Books, 2003, ISBN 0 7176 2737 3 and an electronic version at www.coshh-essentials.org.uk.

16   Substances hazardous to health under COSHH are listed under the Chemicals (Hazard Information and Packaging for Supply) Regulations 2002 (CHIP) and are usually identified by their warning label and safety data sheet which should be provided by the supplier. See also the HSE publication *Approved Supply List*. Substances with workplace exposure limits listed in the HSE publication EH40/2005 *Workplace Exposure Limits* also come under the COSHH Regulations. Biological agents are included if they are directly connected with work, such as farming sewage treatment, or healthcare, or their exposure is incidental to work (e.g. exposure to bacteria from an air-conditioning system which is not properly maintained, any kind of dust if it exceeds COSHH limits, and any other substance which creates a risk to health, not specifically covered by CHIP) (HSE, *COSHH: A brief guide to the Regulations What you need to know about the Control of Substances Hazardous to Health*, 2002a: 1–2).

17   The HSE and local authorities usually get to know about workplace deaths but employers 'do not report all non-fatal injuries' (TUC, 2007: 291).

18   Major injuries include a fracture other than to fingers, thumbs or toes, any amputation, dislocation of the shoulder, hip, knee or spine, loss of sight, a chemical or hot metal burn to the eye or any penetrating injury to the eye, any injury resulting from an electric shock or electrical burn, leading to unconsciousness or requiring resuscitation or admittance to hospital for more than 24 hours. Major injuries also include any other injuries leading to hypothermia, heat-induced illness or unconsciousness, resuscitation or requiring admittance to hospital for more than 24 hours; loss of consciousness caused by asphyxia or by exposure to a harmful substance or biological agent; acute illness requiring medical treatment or loss of consciousness which result from the absorption of any substance by inhalation, ingestion or through the skin or acute illness which requires medical treatment where there is reason to believe that this resulted from exposure to a biological agent or toxins or infected material (HSE, 2005a: 1). Incident reporting in schools (accidents, diseases and dangerous occurrences), EDIS1 (rev1), 06/05.

19   The Health and Safety Executive (HSE) has an HSE Incident Contact Line and facilities to report online or by e-mail, or post. Please see www.hse.gov.uk/riddor/index.htm.

20   See a full list of dangerous occurrences in *A Guide to the Reporting of Injuries, Diseases and Dangerous Occurrences Regulations 1995*, L73 (2nd edn) HSE Books, 1999, ISBN 0 7176 2431 5. See *RIDDOR explained: Reporting of Injuries, Diseases and Dangerous Occurrences Regulations* 1995, Leaflet HSE31 (rev1) HSE Books, 1999, ISBN 07176 2441 2.

21   This is to allow compliance with the Social Security Act (Claims and Payments) Regulations 1979, the Health and Safety at Work Act 1974, the Social Security Administration Act 1992, RIDDOR Regulations 1995 and the Data Protection Act

1998. The accident book can be purchased from HSE Books, PO Box 1999, Sudbury, Suffolk, CO10 2WA.

22 See The Health and Safety Executive (HSE) first aid website at www.hse.gov.uk/firstaid and the HSE web page for latest information on standards and guidance on first aid at www.hse.gov.uk/firstaid/information.htm. The Trades Union Congress also has a web resource on first aid at www.tuc.org.uk/h_and_s/index.cfm?mins=335.

23 Do staff or students work alone or in remote areas, or go on field trips etc. Are staff and students, working or studying in a lecture theatre, classroom, or going on a day trip or canoeing trip? Does the organisation use shared facilities or unfamiliar sites provided by new partners? What are the patterns of annual leave or staff training? Will annual leave/holidays leave the organisation with gaps in first aid provision? See Assessment of First Aid (Paragraph 3 of the Approved Code of Practice and Paragraph 9 of the Guidance to the Regulations).

24 This means attending an HSE approved training course which normally lasts four or five days.

25 The TUC (2007: 303) advise that this is not the same as a statutory accident book. It can be used for identifying trends, inform future first aid assessments, insurance purposes and investigations.

26 Separation can be achieved either by activities being conducted at separate times on the lake or by the use of physical barriers on the lake (Jamieson, 2003: 86).

27 There were other issues including the 'designing of a novice course which was difficult to steer safely, spectators being allowed in the area, failure to have effective supervision and monitoring and failure to have an effective audible warning device' (Jamieson, 2003: 86).

28 See HSE Public Register of Convictions, Education section, Case no. 2012944, HSE Yorkshire and Humberside Region, 2001. See www.hse.gov.uk/prosecutions, accessed 30 November 2007.

29 See R v University of East Anglia (unreported, 2002, Norwich Magistrates' Court) HSE Prosecutions area case no. 2013535. See www.hse.gov.uk/prosecutions, accessed 30 November 2007.

30 See HSE Register of convictions. Case no. 2016631. See www.hse.gov.uk/prosecutions, accessed 30 November 2007.

31 See HSE Register of Convictions case no. 2014925. See www.hse.gov/uk/prosecutions.

32 For example, the 'use of safety bar locking mechanisms which were designed for domestic doors, failing to lubricate locks properly, using a wrongly shaped key to open the locks, a replace when broken policy on locks, rather than checking for wear and tear, failure to record the history of faulty locks and the Ferris wheel timber frame in a poor state of repair and loose footplates' (BBC News online 'Fine for safety breaches theme park' at http://news.bbc.co.uk/l/hi/england/merseyside/6173328.stm, accessed 30 November 2007.

33 See 'Leisure Firm fined over Asbestos' 1/11/2006 bbc.co.uk cited at www.asbetsostech.com/news.asp, accessed 30 November 2007.

34 The Health and Safety Executive (HSE) published the report of the investigation into the drowning of 10-year-old Max Palmer 'so that lessons may be learnt. The HSE considers that naming people will detract from its learning focus. Therefore apart from the deceased, no individuals are named in the report. Neither is the school' (HSE Press Release E034 'Sharing the Lessons Learnt – HSE Publishes web report on Glenridding school trip tragedy' 9 March 2005).

35 The HSE investigation noted that there were 'no DfES, BAALPE, LEA or school

policies or guidance on attendance by non-pupils (other than relating to insurance). It has been suggested that many teachers could not help on visits unless they took their own children. It is an area of considerable ambiguity' (HSE, 2005c: 16). The HSE highlight points that those in charge of educational visits may wish to consider. Bringing additional children may bring conflicts of responsibility, have consequences for supervision levels and risk assessment, due to the implications of different ages or experience and LEAs and schools are strongly advised to have a policy on leaders and helpers bringing additional children on educational visits (ibid: 16).

7 An overview of selected manslaughter cases

1   See the tests for negligence in Chapter 2 and the tests of gross negligence manslaughter in for example, *Adomako* CA 1994 or *Misra* CA 2004.
2   This principle is from the judgment in *R v Church* [1966] 1 QB 59.
3   Molan et al. (2003) raised doubts around the nature of the unlawful act in *Newbury*. The case 'proceeded on the basis that they had committed an unlawful act, but it is not obvious exactly what it was, unless it was the act of dropping the stone' (ibid: 199). Was it a property offence, criminal damage, or a breach of various railway bye-laws? Molan et al. (2003: 199) were of the view that 'criminal damage is a more obvious candidate'.
4   'Under the supervision of Dr Barry Sullman (a house officer), Dr Michael Prentice (a pre-registration house officer) injected vincristine (which should have been given intravenously) into the patient's cerebrospinal fluid, instead of methotrexate. It appears that Dr Sullman misunderstood his role, and believed himself to be supervising only the lumbar puncture, while Dr Prentice believed his colleague to be supervising the overall procedure of administering cytoxic medication. The boy died two weeks later' (Merry and McCall Smith, 2001: 20). Both doctors were convicted of manslaughter but were cleared by the Court of Appeal in 1993. The test of gross negligence (rather than recklessness) was used by the Court of Appeal.
5   However, the location of the Lyme Bay canoe tragedy (the key case later in this chapter), between *Seymour* and *Sullman* (1993) and *Adomako* [1994] 3 All ER 79. In the manslaughter case arising out of the 1993 Lyme Bay canoe tragedy *R v Kite, R v Stoddart, R v OLL Ltd* (unreported, 9 December 1994, Winchester Crown Court, Ognall J) the prosecution appears to be using the offence of reckless (involuntary) manslaughter. A person acts recklessly with respect to 'a) a circumstance, when he is aware of a risk that it exists or will exist; and b) as a result, when he is aware of a risk that will occur, and it is unreasonable, having regard to the circumstances known to him, to take that risk' (Molan et al., 2003: 78), drawing on the proposed 1989 draft Criminal Code and Law Commission definition of reckless (Law Commission 177, cl 18 c). The prosecution in *R v Kite and others* were seeking to prove that the defendants behaved recklessly and created a serious and obvious risk of injury or death.
6   This is adapted from a real hazing (initiation) incident in a sport context in the United States.
7   See the key case later in this chapter *R v Kite, R v Stoddart, R v OLL Ltd* (unreported, 9 December 1994, Winchester Crown Court, Ognall J).
8   See *R v Northern Strip Mining*, The Times, 2, 4, 5 February 1965 (see Wells, 1995: 169) and also an earlier case *R v Cory Brothers and Co Ltd* [1927] 1 KB 810).

9   See *MV Herald of Free Enterprise, Report of Court no. 8074* Department of Transport, 1987. Mr J Sheen.

10 The seven defendants were two former Townsend directors, Wallace Ayers and Jeffrey Develin, deputy chief marine superintendent John Alcindor, senior master John Kirkby, Captain David Lewry, first officer Leslie Sabel and assistant bosun Mark Stanley. A guilty verdict against Ayers and Devlin would have been enough for corporate manslaughter against the company.

11 The Crown Prosecution Service (CPS) was originally considering a charge of murder, but this was later changed to manslaughter.

12 In 1986 Supt George Crawford, who was also an experienced rugby union referee, warned that someone would be killed if severe action was not taken in relation to foul play, particularly punching. See details of his televised protest as a referee, when players continued to punch each other instead of playing rugby, during a Welsh rugby union match in 1985, outlined earlier in Chapter 4 of this text.

13 James (2001) comments on the difficulty of distinguishing between genuine self-defence and retaliation:

> Retaliation would appear to be inconsistent with self-defence. The former is an intentional battery, whilst the latter is a lawful act committed because of apprehension of danger to oneself. In the heat of the moment it is hard enough for the referee to do this, let alone a jury months after the incident has occurred. The argument then becomes whether the players are consenting to violent responses to violent play or acting in legitimate self-defence. The former is illegal, the latter is not.
>
> (2001: 765–766)

14 'Sons watched mother's beach death' BBC News online, 21 September 2004 http://news.bbc.co.uk/1/hi/england/lancashire/3677788.stm, accessed 12/2/05.

15 See BBC News online 'Ferry worker denies death charges' 30 March, 2007 http://news.bbc.co.uk/1/hi/england/hampshire/6310205.stm and Centre for Corporate Accountability website press releases www.corporateaccountability.org/press.htm.

16 'The Horse Pond at Aldershot was placed out of bounds for all training and suitable warning notices were erected soon after this tragic accident' (BBC News Friday 12 July, 2002 'Sergeant "scapegoat" for pond death', http://news.bbc.co.uk/1/hi/england/2117562.stm.

17 The Ministry of Defence had immunity from prosecution for manslaughter.

18 'Man in Court over Caving Death' BBC News online, 25 February 2003 see http://news.bbc.co.uk/1/hi/wales/2795795.stm.

19 See 'Instructor cleared over death' BBC News online, http://news.bbc.co.uk/1/hi/wales/south_west/3543741.stm, accessed 22/7/07.

20 See http://web.lexis-nexis.com/executive 25/11/04.

21 'Teacher jailed over drowned boy' BBC News online, 23 September, 2003 http://news.bbc.co.uk/1/hi/england/lancashire/3132102.stm.

22 See 'Ruling on school trip death', *Birmingham Post* 16 July 2004, http://web.lexis-nexis.com/executive.

23 This marine rocket was 'designed to reach an altitude of 1,000ft in six seconds'. The court heard that sports ground safety legislation did not expressly forbid the taking of flares into matches (*The Guardian* 27 May 1994).

24 Mr Junta apparently 'became incensed because the coach was allowing too much physical contact between the children on the rink. Moreover, his son was allegedly elbowed in the face by another boy as he left the ice' Usborne (2002).

25 Prosecutors told the court that Mr Junta 'repeatedly punched Michael Costin in his head area and then intentionally took his head and hit it into the floor of the arena' (Sheila Calkins, prosecuting):

> Mr Junta, who is a very large and burly man, mercilessly pinned down the coach, who was lighter than him and set about his head. Mr Costin, who was 6ft 1in tall but slight of frame, died after an artery near his spine, ruptured and filled his spinal cavity with blood.
>
> (Prosecution arguments, cited Usborne, 2002)

26 Normally one would expect involuntary manslaughter to be reserved or used for those who cause the death of another human being in the course of a lawful activity – for example, taking part in a sport competition – but engaging in it in such a dangerous or reckless manner as to make it criminal or unlawful. A fight between two adults which is not part of a lawful sport activity would be expected to be labelled as an unlawful act or constructive manslaughter.

27 See 'Hockey dad gets 6–10 years for fatal beating' CNN.com law news at http://archives.cnn.com/2002/LAW/01/25/hockey.death.verdict/index.htm.

28 See Fred Attewill and agencies 'Boys found guilty over stoning death' *The Guardian* 31 August, 2007: 1 at www.guardian.co.uk, accessed 1/9/07.

29 Central Criminal Court (The Old Bailey) London, 30 August 2007. They were later acquitted on appeal in Spring 2008, around issues of proof of causation.

30 See also the private prosecutions brought by the Hillsborough Family Support Group arising out of the 1989 Hillsborough Football Stadium Disaster. See *R v Duckenfield*, *R v Murray* (unreported, July 2001, Leeds Crown Court, Hooper J) in Hartley, 2001b: 169–179. The jury returned a verdict of 'not guilty' on Mr Bernard Murray the deputy match commander on the day of the 1989 Hillsborough Disaster. There was a hung jury (and no retrial) in the case of David Duckenfield, who had been the match commander on the day of the 1989 Hillsborough Football Disaster, at Sheffield Wednesday Football Ground.

31 'Based on the trebuchet used in the Middle Ages to hurl rocks and dead animals over castle walls during sieges, the device uses a form of lead weight to give a see saw effect and propel the volunteers into the air' [and land in a safety net, rather like a smaller version of those nets placed under a trapeze at a circus] (Bruxelles 2004: 11).

32 This ruling came at the end of the prosecution case where Hallet J said that 'she was satisfied that, from the prosecution evidence at its highest, "no reasonable jury could properly convict" and that "the prosecution evidence simply does not come close enough to prove such a grave criminal offence"' (Morgan, 2004: endnote ii).

33 See the Centre for Corporate Accountability www.corporateaccountability.org/press_releases/2004/feb12.htm.

34 BBC News online, 'Court drops manslaughter charges' March 11 2005, http://news.bbc.co.uk/1/hi/england/cumbria/4340159.stm.

35 The Health and Safety Executive (HSE) provides guidance setting out sensible health and safety precautions via the HSE legionnaires website. Practices can be compared with the Approved Code of Practice and Guidance on controlling legionella. See www.hse.gov.uk.

36 Note the date of the incident and the trial. It is in 1993 in advance of CA cases of *Adomako* in 1994 and *Mistra* in 2004 and therefore is located in an era where the law on the meaning of manslaughter, it could be argued, was very unclear.

37 See earlier commentary in this chapter on corporate manslaughter and the collapse of the corporate manslaughter trial of P&O European Ferries in October 1990.

38 See 'Safety "very low" at centre' *The Guardian* 25 November, 1994: 14.
39 See 'Boss admits canoe trip was reckless' *The Guardian* 1 December, 1994: 6.
40 See Bowcott, O. (1994) 'Boss admits canoe trip was reckless' *The Guardian* 1 December, 1994: 6.
41 At the time there was no statutory regulation or any registration scheme for private outdoor activity centres.
42 See Court, C. (1994) 'Canoeing trip instructor not qualified to lead the party' *Western Morning News* 18 December, 1994: 5.
43 See 'Fatal canoe trip left expert staggered' *The Guardian* Saturday 26 November, 1994: 13.
44 In fact the winds that day were *offshore*, a very significant risk factor which will be discussed later in the manslaughter trial.
45 See Bowcott, O. (1994) 'Boss admits canoe trip was reckless' *The Guardian* Thursday December 1, 1994: 6).
46 See 'Head of firm in Lyme Bay canoe tragedy says he is blameless' *The Guardian* 2 December 1994: 6).
47 See Midgely, S. (1994) 'Errors and inexperience cost four young lives' *The Independent* 9 December, 1994: 6.
48 See Court, C. (1994) 'Supervisors in canoe tragedy inappropriate' *Western Morning News* 26 November, 1994: 2).
49 See 'Basic mistakes led to tragedy at sea' *The Guardian* 9 December, 1994: 3.
50 See Midgley. S. (1994) 'Errors and inexperience cost four young lives' *The Independent* 9 December, 1994: 6.
51 See 'The guy in charge has flares and stuff: What tragedy boss allegedly told coastguard' *The Daily Mail* Wednesday 26 November, 1994: 30.
52 See 'Basic mistakes led to tragedy at sea' *The Guardian* 9 December, 1994: 3.
53 See 'Serious breach of rules in canoe deaths' *The Guardian* 23 November, 1994: 3.
54 See 'Canoe trip victims lost lesson in survival' *The Daily Mail* 26 November, 1994: 3.
55 See 'Basic mistakes led to tragedy at sea' *The Guardian* 9 December, 1994: 3.
56 See 'When the waves came we all lifted our heads' *Western Morning News* 18 December, 1994: 6.
57 See 'Urgent action urged to prevent repeat of disaster after jailing of managing director for manslaughter' dossier of mistakes and delays *The Independent* 9 December, 1994: 6 and 'Basic mistakes led to tragedy at sea' *The Guardian* 9 December, 2007: 3.
58 This was later reduced to two years by the Court of Appeal on 8 February 2007.
59 See Midgley, S. (1994) 'Boss jailed over canoe deaths' *The Independent* 9 December, 1994: 1.
60 See Bowcott, O. (1994) 'Director is jailed for canoe deaths' *The Guardian* 9 December, 1994: 1.
61 See Dyer, C. (1994) 'Ruling makes history and opens door for prosecution of more companies' *The Guardian* 9 December 1994: 1.
62 See Midgley, S. (1994) 'Boss jailed over canoe deaths' *The Independent* 9 December, 1994: 1.
63 See Bowcott, O. (1994) 'Director is jailed for canoe deaths' *The Independent* 9 December, 1994: 1.
64 See Midgley, S. (1994) 'Boss is jailed over canoe deaths' *The Independent* 9 December, 1994: 1.
65 See Bowcott, O. (1994) 'Urgent action urged to prevent repeat of disaster after jailing managing director for manslaughter' *The Guardian* 9 December, 1994: 3.

66 See Midgley, S. (1993) 'Taking risks with recreation' *The Independent* 9 December, 1993: 18.
67 See Benson, A. (1993) 'Canoe tragedy inquiry calls for regulation of outdoor centres' *The Guardian* 30 July, 1993: 3.
68 The St Alban's activity centre brochure listed pages on qualified instructors and high safety standards. At the time there were no standardised, legally binding statutory regulation of outdoor activity centres.
69 This made the HSE the 'Adventure Activities Licensing Authority, with responsibility for implementing the Adventure Licensing Regulations'. Although many of the operational aspects were contracted out to the TQS the latter now operates 'on behalf of the Licensing Authority rather than *as* the Licensing Authority' Interim Notice, Marcus Bailie, Head of Inspections, The Adventure Activities Licensing Service, 44 Lambourne Crescent, Cardiff Business Park, Llanishen, Cardiff CF 14 5GG. Website www.aala.org.uk.

8 Natural justice principles

1 See, for example, the Michelle Smith case in this chapter at the 1996 Atlanta Summer Olympics in Beloff (1996) and the case of Evi Sachenbacher-Stehle at the 2006 Winter Olympics in Torino, Italy (see Zagklis, 2006: 47).
2 See, for example, the cases of Diane Modahl, Alain Baxter and Sandra Gasser in this chapter.
3 See, for example, the cases of *Jones v Welsh Rugby Union* [1997] EWCA Civ 3066; and Lee Bowyer and Kieron Dyer in 2005 in Chapter 4 (Gardiner, 2005). In 2007 the manager of the English football team Queen's Park Rangers, Richard Hill, was suspended by the club and arrested on suspicion of actual bodily harm, after he was pictured aiming a punch at a member of the visiting Chinese Olympic football team. The victim, Zheng Tao, was knocked unconscious and suffered a broken jaw (Cass and Barlow, 2007: 74).
4 For example, in February 2007, the Luton Football Club manager, Mike Newell, was fined £6,500 for his sexist comments about assistant referee Amy Rayner, made at a match in November 2006. He is reported to have said 'This is Championship football. This is not park football, so what are women doing here? It is tokenism, for the politically correct idiots. She should not be here. I know that sounds sexist, but I am sexist, so I am not going to be anything other than that. We have a problem in this country with political correctness, and bringing women into the game is not the way to improve refereeing and officialdom'. Mr Newell was fined £5,000 for his specific comments about Rayner and also £1,500 for 'failing to act in the best interests of the game', see 'FA fine Newell for his female linesman jibe' *Daily Mail* 14 February 2007: 74.
5 Kevin Ratcliffe, a coach to the Chester City FC youth squad, was disciplined by his employers for racist comments about a young black football player on the team. This was also the subject of an employment tribunal and civil case (see *Hussaney v Chester City FC and Ratcliffe* (unreported, 15 January 2001, Employment Appeal Tribunal, EAT/203/908, Charles J)).
6 See for example *Keighley RFC v Cunningham* (unreported, 1960) in this chapter.
7 See for example *Jones v Welsh Rugby Union* [1997] EWCA Civ 3066; in Rose and Albertini, 1997; Boyes, 2006.
8 See for example *Modahl v British Athletics Federation Ltd* [2001] EWCA Civ 1447; [2002] 1 WLR 1192.

9   See *Jones v Welsh Rugby Union* [1997] EWCA Civ 3066 in Rose and Albertini 1997; Boyes, 2006.

10 If a sports governing body or club provides an informal grievance process, then, ideally, it should be incorporated into the club policy or constitution, and local officers provided with appropriate training and support.

11 It is partly for these reasons that sports governing bodies tend to provide only formal disciplinary hearings, usually staffed by appropriately experienced volunteers, operating at board level or who sit on a national technical committee. In contrast, large professional organisations or institutions, with appropriate staff resources and training, have traditionally provided an informal grievance procedure.

12 For example, any rules of confidentiality, expectations of behaviour in the meeting. Will both parties be in the room at the same time or heard separately? Can a friend, union or legal representative attend the hearing? If so, what is their role? What happens if one of the parties or someone on the panel is intimidated or threatened in any way, prior to, or during the disciplinary hearing? What is the procedure for dealing with such matters?

13 In professional sports which are well resourced, such as soccer, it is common to find one main disciplinary tribunal, sitting perhaps for three days each week. In a much smaller voluntary organisation, with limited resources, depending on volunteers, panels may differ from case to case, presenting a greater challenge for consistency across panels in the conduct of hearings and application of the rules regarding penalties etc.

14 See www.sportsdisputes.co.uk.

15 Gulland (1995: 10) made these comments in relation to the civil litigation cases brought against the International Amateur Athletics Federation (IAAF) by the athletes in the USA, Butch Reynolds and Randy Barnes, following hearings by their domestic track and field governing bodies. Those cases began in their home towns where, Gulland (1995: 10) suggests:

> they or their lawyers, believed that those courts would have a special sympathy for a local hero appearing on the stand, alone against the faceless, distant, international federation, located abroad.

16 See Beloff 1996, who served on this AHD panel, and provided an overview of the work of the AHD at the 1996 Atlanta Summer Olympic Games. This includes the Michelle Smith (Irish Swimmer) eligibility case, the appeal by a Mr Andrade against the Cape Verde's decision to exclude him from the Olympic Village and from the heats of the 110m hurdles, following an incident in the Opening Ceremony. The AHD also heard an appeal brought by a French boxer (Mendy) and the IABA challenging a decision to disqualify him for a low blow. Since the AHD does not deal with any purely technical matters, the AHD panel decided that this matter was 'non-justiciable'. The most publicised case was that of the Russian swimmer, Korneev, and a Russian wrestler, Gouliev, who challenged 'the decision to strip them of their bronze medals for use of the drug Bromantan' – allegedly classed as a stimulant and 'prohibited by the Rules of the IOC and the Medical Code' (Beloff, 1996: 7–8).The AHD panel referred to the 'overriding importance of the fight against doping in sports' and that 'the offence was one of strict liability' (ibid: 8).

17 This included the well-publicised case of the gold medal winner in snowboarding, Ros Rebagliati, who was appealing against the decision to strip him of his gold medal, following a positive test for marijuana. The CAS AHD panel found that:

> under the Medical Code, that the IOC had no competency to disqualify Rebagliati

in the absence of the requisite agreement the IOC and the international skiing federation (FIS) to provide for tests for cannabinoids (marijuana and hashish). The CAS further found that marijuana was not listed as a banned substance in the Drug Formulatory Guide that had been published for athletes participating in the Nagano Games

(Nafziger, 2004a: 44)

18 See Zagklis (2006) on the CAS AHD at the XX Olympic Winter Games in Turin. There were nine cases, mostly to do with eligibility issues. One unusual and interesting application was that of the German cross-country skier Evi Sachenbacher-Stehle. The FIS filed a 'Notification to Start Prohibition' which followed a blood screening/ testing showing 'haemoglobin levels above the maximum tolerated values' and Ms Sachenbacher-Stehle could not start any competitions for five consecutive days, which meant she would miss her first event (Zagklis, 2006: 47).

The athlete further asked the panel to declare that the levels of haemoglobin were naturally elevated and had no connection with any haematological disease. The Panel refused to make a medical expert's judgment and dismissed the case.

(ibid: 47)

19 See Blackshaw, I. (2006b) 'Another First for the Court of Arbitration for Sport' *International Sports Law Journal* 3–4, p.121. At FIFA's request the CAS created a new AHD to settle disputes arising during the tournament. AHD members were not on site, but could be flown in if necessary and any dispute aimed to be settled within 48 hours (ibid: 121). However, no cases were referred to the AHD during the World Cup, although Blackshaw (2006: 121) suggests that the aftermath of an infamous incident of the head butting of the Italian player, Materazzi, by another player Zidane, 'may result later in an application to the CAS being made under its normal proceedings'.

20 Nafziger (2004b: 5–6) reports that the Australian Olympic Committee (AOC) was 'concerned of possible claims of unfairness at the Sydney Games and asked CAS for an advisory opinion'. The CAS had to consider the compliance of FINA with their own rules and any possible reviewable issues of unfair procedure. CAS held that 'FINA had reached its decision in compliance with its own rules and that its ruling, which was tantamount to approval of bodysuits, did not raise any reviewable issues of unfair procedure, bad faith, conflict with general principles of law, or unreasonableness' (ibid: 7).

21 See Eason, K. (2008) 'Amputee sprinter Oscar Pistorius allowed to compete in Beijing' *The Times* online 17 May 2008: 1, accessed 25/7/08.

22 See Matthieu Reeb Secretary General, CAS Press Release 'Athletics – Case Oscar Pistorius v IAAF. The CAS Hearing is Over – final decision expected in mid May' at www.tas-cas.org, accessed 1 May 2008.

23 See 'Oscar Pistorius banned from the Olympics' *The Times* online, 14 January 2008, accessed 25/7/08.

24 See CAS (2008) 'Athletics – Case Oscar Pistorius v IAAF. The Appeal filed by Oscar Pistorius upheld by the Court of Arbitration for Sport' 16 May at www.tas-cas.org, accessed 20 May 2008.

25 See *Modahl v British Athletics Federation Ltd* [2001] EWCA Civ 1447; [2002] 1 WLR 1192. See also Blackshaw, 2001: 3–4; Hartley, 2004.

26 See the CAS website at www.tas-cas.org.

27 For example see *Modahl v British Athletics Federation Ltd* [2001] EWCA Civ 1447; [2002] 1 WLR 1192 discussed later in this chapter, or *Gasser v Stinson and Another*

(unreported, 15 June 1988, Queen's Bench Division, Scott J) also discussed later in this chapter.

28 For example, note the case of Ros Rebagliati at the 1998 Winter Olympic Games in Nagano, Japan. He tested positive for cannabis and although he won his appeal to the CAS AHD at the Games, the criminal laws of Japan could also have been applied.

29 The allegations against the four included 'providing anabolic steroids, human growth hormone, erythroprotein, or EPO, modafinil and other drugs to a number of track and field athletes, as well as top names from baseball and American football' as well as 'misbranding drugs with intent to defraud and money laundering' (Knight, 2004: 1). Korchemny also coached USA athlete Kelli White, who tested positive for modafinil at the 2004 World Championships. Four of the Oakland Raiders football players also failed tests for THG, which was discovered when an anonymous coach is said to have sent a sample of the drug in a syringe to the United States Anti-Doping Agency (USADA) (ibid: 1).

30 A 'marker' is a compound, group of compounds or biological parameters that indicates the use of a Prohibited Substance or Prohibited Method (Definitions section of the WADA Code, 2007). A 'metabolite' is any substance produced by a biotransformation process (Definition section of the WADA Code, 2007).

31 Alina Kabaeva, a Russian rhythmic gymnast, tested positive for a prohibited substance, 'Furesomide', at a random doping control test at the Goodwill Games in Brisbane, Australia, in August 2001. After the 'A' test result the Russian Federation carried out tests on the new 'hyper' pills bought by Kabaeva's coach on the internet and supplied to her and found that they did contain fluresomide. The FIG did not advise Kabaeva of the date and time of the sample B test and their own rules were based on fault, as opposed to strict liability. The FIG banned Kabaeva for one year, followed by a year's suspension on probation. In addition, her results were annulled from the 2001 World Championships. After the FIG rejected that her appeal, Kabaeva appealed to the CAS who dismissed her appeal (TAS 2002/A/386 23 January 2003). a) Even though a federation may have fault liability rules if the objective elements of the offence are established, that is the doping test has been carried out properly, then an athlete is presumed to be guilty; b) the panel found that Kabaeva could not prove that she was without fault; c) the FIG breached its own rules by failing to inform the athlete of the date and time of the B sample test but 'the objective elements of the doping offence were established without the need to rely on the results of the doping test'. In the circumstances the CAS panel found that a 12-month suspension and 12-month probation were adequate and appropriate (Sport Law Cases Index 2003, *Sport and the Law Journal* 11, 2, 174–176).

32 Article 10.5 only applies to the imposition of a sanction of ineligibility, since the violation itself still stands (WADA Code 2007: 30).

33 This is by no means a straightforward defence. See *International Rugby Board v Keyter* (unreported, 13 October 2006, Court of Arbitration for Sport, CAS 2006/A/1067), 'Sport and Law Journal Reports 12, *Sport and the Law Journal* 14, (3): 117–118.

34 Michelle Verroken, director of Drug Free Sport, speaking on the panel at the British Association for Sport and Law seminar in 2004 see Kelham, A. (2004).

35 On the matter of harmonisation or conflict between sport (doping) rules and human rights or EC rules, see the discussion later in this chapter on rules and harmonisation, where commentators predict that even if strict liability rules are seen as harsh or even unfair they are still likely to be seen through a policy lens and be regarded as HRA compliant.

36 On 21 March 2002, the Disciplinary Commission of the IOC upheld the proposal to disqualify him and remove his bronze medal and diploma. Mr Baxter appealed to CAS which held a panel in London, England on 5–6 September 2002. The FIS suspended Mr Baxter for three months and although he did not challenge the length of the suspension, he challenged the manner of calculating the three-month period.

37 At some stage in the various proceedings related to this case, the makers of the Vicks inhaler, Proctor and Gamble, provided evidence which stated that this substance was not performance enhancing. This however, was irrelevant, as in the case of *Raducan* at the 2000 Summer Olympics in Sydney it was held that 'the governing body did not have to prove the existence of a performance-enhancing effect' (Flint et al., 2003: 955).

38 As Flint et al. (2003: 955) point out, that in the case of *Raducan v International Olympic Committee* (unreported, 28 September 2000, Court of Arbitration for Sport, CAS ad hoc Division OG 00/011) it was held that 'the governing body did not have to prove the existence of a performance-enhancing effect'.

39 This was the conclusion in the case of *Aanes v FINA* (unreported, 9 July 2001, Court of Arbitration for Sport, CAS 2001/A/317A), which Baxter was trying to challenge. The CAS panel in *Aanes* was trying to balance two issues and decided that:

> the interests of the athlete concerned in not being punished without being guilty must give way to the fundamental principle that all competitors must have equal chances.
>
> (pp. 16–17)

40 Nicholson (2004: 5) observes that this is entirely consistent with previous decisions of CAS, including *USA Shooting and Quigley v IUT* (unreported, 13 May 1995, Court of Arbitration for Sport, CAS 94/129) where CAS commented that even in the fight against doping requires strict rules 'the rule-makers themselves must begin by being strict with themselves'. The CAS panel alluded to the importance of rules being predictable, adopted through constitutions from authorised bodies, transparent and understood by all.

41 During the Rugby Football League disciplinary process appeal by the player Ryan Hudson against a two-year suspension by the Rugby Football League in 2005, it appeared that the RFL had not actually formally incorporated the WADA code into their constitution (Richard Cramer and Oliver Marns 'Sports Law – A Practitioners View' visiting lecture to the MA in Sport, Leisure and Equity course, socio-legal studies module, in the Carnegie Faculty of Sport and Education, Leeds Metropolitan University, 14 February 2006).

42 Sandra Gasser, a 1500m competitor in the World Championships in Rome, had a positive dope test for an anabolic steroid. In arguments the strict liability rule was criticised and it was argued that 'a rule which did not allow the athlete to even try to establish his or her moral innocence, either in resisting conviction or in mitigation of sentence, was unreasonable and unjustifiable'. However, Scott. J concluded that 'in the circumstances the restraints were reasonable' (Beloff, 2001: 45). See *Gasser v Stinson and Another* (unreported, 15 June 1988, Queen's Bench Division, Scott J), transcript, paras 8F–G. Following a four-year ban the British field athlete, Paul Edwards:

> brought a claim against the BAF and the IAAF for a declaration that the decision to ban him for four years was contrary to Article 6, 59–66 of the Treaty of Rome. His argument was based on the fact that athletes from other countries would only receive a two-year ban because their national legislation would not allow longer

bans and accordingly that the BAF and the IAAF treatment of him was contrary to various Convention Rights, namely the right to a fair trial and discrimination by nationality. Lightman J. held that the decision of the BAF and the IAAF did not come under this EC law because these rules merely regulated sporting conduct and sporting rules would only be covered by EC law where the rules affect 'an economic activity'.

(Sithamparanathan and Schillings, 2003: 138)

43 Chambers had just made the 100m qualifying time for Beijing the previous weekend and the day of the judgment was at the time of the final decisions of the BOA selection panel.

44 Jacques Rogges, the president of the IOC, vowed to exclude from future Olympics, those federations which fail to observe these regulations. English sports lawyer Nick Bitel criticised such penalties explaining that 'most legal systems in the world abhor this kind of penalty clause, and that more particularly the English courts would be unhappy with this rule' (Cairns, 2003: 119). In addition, Michelle Verroken, director of the anti-doping directorate of UK Sport at the time, who had worked hard to evolve this code, also voiced her reservations:

> Athletes are already concerned about the use of data relating to them. We are strictly governed within the EU, but for it to be conveyed to WADA, as it must be under the Code, it falls under different legislation where it may be difficult to guarantee security. How long can it be kept? Who is able to access it? We don't know.
>
> (ibid: 119)

45 'The USFSA found that she was either involved in the assault or that she knew about it and failed to prevent it, that she failed to notify authorities or that she made false statements about what she knew about of the attack' Janofsky (1994) 'Harding's lawyers prepare strategy', and 'Official says Harding should skate', *New York Times* February, cited in Nafziger (2004a: 83).

46 Nafziger (2004a: 84–85) points out that such a lawsuit raises questions around how a sports governing body might avoid or otherwise respond to such a litigation on the eve of a major competition, when it obviously does not have time to take effective action. See Nafziger (2004a: 85) for changes to the Amateur Sports Act in 1998, which bans injunctions against the USOC within 21 days of the start of a new major competition, as well as encouraging mediation as the preferred route, assisted by the appointment of an ombudsman who is able to mediate disputes (see also Findlay and Corbett, 2002, on Canadian research and developments around domestic arbitration of eligibility issues prior to a major Olympic Games).

9 Legal reform on offences against the person

1 The activities included 'hitting a man's penis with a ruler and holding his testicles in a spiked glove; the application of stinging nettles to the genitals of another man; the dripping of hot wax into someone's urethra and multitudinous incidents of branding, hitting, whipping and flogging' (see McArdle, 1995: 3).

2 The normal general test would be used for recklessness: whether the defendant took the risk of injury of which he was aware, and in the circumstances it was unreasonable for him/her to take that risk. The Law Commission suggested that the reasonableness of a defendant is influenced by the fact that injury occurs in sports and games and may also be influenced by other matters such as:

1 Was the injury inflicted in the course of play, as opposed to after play had ceased or 'off-the-ball'.
2 Where injury is inflicted in the course of play a party will be reckless if he/she takes an unreasonable risk, bearing in mind the requirements of the game, the general expectations of the person playing it, and the ease with which he could have achieved his aim within the game by other means.
3 In assessing whether the player's conduct has been reckless, the conformity of his/her conduct to the rules of the game, if the court judges those rules to be reasonable, will be persuasive but not conclusive as to the reasonableness of his conduct.

(LCCP, 1995: 67, para 46.1)

3 See the Accessories and Abettors Act 1861. 'Whosoever shall aid, abet, counsel or procure the commission of any [offence] . . . shall be liable to be tried, indicted and punished as a principal offender' (Law Commission, 1995: 170, para 12.53).
4 Farrell (1996: 10) notes that 'no reference is made to spectators in a sport context (as in *Coney*) and it would seem sensible to restrict liability to organisers'.
5 See also Gunn and Omerod (1995: 181, 183).
6 'The appellants had been convicted of grievous bodily harm on the victims, but they were acquitted on appeal on the grounds that the trial judge should have allowed their defence – that they had not foreseen that really serious injury would result – to go before a jury even though "if this jury had been given the opportunity of considering this defence they would have had little difficulty in rejecting it"' (1986) 83 Cr App R 379 (per McCowan J.) in McArdle, (1995: 11).
7 See BBC News (2008) '"Beasting" death soldiers cleared' Monday 4 August, 2008 at http://news.bbc.co.uk/1/hi/england/wiltshire/7532516.stm, accessed 5/8/08.

Three soldiers have been cleared of manslaughter of a junior colleague at barracks in Wiltshire. Pte Gavin Williams, 22, of Hengoed, Caerphilly, collapsed and died at Lucknow Barracks in Tidworth in 2006. Sgt Russell Price, 45, Sgt Paul Blake, 37, and Cpl John Edwards, 42, were found not guilty by a jury at Winchester Crown Court. The court heard that Pte Williams died after being made to do an informal punishment known as beasting. During the trial the prosecution alleged Pte Williams was put through an intense session of physical exercise, or beasting, to punish him for his drunken high jinks. The soldier, of the Second Battallion the Royal Welsh Regiment, collapsed and died on one of the hottest days in 2006. He was admitted to hospital where tests showed his body temperature was 41.7C, higher than the norm of 37C.

(BBC News, 4 August, 2008: 1)

8 In the UK there have been regular reports in the media of young boys in informal groups taking part in high risk activities or 'dares' such as lift surfing, fire engine surfing, train surfing and running across railway tracks or experimenting with 'parkour' or 'city running' stunts, or tombstoning off cliffs into shallow water and posting such activities on various internet sites.
9 Doleschal (2000: 16) reports that students and coaches in a Wisconsin school were 'charged with sexual assault as a result of sexually related behaviour that occurred during a hazing incident' laws which are useful in states 'with inadequate hazing laws'.
10 These have now been reduced to six criteria (see www.sportengland.org).
11 There are now eight criteria for recognition of a *sports governing body*. These are: 1. The sport activity must be already recognised. 2. There is no other governing body (recognised or unrecognised) that could better govern and develop the sport

(uniqueness). 3. There is UK/GB support from representative groups. 4. It is sustainable, established for a minimum of two years, with evidence of a signed constitution and AGM minutes. 5. Affiliation to an international governing body for the sport. 6. Governance Structure – appropriate constitution and statement on anti-doping, child protection and equity have been formally adopted by the governing body. 7. Significant membership has been demonstrated. 8. Influence and control. Demonstration of reasonable influence and control, for example, in terms of rule governance and the training and education of coaches and officials.

12 It is worth pointing out that Bledsoe et al. (2006) partly explained this by the significant developments in the rules of MMA competitions in the United States since its introduction in 1993 and the fact that most MMA fights conclude with a technical knockout followed by a tap out. The 'lower knockout rate in MMA, compared to boxing may help prevent brain injury in MMA events' (Bledsoe et al., 2006, cited in Timmins, 2007). It is not clear if there have been similar developments in rules used in MMA events in the United Kingdom.

13 For other examples see www.telegraph.co.uk/arts/main.jhtml?xml=/arts/2008/04/25/nosplit/bvtv25last.

14 See for example www.clubmark.org.uk and the Child Protection in Sport Unit CPSU at www.thecpsu.org.uk.

15 See House of Commons Home Affairs and Work and Pensions Committee *Draft Corporate Manslaughter Bill First Joint Session 2005–06 Vol 1Report* London: The Stationery Office Ltd HC 540–1 20 December 2005. Also see Home Affairs and Work and Pensions Committees *Draft Corporate Manslaughter Bill Written Evidence* HC 540–11. London: The Stationery Office Ltd.

16 See, for example, CCA (2005) Memorandum 69: 153–185. See Hartley (2005) Memorandum 160: 330–332. See Disaster Action, Memorandum 37, Ev 69–71 in House Of Commons Home Affairs and Work and Pensions Committees *Draft Corporate Manslaughter Bill Written Evidence* HC 540–11. London: The Stationery Office Ltd.

17 See 'Manslaughter Bill in Lords for Last Time?' Centre for Corporate Accountability website 16 July, 2007, www.corporateaccountability.org/manslaughter/reformprops/2007/update.htm.

18 See 'Government concedes on custody deaths paving way for Corporate Manslaughter Bill to become law' press release, Centre for Corporate Accountability, 18 July 2007, www.corporateaccountability.org/press_releases/2007/july18mans govtconcession.htm.

19 See www.publications.parliament.uk/pa/ld200607/ldbills/040/07040.1-7.html, accessed 5/8/08.

20 This means any code, guidance, manual or similar publication that is concerned with the health and safety matters and is made or issued (under statutory provision or otherwise) by any authority responsible for enforcement of any health and safety legislation.

21 'In another Hillsborough disaster, the police force could be prosecuted if it resulted in the death of a police officer, but not if it resulted in the death of a member of the public' (CCA, 2008: 18).

22 See Law Commission *Report on Murder, Manslaughter and Infanticide (Law Com No 304) Press Briefing Paper* 29 November 2006.

23 Manslaughter will still include category b) 'killing through gross negligence and causing death'. Second degree murder will encompass a) killing with intent to do serious injury, b) killing with intent to cause some injury or fear risk of injury, in the

awareness that there is a serious risk of causing death, c) killing with intent for first degree murder, but where a defence of provocation, diminished responsibility, or suicide pact succeeds (Law Commission, 2006: 2). Manslaughter b) above and second degree murder a) and b) above may be particularly relevant to sport scenarios. For example, which kind of offence might be applied to *R v Hardy* (unreported, 24 July 1994, Central Criminal Court) if these recommendations became law?

24 See Law Commission press release 'Bringing the law of homicide into the 21st century' 29 November 2006: 1.

25 See 'US Style murder grades proposed' 4 August 2008 at http://newsvote.bbc.co.uk/mpapps/pagetools/print/news/bbc.co.uk/l/uk/4544238.stm, accessed 5/8/08. See Law Commission website. www.lawcom.gov.uk.

Bibliography

Addison, N. (2008) 'Protection from harassment: conned by the Court of Appeal?' *Employment Law Journal* No. 89, April, 19–21.

All Party Parliamentary Group (2004) 'All Party Parliamentary Group on Adventure and Recreation in Society', paper in response to Martin Farrell's presentation 3 November (see Gaskin, 2005).

Ammon Jr, R., (1997) 'Alcohol policies and crowd management strategies as predictors of litigation at multi-purpose stadiums' *European Journal of Sport Management* 4, (2): 40–49.

Anderson, J. (2006) 'Recent developments in tort liability for foul play' *International Sports Law Journal* 1–2: 41–47.

Appenzeller, H. (ed.) (2005) *Risk Management in Sport Issues and Strategies* Durham NC: Carolina University Press.

BAALPE (1985) *Safe Practice in Physical Education* London: BAALPE.

BAALPE (2004) *Safe Practice in Physical Education and School Sport* Leeds: Coachwise Solutions Ltd.

Baker, J. (2001) 'Two high profile sports cases: a view from the Bench, His Honour John A. Baker' *Sport and the Law Journal* 9, (1): 95–103.

Bakker, F. C., Whiting, H. T. A. and Vander Brug, H. (1990) *Sports Psychology: Concepts and Applications* Chichester: Wiley.

Ball, R. T. (2005a) 'Warnings, waivers, informed consent' in H. Appenzeller (ed.) *Risk Management in Sport Issues and Strategies* Durham, NC: Carolina University Press, pp. 49–65.

Ball, R. T. (2005b) 'Product liability for sports products, among other things' in H. Appenzeller (ed.) *Risk Management in Sport Issues and Strategies* Durham NC: Carolina University Press, pp. 93–105.

Barbor, C. (1995) 'Corporate manslaughter: the lessons of Lyme Bay' *Transport and Law Policy* 2, (6): 44–45.

Barker, S. (2006) 'Is there a case for more criminal justice system involvement in sporting incidents?' Opinion and Practice, *Sport and the Law Journal* 13, (2): 13–15.

Baron, R. (2005) *Risk Management Manual* Dallas, TX: The Center for Sports Law and Risk Management.

Barrell, G. R. and Partington, J. A. (1970) *Teachers and the Law* 6th edn, London: Methuen.

Basnett, G. (2005) 'Legion deaths guilty verdict' *The Journal* (Newcastle, UK) 22 April, p.1, at http://web.lexis-nexis.com/professional, accessed 1/11/05.

Bayer, K. (2003) '£13,000 car written off in rugby prank' *Daily Mail* 5 November, p. 1.

BBC News (2007) 'Fine for safety breaches theme park' at http://news.bbc.co.uk/go/pr/fr/-/l/hi/england/merseyside/6173328.stm, accessed 30/11/07.

BBC News (2008) 'Chambers loses Olympic Ban case' BBC Sport, Friday July 18, p.1, at http://news.bbc.co.uk/sport1/hi/olympics/athletics/7503792.stm, accessed 18/7/08.

BBC News (2008) '"Beasting" death soldiers cleared' BBC News online, Monday 4 August at http://news.bbc.co.uk/1/hi/england/wiltshire/7532516.stm, accessed 5/8/08.

BBC News (2008) 'US Style murder "grades" proposed' BBC News online, Monday 4 August, 2008 at http://news.bbc.co.uk/1/hi/uk/4544238.stm, accessed 5/8/08.

BBC 2 (1992) 'Sport in the Dock' *On the Line* series 3 February.

BBC 2 (1994) 'Bad Sports' *On the Line* 26 January.

Beardsall, J. (2008) 'Double Dare' *The Daily Telegraph* (London) 13 September, p. 32, online at www.lexisnexis/frame.do?tokenKey=rsh-20.148125.571735479, accessed 18/11/08.

Beech, J. and Chadwick, S. (2004) *The Business of Sport Management* London: Pearson Educational.

Beloff, M. (1996) 'The CAS at the Olympics' *Sport and the Law Journal* 4, (3): 5–9.

Beloff, M. (2001) 'Drugs, laws and Versapaks' in J. O'Leary (ed.) *Drugs and Doping in Sport: a socio-legal perspective* London: Cavendish, pp. 39–56.

Beloff, M., Kerr,T. and Demetriou, M. (1999) *Sports Law* Oxford: Hart Publishing.

Benedict, J. R. (1998) *Athletes and Acquaintance Rape* London: Sage.

Benson, A. (1993) 'Canoe tragedy inquiry calls for regulation of outdoor centres' *The Guardian* 30 July, p. 3.

Bergman, D. (1991) *Deaths at Work: Accidents or Corporate Crime?* London: Workers' Educational Association, London Hazards Centre.

Bergman, D. (1993) *Disasters: Where the Law Fails* London: Herald Charitable Trust.

Bergman, D. (1994) *The Perfect Crime?* West Midlands: Health and Safety Advisory Committee.

Bergman, D. (1997) 'Weak on crime – weak on the causes of crime' *New Law Journal* 147: 1652, 1665.

Bergman, D. (1999) *The Case for Corporate Responsibility* London: Disaster Action.

Bermingham, V. (2002) *Tort* 6th edn, Nutshells Series, London: Sweet and Maxwell.

Bermingham, V. (2005) *Tort* 7th edn, Nutshells Series, London: Sweet and Maxwell.

Bettman, G. (2000) Full Text of NHL Commissioner Gary Bettman's decision regarding Marty McSorley, November 7, at www.faceoff.com/search/story.asp?f=/news/2000 1107/001107news119128.html.

Bibbings, L. and Aldridge, P. (1993) 'Sexual expressions, body alteration and the defence of consent' *Journal of Law and Society* 20, (3): 456–370.

Bill, K. (2005) 'The prevalence and nature of age discrimination practices in the UK sport and recreation organizations' *Sport and the Law Journal* 13 (1): 4–9.

Bitel, N. (1995) 'Disciplinary proceedings from the point of view of the individual' *Sport and the Law Journal* 3, (3): 7–9.

Blackshaw, I. (2001) 'Modahl loses appeal for compensation' *Sports Law Bulletin* 4, (1): 3–4.

Blackshaw, I. (2003) 'The Court of Arbitration for Sport: An international forum for settling disputes effectively within the family of sport' *Entertainment Law* 2, (2): 61–83.

Blackshaw, I. (2006a) 'Alternative dispute mechanisms in sport' chapter 6 in S. Gardiner, M. James, J. O'Leary, R. Welch, I. Blackshaw, S. Boyes and A. Caiger *Sports Law* 3rd edn, London: Cavendish, pp. 229–268.

Blackshaw, I. (2006b) 'Another first for the Court of Arbitration for Sport' *International Sports Law Journal* 3/4: 121.

Blackshaw, I. (2006c) 'Fair play on and off the field of play: settling disputes through the court of arbitration for sport' *International Sports Law Journal* 3–4: 107–117.

Blackshaw, I. (2006d) 'Provisional and conservatory measures – an underutilized resource in the Court of Arbitration for Sport' *Entertainment and Sport Law Journal* 4, (2): 1–5.

Bledsoe, G. H., Hsu, E. B., Grabowski, J. G., Brill, J. D. and Li, G. (2006) 'The incidence of injury in professional mixed martial arts competitions' *Journal of Sports Science and Medicine* CSSI, 136–142.

Boston Globe (2000) 'A matter of rite and wrong in the wake of the UUM case: debate is renewed over whether initiations are harmless bonding or rituals or outright abuse' February 13.

Boucher, J. (2002) *Student Development and Hazing. Hazing and Higher Education: State Laws, Liability and Institutional Implications* at www.stophazing.org/studentpapers.htm, accessed 8/7/08.

Bourdieu, P. (1987) 'The force of law: towards a sociology of the juridical field' *Hastings Law Journal* 38: 805–853.

Bowcott, O. (1994) 'Fatal canoe trip led by unqualified staff' *The Guardian* Wednesday 16 November, p. 6.

Boxhill, J. (ed.) (2003) *Sports Ethics: An Anthology* Oxford: Blackwell.

Boyes, S. (2006) 'Legal regulation of sports governing bodies' in Gardiner *Sports Law* 3rd edn, London: Cavendish, pp. 179–228.

Brackenridge, C. H. (1997) 'He owned me basically: women's experience of sexual abuse in sport' *International Review of the Sociology of Sport* 32, (2): 115–130.

Brackenridge, C. H. (2001) *Spoilsports: Understanding and Preventing Sexual Exploitation in Sport* London: Routledge.

Brackenridge, C. H. and Kirkby, S. (1997) 'Playing safe: assessing the risk of sexual abuse to elite child athletes' *International Review for the Sociology of Sport* 32: 407–418.

Brackenridge, C. H. and Williams, Y. (2004a) *The Times* 28 September 1995, [1987] 9 Cr App Reports (S) 53.

Brackenridge, C.H. and Williams, Y. (2004b) 'Living in the same household – "Incest" in the family of sport' *New Law Journal* 6 February, pp.179–180.

Brackenridge, C. H., Pitchford, A., Russell, K. and Nutt, G. (2007) *Child Welfare in Football* Oxon: Routledge.

Bradford, M. (2005) 'Sport, gender and the law' *International Sport Law Journal* 1–2: 78–83.

Braithwaite, J. (1984) *Corporate Crime in the Pharmaceutical Industry* London: Routledge.

Brierley, D. (1993) 'Schools Sport and the Law' *Sport and the Law Journal* 1, (1): 19–20.

Browne, K. (1988) *Early Prediction and Prevention of Child Abuse* Chichester: Wiley and Sons.

Bruxelles, Simon De (2004) 'The day a medieval stunt ended in death' *The Times* London (UK) 27 April, p. 11, at http://proquest.umi.com/, accessed 9/6/04.

Burnham, L. (2003) Hazing at www.stophazing.org/devtheory_files/devtheory8.htm, accessed 8/7/08.

Butler, E. (1993) 'Climb down boot boys' *The Observer* 7 November.

Cairns, W. (2002) 'Sports law current survey' *Sport and the Law Journal* 10, (2): 3–137.

Cairns, W. (2003) 'Sports law current survey' *Sport and the Law Journal* 11, (2): 4–151.

Canadian Centre for Ethics in Sport (1999) 'What about violence?' *Building a New Brand of Sport* Discussion paper, Ottawa, Canada, pp. 1–3.

CAS (2008) 'Athletics: case Oscar Pistorius upheld by the Court of Arbitration for Sport' press release 16 May, at www.tas-cas.org.

Cass, S. and Barlow, M. (2007) 'Great Brawl of China: QPR suspend Gregory No 2 over Bust-up' *The Daily Mail* Wednesday 14 February, p. 74.

Cawson, P. (2000) *Child Maltreatment in the UK – A Study of the Prevalence of Abuse and Neglect* London: NSPCC.

CCPR (2008) 'The Disability Discrimination Act' Ethics and Equity at www.ccpr.org.uk/ourcampaigning/uk/ethicsandequity/dda/, accessed 11/7/08.

Cense, M. (1997) *Red Card or Carte Blanche. Risk Factors for Sexual Harassment and Sexual Abuse in Sport.* Summary, conclusions and recommendations. Arnhem: Netherlands Olympic Committee, Netherlands Sports Federation/TransAct.

Centre for Corporate Accountability (2005) Memorandum 69: 153–185. Written evidence submitted to HOC Home Affairs Select Committees *Draft Corporate Manslaughter Bill Written Evidence* HC 540–11. London: The Stationery Office.

Centre for Corporate Accountability (2008) *Guidance on Corporate Manslaughter and Corporate Homicide Act 2007* London: CCA April.

Centre for Sport and Law (1995) 'The standard of care of coaches towards athletes' *Coaches Report* 2, (1):1. Canadian Centre for Sport and Law Inc., P.O. Box 4065, St Catharines, ON L2R 753 Canada, at www.sportlaw.ca/articles/coach/coach3.htm, accessed 14/3/02.

Centre for Sport and Law (1998) 'Restraint of trade: breathing new life into an old legal doctrine' *Coaches Report* 4, 3 at www.sportlaw.ca/articles/coach/coach13.htm, accessed 9/8/2006.

Centre for Sport and Law (2001) 'The responsibilities of supervision' *Coaches Report* summer, 8, (1): 1–3.

Centre for Sport and Law (2002) 'Violence – it's your responsibility too' *Coaches Report* Fall, 9, (2): 1–3 at www.sportlaw.ca/articles/coach/coach36.html.

Charlish, P. (2003) 'Case comment, Richard Vowles – Rugby Case' *Journal of Personal Injury Litigation* 2, (85–9): 1–6.

Christie M. (2003) 'Teacher jailed for school trip death' *Scottish Daily Record* 24 September.

Clancy, R. (1993) 'Judo mats, climbing walls, trampolines and pole vaulters' *Sport and the Law Journal* 3, (1): 28–31.

Clarke, K. S. (2005) 'On issues and strategies' in H. Appenzeller (ed.) *Risk Management in Sport Issues and Strategies* Durham NC: Carolina University Press, pp. 11–22.

Cleary, M. (1995) 'The killing fields' *Rugby World* January, p. 3.

Clinch, P. (2001) *Using a Law Library: A Student's Guide to Legal Research Skills* London: Blackstone Press.

Coakley, J. and Hughes, R. (1991) 'Positive deviance among athletes: the implications of overconformity to the sport ethic' *Sociology of Sport Journal* 8: 307–325.

Colley, J. and Gordon, C. (2002) 'Paralysed rugby player wins high court case' News Press Association, Friday December 13.

Collins, V. (1984) *Recreation and the Law* London: E&FN Spon.

Collins, V. (1993) *Recreation and the Law* 2nd edn, London: Routledge.

Conn, D. (1993) 'When the law cries foul' *The Times* London, June 8 at http://proquest. umi.com/, accessed 9/6/2004, p.1.

Cooke, J. (1995) *The Law of Tort* Harlow: Pearson Longman.

Cooke, J. (2003) *Law of Tort* 6th edn, Harlow: Pearson Longman.

Corbett, R. (2002) 'Risk management for sport organizations and sport facilities' paper presented at the Symposium *Sports Management: Cutting Edge Strategies for Managing Sports as a Business* Toronto: August 2002 (also under articles on the Centre for Sport Law Inc. website at www.sportlaw.ca/articles/.

Corbett, R., Findlay, H. and Lech, D. (2007) *Legal Issues in Sport: Tools and Techniques for the Sport Manager* Toronto: Edmund Montgomery Publications Ltd.

Corrigan, P. (1990) 'The ref is right – right?' *The Observer* Sunday 5 February, p. 9.

Costa, M. and Guthrie, S. (1994) 'Feminist perspectives: intersections with women and sport' in M. Costa and S. Guthrie (eds) *Women and Sport: Interdisciplinary Perspectives* pp. 235–252, Champaign, Illinois: Human Kinetics.

Court, C. (1994) 'Canoeing trip instructor was not qualified to lead party' *Western Morning News* 18 December, p. 5.

CPSU (2002) *Standards for Safeguarding and Protecting Children in Sport* Leicester: CPSU.

CPSU (2008) 'Children involved in Thai (kick) boxing' Guidance letter by S. Boocock, Director of CPSU, Leicester, UK.

Crainer, S. (1993) *Zeebrugge: Learning from Disaster: Lessons in Corporate Responsibility* London: Herald Charitable Trust.

Critcher, C. (1995) 'Running the rule over sport: a sociologist's view of ethics' in S. Fleming and A. Tomlinson (eds) *Ethics Sport and Leisure: Crises and Critiques* 2nd edn, Oxford: University of Brighton, Meyer and Meyer, pp. 25–35.

Crown Prosecution Service (2005) *Draft Guide to Prosecutors and Police Officers – Crime in Sport* London. Stationery Office.

Current Law Yearbook (2001) 'Negligence' p. 1519.

Current Law Yearbook (2002) 'Negligence' p. 1172.

Curry, S. J. (1989) 'Hazing and the "rush" toward reform: responses from universities, fraternities, state legislatures and the courts' *Journal of College and University Law* 16, (1): 93–117.

Daily Mail (2006) 'Judge mauls CPS after it prosecutes rugby player over a bruise' Thursday June 15, p. 24.

Dalton, A. J. P. (1998) *Safety, Health and Environmental Hazards at the Workplace* London: Cassell.

Darbyshire, P. (2007) *English Legal System* 7th edn, London: Sweet and Maxwell.

David, R. (2004) *Human Rights in Youth Sport* London: Routledge.

Day, M. and Hopkins, C. (1994) 'Dirty doings at the beach' *The Times* Law, Tuesday 10 May, p. 33.

DCMS (2007) Letter from Department for Culture, Media and Sport to Stan Timmins.

Deakin, J. (2000) 'Blood sport' *Maclean's* 113, (10): 44–48.

Dellise, J. (1993) 'Hazing and athletics: the state of the law' *Reduce your Risk* 1, 1–4.

Department for Education and Skills (2005) *The Protection of Children Act 1999 A Practical Guide to the Act for all Organisations Working with Children* London: DFES.

Department of Health (1999) *Working Together to Safeguard Children* London: Stationery Office.

Dios Crespo, J. (2006) 'European Law: two swimmers drown the "Sporting Exception"' *The International Sports Law Journal* 3–4: 118.

Disaster Action (2005) Memorandum 37 Ev 69–71 in HOC Home Affairs and Work and Pensions Select Committees *Draft Corporate Manslaughter Bill Written Evidence* HC 540–11. London: The Stationery Office Ltd.

Dobson, P. (2005) *Criminal Law* 7th edn, London: Sweet and Maxwell.

Doleschal, J. (2000) 'When rites become wrongs' *Sports Law Bulletin* 5, (3): 16.

Donnellan, L. (2008) 'Gender testing at the Beijing Olympics' *Sport and Law Journal* 1, (16): 20–28.

Downes, S. (2002) 'Every parent's nightmare' *The Observer Sport Monthly* online Sunday 7 April, p.1, at http://observer.guardian.co.uk/print/0,,4386620-103977,00.html, accessed 22/6/08.

Doyle, B. (2000) 'Sport dispute resolution in Australia' *Sports Law Bulletin* 3, (3): 13.

Drewry, G. (1975) *Law, Justice and Politics* London: Longman.

Driver, D. (2005) 'Paralympic hurdles' *Building* 39: 58–59.

Driver, E. and Droisen, A. (1989) *Child Sexual Abuse. Feminist Perspective* London: Macmillan.

Duce, R. (1996) 'Cantona's kick provoked by abuse from fan' *The Times* London, 1 May, p. 1.

Duff, A. (1995a) 'A hooligan's game played by gentlemen' *Sport and the Law Journal* 2, (3): 13–16.

Duff, A. (1995b) 'Scottish update' *Sport and the Law Journal* 3, (2): 31–34.

Duff, A. (1997a) 'A Scottish update. A brief synopsis of newsworthy matters concerning football, rugby & others from October 1996 to date' *Sport and the Law Journal* 5, (1): 25–30.

Duff, A. (1997b) 'Scottish update. A brief synopsis of newsworthy matters concerning football, rugby & others from July 1997 to date' *Sport and the Law Journal* 5 (3): 43–50.

Duff, A. (1999) 'Reasonable care v reckless disregard' paper presented at Law Society of Scotland's Sport and Law Conference, Ibrox Stadium, 23 March 1999 *Sport and the Law Journal* 7, (3): 44–54.

Duthrie, M. (2004) 'Aussie rules – defining equal opportunities in sport' *World Sport Law Review* 2, (2): 13–16.

Dutta, N. (2006) 'Guilty plea over boys' pool death: Barnet Council admits health and safety breaches' *The Times* Thursday 5 October.

Dyer, C. (1994) 'Commission says pain for pleasure should not be criminal' *The Guardian* 23 February.

Dyer, C. (1996) 'Rugby referee pays for injury –schools and rugby officials ponder landmark ruling *The Guardian* 18 December.

Eason, K. (2008) 'Amputee Sprinter Oscar Pistorius allowed to compete in Beijing' *Times* online 17 May 2008 at www.timesonline.co.uk, accessed 25/7/08.

Edwards, S. (1984) *Women on Trial* Manchester: Manchester University Press.

Elliott, C. and Quinn, F. (2006) *Criminal Law* 6th edn, Harlow: Pearson Education Ltd.

Elliott, M., Browne, K. and Kilcoyne, J. (1995) 'Child sexual abuse prevention: what sex offenders tell us' *Child Abuse and Neglect* 19, (5): 579–594.

Elvin, J. (2003) 'Liability for negligent refereeing of a rugby match' *Law Quarterly Review* 19 October: 560–563.

Farrar, J. (1990) *An Introduction to Legal Method* London: Sweet and Maxwell.

Farrell, R. (1994a) 'Injuries to disabled athletes' *Sport and the Law Journal* 2, (2): 9.

Farrell, R. (1994b) 'Violence in sport and consent to injury – The LCCP Consent and Offences Against the Person' *Sport and the Law Journal* 2, (2): 1–4.

Farrell, R. (1996) 'Consent to violence in sports and the law commission – part two' *Sport and the Law Journal* 4 (1): 5–12.

Farrell, R. (2001) 'Diane Modahl v The Law of Contract' *Sport and the Law Journal* 9, (1): 111–115.

Fasting, K., Brackenridge, C. H. and Sundgot Borgen, J. (2000) *Sexual Harassment In and Outside Sport* Oslo: Norwegian Olympic Committee.

Fattah, E. D. (1997) *Criminology: Past, Present and Future* London: Macmillan.

Felix, A. (1996) 'The standard of care in sport' *Sport and the Law Journal* 4, (1): 32, 35.

Felix, A. (1998) 'The Fleetwood Assassin strikes a blow for female boxing' *Sports Law Bulletin* 1, (3): 1, 6.

Felix, A. (1999) 'Case comment – Watson v Gray, *The Times*, November 26, 1998 (QBD)' *Journal of Personal Injury Litigation* September, 222–224.

Felix A. and Lee T. (1998a) 'Sports Injuries – Smoldon v Whitworth and Nolan: liability of officials, part 1' *Sports Law Bulletin* 1, (2): 8.

Felix A. and Lee, T. (1998b) 'Sports injuries – Smoldon v Whitworth and Nolan: liability of officials, part 2' *Sport Law Bulletin* 1, (3): 8.

Felix A. and Lee T. (1999) 'Case comment: *Watson and Bradford City AFC v Gray and Huddersfield Town FC*' *Journal of Personal Injury Litigation* September, 3: 222–224.

Field, S. and Jorg, N. (1991) 'Corporate liability and manslaughter: should we be going Dutch?' *Criminal Law Review*, pp. 156–171.

Findlay, H. (1998) 'Restraint of trade: breathing new life into an old legal doctrine' Centre for Sport and Law, Canada, Coaches articles Winter, 4, (3): 1–4, at www.sportlaw.ca, accessed 9/8/2006.

Findlay, H. and Corbett, R. (2002) 'Principles underlying adjudication and selection of disputes preceding the Salt Lake City Winter Olympic Games: notes for adjudicators' *Entertainment Law Journal* Spring, 1, (1): 109–120.

Finkelhor, D. (ed.) (1986) *Child Sexual Abuse: New Theory and Research* New York: Free Press.

Fitzgerald, M., McLennan, G. and Pawson, J. (1981) *Crime In Society: Readings in History and Theory* Milton Keynes: Open University Press.

Flint, C., Lewis A. and Taylor, J. (2003) 'The regulation of drug use in sport' in A. Lewis and J. Taylor (eds) *Sport: Law and Practice* London: Butterworths LexisNexis.

Foster, K. (2001) 'The discourses of doping: law and regulation in the war against drugs' in J. O'Leary (ed.) *Drugs and Doping: Socio-Legal Perspectives* London: Cavendish, pp. 181–203.

Foster, K. (2003) 'Is there a global sports law?' *Entertainment Law Journal* Spring 2, (1): 1–18.

Foucault, M. (1980) *Power and Knowledge* London: Harvester Press.

Fraleigh, W. P. (1984) *Right Actions in Sport: Ethics for Contestants* Champaign: Illinois, Human Kinetics.

French, J. R. P. and Raven, B. (1959) 'The basis of social power', in D. Cartwright (ed.) *Studies in Social Power* Ann Arbor, MI: Institute for Social Research, University of Michigan.

Frey, J. (1994) 'Deviance of organizational sub-units: the case of the college athletic departments' *Journal of Sport and Social Issues* 18, (2): 110–122.

Gardner, J. (1993) 'Should coaches take care?' *Sport and the Law Journal* 1 (1): 11–13.

Gardiner, S. (1993) 'Not playing the game: is it a crime?' *Solicitor's Journal* 138: 628–629.

Gardiner, S. (1994) 'The law and the sports field' *Criminal Law Review* July, pp. 513–515.

Gardiner, S. (2005) 'Should more matches end up in court?' *New Law Journal* July, 155, (7183): 998–1000.

Gardiner, S. (2007) 'Sports participation and criminal liability' *Sport and the Law Journal* 15 (1): 19–29.

Gardiner, S. (2008) 'Sports participation in extreme environmental conditions' *Sport and the Law Journal* 15 (3): 7–8.

Gardiner, S. and Felix, A. (1994) '*Elliott v Saunders*: drama in court 14' *Sport and the Law Journal* 2, (2); 1.

Gardiner, S. and Felix A. (1995) 'Juridification of the football field: strategies for giving law the elbow' *Marquette Sports Law Journal* 5, (1): 189.

Gaskin, K. (2005) *Getting a Grip Risk, Risk Management and Volunteering, A Review of Literature. A Report for Volunteering England and the Institute for Volunteering Research* October.

Gentry, C. (2002) *No Holds Barred* Lancashire: Milo Books.

Goose, B. (1997) 'Efforts to end fraternity hazing said to have largely failed' *The Chronicle of Higher Education* [electronic version].

Graff, L. L. (2003) *Better Safe. Risk Management in Volunteer Programs and Community Service* Ontario: Linda Graff Associates.

Grayson, E. (1986) *Safety First for Coaches* Leeds: National Coaching Foundation.

Grayson, E. (1991) All ER Annual Report Sport and Law 2 Lloyds LR 469 CA.

Grayson, E. (1992) 'All England Law Reports Annual Review' *Sport and the Law* pp. 366–367.

Grayson, E. (1994) *Sport and Law* London: Butterworths.

Grayson, E. (1995) 'Drugs in sport – chains of custody' *New Law Journal* January, 20: 44–46.

Grayson, E. (2000) *Sport and the Law* 3rd edn, London: Butterworths.

Grayson, E. (2001) *School Sports and the Law* London: Croner CCH Group Ltd.

Grayson, E. and Bond, C. (1993) 'Making foul play a crime' *Solicitor's Journal* p. 693.

Greenburg, M. J. and Gray, J. T. (1994) 'The legal aspects of the Tonya Harding figure skating controversy' *Sport and the Law Journal* 2, (2): 16–17.

Greenburg, M. J. and Gray, J. T. (1997) 'Designing and implementing a sports based risk management programme' *Sport and the Law Journal* 5 (2): 49–58.

Griffith-Jones, D. (2002) 'The need for a world-wide anti-doping code in my opinion' *Sports Law Bulletin* January/February 2–3.

Griffith-Jones, D. (2003) 'Civil liability for on-field conduct' in A. Lewis and J. Taylor (eds) *Sport: Law and Practice* London: Butterworths LexisNexis, pp. 1027–1069.

Grubin, D. (1998) *Sex Offending Against Children: Understanding the Risk* Police Research Series. Paper 99. London: Research, Development and Statistics Directorate, Home Office.

Gruneau, R. (1999) *Class, Sports and Social Development* 2nd edn, Champaign, Illinois: Human Kinetics.

Gruneau, R. and Whitson, D. (1993) *Hockey Night in Canada: Sport, Identities and Cultural Politics* Toronto: Garamond Press.

Gulland, E. (1995) 'The Reynolds Case and integrity of international dispute resolution' *International Athletics Federation Symposium on Sport and Law*, Monte Carlo, 1991, updated and published 1995.

Gunn, D. and Omerod, D. (1995) 'The legality of boxing' *Legal Studies* 15: 181.

Hale, B. (2008) 'Shocking pictures which show tearful five-year-olds forced to fight in kick boxing contests' *Mail online* 20 April, 14: 37 at www.dailymail.co.uk/news/, accessed 3/7/08.

Halsey, J. S. (2005) 'Risk management and physical educators' in H. Appenzeller (ed.) *Risk Management in Sport Issues and Strategies* Durham NC: Carolina University Press, pp. 151–163.

Hamilton, K. (1995) 'Brawling over brawling: politicians try to finish off human cock-fighting' in G. H. Bledsoe, E. B. Hsu, J. G. Grabowski, J. D. Brill and G. Li (2006) 'The Incidence of Injury in Professional Mixed Martial Arts Competitions' *Journal of Sports Science and Medicine* CSSI, 136–142.

Hargreaves, J. (1986) *Sport, Power and Culture: A Social and Historical Analysis of Popular Sports in Britain* Cambridge: Polity Press.

Harpwood, V. (2003) *Modern Tort Law* 5th edn, London: Cavendish.

Harris, P. (1993) 'Utter folly that cost four lives' *The Daily Mail* Wednesday 16 November, pp. 6–7.

Hartley, H. J. (1996) 'Moments of madness or a normal game?' A socio-legal, philosophical response to the LCCP 1995 Consultation Paper on Consent and the Criminal Law. February.

Hartley, H. J. (1997) 'Moments of madness or a normal game?' paper presented at the *European Association for Sport Management International Conference* Glasgow, September.

Hartley, H. J. (1998) 'Hard men – soft on sport?' *Sport and the Law Journal* 6, (3): 37–59.

Hartley, H. J. (2001a) 'Legal principles and issues: managing disciplinaries in sport and recreation' *Sport Development: Policy, Processes and Practice* London: Routledge, pp. 170–195.

Hartley, H. J. (2001b) *Exploring Sport and Leisure Disasters: A Socio-legal Perspective* London: Cavendish.

Hartley, H. J. (2003) 'An innocent abroad: legal analysis of the Diane Modahl doping case 1994–2001' paper presented to post graduate *juris degree* sports and law students at National Sports Law Institute, Marquette University Law School, Milwaukee, WN, USA 23 September.

Hartley, H. J. (2004) 'An innocent abroad: the Diane Modahl doping case 1994–2001' *International Sports Law Journal* 4, (4): 61–65.

Hartley, H. J. (2005a) 'Collaborations in the curriculum – sport and law: an emerging area?' *LINK* Issue 12: 4–5. Oxford: Higher Education Academy, HLST Subject Network.

Hartley. H. J. (2005b) Memorandum 160 Ev 330–332 in HOC Home Affairs and Work and Pensions Select Committees *Draft Corporate Manslaughter Bill Written Evidence HC* 540–511. London: The Stationery Office Ltd.

Hartley, H. J. (2009) *Sport and Law Learning Resource Guide* HEA HLST Subject Centre at www.hlst.heacademy.ac.uk.

Harvey, S. (2001) 'Cubbin v Minis' *Sport and the Law Journal* 9 (1): 103.

Haylen, P. (2004) 'Spinal injuries in Rugby Union, 1970–2003: lessons and responsibilities' *Viewpoint, Medical Journal of Australia* 161, (1): 48–50.

Hedley, S. (1993) 'Sado-masochism, human rights and the House of Lords' *Cambridge Law Journal* 194–196.

Herbert, D. L. (2002) 'Massachusetts hockey father convicted of involuntary manslaughter' *Sports, Parks and Recreation Law Reporter* Canton, Ohio, March, 15, (4): 59.

Herbert. I (2002) 'HSE to prosecute for deaths of girls on river bank' *The Independent* 2 July at http://education.independent.co.uk/news/story.jsp?story=311149, accessed 30/11/07.

Herbert, S. (1993) 'Consent no defence to acts of violent degradation' *The Guardian* 12 March, p. 7.

Higher Education Academy (2002) *Subject Benchmark Statement. Hospitality, Leisure, Sport and Tourism* Oxford: HEA HLST Subject Centre.

Hill, S. and Revere, C. (2004) 'Boys will be boys' *Solicitors Journal* 148: 1168–1169.

Hinde, A. and Kavanagh, C. (2003) *The Health and Safety Handbook for Voluntary and Community Organisations* London: Directory of Social Change.

Hiscox, W. (2004) 'Ant-doping policy after the Human Rights Act 1998 – is mandatory blood testing compatible with Article 8?' *Sport and the Law Journal* 3, (3): 3–6.

Hollaman, B. B. (2002) 'Hazing: a hidden campus crime' *New Directions for Student Services* 99: 11–24.

Horrow, R. (1980) *Sports Violence? The Interaction Between Private Law-making and the Criminal Law* Arlington, VA: Carlington Press.

HOC (2008a) House of Commons Work and Pensions Committee *The Role of the Health and Safety Commission and the Health and Safety Executive in Regulating Workplace Safety* Third Report of Session 2007–8. Vol. 1 HC 246-I. Monday 21 April. London: Stationery Office.

HOC (2008b) House of Commons Work and Pensions Committee *The Role of the Health and Safety Commission and the Health and Safety Executive in Workplace Safety* Third Report of Session 2007–8 Vol 11. HC 246-II.

HOC (2008c) House of Commons Work and Pensions Committee *The Role of the Health and Safety Commission and Health and Safety Executive in Regulating Workplace Health and Safety: Government Responses to the Committee's Third Report of Session 2007–8* HC 837 2 July 2008. London: Stationery Office.

Hogarth, A. (2005) 'Harassment: foreseeability of injury' *Personal Injury Law Journal* 63: 10–11.

Holt, O. (1998) 'UEFA ignores Bosnich's pleas' *The Times* 7 November.

Hood, C. (2005) 'Where "social risk" meets risk of blame: the architecture of blame avoidance' paper presented at the Third Sector Foresight Seminar *Changing Regulation and Perceptions of Risk*. Seminar Report at www.ncvo-vol.org.uk/3s4, accessed 15/10/05.

Hooper, N. (2006) 'The WADA code is fundamentally flawed – discuss' *Sport and the Law Journal* 14, (3): 21–28.

Hoover, N. (1999) *Initiation Rites in American High Schools: A National Survey* New York University.

Houlihan, B. (2002) *Dying to Win: Doping in Sport and the Development of Anti-doping Policy in Europe* Strasbourg: Council of Europe.

HSE (1995) *A Guide to Reporting of Injuries, Disease and Dangerous Occurrences Regulations* Sheffield: HSE Books

HSE (2001) *Public Register of Convictions* Education Section. Case no. 2012944, HSE Yorkshire and Humberside Region, at www.hse.gov.uk/prosecutions/, accessed 30/11/07.

HSE (2002a) *COSHH: A Brief Guide to the Regulations – What you need to know about the Control of Substances Hazardous to Health*. London: HSE.

HSE (2002b) *The Right Start – Work experience for young people: Health and safety basics for employers*. INDG364 C1500 Sheffield: HSE Books, September.

HSE (2004) *COSHH: A Brief Guide to the Regulations* Sheffield: HSE.

HSE (2005a) *The Control of Substances Hazardous to Health Regulations (as amended). Approved Code of Practice and Guidance L5* 5th edn, Sheffield: HSE Books.

HSE (2005b) *Incident Reporting in Schools* (accidents, diseases and dangerous occurrences) ED1S1 (rev1) June, London: HSE.

HSE (2005c) 'Glenridding Beck –The Investigation' at www.hse.gov.uk/schooltrips/investigation/index.htm, accessed 20/5/08.

HSE (2005d) *Sharing the lessons learnt – HSE publishes web report on Glenridding school trip tragedy* HSE press release: E034. 9 March at www.hse.gov.uk/press/2005/e05034.htm.

HSE (2006a) *Five Steps to Risk Assessment* Risk Management Section of Health and Safety Executive website at www.hse.gov.uk/risk/fivesteps.htm, accessed 29/8/07.

HSE (2006b) 'Principles of sensible risk assessment' at www.hse.gov.uk/risk/principles.htm, accessed 29/8/07.

HSE (2006c) 'HSC tells health and safety pedants to "get a life"'. Statement by Bill Callaghan, Chair of Health and Safety Commission at www.hse.gov/risk/statement.htm, accessed 6/1/08.

HSE (2006d) *Health and Safety Law. What you should know* Sheffield: HSE Books.

HSE (2006e) *HSE Statement on Barrow Legionella* 31 July.

HSE (2007a) 'Myths of the month' at www.hse.gov/myth/index.htm, accessed 6/1/08.

HSE (2007b) *Managing the Causes of Work-related stress. A Step by Step Approach to the Management Standards* Norwich: HMSO.

Illman, J. (1992) 'Death by dirty water' *The Guardian* 27 October, p. 25.

Independent Football Commission (2005) *Report on Child Protection in Football* Stockton-on-Tees: IFC

Jackson, A. (2006) 'Sorority hazing through the lens of Gilligan's Model of Women's Moral Development' at www.stophazing.org/devtheory_files/devtheory11.htm, accessed 8/7/08.

James, M. (2000) 'Player violence and injuries' in D. McArdle (ed.) *From Boot Money to Bosman: Football, Society and the Law* London: Cavendish, pp. 145–172.

James, M. (2001) 'Tort, compensation and alternative dispute resolution for participator violence' in S. Gardiner, M. James, J. O'Leary, R. Welch, I. Blackshaw, S. Boyes, A. Caiger (eds) *Sports Law* 2nd edn, London: Cavendish.

James, M. (2002) 'The trouble with Roy Keane' *Entertainment Law Journal* 3, (1): 72–92.

James, M. (2003) 'Referees, scrums and spinal injuries' *New Law Journal* 53, (7066): 166–167.

James, M. (2006a) 'The criminal law and participator violence' in S. Gardiner, J. O'Leary, R. Welch, I. Blackshaw, S. Boyes and A. Caiger, *Sports Law* 2nd edn, London: Cavendish, pp. 591–627.

James, M. (2006b) 'Tort, compensation and alternative dispute resolution for participator violence' in S. Gardiner, M. James, J. O'Leary, R. Welch, I. Blackshaw, S. Boyes and A. Caiger (eds) *Sports Law* 3rd edn, London: Cavendish, pp. 629–666.

James, M. and Deeley F. (2002) 'The standard of care in sports negligence cases' *Entertainment Law* (1): 104–108.

Jamieson. R. (2003) 'Fair notice: reflections on *R v Lake Estates Water Sports Ltd, Michael Ely and Stuart Ely*' *Entertainment Law* 2, (1): 85–88.

Jefferson, M. (1992) *Criminal Law* London: Pittman.

Jefferson, M. (2000) 'Corporate liability in the 1990s' *Journal of Criminal Law* 64: 106.

Jeffrey, S. (2002) 'Inquest: girls' drownings were accidental' *Guardian Unlimited Education Guardian.co.uk* at http://education.guardian.co.uk/schooltrips/story/0,,664351,00.html, accessed 30/1/07.

Jenkins, R. (2006) 'Judge critical of rugby trial' *The Times* Thursday June 15, p. 8.

Jones, M. A. (2002) *Textbook on Torts* 8th edn, Oxford University Press.

JPIL (2002) *Pitcher v Huddersfield Town FC* unreported 7 July QBD case report, *Journal of Personal Injury Law* 2: 226.

Kay, K. (2002) 'Jail for dad in fatal ice hockey row' *The Times* London (UK) January 26, p. 18, at http://proquest.umi.com/, accessed 9/6/04.

Keely, (2003) 'Teacher tells of pupil's school trip death' *Press Association News* Thursday 8 May.

Kelham, A. (2004) 'BASL Seminar at King's College London: a harmonised approach to the regulation of drug use in sport' *Sport and the Law Journal* 12, (1): 136–139.

Kelly, L., Wingfield, R., Burton, S. and Regan, L. (1995) *Splintered Lives: Sexual Exploitation of Children in the Context of Children's Rights and Child Protection* Ilford, Essex: Barnado's.

Kennedy, H. (1992) *Eve was Framed: Women and British Justice*. London: Chatto and Windus.

Kennedy, K. (2000) 'Stick-headed' *Sports Illustrated* 6 March, 92 (9): 25.

Kerr, A. (1999) *Protecting Disabled Children and Adults in Sport and Recreation: The Guide* Leeds: National Coaching Foundation.

Kerr, G. (2000) 'Bad enough to kill someone' *The Globe and Mail* 23 February, p. S1.

Kerr, J. H. (1997) *Motivation and Emotion in Sport* Hove: Psychology Press.

Kerr, J.H. (2005) *Rethinking Aggression and Violence in Sport* Oxon: Routledge.

Kitchen, J. and Corbett, R. (1995) *Negligence and Liability – A Guide for Recreation and Sport Organisations* St Mary's, Ontario, Centre for Sport and Law, Canada.

Kitson, P. and Allen, S. (1997) 'Personal injuries update' *Sport and the Law Journal* 8, (1): 5–8.

Kirkby, S. and Greaves, L. (1996) 'Foul play: sexual abuse and harassment in sport' paper presented to the Pre-Olympic Scientific Congress, Dallas, USA, 11–14 July.

Kirkup, H. and Solly, B. (2008) 'Anti-doping's brave new world' briefing paper, unpublished, Berrymans Lace Mawyer, Solicitors, Leeds.

Knight, T. (2004) 'Athletics: Chambers' coach on drugs charges' *The Telegraph (Sport)* 13 February at www.sport.telegraph.co.uk/core/Content/display/Printable.jhtml?xml=/sport/.

Lancaster, E. (1996) 'Working with men who sexually abuse children: The experience of the probation service' in B. Fawcett, B. Featherstone, J. Hearn and C. Toft (eds) *Violence and Gender Relations: Theories and Interventions* London: Sage.

Law Commission (1994) 'Consent and offences against the person' A consultation paper. Criminal Law, no.134. London: HMSO.

Law Commission (1995) 'Consent and offences against the person' A consultation paper. Criminal Law, no.139. London: HMSO.

Law Commission (2008) *Reforming the Law: Murder, Manslaughter and Infanticide. An Easy Read Report on Plans to make Changes to the Law about Killing People* London: Stationery Office.

Leahy, T., Pretty, G. and Tenenbaum, G. (2001) 'Once I got into the elite squad it was a lot easier for him to get me'. Sexual abuse in organised sport, a comparison of elite and club athletes' experiences, *Conference Proceedings of the 10th World Congress of Sport Psychology* Skiathos, Greece, 4: 190–192.

Leake, S. and Omerod, D. (2005) 'Contact sports: application of the Defence of Consent' (*R v Barnes* [2004] EWCA Crim 3246; [2005] 1 WLR 910, CA Crim Div) *Criminal Law Review* May, 381–384.

Leaver, P. (2008) quoted in 'Leading figures outline anti-doping changes' National Anti-Doping Panel News, 25 September, at www.sportresolutions.co.uk/news, accessed 26/9/08.

Lee, T. (1997) 'Official's liability and implications of *Smoldon v Whitworth and Nolan* 1996' paper presented at the Annual Conference *British Association for Sport and Law* Lord's Cricket Ground, 17 October.

Lee, T. and Felix, A. (1999) 'Case comment: Smoldon v Whitworth and Nolan' *Journal of Personal Injury Litigation* (3): 218–221.

Lewis, A., Taylor, J. and Parkhouse, A. (2003) 'Challenges in the courts to the actions of sports governing bodies', in A. Lewis and J. Taylor (eds) *Sport: Law and Practice* London: Butterworths LexisNexis, pp. 85–229.

Llewellyn, D. (1996) 'Sports fears after referee decision' *The Independent* London, 20 April, p. 28.

MacLachlan, J. (2000) 'Dangerous traditions: hazing rituals on campus and university liability' *Journal of College and University Law* 26 (3): 511–548.

Matthews, R., Matthews K. J. and Speltz, K. (1989) *Female Sexual Offenders* Orwell: The Safer Society Press.

Maxlow-Tomlinson, P. (1995) 'Ski-ing and the law' *Sport and the Law Journal* 3 (1): 18–25.

McArdle, D. (1995) 'A few hard cases? Sport, sadomasochism and public policy in the English Courts' *Canadian Journal of Law and Society* 10 (2): 1–15.

McArdle, D. (1996) 'Brothers in arms: sport, law and the construction of gender' *International Journal of Sociology of Law* 24: 145–162.

McArdle, D. (1998) 'Discrimination in Sport' *SATLJ* 6 (1): 80.

McArdle, D. (2000) *Football, Society and the Law* London: Cavendish, pp. 141–143.

McArdle, D. (2005) 'The enduring legacy of reckless disregard' CLWR 34, 316.

McArdle, D. (2006) 'Sport, horseplay and the liability of young persons' *International Sports Law Journal* 1–2: 107–109.

McArdle, D. and James, M. (2005) 'Are you experienced?' *Times Law Review* 13 (3): 193.

McClaren, R. (2004) 'The CAS AD HOC Division at the Athens Olympic Games' International Sports Law Perspective *Marquette Sports Law Review* 15, Fall, (1): 175–203.

McCutcheon, J. P. (2000) 'Sports discipline and the rule of law' in S. Greenfield and G. Osborn (eds) *Law and Sport in Contemporary Society* London: Frank Cass, pp. 115–128.

McFarlane, N. (2007) 'Asbestos scandal may cost millions' *The Northern Echo* 4 September at www.asbestech.com/news.asp, accessed 30/11/07.

McFee, G. (2004) *Sport, Rules and Values* London: Routledge.

McGlone, C. and Schaefer, G. R. (2008) 'After the haze: legal aspects of hazing' *Entertainment and Sports Law Journal* 6, (1): 1–14.

McGlove, C. (2005) *Hazing in N C A A Division of Women's Athletics: An Exploratory Analysis* University of New Mexico.

McIlvaney, H. (1993) 'Rough justice puts football in the dock' *The Sunday Times* 26 December, p. 3.

McIntire, J. (2000) 'Curriculum 2000: opportunities for safety & risk education' RoSPA *Safety Education Journal* at www.rospa.com/safetyeducation/curriculum/opportunities.htm, accessed 25/3/08.

McKinnon, C. (1987) *Feminism Unmodified: Discourses on Life and Law* Cambridge: Harvard University Press.

McKinnon, C. (1989) *Towards a Feminist Theory of the State* Cambridge: Harvard University Press.

McNamee, M. J. and Parry, S. J. (eds) (1998) *Ethics and Sport* London: Routledge.

Messner, M. A. (1990) 'When bodies are weapons: masculinity, violence and sport' *International Review for the Sociology of Sport* 25: 203–221.

Messner, M. A. (1992) 'The embodiment of masculinity' in M. A. Messner (ed.) *Power at Play: Sports and the Problem of Masculinity* Boston: Beacon Press.

Messner, M. A. (2002) 'Playing center: the triad of violence in men's sports' in M. A. Messner (ed.) *Taking the Field: Women, Men and Sports*, Sport and Culture Series, vol. 4, Minneapolis: University of Minnesota Press.

Mitchell, K. (1996) 'Sport strangled by the wrong arm of the law' *The Observer, Sport*, 21 April, p. 2.

Molan, M., Bloy, D. and Lanser, D. (2003) *Modern Criminal Law* 5th edn, London: Cavendish.

Moore, C. (2000) 'Sport and the law of tort' in C. Moore (ed.) *Sports Law and Litigation* 2nd edn, Welwyn Garden City: CLT Professional Publishers, pp. 76–110.

Morgan, H. (2004) 'Pair cleared over catapult death' *The Press Association* Friday 7 May, at http://web.lexis-nexis.com/executive/, accessed 24/8/07.

Morris, J. (1998) *Volume 1 – The experiences of disabled children and young people living away from their families* London: The Who Cares? Trust.

Mulrooney, A. and Ammon Jr., R. (1995) 'Risk management practices and their impact on insurance premiums and loss reserves' *Journal of Legal Aspects of Sport* Fall, 5, (2): 57–67.

Myers, J. and Barrett, B. (2002) *In at the Deep End: A new insight for all sports from analysis of child abuse in swimming* London: NSPCC.

NADP (2008) 'Leading figures outline anti-doping changes' 25 September, NADP news at www.sportresolutions.co.uk/news.

Nafziger, J. R. (2004a) *International Sports Law* 2nd edn, Ardsley, NY: Transnational Publishers Inc.

Nafziger, J. R. (2004b) 'Lex Sportiva' *International Sports Law Journal* 3: 3–8.

Nasir, K. J. (1992) 'Nervous shock and Alcock: the judicial buck stops here' *Medical Law Review* 55: 705, 707, 713.

Netherlands Olympic Committee, Netherlands Sports Federation (1997) *Sexual Harassment in Sport, Code of Conduct*, Arnhem: The Netherlands.

Nicholson, M. (2004) 'Cometh the hour, cometh the court' *World Sports Law Report* January, pp. 3–5.

Nicholson, R. (1987) 'Drugs in sport: a reappraisal' *Institute of Medical Ethics Bulletin* August.

NSPCC (2002) 'NSPCC report reveals concern over child abuse in swimming' press release, 4 September, at www.ncpcc.org, accessed 10/8/2004.

Nygaard, G. and Boone, T. H. (1985) *A Coach's Guide to Sport Law* Champaign, IL: Human Kinetics Publishers.

O'Donovan, G. (2008) 'Last night on television heroes BBC 2, Strictly Baby Fight Club' *Telegraph* online live at www.telegraph.co.uk/arts/, accessed 3/7/08.

O'Keefe, R. (2007) 'Pleasureland fined over worker's death. *The Liverpool Echo* 28 November 2007, p. 1.

O'Leary, J. (1998) 'Modahl saga nears conclusion' *Sports Law Bulletin* March/April, pp. 6–7.

O'Leary, J. (1998) 'The regulation of drug abuse in sport' in S. Gardiner, A. Felix, M. James, R. Welch and J. O'Leary (eds) *Sports Law* London: Cavendish, pp.161–197.

Omerod, D. C. and Gunn. M. (1996) 'Consent – a second bash' *Criminal Law Review*, 694–706.

Opie, H. (2002) 'Australian Medico-legal issues in sport: the view from the grandstand' *Marquette Sports Law Review* 13: 113–148.

Padfield, N. (1992) 'Consent and public interest' *New Law Journal* 27 March, pp. 430–432.

Paine, E. A. (1994) 'Recent trends in fraternity-related liability' *Journal of Law and Education* 23, (2): 361–397.

Pannick, D. (1983) *Sex Discrimination in Sport* Manchester: Equal Opportunities Commission.

Pannick, D. (1992) 'Consent and public interest' *New Law Journal* 430–432.

Parker, R. (1995) 'Disciplinary proceedings from the governing body point of view' *Sport and the Law Journal* 3, (3): 3–6.

Parkinson, A. (2008) quotes in 'Leading Figures outline anti-doping changes' National Anti-Doping Panel News 25 September at www.sportresolutions.co.uk/news, accessed 26/11/08.

Parpworth, N. (1996a) 'Sports governing bodies and the principles of natural justice: an Australian perspective' *Sport and the Law Journal* 4, (2): 5–15.

Parpworth, N. (1996b) 'Parliament and the Boxing Bill' *Sport and the Law Journal* 2, (1): 5–9.

Parry, S. J. (1998) 'Violence and aggression in contemporary sport' in M. J. McNamee and S. J. Parry (eds) *Ethics in Sport* London: Routledge, pp. 205–224.

Parsons, S. (2003) 'The doctrine of identification, causation and corporate liability for manslaughter' *Journal of Criminal Law* 76: 69.

Randall, C. (1993) 'Adventure chiefs are charged over four canoe deaths' *The Daily Telegraph* 22 September, p. 3.

Reeb, M. (2000) 'The Court of Arbitration for Sport (CAS)' *Sports Law Bulletin* July/August, pp. 10–11.

Reeb, M. (2005) 'Arbitration CAS 2002/A/376 Baxter/International Olympic Committee (IOC) award of 15 October 2002' *Digest of CAS Awards III* Kluwer Law International, 303–310.

Reid, R. (1995) 'The Modahl case' *Sport and the Law Journal* 3, (2): 6–8.

Roberts, B. (2002a) 'Mum is killed by 70mph sand yacht' *Daily Mirror* 19 August, p. 16.

Roberts, B. (2002b) 'Sand yachting halted on mum death beach' *Daily Mirror* 20 August, p. 20.

Robinson, L. (1998) *Crossing the Line: Violence and Sexual Assault in Canada's National Sport* Toronto: McLelland & Stewart Inc.

Robinson, P. (2003) 'Union boycott call after school trip death' *Yorkshire Evening Post* 18 July.

RoSPA (2006) 'Learning, sharing and moving forwards: advice pack for smaller firms' sheets 1–7 at www.rospa.com/occupationalsafety/smallfirms/, accessed 30/11/07.

RoSPA (2007) 'Young workers – an online resource for young workers. Regulations protecting the health and safety of young people at in the workplace' at www.rospa.org, accessed 28/08/07.

Rose, D. and Weir, C. (2003) 'Discrimination' in A. Lewis and J. Taylor (eds) *Sport: Law and Practice* London: Butterworths LexisNexis. pp. 889–906.

Rose, N. and Albertini, L. (1997) '*Jones v Welsh Rugby Union*: new law for a new era' *Sport and the Law Journal* 5, (1): 20–23.

Rosenberg, D. (2003) 'The banality of violence and the McSorley Affair' *Avante* 9, (2): 30–42.

Rozenberg, J. (1994) 'The rise and fall of legal aid' in *The Search for Justice: An Anatomy of the Law* London: Hodder and Stoughton, pp. 219–224.

Rudgard, N. (2002) 'Controlling the risk – who pays when an event is cancelled?' *Sport and the Law Journal* 10, (1): 130–133.

Ruff, A. (2002) 'Facial injuries and football before school' *Entertainment Law* 2, (1): 89–97.

Russell, Jones and Walker (2008a) 'Bullying and harassment: taking legal action about bullying and harassment at work' handout Russell Jones and Walker (solicitors) website at www.rjw.co.uk, accessed 20/6/08.

Russell, Jones and Walker (2008b) 'Equality Act (Sexual Orientation) Regulations Act 2007' handout on Russell, Jones and Walker (solicitors) website at www.rjw.co.uk, accessed 20/6/08.

Russell, Jones and Walker (2008c) 'Sex Discrimination 2001, 2003 additions: Sex Discrimination in Employment and your legal rights' at www.rjw.co.uk, accessed 20/6/08.

Russell, Jones and Walker (2008d) 'Disability Discrimination: The Disability Discrimination Act 1995 and your legal rights' at www.rjw.co.uk, accessed 20/6/08.

Russell, Jones and Walker (2008e) 'Gender Recognition Act 2004: Transgender, gender recognition-Employment Series' at www.rjw.co.uk, accessed 20/6/08.

Russell, K. (2007) 'Disability football and vulnerable people' in C. Brackenridge, A. Pitchford, K. Russell and G. Nutt (eds) *Child Welfare in Football* Oxon: Routledge, pp. 148–156.

Sanderson, D. (2007) *The Times* online, 4 October.

Scraton, P. (2000) *Hillsborough: The Truth* Edinburgh: Mainstream.

Severs, J., Whitlam, P. and Woodhouse, J. (2003) *Safety and Risk in Primary School Physical Education* London: Routledge.

Sheikh, S. (2007) 'Corporate manslaughter and the corporate homicide bill: part 1' *International Company and Commercial Law Review* 18 (8): 261–278.

Silver, J. R. and Stewart, D. 1994 'The prevention of spinal cord injuries in rugby football' *Paraplegia* 32: 442–453.

Sithamparanathan, A. and Schillings, M. H. (2003) 'Are sporting bodies abusing human rights?' *Sport and the Law Journal* 11, (3): 138–143.

Slapper, G. and Toombs, S. (1999) *Corporate Crime* Harlow: Pearson Education Ltd.

Smith, M. D. (1979) 'Towards an explanation of hockey violence' *Canadian Journal of Sociology* 4: 105–124.

Smith, M. D. (1983) *Violence and Sport* Toronto: Butterworths.

Smith, M. D. (2003) 'What is Sports Violence?' in J. Boxhill (ed.) *Sports Ethics An Anthology* Oxford: Blackwell, pp.199–216.

Soek, J. W. (2001) 'The fundamental rights of athletes in doping trials' in J. O'Leary (ed.) *Drugs and Doping in Sport: Socio-Legal Perspectives* London, Cavendish, pp. 57–74.

Soek, J. W. (2006) *The Strict Liability Principle and the Human Rights of Athletes in Doping Cases* The Hague: Asser Press.

Spengler, J. O., Connaughton, D. and Young, S. (2006) *Risk Management in Sport and Recreation* Champaign, Illinois: Human Kinetics Publishers.

Sport and the Law Journal (1997) 'Law Report' 5 (1): 84–86.

Sport and the Law Journal (2003) 'Sport and the Law Cases Index' 11, (2): 174–190.

Sports Law Bulletin (1998) 'UK Digest Personal Injury, Ear Biting in Sport' pp.1–2 at http://anglia.ac.uk/sportslaw/slbukd2.htm, accessed 9/6/2004.

Sports Law Bulletin (1998) 1 (4): 4.

Sports Law Bulletin (1999a) 'Personal Injury' 2, (6): 4.

Sports Law Bulletin (1999b) 2 (3): 4–5.

Sports Law Bulletin (1999c) 'Drugs and Doping *Modahl v BAF Ltd*' 2: 6.

Sports Law Bulletin (2001a) 'Legal Duties of Sports Governing Bodies' 4, (1): 1.

Sports Law Bulletin (2001b) 'Modahl Compensation Claim Fails' 4 (2): 13.

Sport Law Journal Reports (2006) 'International Rugby Board v Keyter' SLJR 12 CAS 2006/A. 1067, 13 October.

Stinson, R. (1995) 'Harmonisation of laws as they relate to sport' *I.A.F Symposium: Sport and Law* Monte Carlo, January 1991, updated and published 1995.

Stapleton, J. (1994) 'In restraint of torts' in P. Birks (ed.) *Frontiers of Liability* Oxford: Oxford University Press.

Stewart, D. and Silver, J. (1993) 'Rugby – catastrophic injuries, claims and insurance' *Sport and the Law Journal* 2, (1): 15–17.

Suggs, W. (1999) '79% of college athletes experience hazing, survey finds: few coaches and athletics administrators say they are aware of problem' *The Chronicle of Higher Education* [electronic version] in Burnham (2003) *Hazing* at www.stophazing.org, accessed 8/7/08.

Sullivan, P. M. and Knutson, J. F. (2000) 'Maltreatment and disabilities: a population based epidemiological study' *Child Abuse and Neglect* 24: 1257–1273.

Surfers Against Sewage (2005) 'The health risks associated with bathing, surfing and other watersports in contaminated environments' research reports Surfers Against Sewage website www.sas.org.uk, accessed 14/11/05.

Talbot, M. (1988) 'The Sex Discrimination Act: implications for the delivery of physical education, recreation and sport' paper presented at conference *Legal Issues in Physical Education* Leeds Polytechnic, Leeds, England, 4 November.

Talbot, M. (2006) 'Gender stereotypes and discrimination in sport and leisure' lecture to the students on the MA in Sport, Leisure and Equity, socio-legal issues module, 3 March, Leeds Metropolitan University.

Tayfoor, S. (1995) *Tort Law Cartoons* London: Sweet and Maxwell.

Teff, H. (1992) 'The Hillsborough Football Disaster and claims for nervous shock' *Medical Science Law* 32: 251, 253.

The Birmingham Post (2004) Friday 16 July.

The Guardian (1995) 'Ooh ah: a jail sentence too far' 24 March, p. 27.

The Times (2005) 'Whether injury in sport is criminal' Monday 10 January, p. 54.

Thomas, P. and Knowles, J. (2001) *Dane and Thomas How to use a Law Library: an introduction to legal skills* 4th edn, London: Sweet and Maxwell.

Thompson, M. (2000) 'The Michael Watson Case' *Sport and the Law Journal* 8, (2): 7.

Thompson. M. (2006) *Ethics* London: Hodder Education.

Timmins, S. (2007) 'Men or monkeys? Inside the cage: a socio-legal analysis of cage fighting in the United Kingdom and associated practices in the construction of masculinity' unpublished paper in partial fulfilment of the MA in Sport, Leisure and Equity, Carnegie Faculty of Sport and Education, Leeds Metropolitan University, Leeds, England.

Tinmouth, M. (2004) 'Initiation ceremonies in university sport in the UK' University of Southampton, unpublished paper.

Toczek, L. (2002) 'A case of foul play' *New Law Journal* 152, (7035): 868.

Toftegaard, J. (1998) 'Den forbudte zone' (The Forbidden Zone) unpublished MA thesis, Institut for Idraet, Copenhagen, Denmark.

Tomlinson, P. and Strachan, D. (1996) *Power and Ethics in Coaching* Ottawa: Coaching Association of Canada.

Tracey, P. and Baker, T. (2002) 'Sports injuries – is anyone to blame?' Touchline Online, Rugby Football Union official website at www.rfu.com/index.cfm/fuseaction/RFUHome. Touchline_Detail/storyId/958/sectionId/94, 23 January.

TUC (2007) *Hazards at Work Organising for Safe and Healthy Workplaces* London: TUC.

TUC (2008) *Your Rights at Work* 3rd edn, London: Kogan Page.

Turner, C. (2003) *Tort Law* London: Hodder and Stoughton.

Unger, A. (1991) 'Undue caution in the Lords' *New Law Journal* 20 December, 1729–1730.

University of Alberta Legal Resource Centre (1993) 'Could this happen to you? Recreation workers can take steps to prevent injuries and avoid liability' *Law Now* A Publication of the Legal Resource Centre. Centre for Sport and Law Inc. at www.sportlaw.ca/articles/other/article2.htm.

University of Vermont (2000) *Report of the President's Committee on the Prevention of Hazing in Intercollegiate Sports at The University of Vermont* 25 February. VM, US: University of Vermont.

Usborne, D. (2002) 'Father pounded to death ice hockey coach for allowing violence on rink' *The Independent* London (UK) Foreign News section, 5 January, p. 15.

Usher, T. (1996) 'Awareness and application of the rules is paramount' *The Guardian* 20 April, p. 21.

Uttley, R. (1996) 'A game only referees can lose' *The Guardian* 20 April, p. 21.

Van der Smissen, B. (1990) Legal *Liability and Risk Management for Public and Private Entities* Cincinatti, OH: Anderson Publishing Company.

Vrijman, E. (2000) 'Towards harmonisation: a commentary on current issues and problems' (Part One) *Sports Law Bulletin* 3, (2): 13–14.

WADA (2007) *World Ant-Doping Code* Montreal: World Anti-Doping Agency.

Watson, H. (2003) 'Duty of care owed on the playing field – a further incremental step' 13 March published online with consent of consilio at www.spr_consilio.com/arttort5.htm.

Wearmouth, H. J. (1990) 'The prudent coach: legal aspects of gymnastics' in C. Still (ed.) *Women's Gymnastics – Teaching and Coaching Manual* Denby Dale: Springfield, pp. 49–61.

Wearmouth, H. J. (1995) 'Ethical and legal frameworks or evaluating disciplinary processes in sport' *Sport and the Law Journal* 3, (3): 29–35.

Weaver, M. (1996) 'Man crippled in bouncy castle romp awarded £950,000' *The Daily Telegraph* 12 March, p. 1.

Weele, S. (1994) 'Stunt which killed actor was unsafe' *The Guardian* Tuesday 4 October, p. 3.

Weele, S. (1994) 'Spanish hospital held largely to blame for death of film actor' *The Guardian* 22 December, p. 4.

Welch, M. (1997) 'Violence against women by professional football players: a gender analysis of hypermasculinity, positional status, narcissism and entitlement' *Journal of Sport and Social Issues* 21 (4): 392–411.

Welch, M. and Wearmouth, H. J. (1994) *Getting it Right* (A guide to sports ethics, disciplinary procedures and appeals) Running Sport series) London: Sports Council.

Welch, R. (2006) 'Sport and the law of discrimination' in S. Gardiner, M. James, J. O'Leary, R. Welch, I. Blackshaw, S. Boyes and A. Caiger (eds) *Sports Law* 3rd edn, London: Cavendish, pp. 555–588.

Wells, C. (1993a) *Corporations and Criminal Responsibility* Oxford: Clarendon.

Wells, C. (1993b) 'Corporations: culture, risk and criminal liability' *Criminal Law Review* pp. 551–566.

Wells, C. (1995) *Negotiating Tragedy: The Law and Disasters* London: Sweet and Maxwell.

Westcott, H. and Clement, M. (1992) *NSPCC Experience of Child Abuse in Residential Care and Educational Placements* London: NSPCC.

Whitlam, P. (2003) 'Risk management principles' in J. Severs, P. Whitlam and J. Woodhouse (eds) *Safety and Risk in Primary School Physical Education* London: Routledge, pp. 30–42.

Whitlam, P. (2005) *Case Law in Physical Education and School Sport* Leeds, Coachwise 1st4 Sport.

Williams, G. (1962) 'Consent and public policy' [1962] *Criminal Law Review* 74: 80.

Williams, J. M. (2003) 'Case comment – personal injury – sports injuries – adult rugby match' *Journal of Personal Injury Litigation* 2: C49–52.

Williams, R. (2008) 'Judge rules against late upset for "clean" Team GB' *The Guardian* Sport, Friday 18 July, p. 13.

Williams, Y. (2005) *Response to the Home Office and DCMS Consultation on the Scope and Implementation of the Sexual Offences Act 2003 in Relation to Sports Coaches* 4 March.

Williams, Y. (2006a) 'The potential of the Safeguarding Vulnerable Groups Bill for children's sport' *Entertainment and Sports Law Journal* 4 (1): 1–4.

Williams, Y. (2006b) 'Human rights in youth sport by Paulo David' *Entertainment and Sports Law Journal* 4 (2): 1–4.

Winfield, G. and Osborne, S. (2001) *Film and the Law* London: Cavendish.

Wise, A. (1996) 'Strict liability rules – are they legal? *Sport and the Law Journal* 4 (3): 70–82.

Young, K. M. (1993) 'Violence, risk and liability in male sports culture' *Sociology of Sport Journal* 10: 373–396.

Young, K. M. (2004) 'Sport and violence' in J. Coakley and E. Dunning (eds) *Handbook of Sports Studies* pp. 282–407.

Young Workers (2007) 'Young workers – advice for young people: your rights and responsibilities' at www.youngworker.co.uk/youngpeople/responsibilities/index.htm, accessed 28/8/07.

Zagklis, A. K. (2006) 'The CAS ad hoc Division at the XX Olympic Winter Games in Turin' *International Sports Law Journal* 3, (4): 47–52.

Index